The Book of MYTHS & MISCONCEPTIONS

THE TRUTH IS FINALLY REVEALED

D1056344

WEST
SIDE
PUBLISHING

Contributing Writers: Jeff Bahr, Tom DeMichael, Katherine Don, James Duplacey, Emily Dwass, J. K. Kelley, Bill Martin, Susan McGowan, Ken Sheldon, Lawrence Robinson, Bill Sasser, Ilene Springer, Donald Vaughan, and Jennifer Plattner Wilkinson

Additional Contributors: Allison Gaudet, Bruce Herman, Ed Moser, Bill O'Neal, Laura Paskus, and Anna Zaigraeva

Cover Illustration: Adrian Chesterman

Factual Verification: Brenda Bourg, Marci McGrath, Helen Erwin Schinske, Chris Smith, and Leigh Smith

The brand-name products mentioned in this publication are trademarks or service marks of their respective companies. The mention of any product in this publication does not constitute an endorsement by the respective proprietors of Publications International, Ltd., nor does it constitute an endorsement by any of these companies that their products should be used in the manner represented in this publication.

Armchair Reader is a trademark of Publications International, Ltd.

West Side Publishing is a division of Publications International, Ltd.

Copyright © 2009, 2010 Publications International, Ltd. All rights reserved. This book may not be reproduced or quoted in whole or in part by any means whatsoever without written permission from:

Louis Weber, CEO
Publications International, Ltd.
7373 North Cicero Avenue
Lincolnwood, Illinois 60712

Permission is never granted for commercial purposes.

ISBN-13: 978-1-4127-1651-2
ISBN-10: 1-4127-1651-9

Manufactured in USA.

8 7 6 5 4 3 2 1

CONTENTS

❀ ❖ ❀

READING IS BELIEVING!

Haven't we all fallen prey at one time or another to the siren song of juicy gossip, a scandalous rumor, or creepy urban myth? Although it can be painful to discover that our cherished tidbit is actually incorrect, learning the truth often brings with it a feeling of "Aha!" and might even inspire us to question our sources more thoroughly in the future.

In *Armchair Reader™: The Book of Myths & Misconceptions*, we have endeavored to shed light on a wide variety of commonly held but erroneous beliefs. The so-called "facts" that we have assimilated over the years through cultural osmosis are closely examined under the Armchair Reader™ magnifying glass. Join us on this intellectual treasure hunt as we unearth the origins and question the truth behind a dizzying array of topics that include:

- Jack the Ripper's gruesome ties to the British royal family
- Modern-day dinosaurs living right in your neighborhood
- Charles Manson's audition for the TV show *The Monkees*
- Rock Hudson's marriage to Jim Nabors

Controversial? Possibly. Entertaining, interesting, and surprising? We think so, and we're sure you will, too. Please feel free to flop onto your favorite furniture (we know the piece we'd choose) and enjoy the factual feast we've prepared for your delectation!

Until next time,

Allen Orso
Publisher

P.S. If you have any questions, concerns, or ideas pertaining to this book, or if you would like more information about other West Side Publishing titles, please contact us at:
www.armchairreader.com.

HOW DO YOU LIKE
THEM APPLES?

*Johnny Appleseed is often depicted as a happy-go-lucky
farmer who roamed the American frontier barefoot,
wearing a pan on his head and scattering apple seeds.
Although this image fits comfortably with folklore,
Johnny Appleseed was actually a real person.*

Johnny Appleseed was born John Chapman on September 26,
1774, in Leominster, Massachusetts. He made his name by moving west ahead of the first pioneers, mainly in and around western
Pennsylvania, Indiana, and Ohio. He traveled with a supply of
apple seeds that he used to plant orchards (some of which exist to
this day). By the time the first settlers arrived, he had fully grown
apple trees ready to sell to them, along with nutritious fruit and
that intoxicating beverage of choice among weary travelers—hard
cider. Chapman quickly became known for his friendly, outgoing
nature, and settlers welcomed him into their homes both for his
liquid refreshments and his entertaining stories. They nicknamed
him Johnny Appleseed, and along with his popularity, legends
about him began to spread.

Although there's no evidence to support the idea that Johnny
Appleseed wore a cooking pot on his head, he was known to
remain barefoot—even in ice and snow. He preached a liberal
Christian theology called Swedenborgianism, befriended Native
Americans, and espoused a deep love of nature. He believed it
was a sin to chop down trees or kill animals, and he often used
his apple-tree profits to buy lame horses and save them from
slaughter.

Johnny Appleseed died in 1845, but his reputation continued
to grow. In 1871, a story about his life appeared in *Harper's New
Monthly Magazine,* and the depiction served to elevate him from
eccentric tree planter to "patron saint of horticulture."

LIKE A ROCK

❋ ❈ ❋

Rolling Rock has long been one of Pennsylvania's favorite libations, and for years, barroom patrons have bickered over the significance of the number 33 on the beer's label.

Beer drinkers love beer labels almost as much as they love the yeasty, thirst-quenching nectar itself. Each word and turn of phrase is examined, disputed, and questioned in discussions that are usually helped along by concerted suds consumption. Consider, for example, the number 33 on bottles of Rolling Rock beer. Some lager analysts have theorized that the double digits denote the year—1933—that Prohibition was repealed and alcoholic beverages were once again allowed to flow freely. Others contend that "33" refers to the number of steps from the brewmaster's office to the brewery floor. Equine enthusiasts claim that a timely transaction at the track—placing a $33 bet on horse number 33 on the third race on the third day of the third month—provided Rolling Rock's future owner with the funds necessary to buy his brewery. So which one of these tantalizing theses holds the answer?

The truth is, none of the above. In 1939, company executives developed a distinctive description of their product to adorn the label. To ensure that the manufacturer printed the pronouncement correctly, the number of words in the elongated adage—33—was added at the end of the text as a guideline. Only after the first bottles of Rock rolled off the line was it discovered that the number 33 had been mistakenly left at the end of the slogan.

Count 'Em and Weep

"Rolling Rock. From the glass-lined tanks of Old Latrobe, we tender this premium beer for your enjoyment as a tribute to your good taste. It comes from the mountain springs to you. 33"

RETURN TO SENDER

*Kids who procrastinate on homework projects like to justify
the delay by recalling that Abraham Lincoln scribbled
the Gettysburg Address on the back of an envelope shortly before
he gave the speech. Well, those same kids are about to get schooled.*

The Gettysburg Address, given by Lincoln at the dedication of
Gettysburg National Cemetery on November 19, 1863, is considered by most historians to be one of the greatest pieces of oratory
ever presented by a president. Almost everyone knows at least the
opening line, even if they don't know how many years "four score
and seven" equals (it's 87, in case you're curious).

Presidential Procrastination?

One of the most enduring myths surrounding the Gettysburg
Address is that Lincoln wrote it on the back of a used envelope
as he rode a train from Washington, D.C., to the Pennsylvania
cemetery. It's definitely a great story, but historians agree that it's
not true.

To Lincoln, the Gettysburg speech was a minor effort, a necessary honorific that he assumed would quickly be forgotten. Nonetheless, he did spend some time on its creation, writing at least
two drafts and changing the speech slightly as he gave it.

Short and Sweet

During the dedication, the speaker at the podium just before Lincoln, a man named Edward Everett, spent two hours recounting
the Battle of Gettysburg in excruciating detail. The audience was
exhausted by the time Lincoln finally took the dais, not to mention
a little startled when his speech lasted only two minutes. In fact,
some people were confused when Lincoln sat down, unsure that
the speech was actually over. Silence followed, and Lincoln later
confided to a friend that he felt the speech, in its brevity, had dis-
appointed people. Of course, he couldn't have been more wrong
about one of history's most noble expressions of democracy.

LIP'S QUIP

*Long considered to be a placard for the passive and polite,
the saying "Nice guys finish last" is credited to baseball manager
Leo Durocher. For decades he sailed his ship on the wave created
by that quote, but according to Durocher himself,
he merely used the phrase best.*

Known as "The Lip" during his lengthy major league career as
a player and on-field manager, Leo Durocher was always quick
with a quip and a colorful anecdote. On July 6, 1946, when he was
bench boss of the Brooklyn Dodgers, Durocher was shooting the
breeze with sports scribe Frank Graham about that afternoon's
opponents, the crosstown-rival New York Giants. The Dodgers,
known affectionately as "Da bums" by the Brooklyn faithful, were
a motley crew of reprobates who played hard both on and off the
field. When asked to describe the Giants, Durocher supposedly
said: "Take a look at them. They're all nice guys, but they'll finish
last. Nice guys. Finish last." In his summation of the conversation the following day, Graham shortened the quote to "Nice guys
finish last." At the time, Durocher denied making the remark, and
his account of the episode was substantiated by *New York Times*
pundit Lou Effrat, who was adamant that the Lip had actually
lamented, "Nice guys finish eighth," referring to the number of
teams in the league.

In 1992, Ralph Keyes compiled a book of misquotes titled *Nice
Guys Finish Seventh*. In his version of the events, Durocher said:
"Why, they're the nicest guys in the world! And where are they? In
seventh place." Which is where the Giants were in the standings
when the Lip started flapping. Although no one can agree on what
was actually said, Durocher nonetheless titled his 1975 best-selling
autobiography—what else?—*Nice Guys Finish Last.*

THE SEVERED EAR OF VINCENT VAN GOGH

Vincent van Gogh is remembered as a brilliant, temperamental artist who sliced off his left ear in a fit of insanity. But like the ear itself, the veracity of this story is only partial.

A Tortured Soul

Throughout his life, the great Dutch artist was plagued by a wide range of physical and mental ailments, including epilepsy, lead poisoning, bipolar disorder, and depression. As a child, he was withdrawn and suffered from social paralysis, and his anxiety increased greatly after he was sent away to boarding school.

Van Gogh did indeed take a whack at his left ear, but he only severed part of the earlobe. This act of self-mutilation happened when he was spending time with his friend and fellow artist Paul Gauguin in Paris. Actually, the word *friend* may be imprecise here—van Gogh and Gauguin often drank heavily together and ended up in heated arguments. On the Parisian social and artistic scene, absinthe was a popular libation, and van Gogh had a particular fondness for it. At the time, it was thought that people who consumed too much of the powerful liquor were prone to violent behavior.

Fighting Dirty

During a spat with Gauguin on Christmas Eve in 1888, van Gogh attacked him with a razor. When he failed to cause Gauguin any harm, van Gogh filled the emotional void by razoring off a piece of his own earlobe. He gave the bloody chunk to his prostitute friend Rachel, advising her to keep it as something precious. (Laugh if you wish. What would it be worth today?)

The incident happened about two years before van Gogh shot himself to death. It's reasonable to assume that his suicide was connected to a general and final psychological collapse—another irrational, self-harming act.

HITLER'S DANCE FEVER

*When France surrendered to the Nazis during World War II,
did Adolf Hitler really perform an odd little jig?
The Führer was guilty of many things, but inappropriate
dancing wasn't among his crimes.*

In June 1940, as Adolf Hitler accepted the surrender of the
French government at Compiegne, France, he gave the sidewalk
a single stamp with his boot, seeming to punctuate the astonishing turn of history. But people in Allied countries saw something
much different in newsreels: Hitler danced a childish two-step,
seeming to gloat over the German victory. Played over and over
again in movie theaters, the clip ridiculed the Nazi leader while
raising the fighting spirit of the public for the many battles to
come. Although still recorded as fact in many history books, Hitler's jig was in fact the invention of British propagandists who had
simply looped the footage of his single step so that he appeared to
be dancing.

Hitler was also the target of less-remembered hoaxes. In 1933,
a picture supposedly showing him as a baby—with a scowling
mouth and menacing eyes—was published widely in Great Britain
and the United States. The German consulate in Chicago wrote
a letter to the *Chicago Tribune* protesting the photo. Five years
later, the image was identified by a woman named Harriet Downs,
who said it was a baby photograph of her son, John, which had
been obviously retouched and darkened to make the child appear
sinister. The photo was then retracted by Acme Newspictures.

❈ ❈ ❈

- *Since 1927,* Time *magazine has featured a person, place, or thing
  that "for better or worse, has done the most to influence the
  events of the year." In 1938, that person was Hitler.*

PRIORITY SEATING

Most people who fly on planes have little choice about where they sit. If they did, a popular misconception might have the majority of passengers clamoring for the back of the plane rather than the first-class section.

Any traveler will tell you that sitting at the back of an airplane is just a stifling sound track of engine roars punctuated by toilet flushes. But you'd be surprised at the number of people who will weather the annoyances because they are convinced that the back of the plane is a much safer place to sit than the front. After all, they reason, a debilitated plane plunges nose first, so those seated in front would at least be first to redeem their lifetime air miles for a pair of angel wings.

Some aviation experts say the back of a plane is statistically safer by about 10 percent over business class—a small consolation. But others insist that the seats over the wings are the safest ones to occupy, because the structure of the wing section can absorb more impact damage. The prevailing wisdom, however, is that the seats closest to the emergency exits are your best bet.

When most people think of aviation accidents, they conjure up catastrophic midflight events in which mechanical malfunctions send a plane plummeting to the ground or into a mountainside. The fact is that nearly 95 percent of all airplane mishaps take place either at takeoff or during landing, which means the high-altitude cruise is actually the safest part of the journey.

Crashes Are Uncommon

In most airplane accidents, there's an on-board fire, and the biggest threat is actually the toxic smoke, which can spread fast in a closed cabin, obstructing everyone's view of the emergency exits and making it difficult to breathe or speak.

WHO SAYS DINOSAURS ARE EXTINCT?

Dinosaurs vanished from Earth 65 million years ago...or did they? Don't get nervous—you won't see a Tyrannosaurus rex *stomping down your street.*

Recent findings have turned the field of paleontology on its head. Scientists now believe that there is a group of dinosaurs that are not extinct. In fact, they could be flapping around your neighborhood right now!

Look...Up in the Sky!

The dinosaurs that exist today are descendants of theropod dinosaurs, a group that includes such popularly known creatures as velociraptor and *T. rex,* as well as myriad smaller dinosaurs. These living relics are avian dinosaurs—also known as birds.

For hundreds of years, scientists had observed similarities between birds and the fossils of theropod dinosaurs—features such as hollow bones and birdlike feet. The conceptual leap from "birdlike" to "bird" was cemented in 1996, when an extraordinary finding was reported from China's Liaoning Province. Paleontologist Chen Pei Ji presented a fossilized skeleton of a small theropod surrounded by impressions of fuzzy down on the perimeter of its body. Turns out, these were feathers. Since then, hundreds more of these feathered dinosaur specimens have been found all over the world.

Jurassic Zoo

Our understanding of dinosaurs has always been limited by what we can glean from dusty fossilized remains. If you want to learn about how theropod dinosaurs moved, how their bodies were shaped, and even how they cared for their young, you can skip the trip to a natural history museum and go to the zoo instead. An afternoon with an emu could be your day with a dinosaur.

A CRYING SHAME

*A popular public-service campaign
from the 1970s featured a Native American man
named Iron Eyes Cody whose tearful visage
implored people not to litter.
In truth, his heritage was fabricated.*

"People start pollution; people can stop it." Although the public-service campaign was one of the most successful ever created, Iron Eyes Cody's career encompassed much more than that particular spot. He appeared in an estimated 200 movies and dozens of television shows, typically playing a Native American. Offscreen, he worked faithfully and tirelessly on behalf of the Native American community. Throughout his adult life, Iron Eyes Cody claimed to be of Cherokee/Cree lineage. However, the assertion was a lie: Cody was, in fact, a full-blooded Italian.

Of Immigrants Born

His story began in the tiny town of Kaplan, Louisiana, where he was born Espera DeCorti in 1904. His parents, Antonio DeCorti and Francesca Salpietra, had emigrated from Italy at the turn of the century. Espera—who went by the name Oscar—was the second eldest of the couple's four children.

Antonio abandoned his family in 1909 and moved to Texas. Francesca divorced him and married a man named Alton Abshire, with whom she bore five more children. While still in their teens, Oscar and his brothers, Joseph and Frank, joined their father in Texas and, like their father, shortened their last name to Corti. In 1924, following Antonio's death, the brothers moved to Hollywood, where they again changed their last name—this time to Cody—and started working in motion pictures.

Joseph and Frank managed to land a few jobs as movie extras but eventually gave up their acting dreams and moved on to other careers. Oscar, however, had found his niche. He quietly changed his name to Iron Eyes Cody and started passing himself off as a full-blooded Native American.

Who Knew?

At the time, no one had reason to challenge him. Cody had a distinctive Native American look, and he took great pains to embrace his new identity and false heritage. He married a Native American woman named Bertha Parker, and together they adopted several Native American children. Iron Eyes almost always wore his long hair in braids and dressed in Native American attire, including beaded moccasins.

In fact, it was Cody's appearance that made his anti-littering public service announcement such a success. Everyone who saw it assumed that Cody was a real Native American and thus felt tremendous sympathy for him when a bag of garbage was tossed at his feet. Many even thought the tear that ran down his cheek at the ad's conclusion was real, but it was really just a drop of glycerin.

The television ad made Cody a household name and brought him quite a bit of attention. In the years that followed, he repeatedly denied nagging rumors that he was not what he claimed to be, and his story finally unraveled in the mid-1990s when his half-sister sent journalists proof that he was actually Italian. Several newspapers jumped on the story, eagerly pulling back the curtain to reveal the truth behind Cody's ancestral lie. But even in the face of overwhelming evidence (including his birth certificate), Cody stuck steadfastly to his story, which he maintained until his death.

Who Cared?

Ultimately, it didn't really matter to most Native Americans that Iron Eyes Cody had lied. He had spent decades working on their behalf, drawing international attention to their concerns. In 1995, Hollywood's Native American community honored him for his many charitable endeavors.

Iron Eyes Cody—perhaps the most famous Native American who never was—died on January 4, 1999, at the age of 94.

THE REAL DIRT
ON THE DESERT

❋ ❋❋ ❋

Sand dunes, scorching heat, mirages.
If this is your image of the desert, you're in
for a surprise. There are many stories about
the desert that have spawned numerous myths.
Here are two favorites.

Myth: It never snows in the desert.
Fact: Believe it or not, the largest desert on Earth is Antarctica, where it snows a lot—the mean annual precipitation ranges from 5.9 to 10.2 inches. So why is Antarctica considered a desert? The definition of a desert is a region that receives very little rain. To be precise, a desert landscape exists where rainfall is less than 10 inches per year. Rain, of course, is needed to sustain certain types of plants and animals, but snow doesn't count as rain. So Antarctica—with all its wet snow—is dry enough to be considered a desert and too dry for a person to survive without water.

Myth: Most sandstorms occur in hot, dry deserts.
Fact: It's true that dangerous sandstorms commonly occur in hot, dry deserts, including the Sahara and the Gobi. But they also occur frequently in a place you might never consider—North China, particularly around the area of Beijing. Since 2000, there have been 70 sandstorms—with an average of more than 13 per year.

A ten-year research project found that sandstorms affecting China were closely related to the cold front from Siberia, according to the Inner Mongolia Autonomous Regional Meteorological Station. As the cold front swirls through the Gobi and other large desert areas, it often combines with cyclones in Mongolia, consequently bringing sandstorms to China. So if you're planning a trip to the Great Wall of China, prepare to dust yourself off!

THE CAT TOSS

*Cats are curious creatures: Many people believe that
a dropped kitty will right itself and land safely on its feet,
only to step away aloof and unaffected.*

A Belgian legend has it that in A.D. 962, Baldwin III, Count of
Ypres, threw several cats from a tower. It must have been a slow
news year, because the residents of Ypres named the last day of
their annual town fair "Cat Wednesday" and commemorated it
by having the village jester throw live cats from a belfry tower—a
height of almost 230 feet. But there's no need to call PETA: The
last time live cats were used for this ceremony was in 1817, and
since then stuffed animals have been thrown in their place.

As cruel as this custom was, it is unclear whether the cat toss
was meant to kill cats or to demonstrate their resilience. After that
last live toss in 1817, the village record keeper wrote the following:
"In spite of the height of the fall, the animal ran off quickly so that
it might never be caught again in a similar ceremony." How could
the cat have survived such a tumble?

✻✻✻

Twist and Meow

Cats have an uncanny knack for righting themselves in midair.
Even if a cat starts falling head first, it almost always hits the
ground on its paws. The people of Ypres weren't the only ones
amazed and amused by this feline feat. In 1894, French physi-
ologist Etienne-Jules Marey decided to get to the bottom of the
mechanics of cat-righting by taking a series of rapid photographs
of a cat in midfall. Marey held a cat upside down by its paws and
then dropped it several feet onto a cushion.

The resulting 60 sequential photos demonstrated that as the
cat fell, it initiated a complex maneuver, rotating the front of its
body clockwise and then the rear part counterclockwise. This

motion conserved energy and prevented the cat from spinning in the air. It then pulled in its legs, reversed the twist again, and extended its legs slightly to land with minimal impact.

High-Rise Syndrome

The story gets even more interesting. In 1987, two New York City veterinarians examined 132 cases involving cats that had fallen out of the windows of high-rise buildings (the average fall was five and a half stories). Ninety percent of the cats survived, though some sustained serious injuries. When the vets analyzed the data, they found that, predictably, the cats  suffered progressively greater injuries as the height from which they fell increased. But this pattern continued only up to seven stories; above that, the farther the cat fell, the greater chance it had of surviving relatively unharmed.

The researchers named this peculiar phenomenon High-Rise Syndrome and explained it this way: A cat that fell about five stories reached its terminal velocity—that is, maximum downward speed—of 60 miles per hour. If it fell any distance beyond that, it had the time not only to right itself in midair but also to relax and spread itself out to slow down its fall, much like a flying squirrel or a parachute.

Not Quite Nine Lives

Although cats have the capacity to survive great falls, they rarely survive them uninjured. In urban areas, where careless pet owners let their cats sun themselves on the ledges of unscreened windows or stroll on balconies, veterinary hospitals frequently treat cats that have broken their jaws, ribs, or limbs after landing from great heights. Cats may be resilient, but they are not immortal, and despite another popular misconception, they only have one life to live.

BEAM ME UP

❋ ❈ ❋

Star Trek fans who watch as captains Kirk and Picard are "beamed" from the starship Enterprise to a nearby planet want to believe that such instantaneous transport of matter—called "teleportation"—is actually possible. But is it?

What is teleportation? Since 1998, scientists have been applying Einstein's term for teleporting, *spukhafte Fernwirkung,* or "spooky action at a distance," to atoms and beams of light, sending their replicas across space. These experiments in physics are done through a bizarre process called "quantum entanglement."

Laboratory researchers create three charged atoms of an element such as beryllium—let's call them A, B, and C. Like all atoms, atom A has certain unique properties, such as its spin, motion, and magnetic field. Atoms B and C have their own properties. In teleportation, scientists move the properties of atom A to atom C, in essence re-creating atom A.

Yet physicists face a big obstacle in moving atom A's unique characteristics: It's called Heisenberg's Uncertainly Principle. This is the scientific theorem that one cannot know with certainty the properties of a particle, including its location and speed.

To get around the uncertainty, scientists "entangle" atom B and atom C. Through the magic of quantum physics, researchers then can measure the properties of an atom without changing them. Next they transmit the properties of atom A, via atom B, to atom C. Atom C takes on the properties of atom A, in effect "becoming" atom A.

Great! When do we leave? The experiment can be done with photons of light as well as atoms. Atoms can be sent about a foot and a half, and photons can be launched about 20 miles. But here's the disappointing part: This experiment can't yet be done with people. To duplicate a person, you'd need machines smart enough to copy and exactly position the trillions of atoms in the human body.

OSCAR WHO?

❋ ❋ ❋

*Every year, film buffs and celebrity oglers around
the world tune in to watch the Academy of Motion Picture
Arts and Sciences hand out its Academy Awards of Merit.
But why are they referred to as "Oscars"?*

The epic films *Ben-Hur* (1959), *Titanic* (1997), and *The Lord of
the Rings: The Return of the King* (2003) each won 11 of them.
The legendary Katharine Hepburn set the standard for professional acting, having won a record four of them in the category of
Best Actress. Renowned British actor Peter O'Toole was nominated for eight over the course of his career, only to go home
empty-handed every time.

"Them," of course, refers to the Academy Awards of Merit,
the illustrious prizes handed out annually by the Academy of
Motion Picture Arts and Sciences for excellence in the fields of
movie acting, writing, directing, producing, and technology.

The eight-and-a-half-pound gold-plated statuette that sym-
bolizes the epitome of film industry success is formally called the
Academy Award of Merit, or the Academy Award, for short. So,
how is it that the award became known as "Oscar"?

Credit for originating the name is generally given to former
Academy executive director Margaret Herrick. In 1931, as a young
librarian with the Academy, Herrick cheerfully remarked that the
statuette's art-deco figure reminded her of her Uncle Oscar. The
name stuck, and in 1939 the Academy began using both "the Academy Award" and "the Oscar" as the official tag of its prized prize.

❋ ❋ ❋

- *Bette Davis once claimed she coined the name when, after winning the Academy Award for Best Actress in 1935, she nicknamed her statuette "Oscar" after her husband, Harmon Oscar
  Nelson. Nice story, but it's a claim she later withdrew.*

ANOTHER HUMDRUM CONUNDRUM

❋ ❖ ❋

Is conundrum *just a five-dollar word for a perplexing problem, or must it be specifically a word-based riddle? If you have a strong opinion about the matter, some 16th-century academics might just be having the last laugh—at you.*

Picky, Picky...

Conundrum is a word that English majors and self-proclaimed grammarians find deliciously vexing. Most people use it to mean any difficult problem, paradox, or dilemma, but the "grammarati" hold that it can only mean a riddle involving wordplay. These nitpickers are tormented by the prevalent (and incorrect) usage but often enjoy the feeling of superiority that comes with rarified knowledge.

The word first appeared in print in 1596 and was spelled *quonundrum,* reflecting the then-fashionable academic humor of inventing Latin words to poke fun at current events and situations. It initially described someone who was overly pedantic or fussy about a seemingly unimportant point.

By 1646, *conundrum* had evolved to mean any bit of confusing wordplay, especially an insulting one. In the 1700s, it began to refer specifically to a riddle based on a pun or verbal trickery. By the end of the century, it was commonly used in reference to any mind-bending puzzle, especially one without an easy answer.

It's Only a Word

Despite the continued cry from modern English purists to keep *conundrum* from acquiring a meaning beyond that of a punny problem, they lost that battle nearly 300 years ago. The irony is that in railing against the historically accurate meanings and forms of the word, these language sticklers are perceived by the general populace as more than a little *conundrumed* (somewhat crazed) over the issue and are perhaps even—to borrow the original meaning—conundrums themselves.

ABNER STRIKES OUT!

Generations of baseball fans have been led to believe that the game was invented by Civil War hero Abner Doubleday in Cooperstown, New York, in 1839. Historians tell a different story.

The Doubleday myth can be traced to the Mills Commission, which was appointed in 1905 by baseball promoter Albert Spalding to determine the true origins of the game. Henry Chadwick, one of Spalding's contemporaries, contended that the sport had its beginnings in a British game called rounders, in which a batter hits a ball and runs around the bases. Spalding, on the other hand, insisted that baseball was as American as apple pie.

Can We Get a Witness?

The seven-member Mills Commission placed ads in several newspapers soliciting testimony from anyone who had knowledge of the beginnings of the game. A 71-year-old gent named Abner Graves of Denver, Colorado, saw the ad and wrote a detailed response, saying that he'd been present when Doubleday outlined the basics of modern baseball in bucolic Cooperstown, New York, where the two had gone to school together. In his account, which was published by the *Beacon Journal* in Akron, Ohio, under the headline "Abner Doubleday Invented Baseball," Graves alleged to have seen crude drawings of a baseball diamond produced by Doubleday both in the dirt and on paper.

The members of the Mills Commission took Graves at his word and closed their investigation, confident that they had finally solved the mystery of how baseball was invented. The commission released its final report in December 1907, never mentioning Graves by name, and a great American legend was born.

Sadly, Graves's story was more whimsy than fact. For one thing, he was only five years old in 1839, when he claimed to have seen Doubleday's drawings. But even more important, Doubleday wasn't even in Cooperstown in 1839—he was a cadet attending the military academy at West Point. In addition, Doubleday, a renowned diarist, never once mentioned baseball in any of his writings, nor did he ever claim to have invented the game.

Nonetheless, the Doubleday myth received a boost in 1934 when a moldy old baseball was discovered in an attic in Fly Creek, New York, just outside Cooperstown. It was believed to have been owned by Graves and as such was also believed to have been used by Abner Doubleday. The "historic" ball was purchased for five dollars by a wealthy Cooperstown businessman named Stephen Clark, who intended to display it with a variety of other baseball memorabilia. Five years later, Cooperstown became the official home of the Baseball Hall of Fame.

Who Was Baseball's Daddy?

If anyone can lay claim to being the father of American baseball, it's Alexander Cartwright. He organized the first official baseball club in New York in 1845, called the Knickerbocker Base Ball Club, and published a set of 20 rules for the game. These rules, which included the designation of a nine-player team and a playing field with a home plate and three additional bases at specific distances, formed the basis for baseball as we know the sport today. Cartwright's Hall of Fame plaque in Cooperstown honors him as the "Father of Modern Base Ball," and in 1953, Congress officially credited him with inventing the game.

Notable Nonetheless

Abner Doubleday may not have invented baseball, but he was still a man of historical significance. He was at Fort Sumter when it was attacked in 1861 (initiating the Civil War), and he aimed the first Union gun that was fired in the fort's defense. Doubleday also participated in some of the most important battles of the Civil War, including Antietam, Fredericksburg, Chancellorsville, and Gettysburg.

THE MYTH ABOUT BRAIN MATTER

Contrary to popular belief, adults can grow new brain cells.

Neuroscientists used to think that mature human brains could not produce new cells, so the number of neurons you managed to develop by the time you reached adulthood was all you got. But it turns out that the matter is slightly more complicated than that.

Science for the Birds
Oddly enough, some of the first people to recognize that brains are not set in stone were crooked canary sellers. Because male canaries sing and female canaries usually do not, only male canaries fetch a handsome price at pet stores. In the 1940s and '50s, enterprising bird importers took to injecting female canaries with testosterone in hopes of giving them the gift of song. The scam worked: The masculinized female canaries sang just long enough to be sold as males to hoodwinked pet-store owners and their unsuspecting customers.

Elevated Research
In the mid-1970s, when scientists at Rockefeller University repeated the canary sellers' testosterone "experiments," they discovered that the region of the brain responsible for singing was much larger in male canaries than in females. The injected female birds generated glial cells (which give structural support to the brain) and new neurons in that region. Subsequent research at Cornell University confirmed that this was not just stuff for the birds: All vertebrate brains, whether canary or human, house precursor cells, which can be stimulated to develop into new neurons, just as they would during embryonic development. Adult neurogenesis holds the tantalizing promise of rebuilding brain cells destroyed by injury, stroke, or degenerative diseases such as Alzheimer's or Parkinson's—a goal long considered to be the Holy Grail of medical research.

DRUNKEN REFORMERS

*If the squeaky-clean Puritans were known for their disdain
of alcohol, why was there more sour mash than mashed
potatoes at the first Thanksgiving?*

Many people associate the Puritans with the temperance movement that worked so hard to ban alcohol during the 19th and early
20th centuries. After all, wasn't it this fire-and-brimstone group
that did everything it could to squeeze all the fun out of life? The
truth is, the Puritans liked their hooch every bit as much as the
average drunken sailor—and they loaded down their ships with
the evil brew to prove it.

"A Puritan is a person who pours righteous indignation into
the wrong things," says writer G. K. Chesterton. Funny he should
use the word *pour.* When the *Mayflower* sailed to America, its
holds actually contained more beer than water. Although seemingly at odds with their religious precepts, the Puritans maintained
a love affair with alcohol that would span the ages.

After setting up shop in the New World, colonialist Puritans
got busy producing their favorite beverage. Soon, the manufacture
of rum would become colonial New England's largest industry.
Even the hallowed halls of Harvard University included a brewery.
Was nothing sacred?

Apparently not. John Hancock, the first signer of the Declaration of Independence, worked as an alcohol dealer. Thomas Jefferson, the document's author, penned its first draft at a Philadelphia
tavern. Even superpatriot Patrick Henry ("Give me liberty or give
me death") got in on the act as a bartender.

❋❋❋

- *In the 1830s, during the Second Great Awakening of Puritanism,
the average American consumed more than seven gallons of alcohol annually. Today, that figure has plummeted by two-thirds.*

CRACKING THE CASE

*Scare tactics can sometimes get people to give up annoying
habits—and that may be the origin of the misconception
that cracking one's knuckles will cause arthritis.*

Experts insist that there is no medical evidence that frequent
knuckle-cracking leads to the development of arthritic hands, but
that doesn't mean it's a good habit to have. Many people find those
knuckle-cracking noises highly annoying—a lot like fingernails on
a chalkboard.

That distinctive sound is created by a fairly complicated
sequence of events. Our joints are covered by connective-tissue
capsules. Inside them is a thick, clear substance called synovial
fluid, which lubricates our joints and supplies nutrients to our
bones. The fluid also contains gases, including CO_2. When a
knuckle-cracker goes into pre-pop mode and extends the fingers,
the capsule around the knuckles gets stretched out and its volume
increases. This, in turn, lowers the pressure of the synovial fluid
inside the joints and causes CO_2 bubbles to form, a process known
as cavitation. The popping or cracking sound is created when the
bubbles burst. It takes about half an hour before the gases are
reabsorbed into the synovial fluid. Until that happens, the knuckles cannot be cracked again.

Although knuckle-crackers are not at increased risk for arthritis, a long-term cracking habit can cause injury to the ligaments
around the finger joints. One study found that habitual knuckle-
crackers might also end up with decreased grip strength, swelling
of the hands, and soft-tissue damage to the fingers.

Many people who repeatedly crack their knuckles claim it
relieves finger stiffness and gives them greater finger mobility,
especially after typing on a keyboard for an extended period. A
better solution is a simple stretch of the hands—but that doesn't
get much of a reaction from coworkers, does it?

INVENTING THE INTERNET

❀❀❀

*Former vice president Al Gore received a Nobel Peace Prize,
but did he also claim that he invented the Internet?*

On March 9, 1999, while being interviewed by Wolf Blitzer on
CNN, Al Gore said, "During my service in the United States Congress, I took the initiative in creating the Internet. I took the initiative in moving forward a whole range of initiatives that have proven
to be important to our country's economic growth and environmental protection, improvements in our educational system."

It was merely a case of unfortunate wording. Of course, no single person invented the Internet. Its forerunner, ARPAnet, evolved
through the 1960s and '70s from defense researchers' information-sharing needs. In 1983, ARPAnet standardized the basic Internet
information-transfer system still used today: TCP/IP, designed by
Internet legends Vinton Cerf and Robert Kahn. With this, ARPAnet started to resemble the modern Internet.

When Gore joined Congress in 1977, his academic training
was in journalism and law. Alone, he was no more qualified to create an Internet than the average Joe is to create the starship *Enterprise.* What Gore did was push funding to support and expand the
Internet. He didn't invent the term "information superhighway,"
but he was using it back when the Net was still an information
goat path.

In the greater context, Gore meant that he'd gotten off his
congressional backside and done some work to help advance the
country's fortunes. His clumsy way of saying that may have in some
way cost him the presidency, but Cerf himself, considered to be
the real "father of the Internet," has publicly acknowledged Gore's
early legislative efforts on behalf of the technology.

DRIBBLING DRIVEL

*There are numerous rules on how to properly dribble a basketball,
but bouncing the ball with such force that it bounds
over the head of the ball handler is not illegal.*

Although it might fun-up the standard NBA game to see players
drumming dribbles with the exaggerated effort of the Harlem
Globetrotters, it wouldn't do much to move the game along. And
contrary to popular belief, there is no restriction on how high a
player may bounce the ball, provided the ball does not come to
rest in the player's hand.

Anyone who has dribbled a basketball can attest to the fact it
takes a heave of some heft to give the globe enough momentum
to lift itself even to eye-level height. Yet, the myth about dribbling
does have some connection to reality. When Dr. James Naismith
first drafted the rules for the game that eventually became known
as basketball, the dribble wasn't an accepted method of moving
the ball. In the game's infancy, the ball was advanced from teammate to teammate through passing. When a player was trapped by
a defender, it was common practice for the ball carrier to slap the
sphere over the head of his rival, cut around the befuddled opponent, reacquire possession of the ball, and then pass it up court.
This innovation was known as the overhead dribble, and
it was an accepted way to maneuver the ball until the
early part of the 20th century. The art of "putting the
ball on the floor" and bouncing it was used first as a
defensive weapon to evade opposing players.

By the way, there is absolutely no credence
to wry comments made by courtside pundits that
the "above the head" rule was introduced because
every dribble that former NBA point guard
Muggsy Bogues took seemed to bounce beyond
the upper reaches of his diminutive 5'3" frame.

THE FIRST MONOTHEISTIC FAITHS

Judaism is often thought to be the first monotheistic religion—that is, faith in a single, all-powerful God. But the idea of one all-knowing deity may have come along about the same time as another monotheistic creed—Zoroastrianism.

Zoroastrianism is named after its founding prophet, Zarathustra, a Median, or ancient Persian, who is believed to have lived around 1000 B.C. Roughly the same time that Hebrew tribes were beginning to worship a sole deity named Yahweh (or Jehovah), the followers of Zoroaster were taking up a faith with remarkable similarities to the Jewish creed.

The Faith of the Magi

Zoroastrians, of whom there are perhaps 200,000 today, believe in a universal God, Ahura Mazda. He is seen as the opposite of evil (namely, chaos and falsehood), which his worshippers (the forces of light) battle with good deeds, words, and thoughts. Zoroastrians believe that after they die, their souls leave their bodies, dwell in an intermediate world, and then are reunited at the end of time with Ahura Mazda, who judges them for their behavior on Earth. In another parallel with Judeo-Christian tradition, each person has a protecting *fravashi,* or guardian angel. Zoroastrianism was the preeminent religion of the Persian Empire, and Zoroastrian priests, known as Magi, were renowned for their knowledge. In the New Testament, the Magi were the wise men who journeyed to Bethlehem with gifts for the newborn Jesus.

According to scholar Hannah Shapero, the people and the cultures of the ancient Hebrews and Zoroastrians interacted often during and after the Babylonian Captivity—the exile of the Jews from Palestine to Babylon in 586 B.C., which ensued after the Assyrian conquest of the Kingdom of Judah. In 539 B.C., the Jews returned to the land of Zion after the Assyrians were conquered by King Cyrus's Persian Empire.

The trauma of their defeat by the Assyrians, and their exposure to the ideas of Zoroaster, may have bolstered the Jews' sometimes wayward monotheism (remember the golden calf?). Indeed, there are hints of Zoroastrian influence in Jewish thought. Their notion of a *saoshyant,* or savior, influenced the prophet Isaiah, who spoke of a coming messiah. And the biblical word *paradise* comes from the Persian term *pairidaeza,* or enclosed garden.

Shapero suggests that the Jews' time in an alien land made their faith more universal and their view of God less tribal, laying the ground for the universal faiths of Christianity and Islam. After its return from Babylon to Palestine, Judaism was firmly monotheistic, and it has been ever since. So perhaps Jews and Zoroastrians can take dual credit for devising the belief in a single God.

Just Following Akhenaten?

Yet both may have been beaten to the punch by the probable father of King Tut. Centuries before Zoroaster, the Egyptian pharaoh Akhenaten ordered his subjects to bow to a single deity, a sun god called Aten. Around 1353 B.C., Akhenaten and one of his wives, Nefertiti, built vast new temples to Aten and removed from public buildings the images of the old Egyptian gods. But the new religion didn't last, according to Egyptologist Kate Spence. When Tutankhamen took over Egypt, he destroyed the temples of Akhenaten and erased the very name of his blasphemous father from public memory—until the discovery of Tut's famous tomb helped resurrect the facts of his father's eventful reign.

A Second Opinion

Some Egyptian scholars think that Akhenaten's short-lived creed may not have really been monotheism. Because the people's worship of the god Aten was tightly tied to worship of Akhenaten and his family, it was likely more a cult of a king than devotion to one omnipotent God.

A PRESIDENCY CARVED IN STONE

*When something is considered absolute and irrefutable, it is said
to be "carved in stone." In the case of David Rice Atchison,
whose tombstone claims that he was once president
of the United States, you cannot take the granite for granted.*

Read through the list of presidents of the United States, and you
won't find the name David Rice Atchison. This shouldn't surprise
anyone, with the possible exception of those who have seen Atchison's gravesite and noted that his tombstone states emphatically
that the person buried there was president of the United States
for one day, March 4, 1849. The story goes something like this:
The term of President James Polk and his administration, including Vice President George Dallas, expired on Sunday, March 4,
1849. The incoming commander in chief, Zachary Taylor, was a
devoutly religious soul who refused to take the oath of office on
the Sabbath, so the inauguration ceremonies were rescheduled for
Monday, March 5.

According to the Constitution as it existed in 1849, the president pro tempore of the Senate was second in the line of succession to serve as the presiding chief executive, after the vice
president. When Congress was dissolved in 1849, that man was
David Rice Atchison. So in the opinion of some pundits, Atchison
was the acting president until Taylor's inauguration. There was one
problem, however. Atchison's term of office also came to an end on
Sunday. In effect, there was one day—Sunday, March 4—on which
the United States was left in the lurch without a leader.

Atchison does deserve one claim to fame. Because he had
already been selected by his fellow senators to continue his duties
as president pro tempore for another term, he was the first executive to take the oath of office on March 5. So it can be said that he
was "president" for a few minutes—until old Zach placed his left
hand on the Bible.

BABY RUTH'S TRUTH?

Many people believe that the Baby Ruth candy bar was named for baseball great Babe Ruth. Others contend that the honor belongs to President Grover Cleveland's daughter Ruth.

German immigrant Otto Schnering founded the Curtiss Candy Company in Chicago in 1916. With World War I raging in Europe, Schnering decided to avoid using his Germanic surname and chose his mother's maiden name for the business. His first product was a snack called Kandy Kake, a pastry center covered with peanuts and chocolate. But the candy bar was only a marginal success, and to boost sales, it was renamed Baby Ruth in 1921. Five years later the company was selling millions of dollars worth of the bars every day. Whenever pressed for details on the confection's name, Curtiss explained the appellation honored Ruth Cleveland, the late and beloved daughter of President Grover Cleveland. But the company may have been trying to sneak a fastball past everybody.

Cleveland's daughter had died of diphtheria in 1904—a dozen years before the candy company was even started. One questions the logic in naming a candy bar after someone who had passed away so many years earlier. The gesture may have been appropriate for a president, but a president's relatively unknown daughter?

The more plausible origin of the name might be tied to the biggest sports star in the world at the time—George Herman "Babe" Ruth. Originally a star pitcher for the Boston Red Sox, Ruth became a fearsome hitter for the New York Yankees, slamming 59 home runs in the same year the candy bar was renamed Baby Ruth. Curtiss may have found a way to cash in on the slugger's fame—and name—without paying a dime in royalties. In fact, when Ruth gave the okay to use his name on a competitor's candy—the Babe Ruth Home Run Bar—Curtiss successfully blocked it, claiming infringement on his own "baby."

BLUEBEARD VERSUS BLACKBEARD

*There is much confusion surrounding the identity
of Bluebeard, who often gets a bad rap as being
the infamous English pirate Blackbeard. Turns out,
there's good reason for the mix-up.*

Bluebeard

Bluebeard was in fact the title character of a fairy tale written
by Charles Perrault about a violent nobleman who murdered his
wives. The tale was first published in 1698, a few years before
Blackbeard the pirate came to prominence. In the story, the character was a man "so unlucky as to have a blue beard, which made
him so frightfully ugly that all the women and girls ran away from
him." When Bluebeard finally persuaded a woman to marry him,
she was driven by curiosity to discover the contents of a room in
his home that he always kept locked. When she entered the room,
she was greeted by the sight of blood-stained floors and the bodies of her husband's former wives hanging off the walls. Before
Bluebeard could add his new wife to the collection, she was
rescued by her brothers, who slew the murderous nobleman. The
tale of Bluebeard was used as the basic plot for Kurt Vonnegut's
1988 novel of the same name.

Blackbeard

Blackbeard, on the other hand, was the ferocious pirate Edward
Teach, who terrorized the waters of the Caribbean. He's usually
depicted armed to the teeth, often lighting matches off the hemp
woven into his mangy black beard. His most audacious act came
in 1718, when his pirate fleet blockaded the harbor of Charleston,
South Carolina. Without having to fire a shot, Blackbeard plundered merchant ships trapped in the harbor and terrorized the
town. He was later accused of deliberately grounding two of his
own vessels so he had fewer crew members with whom to share
his loot.

THE TENNIS STAR WHO WASN'T

No one can accuse Sports Illustrated *of not having a sense of humor. For laughs, it invented an attractive, camera-ready tennis star to rival Anna Kournikova. Her name was Simonya Popova.*

Sports Satire

A September 2002 issue of *Sports Illustrated* told of an unstoppable 17-year-old tennis force named Simonya Popova, a Russian from Uzbekistan and a media dream: 6'1", brilliant at the game, fluent in English, candid, busty, and blonde. She came from an appealing late-Soviet proletarian background and had a father who was often quoted in Russian-nuanced English. But she wouldn't be competing in the U.S. Open—her father forbade it until she turned 18.

The magazine verged on rhapsody as it compared Popova to Ashley Harkleroad, Daniela Hantuchová, Elena Dementieva, and Jelena Dokic. Editors claimed that, unlike Popova, all of these women were public-relations disappointments to both the Women's Tennis Association (WTA) and sports marketing because they chose to resist media intrusions to concentrate on playing good tennis. As a result, U.S. tennis boiled down to Venus and Serena Williams, trailed by a pack of hopefuls and won't-quite-get-theres. The gushing article concluded with this line: "If only she existed."

Just Kidding!

Popova *was* too good to be true. The biography was fiction, and her confident gaze simply showcased someone's digital artistry.

Some people got it. Many didn't, including the media. They bombarded the WTA with calls: Who was Popova and why wasn't she in the Open? The article emphasized what many thought—the WTA was desperate for the next young tennis beauty. WTA spokesperson Chris DeMaria called the story "misleading and irritating" and "disrespectful to the great players we have." Complaining that some people didn't read to the end of articles, he said, "We're a hot sport right now and we've never had to rely on good looks."

Sports Illustrated claimed it was all in grand fun. It hardly needed to add that it was indulging in puckish social commentary on the sexualization of women's tennis.

Other Great Sports Hoaxes

Sidd Finch. Another *Sports Illustrated* gag was the 1985 invention of a gangly yoga devotee and Mets pitching prospect by the name of Siddhartha Finch. With one foot in cleats and the other bare, Finch was unsure whether pitching was consistent with Tantric principles—but he could hurl an accurate fastball at 168 miles per hour. Author George Plimpton eventually novelized the fictitious Finch.

Michael Strahan fights Tom Arnold. In April 2006, the NFL defensive end and the actor pretended to get into a fight on the program *Best Damn Sports Show, Period.* Amusingly, the bumbling actor "won" the fight. Realistically, of course, Strahan against Arnold would be like Germany against Luxembourg. Strahan and Arnold even fooled their fellow hosts, former pitcher Rob Dibble and retired quarterback Rodney Peete, who rushed to break up the combatants.

Caltech Rose Bowl hoax. The Washington Huskies squared off against the Minnesota Golden Gophers in the 1961 Rose Bowl, and UW's "card section" was part of the halftime show. Fans in Washington's student section were given cards and instructions that told them when to flip the cards to reveal a giant message. They didn't know that some sneaky students from Caltech, a small technical college down the road, had stolen the instruction sheets and substituted a few of their own cards.

Halftime came, and the first 11 planned images went off normally. The 12th was supposed to be a husky but looked like a cartoon beaver—Caltech's mascot. Image 13 was supposed to say "Huskies," but the crowd saw "Seiksuh" and assumed the card-flippers had misread the instructions. Image 14 left no doubt about the gag when it blazoned "Caltech" in bold, black letters to fans in the stadium and to millions of viewers nationwide.

ON TOP OF THE WORLD

✻ ❉ ✻

Think you're at the top of the world when you climb Mt. Everest?
Think again. You'll need to scale Ecuador's Mt. Chimborazo
to make that claim.

You've scaled Mt. Everest and are marveling at the fact that
you're getting your picture taken at the highest point on the
planet. You're as close to the moon as any human being can be
while standing on the surface of the earth. Actually, you're not.
To achieve that, you'd have to climb back down and travel to the
other side of the world—Ecuador, to be exact—so you can schlep
to the summit of Mt. Chimborazo.

It's true that Everest, at 29,035 feet, is the world's tallest
mountain—when measured from sea level. But thanks to the
earth's quirky shape, Chimborazo, which rises only 20,702 feet
from sea level, is about a mile and a half closer to the moon than
Everest's peak.

Earth is not a perfect sphere. Rather, it's an oblate spheroid.
Centrifugal force from billions of years of rotating has caused the
planet to flatten at the poles and bulge out at the equator.

In effect, this pushes the equator farther from the earth's center than the poles—about 13 miles closer to the moon. The farther
you move from the equator, the farther you move from the moon.
Chimborazo sits almost at the equator, while Everest lies about
2,000 miles north—enough to make it farther from the moon than
Chimborazo, despite being more than 8,000 feet taller.

✻ ✻ ✻

• *Here's another geophysical oddity caused by the earth's midriff*
  bulge: Because its source lies 2,300 miles farther from the equa-
  tor than its mouth, the Mississippi River actually flows uphill
  from Minnesota to the Gulf of Mexico—which may explain why
  Old Man River seems to flow so slowly.

BEFORE BARBIE

The Barbie doll is considered by most people to be an American original. But before her, there was Bild Lilli, the German fashion doll that became the prototype for Barbie and friends.

What a Doll!

Barbie—the 11½-inch plastic fashion figure with the unachievable body structure and inexhaustible wardrobe—is the world's most successful toy doll, with more than a billion sold in over 150 countries. Introduced in 1959 at the American International Toy Fair by Mattel Inc., Barbie has staked her place in American pop culture. She's been parodied countless times by the media (notably as the vacuous Malibu Stacy doll on *The Simpsons*) and honored with a section of Times Square renamed Barbie Boulevard. Her unrealistic body image and prissy persona have riled feminists for 50 years, yet her iconic status earned Barbie 43rd place on the list *101 Most Influential People Who Never Lived,* published in 2006.

A German Predecessor

Barbie's indelible mark on the national psyche leads most people to assume that she's a purely American creation. But Barbie had a predecessor whose name was Bild Lilli. This German fashion doll was based on a popular comic-strip character who sassily used men to get what she wanted. The adult-figured Lilli doll was originally sold as a sexy novelty item for men, but it spawned an idea in the mind of Ruth Handler, an American who discovered Lilli while visiting Europe in 1956. Handler set about designing a more wholesome version of Lilli geared toward girls. She named her creation Barbie, after her daughter, Barbara, and pitched the idea to her husband, who was a cofounder of Mattel.

Whatever became of Lilli? Mattel bought the rights to the doll in 1964 and promptly stopped its production—effectively removing the skeleton from Barbie's cavernous closet.

PLAY THAT AGAIN, AND I'LL PUT A CHOPSTICK IN MY EYE

In 1877, 16-year-old Euphemia Allen composed the simple piano composition commonly known as "Chopsticks." But what is the real connection between this annoying ditty and the Asian eating utensils?

The actual name of Allen's composition, "The Celebrated Chop Waltz," stems from her performance note that the piece should be played with the hands held flat, perpendicular to the keys, the little fingers pointing downward and striking the keys in a chopping motion. As the piece became more popular, players began using the forefinger of each hand to strike the keys, an action that called to mind the mechanics involved in using a pair of chopsticks. Because of this, and the non-Western sounds of some of the intervals, the name began to morph into its current reference. This false connection was strengthened by the fact that the work was repeatedly published with images of fans, kimonos, dragons, and pagodas on the cover.

In a strange coincidence, the same year that Allen published her piece, the Russian composer Aleksandr Borodin overheard his daughter playing a similar composition. He called his daughter's composition "The Coteletten Polka" (from the French word for "chop" or "cutlet"). He went on to compose and publish variations on that tune, as did a number of other famous composers, including Nikolai Rimski-Korsakov and Franz Liszt. It seems likely that both Allen and Borodin's daughter were playing their own variations on a simple, one-fingered composition from a popular beginner's piano book, but that composition, if it ever existed, has never been found. A copy of Allen's piece, on the other hand, is owned by the British Museum, published under pseudonym Arthur de Lulli.

THE BEST LAID PLANS

❀ ❀ ❀

*Go ahead, plan all you want—but don't forget what happens
to the field mouse's nest when plowing begins!*

John Steinbeck is often given credit for the saying "The best laid plans of mice and men often go astray." The title of his classic novella *Of Mice and Men* automatically brings this piece of wisdom to mind. But Steinbeck did not dream up the title; rather, he borrowed it from a poem.

Anyone particularly knowledgeable about literature should correctly cite the source of this saying as Robert Burns's 1785 poem "To a Mouse." There was a time back in the early 20th century—the era in which Steinbeck grew up—when every schoolchild in the United States was required to memorize poems. "To a Mouse" was a favorite selection, and Steinbeck would have been familiar with it, as would have most of his contemporaries.

"To a Mouse" describes Burns's sadness at having destroyed a mouse's nest with his plow. He empathizes with the mouse, which had spent so much time and care building its house, only to have it ruined in an instant. Burns writes (in the Scottish dialect): "The best laid schemes o' mice an' men gang aft a-gley," which translates as "The best laid schemes of mice and men go oft astray."

Steinbeck's choice of a title for his novella reflects the story's plot. Two hard-luck Depression-era migrant workers do everything they can to improve their lot in life, only to have their plans struck down by circumstances out of their control. The message of the story is that dreams are fragile and plans can be futile. Robert Burns's life turned out to be proof of this sentiment. Having spent most of his adult years as an unsuccessful farmer, Scotland's National Poet died in poverty at the age of 37.

THE HITLER DIARIES HOAX

✳ ❖ ✳

In 1983, Germany's popular magazine Stern *dropped a bomb: It now had access to Adolf Hitler's secret diaries. Experts soon revealed them as phonies authored by a modern crook, leaving prominent historians and major media looking ridiculous.*

Counterfeit Collectibles

The crook was Konrad Kujau, a man of numerous aliases and lies. He was born in 1938, and after World War II he lived in East Germany. He moved to West Germany in 1957 and began a life of petty crime, quickly specializing in forgery.

A lifetime Hitler fan, Kujau became a noted Nazi memorabilia "collector." Naturally, he manufactured most of his collection, including authentication documents. He built a favorable reputation as a dealer specializing in ostensibly authentic Hitler stuff· signatures, writing, poetry, and art.

The public display of Nazi anything is illegal in Germany, as is Holocaust denial. Even WWII games sold in modern Germany cannot use the swastika. Nazi memorabilia collections remain strictly on the down low. Modern Germans overwhelmingly repudiate Nazism, and those born post-war also dislike association with a horror they didn't perpetrate. It's a painful subject.

Still, every country has closet Hitler admirers, and Germany is no exception. *Stern* journalist Gerd Heidemann was one—he even bought Hermann Goering's old yacht. In 1979, a collector (Kujau under an alias) invited Heidemann to check out his Nazi collection, including a bound copy of a diary supposedly authored by Hitler. The diary, which covered a period from January to June 1935, had been salvaged from a late-war plane crash in East Germany. The collector also claimed that there were 26 other volumes, each covering a six-month period.

Faulty Fact-Checking

Using his journalistic training, Heidemann went to East Germany and found a backstory that verified a plane crash. Although he didn't dig much deeper, he had a good excuse. At the time, the world thought in terms of East and West Germany. In East Germany, a socialist police state, no one nosed around except where the state approved (which it rarely did). Heidemann and *Stern's* West German homeland was the mainstay of NATO, and the border between East and West Germany bristled with a surprising percentage of the world's military power. *Stern* lacked an easy way to verify anything in East Germany.

So Heidemann basically pitched what he had to *Stern*, and the magazine swung from its heels. Salivating at the "find of a generation," *Stern* authorized Heidemann to offer an advance of $1 million (approximate U.S. equivalent) for the diaries. Kujau played coy, explaining that the other 26 volumes hadn't yet been smuggled out of East Germany. In reality, he needed time to forge them. He finally finished in 1981 and handed over the first volume to Heidemann.

At this point, everyone was too excited to bother with that tedious step called "authentication." *Stern* hadn't even learned Kujau's identity; it was too busy counting its future profit from serialization rights. Anyone who voiced worries about fraud was hushed. Some surprisingly big names entered bids, including *Newsweek, Paris Match,* and the *London Times.*

Stretching the Truth

The diaries themselves purported to reveal a kinder, gentler Hitler, a generally okay guy who wasn't even fully aware of the Holocaust. This Hitler is what modern Nazi sympathizers like to imagine existed, not the weird megalomaniac of actual history. But its improbability also spurred skeptics into gear.

In an attempt to deal with the naysayers, *Stern* got a bit hysterical, even insisting that noted British historian Hugh Trevor-Roper had pronounced the diaries authentic. But skeptics faulted the diaries' paper, handwriting, and style. After some controversy,

West German authorities ran forensics. The testing proved that the paper, ink, and even glue were of post-WWII manufacture. *Stern* had been bamboozled.

Because *Stern* is to Germany what *Time* and *Newsweek* are to the United States, it had a significant amount of credibility to lose. Several *Stern* editors were soon looking for new jobs. To say that the West German government was "annoyed" is an understatement. After *Stern* fired Heidemann, the police charged him with fraud. Heidemann, in his smartest move in a long time, implicated Kujau. When this news was made public in the media, Kujau went into hiding. In May 1983, he decided to turn himself into the police, who were anxiously waiting to arrest him. After several days of intense questioning, the authorities learned that Kujau was a reflexive, perpetual liar who invented falsehoods to cover his fictions.

The High Price of Greed

Kujau and Heidemann were each sentenced to several years in jail. The judge said *Stern* had "acted with such naiveté and negligence that it was virtually an accomplice in the fraud." The roughly $5 million the magazine ultimately gave Heidemann to pay Kujau was never recovered. Heidemann's increasingly lavish lifestyle during the forgeries and subsequent investigations suggests that he spent the majority of the money offshore.

After his release, Kujau tried his hand at politics, replica painting, and (again) forgery. He died of complications from cancer in 2000, but his crime is considered one of the most bold and successful hoaxes of the century.

Declassified East German files later showed that Heidemann had been an East German spy, though it's uncertain whether that had anything to do with the hoax. He claims he was actually a double agent working for West German authorities. With his career prospects impaired, he now keeps a low profile. For its part, *Stern* would like to forget the whole thing.

CUT THE FAT

*Exercise enthusiasts and gym-goers everywhere fear it:
Take too long a break from a workout regimen, and those
hard-earned muscles will turn into fat. Luckily for
the lazy, this change is actually impossible.*

Even if you lie on the couch all day eating bonbons, moving only
slightly to reach the remote control, your muscles will not turn
into fat. However, you will most certainly gain weight, and your
muscle strength will diminish.

There are hundreds of different types of cells in the human
body—muscle and fat are just two of them. Like spaghetti and
meatballs, muscle and fat cells are often grouped together, but
they don't have much in common, and one will never turn into the
other. Muscle cells are long, fibrous, and mostly striated, while fat
cells are round and globular. Each type of cell has a different function: Fat cells store energy, and muscle cells burn energy.

When you stop exercising, your muscles begin to shrink, or
atrophy. You don't lose muscle cells; the ones you have just get
smaller and flabbier. If you continue to consume the same number of calories as you did when you were active, your fat cells
will grow and store the excess calories that are not being burned.
The engorged fat cells will take up residence in the territory that
muscles used to occupy, creating the illusion that muscle has
magically converted to fat.

Get Moving!

There are more than 600 muscles in the human body, so if you really
want to get in shape, you have plenty to focus on. You can build and
tone your muscles with the use of fancy gym equipment, but simple
everyday activities such as walking and household chores can help
keep some of them from looking flabby—and that's no illusion.

BILL BLEEPING BUCKNER

*Put "Red Sox" and "1986 World Series" in the same
sentence, and the name "Bill Buckner" is only a few words
away. Despite popular belief, though, the team's collapse
wasn't entirely his fault.*

During Boston's 85 consecutive seasons without a World Series
championship, the word *bleeping* assumed a prominent place in
the lexicon of Red Sox Nation. Commonly inserted between the
first and last names of players who separated the Sox from the
prize, its use reached an alliterative zenith in 1986, when Bill
bleeping Buckner let that bleeping ball roll through his bleeping
legs. Had the first baseman stabbed the easy grounder for the final
out of Game 6, the Series could have ended in Boston's favor, but
it is just as true that the Sox had the chance to take care of business numerous times before and after the miscue.

By the time the contest had snaked to the bottom of the tenth
inning, the Red Sox already had given back two other leads and
left a scandalous 14 runners on base. And even before the New
York Mets' Mookie Wilson trickled the game-winning bouncer,
it was timorous young pitcher Calvin Schiraldi who surrendered
three singles to establish the precarious scenario. It was Schiraldi's
replacement, Bob Stanley, who allowed the tying run to score by
zipping an errant-but-catchable pitch past backstop Rich Gedman.

Then there's manager John McNamara, who was presented with
two situations in which he could've/should've replaced the hobbled
36-year-old Buckner before the game reached critical mass. Three
innings earlier, Mac allowed the left-handed hitter to bat (and pop
out) with the bases loaded against a tough lefty pitcher, despite
having powerful right-hander Don Baylor at his disposal. Protecting
a lead in the tenth, the skipper's obvious move would have been to
insert the more mobile Dave Stapleton at first base. By that time,
however, strategic rigor bleeping mortis had set in.

FALLACIES & FACTS: ST. PATRICK

❀ ❀ ❀

Fallacy: *St. Patrick drove the snakes out of Ireland.*
Fact: *There weren't any snakes in Ireland at that time. Snakes first appeared in the Southern Hemisphere on the supercontinent known as Gondwanaland before it separated into South America, Africa, India, Australia, and Antarctica. From there, snakes migrated north and eventually covered most of the globe. But they never made it to Ireland, which is surrounded by water.*

Fallacy: *St. Patrick was Irish.*
Fact: *Actually, he was born in Britannia, a Roman province that later became what we know as England. From Patrick's own writings, we know that he was captured by Irish raiders when he was 16 and carried off to Ireland, where he was a slave for six years. He escaped and returned to his family but was later inspired by a vision to return to Ireland to spread the Christian gospel.*

Fallacy: *St. Patrick used a shamrock to promote Christianity.*
Fact: *Although many believe St. Patrick used the three-leaf shamrock as a teaching symbol of the Christian trinity, there is no record of this in any of his writings or those of his contemporaries.*

Fallacy: *His name was Patrick.*
Fact: *Some historians say his birth name was Maewyn Succat. He took the name Patrick when he began his missionary work for the Catholic Church.*

Fallacy: *St. Patrick introduced Christianity to Ireland.*
Fact: *Ireland had strong trade relations with the Roman Empire, so it's likely that Christianity existed in the country before Patrick arrived.*

THE MALIGNED MRS. LINCOLN

Mary Todd Lincoln was a lot of things: first lady,
extravagant spender, generous hostess.
And though a Southerner by birth, she was not,
as is widely suspected, a Confederate spy.

Flawed First Lady

Being the president's wife is a grueling job—the hours are long
and the demands are wearisome. Most first ladies manage to get
through it relatively well, but for Mary Todd Lincoln, wife of
Abraham, it was an agonizing experience fraught with relentless
criticism, borderline mental illness, and personal tragedy.

Mary deeply loved her husband, whom she married despite
the disapproval of her family and social peers. She saw in Lincoln
a good, honest, talented man and was delighted when he won the
presidency in 1860. But because Mary was a native of Kentucky and
thus a Southerner by birth, rumors swirled throughout the course of
the Civil War that the first lady was, in fact, a Confederate spy.

Guilt by Relation

It's easy to see how such rumors got started. According to historians and biographers, Mary devotedly agreed with and supported
her husband's political beliefs and, like him, wanted only that the
nation become whole again.

But one of Mary's brothers, three half-brothers, and three
brothers-in-law all served in the Confederate army during the
Civil War. How then, people wondered, could she truly support
the Union? Not surprisingly, certain individuals—including many
of Lincoln's political enemies—started a whisper campaign that
perhaps Mary wasn't the Unionist she said she was.

The entire issue, however, was just scandalous hearsay without
a shred of proof. Even today, with nearly 150 years of hindsight,
there is absolutely no evidence that Mary Todd Lincoln passed
government secrets to the South, or even had the opportunity to

do so. Indeed, Mary's interests as first lady were generally more social than political.

Can't Win for Losing

The whispered allegation that Mary Lincoln was a Confederate spy was just one of many things that made her time in the White House miserable. The belles of Washington society considered her silly and uncouth and took every opportunity to denigrate her. For example, when she hosted a large party in the White House as the war raged, she was condemned for her extravagance. And because two of her sons were ill at the time, she was castigated as being unmotherly and cold.

All of this was made worse by Mary's many emotional and physical problems. She suffered from excruciating headaches that sometimes left her bedridden for days, and she also experienced violent mood swings that caused more than one White House aide to describe her as unpredictable and difficult to get along with.

Mary was also familiar with death. She lost three of her four sons to various ailments and, of course, witnessed the assassination of her beloved husband at the hands of John Wilkes Booth.

Mary Todd Lincoln was a flawed woman who did her best under dire circumstances. It's unfair and inaccurate for her character to be impugned by untrue rumors regarding her patriotism.

Varina Howell Davis

Varina Howell Davis, the young wife of Confederate president Jefferson Davis, suffered similar indignities over the course of the war. Though she was born in Mississippi, her father, a wealthy plantation owner, had deep Northern roots—his father was an eight-term governor of New Jersey. As a result, many within the Confederacy wrongly condemned Varina as a Union sympathizer.

FOR CRYING OUT LOUD!

*Every new parent dreams about getting
a good night's sleep, but there's a lot of disagreement
over the best way to help a baby sleep soundly.*

Of course, no one expects a newborn or young infant to sleep
through the night. But according to some experts, how parents put
their infants to bed and how they tend to them when they awaken
may make a difference in their sleep habits in the long run.

There are two main schools of thought on the subject.
Respected medical experts continue to weigh in with differing
theories and studies. Well-meaning—and experienced—friends
and family add to the confusion by offering their surefire bedtime
strategies.

To Soothe or Not to Soothe?

On one side of the debate are proponents of routines that purportedly train a baby to fall asleep by himself. This approach advises
parents to let the baby cry for short intervals of time. On the other
side are those who don't believe a crying infant should ever be left
alone and that it's a parent's responsibility to make the baby feel
secure enough to fall asleep.

The controversy over sleep routines escalated in 1985 with
the publication of *Solve Your Child's Sleep Problems,* by pedia-
trician Richard Ferber. He advocates allowing babies to soothe
themselves to sleep, starting around four to six months of age.
The basic idea of "Ferberizing," as it has come to be known, is to
put the baby in the crib while still awake, after a calming bedtime
routine. Parents are told to not pick up the baby or feed him, even
if he cries. Instead, Ferber advocates letting the baby cry for a few
minutes before returning to the room to comfort him. Parents are

instructed to gradually increase the amount of time the baby is left alone. Ferber calls this approach "progressive waiting," and he believes it eventually teaches the baby to fall asleep without parental intervention. Successfully Ferberized babies will be able to fall back asleep without crying out for their parents when they awaken during the night.

Critics of the Ferber method (which was somewhat revised in the 2006 edition of his book) argue that letting a baby "cry it out" only teaches an infant that nobody cares about him. Two Harvard researchers have gone so far as to say that leaving crying babies alone in their cribs can be traumatic, leading to emotional problems later in life.

Parental Prerogative

There is much anecdotal evidence from parents to support both points of view. Many moms and dads praise Ferber's system, saying that their babies began sleeping through the night after following the routine for a few days. Other parents tell horror stories of letting a baby cry himself to sleep, only to later discover that the child was suffering from, say, a painful ear infection.

The American Academy of Pediatrics says that it is perfectly normal for babies to wake up during the night. A newborn is hungry every one and a half to three hours and needs nourishment in order to fall back asleep. Around the age of six months, most babies can sleep a span of six to eight hours without nursing or having a bottle. However, some doctors insist that it is unreasonable to expect an infant to sleep soundly through the night before he turns a year old.

A Filling Idea

A common misconception is that introducing solid food early will help solve a baby's sleep problems. But some pediatricians say babies should be given only breast milk or formula until they are six months of age. Younger babies cannot properly digest solid food and may end up getting a stomachache instead of a good night's sleep.

THE CURSE OF KING TUT

❋ ❋ ❋

Many people still believe that anyone associated with the excavation and unsealing of King Tutankhamen's tomb suffered an untimely death. Here's the truth about one of the most infamous "curses" from the ancient world.

Myth: Lord Carnarvon died because of his association with King Tut's tomb.
Fact: Medical records say he succumbed to pneumonia, but when Lord Carnarvon—the financial backer of the Tutankhamen excavation—died on April 5, 1923, people genuinely believed he was the victim of a curse from King Tut's tomb.

The idea of a curse was already afoot before Lord Carnarvon died. As soon as archaeologist Howard Carter discovered Tutankhamen's tomb, people started predicting that terrible things would happen to anyone who entered it. The public's fears were realized when there was report of a cobra that devoured Carter's pet canary the very day he entered the secret sanctuary. In Egyptian lore, cobras were the protectors of the pharaohs.

Things got even more sensational when Lord Carnarvon died. The thrill of the curse soon matched the obsession over the glorious treasure Carter found in the young pharaoh's tomb. Newspapers of the day feasted on it, and so did the public. Even Sir Arthur Conan Doyle, the creator of Sherlock Holmes, believed in the curse, postulating that Egyptian priests frequently placed deadly spores in tombs to punish grave robbers. The frenzy over Carnarvon's curse-caused death escalated despite the knowledge that the lord had been in poor health for at least 20 years before he set foot inside Tutankhamen's tomb.

Myth: Everyone associated with Tut's tomb met untimely deaths. **Fact:** The existence of a curse would be more believable if many people had died soon after their association with the tomb. In reality, only a handful of individuals died in the decade after. Howard Carter lived 17 more years—after working in the tomb for almost 10 years. Richard Adamson, a guard who slept in the tomb, died in 1982 at the age of 81. And the daughter of Lord Carnarvon, Lady Evelyn Herbert, entered the tomb with her father, but she died in 1980 at the age of 78. Despite these facts, tales of the curse of King Tut live on.

Media Myths

Just as they do today, the media of old often invented the news. In fact, the press invented the phrasing of the curse itself: *"They who enter this sacred tomb shall swift be visited by wings of death."* Those words were never found inside Tut's tomb, but all ancient Egyptian tombs contained inscriptions and magic spells to assist the deceased to the other world. On the statue of Anubis, representing the god of death, the following words were inscribed in Egyptian hieroglyphics: *"It is I who hinder the sand from choking the secret chamber. I am for the protection of the deceased."* This message can be viewed on the statue displayed in the collection of Tutankhamen's treasures in Cairo's Egyptian Museum. But one reporter back then added his own interpretation with an extra line in the inscription that wasn't originally there: *"I will kill all those who cross this threshold into the sacred precincts of the Royal King who lives forever."*

The media also reported that at the moment of Lord Carnarvon's death in Egypt, the lights went out in Cairo, and that back in England, Carnarvon's dog howled and dropped dead at the same time as its master. Did those things happen? No one really knows. As for the alleged blackout, the lights in modern Cairo often go out—and it was likely more frequent in the 1920s.

DON'T BOTHER SAVING THE DATE!

*A lot of outrageous Hollywood couples have gotten hitched
over the years, but Jim Nabors and Rock Hudson?
That rumor was rampant in the 1970s, and Hudson
went to his grave trying to live it down.*

The story apparently started as a joke that quickly became an urban myth. According to Hudson, the instigators were a gay couple living in California who often promoted their annual parties with wacky invitations. One year the notice read: "You are cordially invited to the wedding reception of Rock Hudson and Jim Nabors." And a lot of people took it seriously.

The obviously whimsical invitation was distributed all over the country and eventually found its way into a movie magazine. Other publications picked up on it, and off it went.

The joke took a jarring toll on Hudson and Nabors, who were friends but nothing more. In fact, once the rumor started to spread, the men realized they could never again be seen in public together without giving it legitimacy.

Hudson was especially hard-hit. He had always made an effort to keep his sexual preference a secret, lest it negatively affect his career. In fact, at the time the rumor surfaced, Hudson was just beginning a long and successful stint on the television show *McMillan & Wife* (with Susan Saint James), a gig that depended on his "wholesome" reputation. It wasn't until he was diagnosed with AIDS that Hudson went public with his homosexuality.

Nabors, too, had a lot to lose. He had been horribly typecast because of his role as Gomer Pyle on *The Andy Griffith Show* and *Gomer Pyle, USMC*, and was struggling to reinvent himself. Scandalous rumors of an alleged marriage to a man were the last things he needed.

Celebrity gossip certainly isn't new, but this lingering tale proves that it still dies hard.

THOSE POOR PIRANHA!

*One of the most popular myths in the animal kingdom
is that of the ferocious piranha, a fish so mean that
it has stricken terror in the hearts of South American
explorers for nearly a century.*

These fish certainly look menacing, with their beady eyes and
mouthful of razor-sharp teeth. But piranha aren't the Amazonian
killing machines everyone thinks they are. In fact, experts say
that piranha are quite timid and fear humans more than we
fear them.

Teddy Tells a Tale

You can thank President Theodore Roosevelt for his help in
spreading the myth of the piranha as a relentless, bloodthirsty
carnivore. During a trip through Brazil in 1913, Roosevelt witnessed a piranha feeding frenzy that caused him to label the fish
"the embodiment of evil ferocity." But according to historians,
Roosevelt was the victim of a setup. Because his hosts wanted to
give him a good show, Brazilian ichthyologist (one who studies
fish) Miranda Ribeiro had a small section of a local river blocked
off with nets and stocked with thousands of pole-caught piranha,
which were left unfed for several days.

When Roosevelt and his entourage arrived by boat, they were
warned not to stick their hands in the water because of the vicious
fish that lived there. Skeptical, Roosevelt and
the journalists who were with him demanded
proof, so an ailing cow was driven into
the water, where it was immediately
devoured by the starving piranha.
Roosevelt was awestruck by what he
had seen, and he went home with a
tale of aquatic terror that remains
popular to this day.

Chicken Fish

Most people assume there is only one kind of piranha. However, the fish come in a variety of colors and sizes, ranging from six inches to two feet. They swim in schools, but this is more for protection—safety in numbers, after all—than to help them hunt prey.

Although piranha wouldn't turn down a steak dinner if presented with one, they are actually scavengers rather than aggressive hunters. If there happens to be flesh in the water, such as a dead animal, they will happily graze on it, but they're just as content to dine on insects, smaller fish, and plantlife. Feeding frenzies do occur, but usually only when food is scarce. Attacks on humans are relatively uncommon and are generally attributed to an intrusion into the piranha's breeding grounds. In other words, we should watch where we're sticking our toes.

It's interesting to note that while humans are fearful of piranha because of their nasty reputation, the fish are actually much more frightened of us and will flee rather than attack if given the opportunity. In fact, one scientist who was studying wild-caught piranha in a tank had to erect a special screen around the aquarium because the fish became terrified and dangerously stressed every time she and her colleagues got too close.

The Real Stone-Cold Killer

Biologists warn that though the piranha is (erroneously) considered in a league with the great white shark as a natural killing machine, there are many other fish that are much more dangerous to humans. The stonefish, for example, carries in its dorsal fins a venom that can cause excruciating pain, swelling, and tissue death that can require amputation. In severe cases, the venom of the stonefish can even result in death if the victim is not treated promptly.

Most troubling about the stonefish, however, is its highly effective camouflage. It looks just like a rock on the ocean floor—until you step on it. And its dorsal fins are so sharp that they can pierce a shoe. So the next time you see a piranha, remember: There are far more terrible creatures in the water.

A FINE FINNISH

❋ ❖ ❋

When Reuters presented a story about Russian scientists
exploring the ocean under the North Pole—and provided
visual evidence to back the boasts of the expedition—few
people doubted the validity of the claim. But was
the polar-cap caper really a Russian ruse?

In August 2007, Reuters news agency reported that a group of
Russian scientists had successfully explored the bottom of the
Arctic Ocean bed, a little more than two and a half miles beneath
the North Pole. The story was accompanied by dramatic footage
of two Finnish-built *MIR-1* and *MIR-2* submersibles in active
exploration of the area. The feat was heralded around the world,
and accolades poured in to the Russian Academy of Sciences
for its researchers' achievements. Shortly after the story hit the
airwaves, a 13-year-old Finnish film fan by the name of Waltteri
Seretin noticed peculiar similarities between the footage exhibited by Reuters and some key scenes in the 1997 blockbuster
movie *Titanic*.

After careful scrutiny, it was discovered that the footage
Reuters used, which purported to prove that the submersibles had
reached the bottom of the ocean under the polar cap, consisted of
segments from *Titanic* that showed the deep-sea machines exploring the wreckage of the famed ocean liner. Amid howls of a hoax,
it was eventually determined that the filmed fodder, sent by the
Russian organization merely as an example of what the undersea
vessels were capable of accomplishing, had been mislabeled. The
usually meticulous medium assumed the footage was faithful
and used it to provide a visual accent to a remarkable news item.
Embarrassed by the error, Reuters later provided further evidence
that the expedition had indeed taken place and that the Russian
Academy deserved the praise it had received.

"RUM, SODOMY, AND THE LASH"

※ ※※ ※

*Is it possible that Prime Minister Winston Churchill,
whose favorite port in a storm was any one with
abundant alcohol, would dish out a disparaging
dictum about the British Royal Navy?*

When Great Britain was a dominant naval power, it was said that
Britannia ruled the waves with a navy rich in resources and bathed
in tradition. Therefore, it came as a shock to the British population
when it was widely reported that Winston Churchill was of the
opinion that the only true traditions that the Royal Navy observed
were "rum, sodomy, and the lash."

In fact, Churchill's dissenters perpetrated the origin of this
myth-quote. In the 1940s, while he was serving as prime minister and his country was fighting for its very survival, Churchill's
political foes concocted an amusing smear campaign that focused
on his apparent disdain for and distrust of the navy. According to
Churchill's competitors, young Winston had been denied entry
to the Royal Naval College because he suffered from a speech
impediment, and the scars from that snub never healed.

That wound still riled him when he allegedly rose in the House
of Commons and delivered a scathing speech that ridiculed the
Royal Navy and its traditions, which he summarized as the equivalent of alcohol, sex, and torture. But the entire incident proved to
be fabricated. Records show that Churchill never attempted to
join the navy, and documents concur that he never used the House
of Commons as a platform to voice his opinions on the Admiralty.
Yet, the line remains one of the most popular quotes attributed to
Churchill. Its fame was cemented when he supposedly confided
to his assistant, Anthony Montague-Browne, that although he had
never spoken those words, he certainly wished he had.

PLAY IT AGAIN...RONALD?

※ ※※ ※

One of the most enduring Tinseltown myths is that Ronald Reagan was under serious consideration for the role of Rick Blaine in Casablanca—*a character forever associated with Humphrey Bogart.*

It turns out that the Reagan-as-Rick story was a clever publicity stunt perpetrated by Warner Bros. No actor other than Humphrey Bogart was ever considered for what would become one of cinema's most iconic roles. The rumor started when the publicity department at Warner Bros. planted a false press release in the *Hollywood Reporter* on January 5, 1942, announcing that Ronald Reagan and Ann Sheridan were set to costar in *Casablanca,* which was still in the script stage at the time.

Why would a major studio intentionally plant such a falsehood? To protect its property—in this case, Ronald Reagan. Under the old studio system, production houses such as Warner Bros. worked hard to keep the names of their best talent in the public (and professional) eye. Planting false news items in the industry press and elsewhere was an easy way to accomplish this.

Interestingly, Reagan couldn't have appeared in *Casablanca* even if the role of Rick Blaine had been up for grabs. He was a second lieutenant in the Army Reserve, and Warner Bros. had been getting deferments for him for several months. But when the United States entered World War II on December 8, 1941, there was no question that the actor would be called up for active duty long before *Casablanca* began filming in April. And that's exactly what happened.

The Lost Role

The Hollywood landscape is littered with the names of actors who were up for important roles that ultimately went to someone else. Tom Selleck, for example, was Steven Spielberg's first choice to play Indiana Jones in *Raiders of the Lost Ark,* a role that helped make Harrison Ford a superstar.

THEY WAS ROBBED!

*It's reasonable to assume that Superman's creators,
Jerry Siegel and Joe Shuster, made millions off their
Spandex-clad hero. Unfortunately, that was not the case.*

Is there anyone in the world who isn't familiar with Superman?
Over the years, the character has graced countless comic books,
appeared in several movies, and seen his iconic "S" emblazoned on
everything from underwear to snack cakes.

"Man of Steel" Was a Real Steal

You'd think the creators of Superman profited greatly from their
brainchild. However, Siegel and Shuster were nearly penniless in
their later years, until friends and fate intervened.

The boys were barely out of their teens when they created
Superman, which they initially hoped to sell as a syndicated comic
strip. When that didn't pan out, they presented Superman to the
editors at DC Comics (known then as Detective Comics).

Their timing couldn't have been better. DC was getting ready
to launch a new title called Action Comics, and it desperately
needed a lead feature, something new and different. Superman fit
the bill perfectly.

Amazingly, Siegel and Shuster sold all rights to Superman for
a paltry $130. Such an arrangement was standard at the time, and
the boys didn't mind at first because they were making pretty good
money writing and drawing the Man of Steel. Indeed, those were
heady times for a couple of science-fiction geeks from Cleveland.
Every comic book in which Superman appeared sold through
the roof, and Siegel and Shuster became minor celebrities by
association.

Up Against the Big Guys

In 1947, it became apparent to the boys just how much money
Superman was raking in for DC. Unhappy with the deal as it stood,
they took the company to court for a much bigger piece of the pie.

It was a grandiose plan, but one that was destined to fail. Despite the boys' best hopes, the suit was settled in DC's favor. Siegel and Shuster were fired from the company and spent the following years doing piecemeal work for a variety of lesser comic-book publishers. Eventually, Shuster developed vision problems that prevented him from drawing, and Siegel was forced to take a $7,000-per-year civil-service job for the health benefits. By the early 1970s, both men were living in near poverty.

Righting Wrongs

In 1975, months after Siegel had mailed out a thousand copies of an angry, ten-page press release he had written, the national media finally started reporting how horribly the creators of Superman had been treated over the years.

Siegel was first interviewed by a Los Angeles arts newspaper called *Cobblestone,* and in October the *Washington Star* came calling. An appearance on *The Tomorrow Show* with Tom Snyder followed, and shortly after that, the National Cartoonists Society took up the men's cause, enlisting the aid of such literary lions as Norman Mailer, Jules Feiffer, and Kurt Vonnegut. All demanded that Warner Communications, which owned DC Comics, do the right thing for the men who had helped make the company wealthy.

After weeks of negotiation, Warner Communications finally acquiesced. The company offered Siegel and Shuster $20,000 per year with built-in cost-of-living increases, provisions for their heirs, and—most important—creator credit on almost everything on which Superman appears. As the character made money, so did the men who created him. In their final years, it is estimated that Jerry Siegel and Joe Shuster were each pulling down approximately $100,000 annually.

❋ ❋ ❋

- *The good fight continues. In March 2008, again after years of litigation, a federal court ruled that Siegel's family was entitled to a share of the Superman copyright—and a chunk of the cash the character has made in recent years. Most agree it was a big win for truth, justice, and the American way.*

OPTICAL CONFUSION

❀ ❈ ❀

*Do hair and nails continue to grow after
your ticker has taken its final tock? It's not just
your mortician who knows for sure!*

The macabre myth that hair and nails continue to grow after we depart for our heavenly voyage is a tall tale fueled by an optical illusion. Even though hair and nails appear to grow to some extent after death, there is a simple explanation—and seeing should not lead to believing.

- After we die, all blood flow ceases, and slowly but surely, the body begins to dehydrate. The skin surrounding the fingernails and toenails dries out and retracts, exposing more of the nail plate. So while the nail remains the same length it was when the soul took its final flight, the shrinkage creates the illusion that it is still very much alive and growing.

- The same notion applies to the hair on your head. It's not that the follicles around the forehead are flourishing—instead, the scalp is contracting. We are so accustomed to seeing nails and hair getting longer that we fail to comprehend that the moisture in the skin on the head, hands, and feet is actually dissipating.

- Here's a similar illusion to illustrate the idea: Picture a tree growing in a swamp. When the water level drops, the tree dramatically and magically appears to soar. But the tree hasn't grown; more of its trunk simply has been exposed.

So rest easy. The family of the deceased does not need to hire a barber and a manicurist to ensure their beloved greets St. Peter at the golden gates in fine form and fettle.

CROSSING SWORDS

Confederate General Robert E. Lee's surrender to Union Lieutenant General Ulysses S. Grant on April 9, 1865, marked the end of the Civil War. For such an important moment in American history, though, the event is shrouded in misconceptions.

The surrender took place in a private home in a town called Appomattox Court House, not in the courthouse of the town of Appomattox. It's easy to see how this misconception arose. There is a town in Virginia named Appomattox, and it does have a courthouse. But it was the private home of Wilmer McLean in the town of Appomattox Court House, Virginia, that housed the historic meeting between the two leaders.

At no time did Robert E. Lee surrender his ceremonial sword to Grant, only to have the Union leader magnanimously return it. General Lee did arrive in full military uniform, which included his ceremonial sword. General Grant, on the other hand, arrived wearing only a dirty private's uniform. In Grant's own words: "The much repeated talk of the surrendering of Lee's sword and my handing it back . . . is the purest romance. The word *sword* or *sidearms* was not mentioned by either of us until I wrote it in the terms." These terms were written during the meeting in Appomattox Court House, but they did allow the Confederate officers to keep their sidearms. The misconception surrounding the sword could have arisen after a different magnanimous act by Grant. As General Lee left McLean's house after surrendering, Grant's men outside cheered in celebration. Grant immediately ordered the cheering to stop. "The Confederates were now our prisoners," he said later, "and we did not want to exult over their downfall."

By all accounts, Lee greatly appreciated Grant's behavior during the surrender, and the site is now appropriately part of a national historic park. But there is still no sign of a courthouse.

WHEN COLD BURNS

Frostbitten skin may feel like it's burning, but that doesn't mean you should try to cool it down.

If your mother told you to rub snow on frostnipped digits or appendages, chances are she was born before the 1950s—or else she was getting her treatment advice from a very old first-aid manual.

Rubbing snow on frostbitten skin had been standard treatment since Napoleon's army surgeon, Baron Larrey, proposed it in the frigid winter of 1812–13, during the retreat from Moscow. Larrey saw the disastrous results when soldiers defrosted their hands and feet by holding them over fires, and he decided that using snow was a better way to minimize infection.

The good doctor had it wrong, however. Physicians' discoveries during another military endeavor, the Korean War, followed by a landmark study a few years later, debunked the popular snow-on-frostbite treatment theory.

Frostbitten skin should not be thawed unless it won't be refrozen. Refreezing warmed frostbitten tissue is more harmful than leaving it alone. Of course, the soldiers did not have an option. They were stuck outdoors on the battlefield, and a great number of them ended up amputees.

Treating Frostbite

There are four degrees of frostbite, according to the extent of injury, just like there are four degrees of burns. As frostbite advances, your skin may throb or even burn. Eventually it will become numb, white, and hard because your body shuts off blood flow to the skin to conserve heat for your internal organs. Severely frostbitten skin will develop blisters, swell, and turn black.

Slow thawing teamed with oral medications for pain, which can be severe, is the appropriate treatment. You wouldn't consider putting a heating pad on burned skin—apply the same logic to frostbite.

Hey, I Never Said That!

DON'T BE FOOLED

❀❀❀

Abraham Lincoln is reputed to have said, "You can fool all of the people some of the time and some of the people all the time, but you cannot fool all the people all the time." But any fool knows that the true sources of famous quotes are often difficult to track.

Although this legendary quote may make a wise point about lies and politics, it is unwise to assume it came from the sage mouth of our sixteenth president. Historians have been unable to confirm that Lincoln ever spoke these words. The first written reference that attributes the quote to Lincoln is in 1901's *"Abe" Lincoln's Yarns and Stories,* by Alexander K. McClure, in which the author claims the president made the remark in casual conversation. The quote pops up again in a 1905 compilation book called *Complete Works of Abraham Lincoln.*

According to the most common story, Lincoln spoke these words on September 2, 1858, in a speech made in Clinton, Illinois. This was during the famous Lincoln–Douglas debates, when the two contenders for an Illinois seat in the U.S. Senate took part in eloquent political wrangling, mostly over the issue of slavery. A complete record of the speech does not exist, so no one can prove or disprove whether the future president ever said anything about the relative ease of foolery. The quote definitely does not appear in any of Lincoln's writings.

Lincoln scholars generally deny that he is the true source of the quote, but others believe he may have said something like it in one of his speeches, and the words then became a sound bite. Whether Lincoln said it or not, the confusion over this quote does prove that, unless you have it in writing, nowadays it's difficult to fool anyone about anything.

THE PHANTOM PUNCH

*When Sonny Liston hit the canvas less than
two minutes into his second heavyweight-belt bout
with Muhammad Ali, pundits immediately accused
the former champ of taking a dive. Did the
lumbering Liston really fake a fall?*

Even without the controversial conclusion to the widely publicized Sonny Liston–Muhammad Ali rematch on May 25, 1965, there was enough ink and intrigue to fill a John LeCarre spy novel. The bout against Ali—who had just joined the Nation of Islam and changed his name from Cassius Clay—was held in a 6,000-seat arena in Lewiston, Maine, after numerous states refused to sanction the fight because of militant behavior associated with the Muslim movement.

Robert Goulet, the velvet-voiced crooner entrusted with singing the national anthem, forgot the words to the song, and the third man in the ring, Jersey Joe Walcott, was a former heavyweight champion but a novice referee. One minute and 42 seconds into the fight, Ali threw a quick uppercut that seemed to connect with nothing but air. Liston tumbled to the tarmac, though no one seemed sure whether it was the breeze from the blow or the blow itself that put him there. Liston was ultimately counted out by the ringside timer, not the in-ring referee.

Since it was a largely invisible swing (dubbed the "phantom punch" by sports scribes) that floored Liston, he was accused of cashing it in just to cash in. Evidence proves otherwise. Film footage of the bout shows Liston caught flush with a quick, pistonlike "anchor" punch that Ali claimed was designed to be a surprise. Liston actually got back up and was trading body blows with the Louisville Lip when the referee stepped in, stopped the fight, and informed Liston that his bid to become the first boxer to regain the heavyweight title was over.

THE PAPACY AND THE EX-WIVES CLUB

❋ ❖ ❋

Many believe that popes in the Catholic Church have never been allowed to marry. But celibacy has not always been Church doctrine, and past popes-to-be simply left their wives before ordination.

Pope, Plus Wife and Child

The furthest things from anyone's mind upon hearing the word *pope* are marriage and its close companion, sex. Yet there have been married popes, sexually active popes, and even popes with brothels. The relationship between popes and celibacy has changed drastically over time.

Records indicate that St. Peter, considered by some to be the first pope, was married. Christian communities at that time were small, scattered, and based largely on close familial relationships. Yet when Christianity became the official religion of the Roman Empire, the attitude toward betrothed clergy evolved from "the more, the merrier" to "one is the holiest number." As the Church became married to politics, the powers-that-be feared wedded clergy would leave money and land to their families rather than the Church. This became pressing in the Middle Ages, when bishops and priests received land and money in exchange for allegiance to the local lord. Various Church regulations discouraged the clergy from marrying, but marriage itself was still allowed.

Resisting Temptation

Despite regular resistance to the Church's anti-marriage mandates, throughout the first millennium A.D., some clergy members embraced the doctrine of celibacy. Popular Christian philosophy saw the spiritual as pure and the material as fleeting and corruptive. Hence St. Augustine's fifth-century claim that "Nothing is so powerful in drawing the spirit of a man downwards as the caresses of a woman." Carnal relations were considered incompatible with sacred ritual, and therefore clergy were not allowed to perform their duties within certain time periods of having sex. The ascetic monastic traditions that were imported from the Orient also emphasized the spiritual transcendence associated with celibacy.

Overall, then, it was considered a good thing to resist sexual temptation, and in many circles, celibate priests had a one-up on their married counterparts. Finally, there was good old-fashioned misogyny, illustrated by Pope Gregory VII's insight that "the Church cannot escape the clutches of the laity unless priests first escape from the clutches of their wives."

Pope, the Perpetual Bachelor

The higher-ups in the Church had a vested interest in encouraging celibacy among the priests, yet this meant the popes and bishops had to practice what they preached. This was a problem for those who were already married, and the solution was to declare a pope's marriage retroactively invalid on the day of his ordination. Pope Siricius of the fourth-century A.D. left his wife and child when he was ordained. Other popes kept their families nearby, but their wives were technically demoted to concubine status. Thus, despite apparent efforts to shield the papacy from nepotism, between A.D. 400 and 1000, six popes were sons of popes and nine popes were sons of bishops or priests.

The issue came to a head in A.D. 1139, when the Second Lateran Council finally and officially outlawed marriage within the clergy. All existing marriages were declared null and void, and any new clergy hopefuls had to sever their matrimonial unions.

Many popes continued to nurture their own nests of illegitimate children, including Innocent VIII, Alexander VI, Pius IV, and Gregory VIII. It was in part the liaisons of Renaissance-era popes that prompted the Catholic Counterreformation of 1560. Since that time, no pope has been known to be sexually active during his papacy, and certainly none were married. The actual number of married popes in history is difficult to quantify, as the nuances of Catholic law in this area have fluctuated. Of history's 266 popes, approximately 35 were married at some point in their lives.

NO PICNIC

❋❋❋

When the Japanese attacked Pearl Harbor on December 7, 1941,
2,390 lives were lost and the United States was dragged into World
War II. But it is a mistake to believe that no one was
killed on the U.S. mainland as a result of the war.

On May 5, 1945, a Japanese balloon bomb killed six Americans
picnicking near the town of Bly, Oregon. The Japanese launched
some 9,000 balloon bombs against the United States during World
War II. They attached incendiary and anti-personnel bombs to
large hydrogen-filled balloons and released them into the jet-
stream winds to float 5,000 miles across the Pacific Ocean and
explode in the forested regions of Western states. This, they
hoped, would cause widespread forest fires and divert U.S. man-
power and resources away from the war in the Pacific.

Officially, only 285 of the balloon bombs reached North
America, though experts estimate that approximately 1,000 made
it across the Pacific Ocean. The U.S. military successfully orchestrated a media blackout of the bombings to deny the Japanese
any publicity of success. The first balloon landed near San Pedro,
California, on November 4, 1944. The bombs traveled as far north
as Canada, as far south as the Arizona border with Mexico, and as
far east as Farmington, Michigan, just ten miles from Detroit. The
U.S. military shot some down, while others landed without exploding. None, however, succeeded in creating the major forest fires
Japan desired.

When a 13-year-old girl on a church picnic in the woods near
Bly, Oregon, discovered one of the balloon bombs, she attempted
to pull it from a tree. It exploded, killing the girl, the church
minister's wife, and four other children. These six were the only
war casualties on the U.S. mainland during World War II. Had the
Japanese perfected the balloon bombs and used germ or biological weapons, that statistic, and the outcome of the war, might have
been very different.

DEMONIZED BY MYTHOLOGY: LUCREZIA BORGIA

※ ◈ ※

In public perception, she rates alongside Jezebel and Messalina for conniving promiscuity. But who was the real Lucrezia Borgia, and how depraved was she?

Backdrop

Lucrezia Borgia's life was orchestrated by the intense political and military competition of the Italian Renaissance. Italy was a gaggle of city-states and noble families, with foreign neighbors butting in, all jostling for advantage in a sleazy multiplayer chess game of shifting alliances, fiefdom grants, political marriages, excommunication, and warfare. The Vatican sat at that chessboard, and Lucrezia was a pawn.

The Borgia Family

Lucrezia's father was Cardinal Rodrigo Borgia, later Pope Alexander VI, the poster boy for corrupt, lascivious popes. His Holiness fathered Lucrezia and her three brothers with a mistress; her most prominent brother, Cesare, was ambitious and ruthless even by the inflated standards of the Renaissance. Lucrezia had the misfortune of being born into a family whose name evoked fear and loathing, with good cause.

Lucrezia's Marital Career

When Lucrezia reached the age of 13 in 1493, her father married her off to Giovanni Sforza to cement an alliance with Sforza's powerful Milanese clan, thus boosting Cesare's fortunes. When Alexander no longer needed to make nice with the Sforzas, he had Lucrezia's marriage to Giovanni annulled.

It was rumored that Lucrezia had a love affair and bore a son out of wedlock. In 1498, she entered an arranged marriage to Alfonso of Bisceglie, this time to ingratiate Cesare with the king of Naples. When that notion soured, "unknown assailants" (probably her brother Cesare's henchmen) assassinated Alfonso. Lucrezia had grown to love her husband, and she went into a deep depression.

In 1501, Alexander brokered Lucrezia's marital hand to Alfonso d'Este, Prince of Ferrara. The new bride's sister-in-law, Isabella, delighted in snubs and snippy comments, but Lucrezia now knew the game. While keeping up appearances as a noble, dutiful Ferrarese matron, she carried on with Isabella's husband. After the deaths of Alexander (1503) and then Cesare (1507), Lucrezia could finally settle down. She died on June 24, 1519, at the age of 39, of complications from childbirth.

Heinous Allegations

Detractors love to paint Lucrezia as a Renaissance floozy with a poison-filled ring who had incestuous relations with her father and brother. It makes lurid reading, but the sliver of truth in such allegations is rather dull and tame. She did have lovers between marriages and outside of wedlock, as did many in her time. Living as a political pawn, can anyone blame her for wanting romantic flings? It would be peculiar if she hadn't.

There's no evidence supporting the incest slander—but there is good reason to reject it. Unlike her father and Cesare, Lucrezia had authentic religious scruples. Her consent would be unthinkable. She remained fond of each unto his death and mourned both. Would she have lamented those who'd traumatized her? Her later life is inconsistent with childhood molestation: She adjusted well, had a healthy love life when she could, and was never self-destructive.

The Origins of Slurs

Some aspersions were bandied during her life, mainly as weapons against the Borgias, spurred by Cesare's atrocious conduct. In 1833, Victor Hugo wrote a play that painted Lucrezia as a princess of poison, reveling in each toxic takedown. This, not actual history, has adhered to the public perception. It libels a pleasant, loving woman whose fortunes were dictated mainly by men of great power and limitless greed.

3 PIRATE MYTHS BLAMED ON R. L. STEVENSON

❋ ❈ ❋

If Robert Louis Stevenson is unlucky enough to be sharing the afterlife with pirates, he's likely answering some uncomfortable questions. His novel Treasure Island *gave us a host of pirate myths that would make real pirates shiver their timbers.*

1. Pirates had parrots perched on their shoulders. The idea that pirates and parrots go together is not entirely unfounded. Like other seafarers of the time, pirates were awestruck by colorful birds in tropical ports. Parrots made good souvenirs, bribes, or gifts, and they fetched a nice price back in Europe. But other than Long John Silver, pirates didn't stomp around with parrots secured to their shoulders. A large, squawking bird would have made firing a cannon or running the rigging difficult, to say the least.

2. Pirates ran around yelling, "Fifteen men on the dead man's chest. Yo-ho-ho and a bottle of rum." Most every sailor sang sea shanties, which provided both a diversion and a rhythm for hoisting anchors and hauling bowlines. But fictional pirates and pirate wannabes have been singing this particular song only since Stevenson made up a few lines for *Treasure Island.* A writer named Young E. Allison later expanded the snippet into a six-stanza poem titled "The Derelict." In 1901, the tune was added when the poem was used in a musical version of *Treasure Island.*

3. Pirates marked treasure maps with an "X." To pass the time in the rainy Scottish Highlands, Stevenson drew a treasure map and then made up stories (which he later wrote down) for his stepson. But it is unlikely that real pirates ever drew maps to locate their buried treasure. Not a single pirate treasure map has ever been found, and pirates would not likely have risked alerting others to their booty. Scholars doubt that pirates buried much treasure in the first place. Although they returned from raids flush with loot, they blew through it quickly because they didn't expect to live long enough to spend it in retirement.

FRAN'S FATHER

It is said that the death of Fran Tarkenton's father was caused by officiating miscues in the 1975 playoff game between Minnesota and Dallas. Tarkenton's father did die during the game, but it was before the referees made their blunders.

One must approach such a macabre myth delicately, which is more than can be said for the perpetrators of this tall tale, who were probably the same lunatics who plunked an on-field official with a whiskey bottle during the tumultuous NFL contest that was played on December 28, 1975.

That year, the Minnesota Vikings had pillaged their way through the regular season, posting a 12–2 record. Bolstered by quarterback Fran Tarkenton, the Vikings were not expected to have any trouble subduing the Dallas Cowboys when they clashed in Minnesota on that solemn Sunday. Less than six minutes remained on the clock when the men in stripes began their football follies. The first questionable call came when Dallas receiver Drew Pearson appeared to step out of bounds before snagging a do-or-die pass on a fourth-and-sixteen play. The officials ruled that Pearson had kept both feet in play. With only a handful of ticks left in the game and Dallas still trailing 14–10, Roger Staubach pitched a prayer toward the end zone before disappearing under a mound of Minnesota muscle. Pearson caught the ball, but he appeared to push Viking defender Nate Wright to the ground before grabbing the toss. Once again, the on-field zebras ignored the malfeasance and signaled a touchdown. A shower of debris rained onto the field, including the well-flung bottle that bopped field judge Armen Terzian. After the contest, Tarkenton learned that his father had suffered a fatal heart attack during the third quarter of the game, long before the tables had turned.

Staubach's miracle missile was later described as a "Hail Mary," the first time that divine designation was applied to a flying football.

GONE WITH THE WIND: MYTHS ABOUT TORNADOES

*It's a warm afternoon, and the skies have turned
a greenish-gray color that can only mean trouble. Many
misconceptions swirl around the subject of tornadoes.
What many believe to be fact may actually be fiction.*

The southwest corner of your house is the safest place to be during a tornado. In fact, occupying the area that is closest to the approaching tornado—whether it's above ground or in the basement—results in the most fatalities. A prominent study in the 1960s showed that the north side of a house is the safest area, both on the ground floor and in the basement. Many homes shift from their foundations during a tornado, toppling walls in the same direction as the storm's path. If the storm approaches from the southwest, then the home's southwest walls will fall into the structure, while north and northeast walls will fall away from the interior as the tornado moves away.

During a tornado, you should open all windows to equalize air pressure and reduce damage. The question of air pressure differences is really no question at all. Engineers agree that a storm with 260-mile-per-hour winds—classified as an F4, or "devastating," tornado—creates a pressure drop of only 10 percent. Homes and buildings have enough vents and natural openings to easily accommodate that. In fact, running around opening windows can increase the possibility of interior damage and personal injury, and it can take valuable time away from finding a safe place to ride out the storm.

A highway overpass is a safe place to wait out a storm when you're on the road. A video clip of a TV news crew surviving a tornado by huddling under an overpass was seen around the world in the 1990s, leading many to believe this was a location out of harm's way. But most trained storm chasers consider highway overpasses extremely dangerous places to be when a tornado strikes. National Weather Service meteorologists judge overpasses to be poor shelters from severe weather because high winds essentially channel themselves under these structures, carrying with them flying debris.

Tornadoes never strike large cities. The following big cities (populations of at least 300,000) have witnessed tornadic activity:

On a single day in 1998, three major tornadoes struck Nashville, Tennessee. St. Louis, Missouri, witnessed ten tornadoes between 1871 and 2007, resulting in more than 370 deaths. An F3 tornado roared through Dallas in 1957. In 1997, tornadoes touched down in Miami and Cincinnati, and another tore through Fort Worth, Texas, in 2000.

Yet, this myth about large cities persists. The combination of traffic, dense activity, and considerable amounts of concrete and asphalt in large cities creates what is known as a "heat island." This rising warm air has the potential to disrupt minor tornadic activity, but it's no match for the fury of larger tornadoes. Cities occupy a much smaller geographic area than rural regions of the country, so the chance that a tornado will strike a city is relatively small.

You should use your vehicle to outrun a tornado. Experts say that you can try to drive away from a tornado—but only if it's a long way off. Tornadoes can travel as fast as 70 miles per hour and can easily overtake a vehicle. Even if a tornado is traveling at a much slower speed, the accompanying storm will likely produce strong winds, heavy rain, and hail that make driving difficult, if not impossible. What's more, tornadoes are dangerously erratic and can change directions without warning. If you're caught in a vehicle during a tornado, your best bet is to abandon it and seek shelter in a building or nearby ditch or culvert.

FALLACIES & FACTS: ANIMALS

❀ ❖ ❀

Fallacy: *On your African safari, you'll see lions and tigers.*
Fact: *You would need to go on one heck of a long safari, because lions and tigers don't share the same range. Lions live primarily on the plains in Africa, while tigers are found only in Asia.*

Fallacy: *According to popular soda commercials, polar bears and penguins hang out on the same frozen beaches.*
Fact: *Sadly, there are no arctic (or subarctic) beach parties going on, since polar bears and penguins never come face-to-face. Polar bears live in the Northern Hemisphere, and penguins reside in the Southern Hemisphere.*

Fallacy: *Puffins are hybrid fish-birds.*
Fact: *Puffins are roly-poly little birds that live along northern coastlines in North America and Europe. Often mistaken for penguins because of their black-and-white markings, they lay eggs, have feathers, and can even fly. The fish-bird myth can be traced to early Catholics who lived in puffin-infested regions and declared the flesh of fish-eating puffins to be fish itself so that they might be eaten during Lent. The bird's superb ability to swim under-water contributes to its fishy reputation.*

Fallacy: *Cats will try to suffocate a baby by sucking out its breath.*
Fact: *Cats like to sleep on warm things (appliances, sun-bathed beds, babies, etc.), and they favor things that smell like milk (cereal bowls, babies, etc.)—so the fear that a cat might sleep on and suffocate a baby isn't entirely crazy. Despite centuries of anti-cat folklore, however, it's unlikely Mittens would harm Junior intentionally.*

Fallacy: *A bird will abandon its baby if a human touches it.*
Fact: *Contrary to what your parents told you when you asked if you could please pet the baby robin, a mother bird will not abandon her baby if she smells evidence of human touch. Most birds have little or no sense of smell. This isn't permission to go groping around in nests, however, as human-bird interaction can put dangerous levels of stress on mama bird and baby bird.*

Fallacy: *Hummingbirds have no feet.*
Fact: *Although hummingbirds belong to the scientific order* Apodiformes, *which in Latin means "no feet," they have legs, feet, and toes. Their legs and four toes are the same length and are used for perching, not for walking.*

Fallacy: *Polar bears are white.*
Fact: *Although polar bears appear white, yellow, or some shade in between, the hairs that make up their outer coat are actually clear, hollow tubes that trap the sun's heat and light so they can reach the skin. Some light reflects off these hairs, making the bears appear a shade of white, but their actual color depends on the angle of the refracted light, the season, and the texture of the fur. The skin under a polar bear's fur is black.*

Fallacy: *Elephants are afraid of mice.*
Fact: *Sadly for cartoonists everywhere, most elephants show little fear of mice. Because of an elephant's size and poor eyesight, it probably wouldn't even notice a mouse. If an elephant does see such a critter, it would likely approach it cautiously, as it does most "unknowns."*

Fallacy: *A stag is as old as the number of points on its antlers.*
Fact: *This may be true of young stags, but how much and how fast the antlers develop depends on the animal's health and genetic makeup.*

WHOSE WAY?

❈ ❈❈❈ ❈

Frank Sinatra's signature number "My Way" is one of the most popular songs of all time. Paul Anka wrote the lyrics to the song with Sinatra specifically in mind, but he did not write the tune.

"My Way" is based on the French song *"Comme d'habitude,"* composed by Claude Francois and Jacques Rivaux. Known as Clo-Clo, Francois was one of the most successful pop stars in France during the 1960s and '70s, overshadowed only by Johnny Hallyday, the French version of Elvis Presley.

In 1967, Rivaux, an aspiring songwriter, presented Francois with a ballad called "For Me." CloClo adjusted the melody, rewrote the lyrics, and released the song as *"Comme d'habitude,"* a requiem to fading love. Paul Anka heard CloClo's original version while on vacation in Paris and subsequently acquired the publishing rights. He made subtle changes to the melody and completely rewrote the lyrics, tailoring them for Sinatra and, unwittingly, for tone-deaf karaoke crooners the world over.

Sinatra included "My Way" on his 1969 album of the same name, and versions of the song have since been released by artists as diverse as Dorothy Squires, Sid Vicious, and Jay-Z. In the Philippines, the song has caused numerous incidents of violence among drunken karaoke fans, and in Britain it has become the most popular contemporary song played at funerals.

CloClo ended up becoming a ruthless business tycoon who owned a record label and an erotic magazine, among other successful ventures. Although his greatest love was singing, he never had a hit outside of the French-speaking world, a fact that tortured him until his death in 1978. One cool spring evening, while taking a bath, Francois decided to change a flickering light bulb above the tub and in the process was electrocuted. It was certainly a foolish act, and some people speculated suicide. What's more likely, however, is that CloClo was just doing things as he always did—his way.

NO "LIGHTBULB" MOMENT FOR EDISON

✳ ◈ ✳

*Although Thomas Alva Edison was one of the most prolific
inventors in history, the lightbulb was not one of his brainstorms.*

Edison reportedly conducted more than 3,000 experiments in an
attempt to perfect the filament for a lightbulb, but his research
was based on the work of diligent inventors before him. Historians cite at least 22 people who had presented various forms of
the incandescent lamp prior to Edison. They include Englishman
Humphry Davy, who in 1802 demonstrated the world's first incandescent light. In 1835, Scotsman James Lindsay demonstrated
a constant electric light, and in 1841, Frederick de Moleyns of
England was granted the first patent for an incandescent lamp. In
1845, American John W. Starr acquired a patent for an incandescent bulb that used carbon filaments.

These early inventors were followed by Joseph Wilson Swan,
an English physicist who in 1850 demonstrated a workable,
though short-lived, vacuum bulb. As Swan turned his attention
to producing a better carbon filament, Edison began his own
research. In 1879, he successfully demonstrated a carbon filament
bulb that lasted 13 hours. When he began commercializing his
invention in Great Britain, however, Swan sued him. Eventually,
their two companies merged, as Ediswan. In America, Edison lost
his patent in 1883 when the U.S. Patent Office ruled that his work
was based on the prior research of inventor William Sawyer. After
a number of court hearings, that ruling was overturned in 1889.

Slowly Lit

Although Edison's lightbulb became the first commercially viable electric lamp in the United States, the technology took decades to become
widely used. In 1925, 46 years after Edison patented his lightbulb, only
25 percent of the U.S. population used electric lighting.

THE TRUE STORY OF THE WORLD'S FAVORITE RODENT

*Walt Disney long held that the inspiration for his most famous
creation sprang from a cute little field mouse that visited
him at his drawing board in his Kansas City studio.
The real story is far more interesting.*

In truth, Mickey Mouse was born from a bad business deal. Walt
Disney had originally pinned his cinematic success on an animated
rabbit named Oswald, only to have the rights to the character stolen from him by New York film distributor Charles Mintz. Desperate for another moneymaking character, Disney brainstormed with
his brother, Roy, and lead animator Ub Iwerks. Various animals
were proposed and rejected, until the trio finally settled on a
mouse—basically because the only other cartoon mouse at the
time was George Herriman's Ignatz, of "Krazy Kat" fame. Disney
originally wanted to call his new creation Mortimer, but on the
advice of his wife, Lilly, he changed it to Mickey.

Mickey's first cartoon was a silent effort titled "Plane Crazy,"
inspired by Charles Lindbergh's 1927 transatlantic flight. It was
quickly followed by "The Gallopin' Gaucho," also a silent cartoon.
Distributors were unenthusiastic, so Disney decided to make
one more cartoon, this time with synchronized music and sound
effects. It was a huge gamble—if the third cartoon failed, Disney
would lose everything he had worked so hard to build.

"Steamboat Willie" premiered at New York's Colony Theater
on November 18, 1928. It was an immediate hit and inspired
Disney to add music and sound effects to "Plane Crazy" and "The
Gallopin' Gaucho," so the three shorts could be sold to theaters
as a package. More cartoons followed, and within just a few years,
Disney was head of one of Hollywood's most successful and
groundbreaking movie studios. All that, thanks to a mouse almost
named Mortimer.

HORSING AROUND

According to folk wisdom, the position of a horse's hooves on an equestrian statue—specifically, a statue of a military figure on horseback—reveals the way in which the rider died. It's an interesting theory, but it's not always accurate.

According to the most common version of the legend, if one hoof is raised, the rider was wounded in battle and may or may not have died from his wounds; two raised hooves means the rider died in battle; four hooves on the ground means the rider survived all of his battles without injury.

A good place to test this theory is Washington, D.C., which has more equestrian statues than any other city in the United States. A quick examination shows that many of the statues there follow this convention. For example, the horse in the statue commemorating Ulysses S. Grant has four hooves on the ground, and of course Grant survived the Civil War unharmed and went on to become the nation's eighteenth president. The statue commemorating Major General John A. Logan has one hoof raised, and Logan was twice wounded in battle but survived.

However, a great many other equestrian statues around the city do not accurately reflect the legend. For example, the statue of General Simon Bolivar features a horse with one hoof raised, yet Bolivar sustained no battle wounds and died of tuberculosis in peacetime. And the statue honoring Major General Andrew Jackson features a horse with two hooves raised, yet Jackson also died in peacetime long after he'd left military service.

❈❈❈

- *A similar legend applies to statues of medieval knights: An effigy depicting a knight with his arms or legs crossed supposedly indicates that he was a Crusader. But there are many straight-legged statues of Crusading knights, indicating that legends involving cryptic "codes" are often inaccurate, yet timelessly fascinating.*

SETTING SAKE STRAIGHT

*Most Americans consider sake a Japanese rice wine, but it is
actually more akin to beer. Furthermore, a look back in time
suggests that sake may have originated in China, not Japan.*

What Is Sake?

The Japanese word for sake, *nihonshu*, literally means "Japanese
alcoholic beverage" and does not necessarily refer to the specific
rice-based beverage that foreigners exclusively call sake. What
differentiates sake from other alcoholic beverages is its unique
fermentation process. Although all wines are the result of a single-
step fermentation of plant juices, sake requires a multiple-step
fermentation process, as does beer. The requisite ingredients are
rice, water, yeast, and an additional substance that will convert
the starch in the rice to sugar. People have always found ways to
make alcohol with whatever ingredients are available, so it is likely
that beverages similar to sake emerged soon after rice cultivation
began. The most popular theory holds that the brewing of rice into
alcohol began around 4000 B.C. along the Yangtze River in China,
and the process was later exported to Japan.

The Many Ways to Ferment Rice

The sake of yore was different from the sake that's popular today.
At one time it was fermented with human saliva, which reliably
converts starch to sugar. Early sake devotees chewed a combination of rice, chestnuts, millet, and acorns, then spit the mixture
into a container to ferment. This "chew and spit" approach to
alcohol production has been seen the world over in tribal societies.
Subsequent discoveries and technological developments allowed
for more innovative approaches to fermentation. Sometime in the
early centuries A.D., a type of mold called *koji-kin* was discovered
to be efficient in fermenting rice. In the 1300s, mass sake production began in Japan, and it soon became the most popular national
beverage.

GEORGE WASHINGTON'S HATCHET JOB

❀ ❖ ❀

*For 200 years, schoolkids have been taught that George
Washington couldn't tell a lie. Considering the endurance
of this story, today's political flacks could learn a thing
or two from the man who made up the tale.*

According to legend, six-year-old George tried out his hatchet on
everything within reach, including his father's beloved cherry tree.
When his father saw the remains of his tree, he asked George if he
knew who had chopped it down. The boy famously cried, "I can't
tell a lie, Pa; you know I can't tell a lie. I cut it with my hatchet."
Father embraced son, declaring that his honesty was worth more
"than a thousand trees, though blossomed with silver, and their
fruits of purest gold."

Although the first U.S. president was renowned for his honor,
virtue, and sense of duty, he often came across as cold, dull, and
uninspiring—hardly the stuff of legend. Mason Locke Weems,
a fiery pastor and bookseller, took it upon himself to spice up
Washington's image. His book *The Life and Memorable Actions
of George Washington* was first published in 1800, a year after
Washington's death. It was an instant hit and was republished several times, with each edition boasting additions to a section titled
"Curious Anecdotes Laudable to Himself and Exemplary to his
Countrymen." The fabricated cherry tree story was included in the
fifth edition (1806) and every edition thereafter.

The damage done by Weems's well-intentioned tale is immea-
surable. First, he set the bar uncomfortably high, both for six-year-
olds who are naturally inclined to fib and for parents pressured to
value a misbehaving child's honesty above retribution. But the real
harm comes in hoodwinking children into ignoring their sense of
self-preservation. In 200 years, how many miscreants have bravely
told the truth and received nothing but a sound scolding?

HAIR TODAY

Nearly 80 percent of people in the United States say they spend more money on hair products than any other grooming goods. But no matter what that bottle of expensive shampoo says about nourishing your hair, it can't feed something that isn't alive.

- Despite all the effort we put into coifing and pampering our locks, the hair we see is biologically dead. Hair is alive only in the roots, which are fed by small blood vessels beneath the skin's surface. Hair cells travel up the shaft and are eventually cut off from the blood supply that is their nourishment. The cells die before being pushed out of the follicle onto the head—or back, arm, or anywhere else.

- Even though it's dead, hair is incredibly strong. The average head of hair can support roughly 12 tons of weight—much more than the scalp it's attached to. The tough stuff grows in cycles: During the first phase, hair is actively growing. In the second phase, it rests in the follicle until it is pushed out of the root. Healthy hair grows about .39 inch in a month.

- Each hair is completely independent from the others. When a hair falls out (the average person loses between 50 and 100 resting hairs each day), another one may not grow directly in its place. We are born with every hair follicle we'll ever have, though the composition, color, and pattern of the hair changes over the years. A characteristic full head of hair averages about 120,000 to 150,000 individual hairs (about 250 hairs on each square centimeter of scalp).

- Eating a healthful diet that contains sufficient protein (hair is made of protein), vitamins, minerals, and water is the best way to ensure healthy hair. A better investment is on nutrient-dense foods rather than hair products. Lathering, rinsing, and repeating will only wash a lot of money down the drain.

P. T. BARNUM'S GIANT SUCKER

P. T. Barnum, the consummate huckster, supposedly laughed at the audiences he tricked, saying, "There's a sucker born every minute." But have we misjudged America's Greatest Showman?

The phrase—which suggests that every scam, no matter how obvious, will find a gullible mark—has been attributed to several late-19th-century sources, including con man Joseph "Paper Collar Joe" Bessimer and humorist Mark Twain. Most often, it is attributed to P. T. Barnum.

What a Circus!

Phineas Taylor Barnum (1810–91) both amused and appalled audiences with his collections of freaks, oddities, and wonders. Writer Herman Melville boldly declared him "sole heir to all . . . lean men, fat women, dwarfs, two-headed cows, amphibious sea-maidens, large-eyed owls, small-eyed mice, rabbit-eating anacondas, bugs, monkies and mummies." In the name of entertainment, he promoted "humbugs"—obvious hoaxes designed to delight and entertain, such as the "Feejee Mermaid" and a woman he claimed was George Washington's 161-year-old nanny.

Barnum insisted that people enjoyed being fooled so long as they got "several times their money's worth." Though it seems likely that such a showman would utter this dismissive phrase, Barnum's acquaintances denied it upon inquiry from his biographer, saying that Barnum treasured and respected his patrons.

Start of the Punchline

The true story behind the phrase can be traced to George Hull, a businessman from Binghamton, New York. In 1868, Hull (a fervent atheist) argued with a fundamentalist preacher who insisted the Bible be taken literally, including Genesis 6:4 ("There were giants in the earth in those days"). Hull purchased an enormous slab of gypsum and hired a stonecutter to carve it into a ten-foot-tall statue of a giant with lifelike details such as toenails, fingernails, and pores. The statue was stained with sulfuric acid and ink and shipped to a farm near Cardiff, New York, where it was then buried.

A year later, Hull hired workers to dig a well near the spot where the statue was buried. As he intended, the workers discovered the statue and were excited by their find. (Six months earlier, fossils had been unearthed—with much publicity—at a nearby farm.) Hull had the workers excavate the statue, and then he charged people to see the Cardiff Giant, as it had become known.

Hull sold his statue for nearly $40,000 to a group of exhibitors headed by David Hannum. Barnum became interested in the find and offered to rent it for $50,000, but Hannum refused. Rather than make a higher offer, Barnum built his own Cardiff Giant, which he put on display, declaring that Hannum had sold him the giant after all and that Hannum's was the forgery. Newspapers widely publicized Barnum's story, causing audiences to flock to Barnum while Hannum bitterly declared, "There's a sucker born every minute," in reference to the duped crowds.

Careful What You Sue For

Hannum sued Barnum for calling his giant a sham. At trial, Hull admitted that the original giant was a hoax. The judge ruled in Barnum's favor, saying that it is not a crime to call a fake a fake.

Afterward, one of Barnum's competitors, Adam Forepaugh, mistakenly attributed (or intentionally misattributed) Hannum's phrase to Barnum. The consummate showman didn't deny saying it; in fact, he thanked Forepaugh for the publicity.

Barnum Knew Best

The quotation, and its link to Barnum, has long outlasted Forepaugh, Hannum, and even Hull. As for the Cardiff Giants, both still exist and are on display. Hull's resides at the Farmer's Museum in Cooperstown, New York, while Barnum's is housed at Marvin's Marvelous Mechanical Museum in Farmington Hills, Michigan.

THE HEISMAN CURSE

✹ ◈ ✹

After being named best college football player in the nation, one's best position might be "fallback." Those who believe the Heisman Curse is just a sports myth should consider the following.

During a football game in 1934, University of Chicago running back Jay Berwanger collided with University of Michigan defender Gerald Ford, bloodying the tackler's left cheek. The resulting scar on the future U.S. president would be permanent—as would, some say, the so-called Heisman Curse it begat.

A year later, Berwanger was awarded the first Heisman Trophy, emblematic of the best player in college football. Although he also became the first man ever drafted by the NFL, the "Genius of the Gridiron" never played another snap. Surprisingly few of the six dozen trophy recipients since have made more of an impact.

In recent years, the list of Heisman honorees has included several pro football busts, especially at the marquee quarterback position. Charlie Ward (1993), Eric Crouch (2001), and Jason White (2003) never played an NFL game. Danny Wuerffel (1996) earned just ten starts, and though Chris Weinke (2000) made 19, his team won just one of them.

Berwanger himself tacitly acknowledged that the Heisman wasn't worth the 25 pounds of bronze used to cast it. Until he eventually donated it to his alma mater, the trophy was displayed in his aunt's library—as a doorstop.

✹ ✹ ✹

• *Only eight Heisman winners have been enshrined in the Pro Football Hall of Fame—despite the fact that twice that many had been the first overall picks of the draft. Just two have been NFL Rookies of the Year, and a mere seven have started for a Super Bowl champion team.*

CELEBRATING COLUMBUS DAY

Columbus Day is a holiday that honors the fact that Columbus discovered America. But according to historians—and Columbus himself—he missed the mark.

Christopher Columbus crossed the Atlantic in 1492, convinced he could find a route to the Far East (or "the Indies") that wouldn't require him to sail all the way around the Horn of Africa. On October 12, he landed on a small body of land, believing it was one of the outlying islands of the Orient. Today, we celebrate Columbus Day to honor the fact that Columbus discovered America.

But did he? The truth is that Columbus landed somewhere in the Bahamas—there is disagreement as to exactly which island he set foot on—and from there went on to Cuba (he thought it was China) and Hispaniola (present-day Haiti and the Dominican Republic, which he thought was Japan). On his second trip, Columbus returned to Hispaniola, and it wasn't until his third voyage that he finally landed in America—South America, that is, in what is now Venezuela.

Columbus made one last voyage across the Atlantic in 1502, hoping for definitive proof that he'd found a western route to the Indies. Instead, he discovered St. Lucia, Honduras, Costa Rica, and the Isthmus of Panama. By that time, another Italian mariner, Amerigo Vespucci, had sailed along the coast of South America and proposed that it was not Asia at all but an entirely new continent.

Columbus was nothing if not resolute. He continued to insist that he had discovered a new route to the Indies until the day he died in 1506. A year later, a German mapmaker included the newfound lands on a world map and called them America, in honor of Vespucci. It was the first time the name had been used. Columbus wasn't around to complain, and the name stuck.

THE BOSTON TEA PARTY

*We've all learned that our colonial forebears helped touch
off the American Revolution by turning Boston Harbor into
a big tea caddy to protest "taxation without representation."
In fact, wealthy smugglers set the whole thing up.*

Is the original not a great tale of democracy? Angry patriots,
righteously fed up with burdensome taxes and British oppression,
seize a British ship and spoil the cargo. In reality, there's much
more to the story.

The Backdrop

This tale begins with the 1765 Stamp Act, eight years before the
start of the Revolution. Because it cost Britain money to defend
the colonies, the king wanted help paying the bill. This would
happen through tax stamps, similar to modern postage stamps,
required on various documents, printed materials, goods, etc. For
the same reason that proclaiming "I will raise taxes" is the same
as saying "Don't elect me" 12 generations later, this caused an
outcry. Then, as now, most Americans would rather part with their
lifeblood than pay an extra dime in taxes.

The colonists resorted to various forms of terrorism. Mobs
tarred and feathered government officials, burned them in effigy,
and torched their homes and possessions. Within months, the horrified British gave up on the Stamp Act fiasco.

What's the Price of Tea?

Next the British tried the Townshend Act (1767), imposing
customs duties and hoping the average citizen wouldn't notice.
Tea, much loved in the colonies, was among the taxed imports.
Of course, Britain lacked the resources to patrol the entire colonial coastline against enterprising Dutch smugglers, who snuck
shiploads of tea past customs officials. Seeing opportunity, clever
colonial businessmen bought and distributed smuggled tea; like

teen-clothing branders two centuries later, they marketed their product by associating it with defiant rebellion. It worked: Colonials boycotted legally imported tea, often refusing to let it be unloaded from ships.

The Boston Massacre of 1770 (a shooting incident that escalated from heckling and a snowball fight) didn't help. The British realized that the Townshend Act wasn't working, but they maintained the tea tax as a symbol of authority. The British East India Company (aka John Company), which monopolized the importation of Indian tea to America, was losing a lot of money. In response, Parliament passed the 1773 Tea Act, which relaxed customs duties and allowed John Company to bypass costly London middlemen. It was a brilliant idea: John Company could unload ruinously vast inventories of tea while pacifying the tax-hating, bargain-hunting colonials.

Tea and Cakes in the Harbor

In November 1773, three British merchant ships anchored in Boston Harbor with the first loads of tea. Amid much social brouhaha, the smugglers roused mobs that prevented the tea from being unloaded. But by December 16, it was clear that the ships would land their tea the next day.

One group of protestors fortified itself with lots of liquor, dressed up in "Indian" costumes, and staggered toward the wharf in an outrage. Those who didn't fall into the water along the way boarded the British ships and began dragging the cargo up from the holds, cracking open designated cases and heaving tea leaves into the water. By the end of the night, approximately 45 tons of tea had been dumped overboard, and tea leaves washed up on Boston shores for weeks.

Afterward, the Sons of Liberty wandered home, proud of their patriotic accomplishment. Similar tea "parties" occurred in other colonial ports. The colonies had successfully impugned King George III and maintained a healthy business climate for smugglers.

BEER TIME

In 1933, when newly elected president Franklin D. Roosevelt lifted the ban on alcohol, he famously said, "I think this would be a good time for a beer." For some states, however, Prohibition continued long after that proclamation.

The Volstead Act, also known as the Prohibition Act of 1919, gave U.S. authorities power to enforce the 18th Amendment to the Constitution, which banned the sale, manufacture, and transportation of intoxicating beverages. These were defined as any drink containing more than 0.5 percent alcohol by volume. The 18th Amendment took effect in 1920 and heralded an American era forever associated with gangsters, bootleggers, and speakeasies.

The Prohibition movement evolved from the religion-based Temperance movement of the late 19th century, in part as a response to the explosion in the number of saloons around the time of World War I. A number of individual counties and states, particularly in the South, adopted their own local Prohibition laws prior to the national ban on alcohol in 1920. Prohibition quickly became unpopular, though, and created a nightmare for law-enforcement officials. In March 1933, shortly after he was elected president, Franklin Roosevelt amended the Volstead Act with the Cullen-Harrison Act, which allowed the manufacture and sale of "light" wines and 3.2 percent beer. In December of that year, he ratified the 21st Amendment to the Constitution, ending national Prohibition.

As well as being the first and only amendment to repeal a previous amendment to the Constitution, the 21st Amendment enabled individual states to use their own discretion in deciding when to repeal Prohibition. So, depending on where you lived, Prohibition may not have ended in 1933. Mississippi, the last dry state, did not repeal it until 1966.

THE PYRAMIDS OF EGYPT

Ask most people what they consider the oldest, most magnificent architecture in the world, and the pyramids of Egypt are sure to be part of the answer. Magnificent they are, but they are not the oldest.

The Pyramids of Giza are the most famous monuments of ancient Egypt and the only structures remaining of the original Seven Wonders of the Ancient World. Originally about 480 feet high, they are also the largest stone structures constructed by humans. They are not, however, the oldest.

What's older than the pyramids? That glory goes to the prehistoric temples of Malta—a small island nation south of Sicily. The temples date from 4000 to 2500 B.C. At approximately 6,000 years old, they are a thousand years older than the pyramids. Not much is known about the people who built these magnificent structures, but they were likely farmers who constructed the temples as public places of worship.

Because the Maltese temples were covered with soil from early times and not discovered until the 19th century, these megalithic structures have been well preserved. Extensive archaeological and restorative work was carried out in the early 20th century by European and Maltese archaeologists to further ensure the temples' longevity. The major temple complexes are now designated as UNESCO World Heritage Sites.

Which pyramid is the oldest? That would be the Step Pyramid at Saqqara. It was built during the third dynasty of Egypt's Old Kingdom to protect the body of King Djoser, who died around 2649 B.C. It was this architectural feat that propelled the construction of the gigantic stone pyramids of ancient Egypt on a rocky desert plateau close to the Nile. These pyramids, known as the Great Pyramids, were built around 2493 B.C. The largest structure served as the tomb for Pharaoh Khufu.

POP! GOES YOUR STOMACH

Although eating the explosive candy Pop Rocks while drinking a soda isn't considered a healthful way to snack, it isn't fatal—despite what a persistent urban legend would have us believe.

In 1975, to the delight of bored kids across the country, General Foods unveiled Pop Rocks, aka Space Dust. These tiny pebbles of fruit-flavored candy release a bit of carbonation when held on the tongue, causing an "exploding" sensation.

Death by Pop Rocks?

Although the candy was invented in 1956 (thus allowing ample time for testing), its startling novelty caused the Food and Drug Administration to set up a Pop Rocks hotline to reassure parents who were concerned about product safety. Despite these efforts, it became widespread playground knowledge that consuming the candy along with a carbonated beverage would cause one's stomach to explode. By 1979, the rumor was so pervasive that General Foods put full-page ads in 45 major-market publications, wrote more than 50,000 letters to school principals, and sent the inventor on a "goodwill tour" to debunk the myths. When General Foods stopped marketing Pop Rocks in 1983, many took it as proof that the confection was too dangerous to sell.

Adding fuel to Pop Rocks's fire was the widely rumored death of a child star who supposedly died after consuming a combination of the candy and soda. The kid, known to most only as "Mikey" (his character in a long-lived Quaker Life cereal commercial), was actor John Gilchrist. Although rumormongers claimed that Gilchrist mysteriously "disappeared" from the public eye after the commercial's 1972 debut (proof, of course, of his death), he actually continued making commercials through 1988 before retiring from acting. He is alive and well today and works in radio advertising, though talk of his unfortunate demise persists.

After General Foods stopped marketing the candy, Kraft Foods purchased the rights to it in 1983 and sold it under the name Action Candy. Today, Pop Rocks are back on the market under their original name, available for purchase online and in stores—without so much as a warning label.

Rumors about the candy have died down, likely due to the high-profile debunking it has received on TV shows and Web sites. However, in 2001, a lawsuit revived some of the original concerns. The suit was filed on behalf of a California girl who was rushed to a hospital in considerable pain after swallowing Pop Rocks that were blended into a special Baskin-Robbins ice-cream flavor. Doctors had to insert a tube into the child's stomach to help relieve gas pressure, but the ice cream was never determined to be the cause.

As "Pop"ular as Ever

Despite that incident, Pop Rocks have enjoyed a revival, finding their way to the table as a mix-in for applesauce or yogurt and even as a garnish at retro-hip eateries (Pop Rocks–studded foie gras, anyone?). General Foods still holds U.S. patent number 4289794 for the "process of preparing gasified candy in which flavored sugar syrup—such as is used to make hard candy—is mixed with CO_2. The gas forms bubbles, each with an internal pressure of 600 pounds per square inch (PSI). As the candy melts on your tongue, the bubbles pop, releasing that pressure."

Although the thought of pressurized candy exploding into shards of crystallized sugar in your mouth or stomach sounds dangerous, it isn't. The amount of gas in a package of Pop Rocks is only one-tenth as much as there is in about an ounce of carbonated soda. Even if you combine Pop Rocks with a carbonated beverage, the pressure is not enough to make your stomach explode.

Mentos Cocktail

A similar but more explosive combination of soda and breath mints has prompted people to create homemade "geysers" by mixing Mentos and Diet Coke. In 2008, students in Leuven, Belgium, dropped Mentos into two-liter bottles of Diet Coke, creating 1,360 simultaneous fountains and setting a world record.

THE STORY OF THE TASADAY

❊ ❊ ❊

*A 1972 National Geographic article announced the discovery of a
gentle, pristine Stone Age people in the Philippines: the Tasaday.
Skeptics say the Tasaday were a hoax perpetrated by the
Marcos government—but are they right?*

In 1971, strongman Ferdinand Marcos was dictator of the Philippines. His wealthy crony, Manuel Elizalde, Jr., was head of
Panamin, a minority-rights watchdog agency. In a nation with
7,107 islands, 12 major regional languages, and hundreds of ethnic
groups, such an agency has its work cut out for it.

The Discovery
The Philippines' second largest island, Mindanao, is bigger than
Maine, with lots of jungle. According to Elizalde, a western Mindanao tribesman put him in contact with the Tasaday. The tribe
numbered only a couple dozen and lived amid primitive conditions. Their language bore relation to nearby tongues but lacked
words for war and violence. They seemed to be living in gentle
simplicity, marveling at Elizalde as a deity and protector. For his
part, Elizalde clamped the full power of the Philippine state into
place to shield his newfound people. One of the few study groups
permitted to examine the Tasaday was from *National Geographic,*
which introduced the Tasaday to the world in 1972.

After Marcos fell from power in 1986, investigators studying
the lives of the Tasaday revealed that it was all a fraud. According to
reports, Elizalde had recruited the Tasaday from long-established
local tribes and forced them to role-play a Stone Age lifestyle. The
Tasaday eventually became the "Tasaday Hoax."

A Scam Revealed?
A couple of Tasaday told a sad story: They normally farmed
nearby, living in huts rather than caves, but Elizalde made them

wear loincloths and do dog-and-pony shows for paying visitors. The poorer and more primitive they looked, the more money they would get. In one instance, a group of German journalists who set out to document the Tasaday found them dressed primitively—sort of. They were wearing leaves, but they had stuck them onto their clothing, which was visible beneath the foliage. Scientific skepticism soon surfaced as well: How could they have remained that isolated for so long, even on Mindanao? Why didn't modern disease now decimate them? Why did their tools show evidence of steel-knife manufacturing?

Elizalde didn't back down easily. In an attempt to keep up the charade, he flew a few Tasaday to Manila to sue the naysayers for libel. With Marcos ousted, however, Elizalde was less able to influence investigators or control what they had access to. Eminent linguist Lawrence Reid decided that the Tasaday were indeed an offshoot of a regional tribe—but one that had been living in the area for only 150 years, not more than a thousand as was claimed. Likely as confused as everyone else at this point, previous Tasaday whistleblowers now confessed that translators had bribed them to say the whole thing was a hoax.

The Aftermath

Elizalde later fled to Costa Rica, squandered his money, and died a drug addict. If he had indeed fabricated the history of the Tasaday, what was his motivation? It could have been a public-relations ploy, because the Marcos government had a well-earned reputation for repression. A strong minority-rights stance in defense of the Tasaday could be expected to buff some tarnish off the government's image. Commerce likely played a role, for the Tasaday episode denied huge tracts of jungle to logging interests. Perhaps those interests hadn't played ball with Marcos and/or Elizalde.

Elizalde did not "discover" the Tasaday, but that doesn't mean they were total fakes. What is clear is that they were pawns in a sociopolitical chess game far greater than the jungle of Mindanao.

SOUNDLY WHIPPED

❈ ❈ ❈

Was U.S. Air Force captain Chuck Yeager first to break the sound barrier? The answer may surprise, mesmerize, or antagonize.

Many believe that celebrated test pilot Chuck Yeager was first to punch through the elusive sound barrier. They are correct—at least in part. When Captain Yeager's Bell X-1 rocket plane hit Mach 1.07 (just beyond the speed of sound) on October 14, 1947, the grinning West Virginian became the first *human* to conquer the sound barrier in level flight. Although the feat was a crowning achievement for humankind, Yeager's X-1 was far from the first *object* to surpass the speed of sound.

That title goes to something far less glamorous than a celebrated aviator—a plain old bullwhip. As far back as 5000 B.C., the Chinese were producing these long, handheld implements to drive cattle. When the whip uncoiled to its fully extended length, a noticeable "crack" would encourage the animals to fall in line. The question has always been: Why does the whip issue such a sound, even when it is striking nothing more than thin air?

In 1927, high-speed photography of a whip-stroke solved the mystery. The pictures showed that a sonic boom was being created as the extreme tip of the whip "snapped" out to its full length. Because the speed of sound is dependent upon elevation (greater speed is required to break through at sea level than at higher altitudes), the whip had to be traveling at an even faster speed than Captain Yeager.

❈ ❈ ❈

- *Some studies suggest that dinosaurs had what it took to create a sonic boom more than 150 million years ago. Sauropods (the dinosaur family featuring such beasts as Brontosaurus and Diplodocus) used their long, tapered appendages to defend themselves. And with tails that weighed as much as 3,500 pounds, these dinosaurs could have done some serious whip-cracking!*

❀ ❖ ❀

Fallacy: *Baking soda eliminates odors in the refrigerator.*
Fact: *Chemically speaking, the alkaline composition of baking soda may absorb and neutralize a bit of an acidic odor. But the humidity in a fridge can cause the baking soda to develop a hard crust, further reducing its already weak ability to tame tough odors. Replace the baking soda with an open canister of charcoal, which will do a much better job of soaking up smells.*

Fallacy: *Lobsters scream in pain when dropped into boiling water.*
Fact: *First, lobsters have no vocal cords. Second, lobsters, crabs, and other invertebrates have ultrasimple nervous systems that lack the receptors to feel what humans call "pain." Here's the explanation for the sound you hear: Air that is trapped under the lobster's shell expands rapidly in boiling water and escapes through small openings. So in the same way that teapots don't actually whistle, lobsters don't really scream.*

Fallacy: *Thanksgiving turkey makes you sleepy.*
Fact: *Although many people believe that the culpable compound in turkey is the natural sedative known as tryptophan, plenty of other foods (including beef, pork, and cheese) contain similar or higher amounts of the amino acid. Most likely, the other things you consume at your holiday table, including the alcoholic beverages and carbohydrates that accompany Mom's turkey, can slow your metabolism. This, along with a heavy meal that forces your diaphragm to work harder (it pulls the lungs down and hinders breathing), can leave you snoring on the couch after dinner.*

Fallacy: *Raw eggs carry* salmonella.

Fact: *According to the U.S. Department of Agriculture, 1 in 3,600 eggs is contaminated with* salmonella. *That's 300 dozen—if your family eats a carton every week, you may get one bad egg every six years. In many cases, the contamination is on the shell rather than in the egg itself (chickens aren't the cleanest creatures in the barnyard). The process of pasteurization, which many commercial egg plants employ, uses hot water baths to kill bacteria while keeping the egg inside the shell uncooked. When in doubt, always cook eggs completely, and be sure to purchase in-shell eggs from a dependable vendor. Also, while you're checking the carton for cracked eggs before you buy them, check the expiration date!*

Fallacy: *Food that falls on the floor is okay if picked up within five seconds.*

Fact: *Granted, the longer the contact time, the greater the amount of contamination, but food products that come into contact with any unsanitary surface can pick up pathogens in as little as two seconds. A quick retrieval may mean fewer harmful germs, but it's no assurance of safety. Bacteria can thrive on surfaces for as long as a month, so cleaning floors and countertops with a disinfectant can go a long way toward keeping your meals down—for good.*

Fallacy: *Dishes made with mayonnaise spoil quickly if not refrigerated.*

Fact: *Your family picnic may have made you queasy, but don't be too quick to blame Uncle Leo's potato salad. The commercial mayonnaise used by many home cooks contains vinegar, which inhibits the growth of the bacteria that cause food poisoning. Chances are that if you got sick from a dish made with mayo, it was because of another ingredient, such as contaminated chicken.*

THE NOT-SO-WINDY CITY

※ ◈ ※

Called the "Windy City" for well over a century, Chicago is famed for its swirling wind currents. But all may not be as it seems. Both the city's nickname and the assumptions behind it are "airy" affairs.

Perhaps the most interesting aspect of Chicago's "Windy City" nickname is the fact that there's no certainty about its origin. But there are theories. One possible explanation appeared in an article in the September 11, 1886, edition of the *Chicago Tribune*. It claimed that the nickname referred to the "refreshing lake breezes" blowing off Lake Michigan. Another explanation completely ignores climate and credits 19th-century Chicago promoters William Bross and John Stephan Wright with inspiring the phrase. In this colorful version of the story, witnesses to the duo's loud boasts eventually branded them "windbags." The backhanded term "Windy City" grew from this, and the rest is history.

A Lot of Hot Air

The origin of Chicago's nickname may be up for debate, but the veracity of its claim is not. One need only consult weather records that display average annual wind speeds for U.S. cities. Certainly, if Chicago's "Windy City" tag derives from its much-celebrated wind currents, this would be the place to confirm it.

According to National Climatic Data Center findings from 2003, Blue Hill, Massachusetts, blows harder than all other U.S. cities, with a 15.4-mile-per-hour average annual wind speed. Dodge City, Kansas, and Amarillo, Texas, nab second- and third-place honors, with wind speeds of 14.0 mph and 13.5 mph, respectively. Lubbock, Texas, comes in tenth on the center's top-ten list with a 12.4-mph clocking.

※ ※ ※

- *How fast do air currents move in the notorious Windy City? With average annual winds pushing the needle to just 10.3 mph, it appears that Chicago's blustery status is full of hot air.*

TIME FOR A RECOUNT?

❀❀❀

Some people can bend themselves into mind-boggling positions.
Others have one cool trick, such as wrapping their legs
behind their neck or bending their thumbs backward.
Talented? Maybe. Double-jointed? No.

To explain such feats, people boast that they're "double-jointed," as though they either have more joints than the rest of us or have joints with twice the normal range of motion. Even if you can twist yourself into the shape of a pretzel, you are not, in fact, double-jointed.

Bend Me, Shape Me

Circus promoters often claim that their star contortionists have a little extra in their anatomy, but that's just to sell tickets. In fact, we all have the same number of joints. Those dramatic twists and turns are a combination of genetic flexibility—which allows for extra movement in the joints—and intense training. The technical term for extraordinary joint flexibility is *hypermobility*.

Hypermobility is most often seen in children. Most of the time, the condition doesn't cause any problems, but in some cases, it can be a sign of an underlying medical condition. When hypermobility causes dislocations and sprains, or pain and swelling in the joints, the diagnosis is Benign Hypermobility Syndrome. Also called "looseness of joints," this condition is characterized by loose and weak ligaments, which do a poor job of providing stability to the joints.

Experts do not know why some hypermobile individuals are pain free while others experience discomfort. Treatment varies but may include exercises to increase muscle strength and training to prevent hyperextension.

In rare instances, hypermobility can indicate the presence of serious systemic genetic diseases such as Marfan Syndrome or Ehlers-Danlos Syndrome.

SACAJAWEA'S STORY

❀ ❖ ❀

There aren't many tour guides as famous as Sacajawea,
but in truth, she wasn't a guide at all—she had no idea
where she was going, and she didn't even speak English!

Hooking Up with Lewis and Clark

Meriwether Lewis (a soldier) and William Clark (a naturalist) were
recruited by President Thomas Jefferson to explore the upper
reaches of the Missouri River. Their job was to find the most
direct route to the Pacific Ocean—the legendary Northwest Passage. Setting out in 1803, they worked their way up the Missouri
River and then stopped for the winter to build a fort near a trading
post in present-day North Dakota. This is where they met the
pregnant Shoshone teenager known as Sacajawea.

Actually, they met her through her husband, Toussaint Char-
bonneau. He was a French fur trader who lived with the Shoshone
(he is said to have purchased Sacajawea from members of another
group who had captured her, so it may be inaccurate to call her
his "wife"). Although Sacajawea is credited with guiding Lewis
and Clark's expedition to the Pacific, the only reason she (and her
newborn baby) went along at all was that her husband had been
hired as a translator.

Pop Culture Icon

The myth of Sacajawea as the Native American princess who
pointed the way to the Pacific was created and perpetuated by the
many books and movies that romanticized her story. For example,
the 1955 movie *The Far Horizons,* which starred Donna Reed
in "yellow-face" makeup, introduced the fictional plotline of a
romance between Sacajawea and William Clark. Over time, she
has evolved to serve as a symbol of friendly relations between the
U.S. government and Native Americans. In 2000, she was given
the U.S. Mint's ultimate honor when it released the Sacajawea
Golden Dollar. At the same time, though, the Mint's Web site

incorrectly states that she "guided the adventurers from the Northern Great Plains to the Pacific Ocean and back."

The Real Sacajawea

The only facts known about Sacajawea come from the journals of Lewis and Clark's expedition team. According to these, we know that she did not translate for the group—with the exception of a few occasions when they encountered other Shoshone. But because she did not speak English, she served as more of a go-between for her husband, the explorers, and members of other tribes they encountered in their travels. Concerning her knowledge of a route to the Pacific, Lewis and Clark knew far more about the land than she did. Only when they reached the area occupied by her own people was she able to point out a few landmarks, but they were not of any great help.

This isn't to say that she did not make important contributions to the journey's success. Journals note that Sacajawea was a great help to the team when she took it upon herself to rescue essential medicines and supplies that had been washed into a river. Her knowledge of edible roots and plants was invaluable when game and other sources of food were hard to come by. Most important, Sacajawea served as a sort of human peace symbol. Her presence reassured the various Native American groups who encountered Lewis and Clark that the explorers' intentions were peaceful. No Native American woman, especially one with a baby on her back, would have been part of a war party.

There are two very different accounts of Sacajawea's death. Although some historical documents say she died in South Dakota in 1812, Shoshone oral tradition claims she lived until 1884 and died in Wyoming. Regardless of differing interpretaions of her life and death, Sacajawea will always be a heroine of American history.

THIRSTY FOR KNOWLEDGE

Medical experts have been warning people for years: If you wait until you're thirsty to drink, it may be too late because dehydration may have already set in. This topic still generates controversy, but here are the prevailing thoughts on thirst.

To drink or not to drink before you're thirsty: That's the question some physicians, nutritionists, and athletes still debate. Although many people worry about becoming dehydrated, most experts believe that if you drink when you're thirsty, you'll be well hydrated.

Kidney expert Heinz Valtin, M.D., of Dartmouth Medical School, disputes the idea that people are already dehydrated by the time they are thirsty. He believes thirst begins when the concentration of blood (an accurate indicator of our state of hydration) has risen by less than 2 percent. However, other experts define dehydration as beginning when that concentration has risen by at least 5 percent.

How did the thirst-dehydration debate start? It could have simply been the result of a successful marketing campaign. Look at all the products devoted to continuous water intake—spring water, demineralized water, fancy water-bottle holders, and water tubes for athletes, just to name a few.

Dr. Valtin thinks the notion may have begun when the Food and Nutrition Board of the National Research Council recommended approximately "one milliliter of water for each calorie of food," which would amount to roughly two to two and a half quarts per day (64 to 80 ounces). The council also said most of that amount is contained in prepared foods, but that fact likely was missed or misinterpreted, leading to the "8 × 8" rule—8 eight-ounce glasses of water per day. To consume that amount, you would obviously have to drink before you were thirsty.

So unless you need lots of water to prevent kidney stones, or for running marathons or living in a hot, dry climate, listen to your body: Drink when you're thirsty.

HORACE GREELEY'S GRIPE

Did this 1800s news mogul and presidential hopeful coin the phrase "Go West, young man"? We know he wrote it, and Greeley was certainly the most prominent person to say it in a memorable way.

Horace Greeley was a self-made newspaperman, social critic, and advocate who built the influential *New York Tribune* into a mighty voice for change. He opposed monopolies, the death penalty, and slavery, and he advocated homestead land grants and egalitarianism. In a *Tribune* editorial dated July 13, 1865, Greeley wrote, "Washington is not a place to live in. The rents are high, the food is bad, the dust is disgusting and the morals are deplorable. Go West, young man, go West and grow up with the country."

Although he was a solid advocate for Western settlement, Greeley was attempting to speak to a different issue. He was addressing disgruntled civil servants in D.C. who had complained at length about low pay and high living costs in their city of employment. What Greeley meant was, "If you don't like it here, go somewhere else."

A number of historians credit the phrase to John B. Soule, writing in the *Terre Haute Express* in 1851. That credit lacks one key component: a specific date. If we're sure someone said or wrote something, we usually know exactly when. With Soule, we do not, so a firm credit becomes problematic. He probably did say it, but just as likely, so did others before and after. In the 1800s, many thousands sought their fortunes out West. "Go West" was the era's equivalent of saying, "Apply to college."

Greeley's own story ended less optimistically. He ran against Ulysses S. Grant for president, was soundly defeated, lost his mind and his newspaper, and died insane. His assessment of Washington, D.C., however, has in many ways endured the test of time.

STRETCHING THE TRUTH

❊ ❊ ❊

*In a time-honored tradition, baseball fans rise from their seats
between the top and bottom of the seventh inning to sing a hearty
rendition of "Take Me Out to the Ball Game." Was this custom really
started as a nod of respect to President William Howard Taft?*

Rather than being remembered for his
one-term residency in the White House
and for being the only man to serve as
both president and chief justice of the
Supreme Court, Taft is probably best
known as the fattest man ever to serve as commander in chief.
Indeed, Taft's girth was impressive, and it sometimes restricted
his movements, especially when he attended Washington Senators
baseball games (a pastime pursuit that was his preferred method
of relaxation). After sitting through a few innings of action, Taft
would extract himself from the compressed confines of his chair,
stand, stretch, and waddle off to the men's room. The denizens
sitting near him would also rise, showing a measure of respect
for their honored guest. This presidential pause for the cause was
rumored to have occurred in the seventh-inning break.

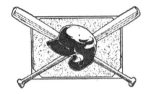

However, there's no proof that the president was responsible
for instituting or influencing the tradition. Taft attended many ball
games, but he rarely stayed as late as the seventh inning. It's been
said he had more pressing matters on his home plate—running
the country, for instance.

Presidents Who Pitch

On April 14, 1910, Taft became the first president to toss the first
pitch on opening day of the season, a convention that has since been
followed by every chief executive, with the exception of Jimmy Carter—
an ironic twist when one considers the relationship between Carter,
peanuts, and baseball.

CROSS PURPOSES

According to Christian tradition, the True Cross consists of the remnants of the cross on which Jesus Christ was crucified. But careful examination reveals that the "pieces" of this story don't add up.

During the 16th-century Reformation that broke Christianity into Protestant and Catholic factions, the Catholic Church was much criticized for its commercialization of holy relics. According to *Forgery in Christianity,* even the supposed baby teeth and umbilical cord of the infant Jesus were put up for sale. Perhaps the most revered object that pilgrims were charged money to see were the reputed remains of the True Cross.

Critics charged that chapels and abbeys had enough fragments of the True Cross to constitute many crosses, undermining the Church's claim that it possessed the real thing. In *Treatise on Relics,* Protestant theologian John Calvin states: "If all the pieces that could be found were collected together, they would make a big ship-load. Yet the Gospel testifies that a single man was able to carry it."

But it appears Calvin may have been wrong. A 19th-century tally of all the known fragments of the True Cross added up to far less wood than it would take to make a single cross.

In 1870, French architect Rohault de Fleury, a devout Catholic, estimated the volume of wood in a complete cross, as cataloged in his book *Les Instruments de la Passion.* A large cross of the type the Romans used for executions would measure about four meters high by two meters across, or 178 million cubic millimeters. Fleury next added up the volume of the alleged pieces of the True Cross in Europe's churches, cathedrals, and monasteries, including the pieces that had been lost to time. Fleury arrived at a total of 4 million cubic millimeters. That is only about 2 percent of the amount of a complete cross.

We can't know for certain whether the fragments that the architect studied were part of the cross on which Jesus Christ died. However, they do make up far less than a complete cross.

THE KU KLUX KLAN: A SOUTHERN PHENOMENON?

❋ ❋❋ ❋

Since the first Ku Klux Klan formed in Tennessee in 1865,
the white sheet and hood have symbolized intimidation
and ethnic hatred. Although the Klan was born in Dixie,
many of its power bases have been—and remain—
far outside the former Confederacy.

The First Klan: Politics by Other Means

To understand the first Ku Klux Klan, one must understand the times. The same year that Robert E. Lee surrendered to Ulysses S. Grant, numerous former Confederate citizens decided that if they couldn't have their old status quo on paper, they'd have it in practice. This meant keeping the Democratic Party in state and local power, which would occur only if Republican-sympathizing African Americans didn't vote. The Ku Klux Klan's primary aim was to suppress black voting.

The first KKK was less a centralized organization than a handy label adopted by ad hoc local political terrorists and racists. Those types also existed in non-Southern states but were less likely to call themselves Klansmen. General public revulsion at Klan tactics led to the Ku Klux Klan Act of 1871, which started sending members to jail for civil-rights violations. Membership waned to a few die-hards.

The Second Klan: Loyal Order of Hoodlums in Hoods

This Klan, born from the general hoopla over the 1915 film sensation *Birth of a Nation,* soon went mainstream and national. Its focus was anti-Catholic, anti-Communist, anti-immigrant, anti-Semitic, and anti–African American. Some KKK members lynched and burned, but for most it was a social pastime much like a fraternal lodge. This Klan boasted millions of members.

Politically and numerically, the Klan was strongest in Illinois, Indiana, and Michigan, with lesser power bases in California,

Oregon, and the South. Woodrow Wilson praised it, and evidence indicates that Warren G. Harding joined it. Its downfall began with a 1925 violent-assault scandal, then accelerated with the onset of the Depression and the rise of Hitler in Germany. This was the deepest KKK penetration of government and society, but it was more Midwestern than Southern; by World War II, it had subsided to a few thousand hardcore bigots.

The Civil Rights–Era Klan: White Supremacy

The 1950s brought a national movement toward any good Klansman's worst nightmare: African Americans as equal participants in society. Again the Klan rose, though in nothing resembling the numbers of the 1920s. This version was much like the first Klan—mostly Southern, with tentacles in other regions, balkanized into numerous groups competing for the sympathies of militant racists.

This time the atrocities occurred in the light of modern mass media, as the nation watched Klan violence on the nightly news. Anyone trying to excuse the Ku Klux Klan as a harmless social club looked delusional, and in the mainstream American psyche, the Klan bedsheet came to emblemize terrorism. After losing the war against the civil-rights movement, the Klan once again receded to several thousand members.

The Modern Klan: Stolen Thunder

By the 1980s, the Klan had become a minor player in racist subculture. Christian identity, neo-Nazism, and the skinhead movement attracted many who would have raided their linen closets in another era. In the past, police had at least attempted to protect civil-rights demonstrators from Klan violence; now angry crowds rained scorn on KKK rallies. Only police protection shielded Klansmen from the brand of violence their ideological forebears used to dish out.

By 2006, the Ku Klux Klan consisted of scattered islets dotting the map from Maine to Louisiana to California. Thus, the Klan does have Southern roots and a Southern presence, but it has often taken on a decidedly Northern and Western character.

GHOST SHIP AHOY!

*Pirates of the Caribbean movies have renewed interest
in such folkloric figures as Davy Jones and* The Flying Dutchman
*while simultaneously muddling their stories. At no time was
Davy Jones captain of the famed ghost ship.*

Davy Jones

"Davy Jones's Locker" is an old seafaring term for the bottom
of the ocean, the grave of all those who perish at sea. There are
numerous tales about the origin of the expression, most of which
attempt to identify a real Davy Jones. One version has Jones running a pub in London, where he press-ganged unwary customers
into serving aboard pirate ships by drugging them and then storing
them in the pub's ale cellar or locker. Other stories relate Jones to
Jonah, the biblical figure who spent three days and nights trapped
in the belly of a big fish.

The Flying Dutchman

This term is often used to refer to a ghost ship that is doomed to
sail the oceans forever, but it is more accurately a reference to
the captain of the ghost ship. Legend holds that in 1680, Dutch
captain Hendrik Van der Decken's ship was wrecked in a terrible
storm off the Cape of Good Hope at the southern tip of Africa. As
the ship sank, the captain's dying words were a vow to successfully
round the infamous Cape even if it took him until doomsday.

Over the years, whenever there is stormy weather off the
Cape, seafarers have reported seeing a phantom ship battling the
waves, with a ghostly captain at the wheel.
In 1939, dozens of bathers on a South
African beach reported sighting a
17th-century merchant vessel off
the coast and then seeing it suddenly vanish into thin air.

THE RUMOR OF OZ

It's said that if you watch The Wizard of Oz *closely enough, you'll see an actor who played one of the Munchkins commit suicide on the set. Or is that just an urban legend?*

In one of the most famous scenes in *The Wizard of Oz,* Dorothy links arms with the Scarecrow and the Tin Man and the three dance off along the yellow brick road singing, "We're off to see the wizard, the wonderful wizard of Oz." Almost as famous as the scene itself is the rumor that has long accompanied the classic 1939 movie. Take your eyes off the central characters for a moment and you can clearly see something move in the background among the trees. Look closely enough, say some people, and you'll see that the movement is created by an actor, playing one of the Munchkins, as he hangs himself. Apparently, the man in question was distraught over being romantically rejected by a fellow Munchkin.

A Flap Over Nothing

Soon after the release of *The Wizard of Oz,* rumors began to circulate about Munchkin unruliness on the set. The suicide story, however, didn't gain ground until the movie was released on video and viewers were able to pause and watch the scene repeatedly in slow motion. Morbid imaginings aside, the movement is not a suicide in progress but the flapping wings of an oversize bird.

To make the forest scenes seem more realistic, filmmakers borrowed large birds from the Los Angeles Zoo and allowed them to roam around the set. The birds can be seen more clearly in earlier scenes: As Dorothy and the Scarecrow are reviving the Tin Man with oil outside his cabin, a peacock leisurely strolls by. In the scene in question, however, the bird (either an ostrich or a crane) is visible only as a blurry background image. Furthermore, the forest scenes were filmed before those that took place in Munchkinland, so no Munchkins would have been on set at the time.

WELL, BLOW ME DOWN!

Will a house survive a tornado if its windows are opened?
Explosive evidence reveals the crushing answer.

With roaring winds that can exceed 300 miles per hour, anything in a tornado's path is in peril. Accordingly, people have devised ways to protect themselves and their homes should this whirlwind come visiting. The idea that opening windows will save one's home represents humankind's hubris against a clearly overwhelming force.

Breezy Logic

A popular idea, aimed at saving a dwelling, instructs occupants to open windows to equalize pressure differentials between their structure and the storm. This, it is said, will keep the home from exploding should the funnel cloud pass overhead. This may sound plausible, but it stems from logic that's severely flawed. In fact, insurance adjusters reserve a name for homes "protected" in such a manner. They are labeled "destroyed." Here's why.

Before a tornado's low-pressure effect is encountered (at the very center of the vortex), winds ranging from 100 to 200 mph will be felt. These gusts usually contain flying debris from devastated structures and other objects. Such projectiles will create vent holes in a building that would theoretically protect it from a drop in pressure. Yet such homes are routinely smashed.

Don't Bother

A study by Texas Tech's Institute for Disaster Research found that the pressure drop experienced in a 260-mph tornado is about 10 percent less than that of surrounding pressures. Most dwellings can vent this difference through existing openings. But the point is moot, anyway. A violent tornado will blow a house apart quicker than you can read this sentence. Open windows have little effect against such devastating fury.

RATS! THEY'RE...EVERYWHERE?

❋❖❋

Urban folklore would have us believe that we're never farther than a few feet from a rat. The thought is enough to make your skin crawl, but are there really that many rats around us?

Why are rats so reviled? Not everyone hates rats. The Jainist religious sect of south Asia honors all life—even that of a rat. People love their pet rats. Your weird friend (you know which one) even likes wild rats. Of course, that might change when he contracts bubonic plague.

Beyond that, the only creatures that like rats are rat predators. The same animal lover who would feed and care for stray dogs would likely pay an exterminator good money to dispose of stray rats. Wild rats carry diseases and filth, eat unspeakable things, are very difficult to kill, can grow to an enormous size, and run in large packs that could overwhelm any human. To the majority of people, rats are the stuff of nightmares, as Winston Smith finds in George Orwell's *1984*.

So just how close to us are they? Do you spend a lot of time in the alleys of a large city's slums, cuddled up next to a garbage can, drinking in the smell of fermenting everything? Do you often seek shelter in the cool, tranquil comfort of your favorite sewer pipe? Do you spend idle afternoons sifting through that landfill you love so well in search of rare treasures?

If you answered yes to any of these questions, you've been in real close proximity to rats. Then again, if these are your preferred haunts, you know that already. For your safety, you might want to peruse the February 13, 1998, *Morbidity and Mortality Weekly Report*. In it you'll find an article that describes a couple of bonafide cases of rat-bite fever.

Then we'll just avoid those places. Unfortunately, rats aren't picky about where they live. Some estimates say there is one rat per U.S. resident, which is hard to confirm because vermin don't answer the Census. But suppose there are that many. They'd be concentrated in big cities where there's also a lot of food and places to hide and scurry. Any poorly secured storage of food, either fresh or discarded, will attract them. People living in immaculate suburban mansions probably don't have a homey woodpile or trash heap in their backyards, but that's not to say rats don't roam idyllic family neighborhoods.

What do we do if we encounter a rat? The number of rats reported to health officials in the suburbs has been steadily increasing, and it's now common for municipalities to offer some sort of "rat patrol" to assist citizens in the fight against these critters. Have you heard the horror stories about rats that get into residential toilets after swimming up through sewer pipes? We'd like to say that those are also urban folklore—but they're not.

Rat Facts

- Rats live from two to seven years, but they rarely reach the upper end of that range.

- Rats have lousy eyesight, but they make up for it with their acute senses of smell and hearing.

- A single female rat can birth more than 60 offspring per year.

- Rats keep their teeth sharp partly by grinding them. They develop a chiseled edge with the beveling in back.

- Rats use their tails somewhat like monkeys do, for balance and gripping on narrow perches.

- According to some estimates, rats destroy a fifth of the food that people produce each year.

- Rats aren't kosher (permitted food for observant Jews), nor are they halal (edible by Muslims). Nonetheless, throughout history rats have been a last-resort food source during many sieges and famines.

NEWTON'S APPLE

Could a falling apple have triggered one of the greatest scientific discoveries of all time? Probably not—but it's a cute story.

The tale of the apple landing on Isaac Newton's head during an afternoon nap has been told for hundreds of years as the explanation for his discovery of the law of gravity. If only it were so simple. Newton enjoyed taking walks in his orchard and probably even indulged in a nap or two under an apple tree. But his understanding of gravity did not come to him as a flash of insight. Rather, it was the result of years of painstaking study.

The Plague of 1665 probably had more to do with Newton's intellectual feat than a round, red fruit. Newton was a 23-year-old student at Cambridge when the plague gripped England. As a result, the university closed and students were sent back to their homes in the countryside. Newton used this time to devote himself to his private studies, and in later years, he would refer to this period as the most productive of his life. He spent days working nonstop on computations and nights observing and measuring the skies. These calculations provided the seeds for an idea that would take years of covert and obsessive work to formulate—his Theory of Universal Gravitation.

Accounts of the apple story began appearing after Newton's death in 1727, probably written by the French philosopher Voltaire, who was famous for his wit but not his accuracy. He reported having heard the story about the apple from one of Newton's relatives, but there is no sound evidence to support that claim.

The falling apple will always be associated with Newton's great discovery. Many universities claim to own trees grown from grafts of trees from Newton's orchard, perhaps to remind overworked students that the theory of gravity was no piece of pie but, rather, the fruit of hard labor.

THE BEATLES' ODE TO LSD

It's a catchy tune with mind-blowing lyrics and a trippy melody. Despite what the drug-devouring flower-power generation speculated (and many still believe), however, "Lucy in the Sky with Diamonds" is not a song about LSD.

"Lucy in the Sky with Diamonds" is the third track on the Beatles' magnificent album *Sgt. Pepper's Lonely Hearts Club Band,* which was released in April 1967. That was the beginning of the so-called Summer of Love, when hippies, freaks, and counterculture types were experimenting with all kinds of mind-expanding hallucinogens, including the trip-inducing drug lysergic acid diethylamide, or LSD.

To some chemically altered minds, "Lucy in the Sky with Diamonds" was a cleverly coded reference to LSD, evidenced by the first letter of each of the key words in the song's title. Furthermore, believers were convinced that John Lennon's evocative lyrics and airy vocals were the perfect musical expression of an acid trip. The myth of "Lucy in the Sky with Diamonds" as the Beatles' ode to LSD was born.

Each of the Beatles has readily admitted to using acid during this period in their lives, but all of them have denied that "Lucy in the Sky with Diamonds" was inspired by the drug. The true inspiration for the song, as consistently stated by Lennon, was a drawing made by his then-four-year-old son, Julian, depicting a little girl surrounded by twinkling stars. The drawing, Julian explained to his father, was of his schoolmate Lucy O'Donnell—who was floating through the sky among diamonds. Lennon said the image reminded him of Lewis Carroll's *Through the Looking-Glass,* which in turn inspired the lyrics in the iconic Beatles song.

"Lucy in the Sky with Diamonds" isn't, as many believe, a song about LSD. Given the context of the times, however, it's not inconceivable that Lennon dropped a hit while writing it.

OUT OF THIS WORLD!

※ ※ ※

The original Star Trek *series brought us two popular quotes:
Captain James Kirk's "Beam me up, Scotty," and Dr. Leonard
"Bones" McCoy's "Damn-it, Jim, I'm a doctor, not a...."
But any Trekkie worth his or her dilithium crystals
knows that neither quote is exact.*

A Universe of One-Liners

Captain Kirk said a lot of things in the original series (when he
wasn't busy smooching green-skinned space women), but he never
said, "Beam me up, Scotty." He did, however, utter a number of
variations on that statement over the course of the series and in
subsequent movies. These included: "Beam me up," "Beam us up,
Scotty," "Beam them out of there, Scotty," and "Scotty, beam me
up." It's a minor point, to be sure, but one of great importance to
the legions of die-hard *Star Trek* fans.

The quote most often attributed to Dr. McCoy has had its
variations, too. Most people put a "Damn-it" in front of the line, but
Bones never uttered that expletive in the TV series (a product of
the 1960s, *Star Trek* was almost devoid of curse words). However,
the doctor did mutter, "Damn-it, Jim!" and "Damn-it, Spock!" on a
number of occasions in various *Star Trek* movies.

The "I'm a doctor, not a..." routine was used a couple of
times during the original series, most evidently in the episode
titled "The Devil in the Dark," in which Captain Kirk orders Dr.
McCoy to attend to an injured Horta, a creature that is essentially
a sentient rock. McCoy's response is typical of his character: "I'm a
doctor, not a bricklayer!" Bones made similar sarcastic comments
whenever he was required to perform a task that was outside his
expertise. In the case of the Horta, he did as he was instructed and
ably patched up the wounded creature with cement.

Knowing a good quote when it hears one, the *Star Trek* franchise used Dr. McCoy's popular catchphrase throughout later series and motion pictures. For example, the holographic doctor in *Star Trek: Voyager* (played by Robert Picardo) used the phrase on a couple of occasions. And so did others. In one episode in which Picardo's doctor asks another holographic physician for help after their ship has been taken over by Romulans, the second doctor replies, "I'm a doctor, not a commando!"

Likewise, in the series *Star Trek: Deep Space Nine* (the episode titled "Trials and Tribble-ations"), when Dr. Bashir (Alexander Siddiq) is asked about events in the 23rd century, he quips, "I'm a doctor, not a historian."

There are additional variations of the "I'm a doctor, not a..." statement. In the movie *Star Trek: First Contact,* a holographic doctor says, "I'm a doctor, not a doorstop." And in the video game *Star Trek: Bridge Commander,* players who try to engage engineer Brex in too much chitchat are eventually scolded with, "Damn-it, Jim! I'm an engineer, not a conversationalist!"

Long-Lasting Legacy

Star Trek has given viewers much over the 40-plus years it has been around, including innovative scientific concepts that are actually starting to become reality. Its influence even reached NASA, which named its prototype space shuttle *Enterprise,* after the starship featured in the show.

The Show Must Go On

There have been few television shows that have had the cultural impact of Gene Roddenberry's *Star Trek.* When the original series was cancelled in 1969 after just three seasons, dedicated fans went into hyperdrive in an effort to force producers to put the beloved show back on the air.

It took a while, but their efforts paid off. Today, *Star Trek* has spawned six television series (including one animated cartoon series), 12 motion pictures, numerous books, international conventions, and an eclectic array of merchandise.

A MONSTROUS MYTH!

*Frankenstein's monster is usually portrayed
as a shambling, dumb brute who growls
and terrorizes fearful villagers. But that's
an entirely inaccurate representation.*

Frankenstein's monster is one of the best-known fictional fiends
ever created. But in the 1818 novel *Frankenstein,* by Mary Woll-
stonecraft Shelley, the monster is at first gentle, almost childlike—
and much more eloquent than the beast played by Boris Karloff in
the 1931 movie of the same name.

Indeed, Victor Frankenstein's creation is initially an object of
pity who is given life and then abandoned and disavowed by his
horrified creator. Uncertain who or what he is, he wanders the
countryside and eventually learns to speak by spying on a peasant
family as they try to teach English to a relative. And he learns to
speak remarkably well!

A Monster by Any Other Name...

In chapter 11, for example, the creature (who is never given a
name but is alternately referred to as a fiend, demon, wretch, zom-
bie, devil, and ogre) describes for Victor Frankenstein his recollections of his own "birth": "It is with considerable difficulty that
I remember the original era of my being. All the events of that
period appear confused and indistinct. A strange multiplicity of
sensation seized me, and I saw, felt, heard, and smelt at the same
time and it was, indeed, a long time before I learned to distinguish
between the operations of my various senses..." He's definitely a
monster who has a way with words.

Of Stage and Screen

Interestingly, the novel, which Shelley wrote when she was a teenager, was an instant hit that resulted in numerous adaptations for
the stage. *Presumption; or the Fate of Frankenstein* premiered in

London in 1823, just five years after the book's initial publication. The first movie version was a ten-minute short produced in 1910 by Thomas Edison's film company. It starred Charles Ogle as the pitiful monster and was long listed by the American Film Institute as one of the "most culturally and historically significant lost films."

The 1931 Universal Studios version—undoubtedly the best known to moviegoers—was based more on a 1927 theatrical adaptation by Peggy Webling than on Mary Shelley's book. Almost all subsequent film versions continued to portray the monster as an inarticulate brute. Only a handful have made an attempt to stay true to the novel in portraying the creature as intelligent and sensitive.

Curious Adaptations

Over the years, the story of Frankenstein's mad science project has been the source material for hundreds of movies. The monster duked it out with a werewolf in *Frankenstein Meets the Wolfman* (1943), yukked it up with comedians in *Abbott and Costello Meet Frankenstein* (1948), and even encountered cartoon varmints in *Alvin and the Chipmunks Meet Frankenstein* (1999). Peter Boyle played the creature for laughs in Mel Brooks's *Young Frankenstein* (1974), which was later adapted into a successful Broadway play.

Although Boris Karloff's portrayal of Frankenstein's monster is considered a cinematic classic, the character suffered mightily in a slew of less prestigious productions. In the 1965 Japanese monster epic *Frankenstein Conquers the World,* for example, the creature's heart is transplanted in a young Japanese boy who then grows to 20 feet tall and battles a huge prehistoric monster. Other awkward adaptations include *I Was a Teenage Frankenstein* (1957), *Frankenstein Meets the Space Monster* (1965), *Jesse James Meets Frankenstein's Daughter* (1966), and *Blackenstein* (1973).

Turning the Page

Frankenstein's monster has become an ubiquitous feature in American popular culture. But if you want to enjoy the story in its purest form, read Shelley's novel. You'll find it a less horrific experience than many of the aforementioned movies.

LIQUOR LOGIC

Sit back with a glass of your favorite adult beverage and ponder some of the many misconceptions about alcohol.

Red wine is made from red grapes and white wine is from white grapes. "White" grapes, of course, are more yellow or green than white. Most white wine is produced from these grapes, but some varieties are in fact made from black grapes. The skins of black grapes are varying shades of purple or red, but the pulp is actually gray. White wines are made only from the juice of grapes, whereas red wines include the crushed skins and stems. During fermentation, the pigment from the grape skins colors the wine red. This also infuses the wine with the tannins that create each particular flavor of red wine.

Rosé or blush-colored wines, such as White Zinfandel, are produced from black grapes either by allowing limited contact with the grape skins during the fermentation process or, more likely, by simply adding a specific amount of red wine to the finished white wine.

※※※

"Liquor before beer, you're in the clear; beer before liquor, you'll never be sicker." Anyone who has been to a college party has probably heard similar drinking tips, but the fact is that mixing different types of alcohol will not make you more intoxicated. It's possible that combining a variety of different-flavored cocktails will upset your stomach and make you feel sick, but it will not make you any drunker. A unit of alcohol is a unit of alcohol, whether it is consumed in the form of beer, wine, or liquor, or is disguised in a sweet fruit punch or a puddle of cream.

A standard drink is the equivalent of a 12-ounce bottle of beer, a 4-ounce glass of wine, a 3-ounce glass of fortified wine such as sherry or port, or a 1-ounce shot of hard liquor. Each drink contains the same amount of alcohol, so whether you consume four of the same standard drinks or four different ones, you will have swallowed the same amount of alcohol and will therefore be equally drunk.

The misconception that mixing drinks will make you more intoxicated stems from the fact that flavored shots of hard liquor are often consumed much faster than a beer or glass of wine. Drink a couple of beers and throw back a few watermelon shots in an hour and, yes, you could end up on the bathroom floor while your friend who nursed just beer stands over you. She's able to hold your hair and laugh at you simply because she consumed fewer units of alcohol. And if you think that a sandwich and a cup of coffee will get you sober, you've got a few more things coming—up.

❀❀❀

Alcohol evaporates when it's heated. Many cooks who add spirits or wine to a dish do so with the belief that all of the alcohol burns off in the cooking process. In fact, the amount of booze that remains in the dish depends on how—and how long—the ingredients are exposed to heat. For example, if you deglaze a pan by adding wine to a boiling liquid and then remove the dish from the heat source, about 85 percent of the alcohol will be retained. If you flambé a crepe or plum pudding by dousing it in brandy and then lighting it, the flame will die out within a minute or so—but as much as 75 percent of the alcohol will remain. Baking and stewing are the most effective ways to remove the booze from a dish, but depending on the length of time the food spends in the oven or on the stovetop, it will still retain some alcohol. Bake a rum cake for an hour, and about 75 percent of the alcohol will cook out, whereas simmering a beef bourguignonne for two and a half hours will burn off 95 percent of the wine.

WASHINGTON'S TAB

Some people believe that as commander in chief of the Continental Army, General George Washington "selflessly" refused a salary in favor of an expense account. Talk about shrewd moves.

When Washington took over leadership of the Continental Army in 1775, he refused to accept a salary. Perhaps he did so to demonstrate sacrifice and to forge solidarity with the "have-nots," a group that included soldiers under his command. Many applauded Washington for his noble gesture without knowing that the general had just been granted carte blanche to use and perhaps even abuse government funds.

From September 1775 to March 1776, Washington spent more than $6,000 on alcohol alone. And during the harsh Valley Forge winter of 1777–78, when his weary troops were perishing from hunger and exposure, Washington indulged his appetite for extravagant foods. An expense-account entry included "geese, mutton, fowls, turkey, veal, butter, turnips, potatoes, carrots, and cabbage."

By 1783, Washington had spent almost $450,000 on food, saddles, clothing, accommodations, and sundries. In today's dollars, that's nearly $5 million. When he became president, Washington again gallantly offered to waive his salary in favor of an expense account. The offer was politely refused, and he was paid a $25,000 stipend. It seems America could no longer afford the general's brand of sacrifice.

Taking Advantage

In 1753, the Iroquois Indians nicknamed George Washington the "town taker" in reference to their belief that he had swindled them out of their land. After examining Washington's expense accounts, however, "taker" assumes a whole new meaning.

AN INFECTIOUS PERSONALITY

Typhoid Mary was bad—but not as bad as most people think.

Who was Typhoid Mary? Mary Mallon was an Irish cook who is often blamed for a multitude of deaths. She was feared and vilified, accused of consciously spreading typhoid fever. But contrary to legend, the feisty immigrant who earned the Typhoid Mary moniker likely infected just 47 people, only three of whom died.

Typhoid fever is rarely seen today in industrialized countries because of improvements in sanitation. The bacteria that cause it are carried in the bloodstream and intestinal tract, and they are deposited in food and water by people who are infected. Typhoid is contracted by eating or drinking something handled by a carrier who is not meticulously clean or from drinking contaminated water. Mary—a "healthy carrier" who had no symptoms herself—unwittingly made her victims sick.

Her condition was discovered in 1907 when New York public health officials linked her to an outbreak of typhoid in a family that had hired her as a cook. But Mary refused to believe that she was the cause. When a civil engineer experienced in typhoid outbreaks went to her workplace to ask for blood, stool, and urine samples, she ran him off with a carving fork!

What became of her? Mary was eventually institutionalized and held in isolation to prevent her from spreading the disease further. She was freed three years later, after promising not to work as a cook again—a promise she didn't keep. A typhoid outbreak at Sloane Maternity Hospital in Manhattan five years after her release was traced to a cook named Mrs. Brown, who turned out to be Mary using a pseudonym. This time, public outrage forced authorities to send Mary away for good. She lived the last 23 years of her life in the isolated community of North Brother Island.

Mary Mallon died on November 11, 1938—not from typhoid but from complications brought on by a stroke.

THE PROOF OF THE PUDDING IS IN THE MEANING

*During any argument in which one party makes
generalizations and the other contradicts them,
someone eventually yells, "The exception proves the rule!"
Is this claim ironclad logic, or is it a rhetorical device
as sophisticated as "I'm rubber and you're glue"?*

The phrase "the exception proves the rule" began appearing in English in the 17th century and has been misused ever since. Even the great lexicographer H. W. Fowler admitted to being uncertain about its meaning. The two most common interpretations of the phrase argue that the item that breaks the rule is actually what shows the rule to be true, which, of course, makes no logical sense.

Exceptions Make the Rule Stronger

The first misuse suggests that a rule is valid specifically because it doesn't apply to all cases. This tactic is particularly brilliant in that it can be used to justify any argument that otherwise flies in the face of reason and logic. Often, it's used to deflate an opponent's argument when there isn't a fact-based leg on which to stand. For example, John argues that all butterflies are blue. Mary points out that Monarch butterflies are not blue, to which John responds that Monarchs are the exception that prove the rule. John is content, sticking to his belief that all butterflies but for those pesky Monarchs are blue (conveniently ignoring all the other non-blue butterflies). Meanwhile, Mary thinks John is a chucklehead. Despite its popular use, this clearly is not a logical argument.

Except in this Case

The second misuse of the proverb uses a different meaning of the word *prove*, but it's wrong nonetheless. In interpreting the word *prove* as "to test or check" (as in *proving grounds* or *mathematical proofs*) rather than as "to show as true," it is explained that having an exception actually helps test the validity of the rule. But in John's all-butterflies-are-blue argument, the Monarch exception would not help him test the strength of his rule because it in fact pokes a gigantic hole in it. This usage, therefore, is also illogical.

Proverbial Prosecution

The proverb was originally based upon a point of Latin law. In 56 B.C., Cicero was charged with defending Lucius Cornelius Balbus against accusations of having gained Roman citizenship illegally. The prosecution argued that treaties with some non-Roman tribes actually prohibited granting them citizenship, which should be then treated as the standard, to which Cicero replied, *"Quod si exceptio facit ne liceat, ubi <non sit exceptum, ibi> necesse est licere."* For those who may have missed that day in Latin class, he was arguing, "If the exception makes such an action unlawful, where there is no exception the action must necessarily be lawful." Point and match to Cicero.

Who Made Up Theses Rules, Anyway?

The misunderstanding of the English phrase began in interpreting the word *exception* as an object (something to be excluded) rather than an action (the act of making something a special case). The proverb actually says that by spelling out an exception to a rule, one implicitly acknowledges that a rule exists in the first place. The exception gives authority and strength to the original rule. We all understand that "Free Parking on Sundays" means we'd better be cramming quarters into the meters all other days of the week.

Whether you're listening to someone loudly claim that exceptions only make his or her argument stronger, or that all rules need exceptions to be true, you have a choice: You could smile, take the high road, and walk away, or you could enthusiastically offer the correct use of the phrase, explaining that while you can have a rule without an exception, you cannot have an exception without a rule. But understand that the latter choice involves a considerable commitment of time and patience.

THE NEW "NORMAL"

*The next time you anxiously await the readout
on your thermometer, consider this: 98.2, 98.8—and
even 99.9—are the new 98.6.*

Normal human body temperature used to be defined by just one
number: 98.6 degrees Fahrenheit. But now medical experts say
that a range of numbers can be considered normal body temperatures for healthy individuals.

Researchers have found that the new "normal" for adults can
range from 98.2 degrees Fahrenheit (36.8 degrees Celsius) to
99.9 degrees Fahrenheit (37.7 degrees Celsius). That's good news
for worrywarts and bad news for children hoping that a thermometer reading of 99 degrees is a get-out-of-school-free card.

What Is "Normal"?

Carl Wunderlich, a 19th-century German doctor, is responsible
for designating 98.6 as normal temperature. He studied the body
temperature of 25,000 adults, took 1 million temperature readings, and determined that body temperature averaged 98.6 among
people in good health.

We now know that many factors can affect the number that
shows up on a thermometer. Your temperature changes throughout the day: It's usually lower in the morning and higher in the
evening. Eating, drinking, exercising, and taking a hot shower can
all skew a body temperature reading if it's taken just after those
activities. Women's body temperatures fluctuate during the menstrual cycle and ovulation. People who have a higher metabolic
rate often will have a higher body temperature than those with
"slower" metabolisms. And, like everything else in our bodies, our
core temperature can change as we age. One study found that
seniors have a lower average thermometer reading than younger
adults.

Thermometer Barometer

How your temperature is measured and what kind of thermometer is used also can make a difference in the number that pops up. Most adults prefer to take their temperature orally, by putting a thermometer under the tongue for a few minutes. In the doctor's office, a tympanic ear probe is often the thermometer of choice. Temperature readings can also be taken by placing a thermometer under the arm (called an axillary reading) or in the rectum. Any of these methods can give an accurate measurement, but different body sites will yield different results. An axillary reading, for example, can be a full degree lower than a reading taken from the ear.

In the past, medical thermometers were made of glass and filled with mercury. Today, there are many more choices with better technology, such as digital electronic thermometers, mercury-free oral thermometers, and infrared ear thermometers.

Feeling Hot, Hot, Hot

Our body temperature is an important reading. It's one of the vital signs, along with pulse rate, breathing rate, and blood pressure, that give doctors an overview of how a patient is doing. If any one of those readings is off, it can be a signal that something is awry.

A fever can occur for many reasons, most commonly when the body is fighting an infection. A doctor should be consulted when a baby's temperature is above 100 degrees Fahrenheit (37.8 degrees Celsius). Most pediatricians want to see any child who seems to be under the weather and is running a fever. In adults, fevers usually are evaluated in the context of other symptoms, such as headache, sore throat, cough, or chills. If a fever persists, it's a good idea to call your doctor.

What's Your 98.6?

Curious about what your normal core body temperature is? On a day when you are healthy, take your temperature several times to get a baseline. But wait at least 30 minutes after eating or drinking and one hour after exercising or bathing to get an accurate reading.

WHAT ABOUT
THE FOOTBALL GAME?

Most people were taught that Thanksgiving originated with the Pilgrims when they invited local Native Americans to celebrate the first successful harvest. Here's what really happened.

There are only two original accounts of the event we think of as the first Thanksgiving, both very brief. In the fall of 1621, the Pilgrims, having barely survived their first arduous year, managed to bring in a modest harvest. They celebrated with a traditional English harvest feast, with food, dancing, and games. The local Wampanoag Indians were there, and both groups demonstrated their skill at musketry and archery.

So that was the first Thanksgiving, right? Not exactly. To the Pilgrims, a thanksgiving day was a special religious holiday that consisted of prayer, fasting, and praise—not at all like the party atmosphere that accompanied a harvest feast.

Our modern Thanksgiving, which combines the concepts of harvest feast and a day of thanksgiving, is actually a 19th-century development. In the decades after the Pilgrims, national days of thanksgiving were decreed on various occasions, and some states celebrated a Thanksgiving holiday annually. But there was no recurring national holiday until 1863, when a woman named Sarah Josepha Hale launched a campaign for an annual celebration that would "greatly aid and strengthen public harmony of feeling."

Such sentiments were sorely needed in a nation torn apart by the Civil War. So in the aftermath of the bloody Battle of Gettysburg, President Lincoln decreed a national day of thanksgiving that would fall on the last Thursday in November, probably to coincide with the anniversary of the Pilgrims' landing at Plymouth. The date was later shifted to the third Thursday in November, simply to give retailers a longer Christmas shopping season.

WHICH WITCHES BURNED?

*Contrary to popular belief, no witches were burned at the stake
during the Salem witch trials, and men (and even dogs!)
were not immune from punishment.*

Blame it on Tituba

In the eyes of 17th-century colonists in Salem, Massachusetts,
Satan was constantly seeking to tempt God-fearing locals into
witchcraft. In 1692, the town pastor owned a slave from Barbados
named Tituba, who entertained the local children with fortune-
and story-telling. No one knows the actual reason, but the girls
among the group soon began to claim that they were being spiritu-
ally tormented. They also began to exhibit such strange behaviors
as hysteria, seizures, and apparent hallucinations. Some people
identified the "illnesses" as a toxic condition known as ergotism,
which is caused by a rye fungus. But the more likely explanation is
much simpler. These were just children being children—eager for
attention, imitating one another, and aware that the attention ends
once the charade does.

Nonetheless, Tituba was quickly identified as the source of the
beguiling "spells," and she ultimately confessed under pressure.
But rather than being burned at the stake, her punishment was
that she was indentured for life to pay the costs of her jailing. Her
arrest was the snowball behind an avalanche of accusations. Those
subsequently charged with being witches were either "proven
guilty" or "soon to be proven guilty."

Witches Take Many Forms

Approximately 150 people (and two dogs) were arrested during the
Salem witch trials, and 19 people (including six men) were hanged.
One gent who refused to enter a plea was subjected to "pressing,"
a form of torture in which rocks are slowly placed atop a person's
body until he or she finally suffocates—a process that can take as
long as three days. Suddenly, incineration doesn't look so bad.

SLOTS O' LUCK

Do slot machines, or "one-armed bandits,"
have predetermined pay cycles? Don't bet on it.
The money you lose may be your own.

As Jake wearily feeds quarters into a humming slot machine, a thought occurs to him: "I think this machine is dead. I'd like to try a different one, but I've heard they all have fixed pay cycles. I've been on this one for two hours, so it should be about ready to cough it up. I guess I'll stay put."

The fact is that many such thoughts steer gamblers into repetitive or superstitious habits that have little to no bearing on reality. A modern slot machine just generates numbers. It can't discern between its first spin and its twenty-thousandth, so Jake could easily spend weeks "babysitting" it, hoping for the big payoff. Slot machines do have certain payout percentages, but these are based on millions of spins to reach a jackpot.

Frustrated by its stinginess, Jake finally walks away from his slot machine. An instant later another patron takes Jake's seat, plops in a coin, and hits the super jackpot. If Jake had simply stuck it out, would he be the rich one? Not unless he had pushed the spin button or yanked the handle at precisely the same microsecond as the winner had. The reason is that changes in timing yield completely different results—a phenomenon referred to as the "hero or zero" rule.

Disgusted, Jake decides to rely on another tactic: He'll come back when the place is jam-packed, knowing that more jackpots are won when the casino is crowded. At this point it would be easy to again call Jake a loser, but we won't go there. The reason a casino gives up more jackpots when it's busy is obvious: More people are playing, so more spins are taking place—which means more jackpots will be hit. In the end, Jake might want to stick to scratch-offs.

WHO BUILT THE PYRAMIDS?

❀ ❀ ❀

The Great Pyramids of Egypt have maintained their mystery through the eons, and there's still a lot we don't know about them. But we do know this: Slaves, particularly the ancient Hebrew slaves, did not build these grand structures.

It's easy to see why people think slaves built the pyramids. Most ancient societies kept slaves, and the Egyptians were no exception. And Hebrew slaves did build other Egyptian monuments during their 400 years of captivity, according to the Old Testament. Even ancient scholars such as the Greek historian Herodotus (fifth century B.C.) and the Jewish historian Josephus (first century A.D.) believed that the Egyptians used slave labor in the construction of the pyramids.

Based on the lifestyles of these ancient builders, however, researchers have discredited the notion that they were slaves (Nubians, Assyrians, or Hebrews, among others) who were forced to work. They had more likely willingly labored, both for grain (or other foodstuffs) and to ensure their place in the afterlife. What's more, we now know that the Great Pyramids were built more than a thousand years before the era of the Hebrews (who actually became enslaved during Egypt's New Kingdom).

Archaeologists have determined that many of the people who built the pyramids were conscripted farmers and peasants who lived in the countryside during the Old Kingdom. Archaeologist Mark Lehner of the Semitic Museum at Harvard University has spent more than a decade studying the workers' villages that existed close to the Giza plateau, where the pyramids were built. He has confirmed that the people who built the pyramids were not slaves— rather, they were skilled laborers and "ordinary men and women."

❀ ❀ ❀

• *The first recorded labor strike in history occurred during the construction of the Great Pyramids, when workers stopped building until their grain payments came through.*

AND THE OSCAR GOES TO...?

In 1992, when the relatively unknown Marisa Tomei won an Oscar for best actress in a supporting role, she had little reason to celebrate. The media reported that she'd received it by mistake.

Poor Marisa Tomei. Winning an Academy Award is supposed to be the highlight of any actor's career. But when she picked up the 1992 Oscar for her portrayal of Mona Lisa Vito in the comedy *My Cousin Vinny,* rumors immediately began to circulate that presenter Jack Palance had read the wrong name at the podium.

A Peculiar Presenter

Palance has an interesting history at the Oscars. In 1991, at the age of 73, he won the Best Supporting Actor award for his role as Curly in the Billy Crystal comedy *City Slickers.* Up on stage, he memorably celebrated the win by dropping to the floor and performing one-handed push-ups. Such eccentric behavior probably contributed to the idea that, when asked to return the following year as a presenter, he *could* have announced the wrong person as the winner. In fact, when he read the names of nominees for the Best Supporting Actress category, he mistakenly called Judy Davis "Joan" Davis.

Upset About the Upset

Tomei, though inexperienced, was up against acting stalwarts who were nominated for their roles in much more critically acclaimed films. Along with Judy Davis in *Husbands and Wives,* the nominees were Joan Plowright for *Enchanted April,* Vanessa Redgrave for *Howards End,* and Miranda Richardson for *Damage.* It was understandably perceived to be a huge upset when Tomei won. But it wasn't a mistake. At every Oscar ceremony, the accounting firm PricewaterhouseCoopers (which collates the results) stations two employees in the wings with instructions to immediately correct a presenter if an error is made. As of yet, they have not been called upon to do so.

TO WHERE ARE
THE ABORIGINES ORIGINAL?

The term Aborigine *conjures images of loincloth-clad spear-throwers running across a sweltering savanna. Yet some people are unsure what an Aborigine actually is, and most Aborigines prefer to be called by a different name.*

Semantic Antics

Ask somebody in the United States what *aboriginal* means, and it is likely that flustered confusion will ensue. In common usage, *aboriginal* (or *aborigine*) refers to the indigenous population of Australia, but *aboriginal* is also sometimes used to refer to the indigenous populations of other countries. When the word begins with a lowercase *a,* it can refer to a wide variety of people, places, and things. When it begins with a capital *A,* it refers only to the indigenous population of Australia. The solution to this semantic puzzle lies in the nuanced differences between the words *indigenous* and *aboriginal.*

The word *aboriginal* means "the first or earliest known of its kind in a region." The word derives from the Latin for "from" combined with the Latin for "the beginning." The word *indigenous* means "having originated in and being produced, growing, or living in a particular region or environment," and it derives from the Latin for "in" combined with the Latin for "born."

Aboriginal, therefore, is a less-inclusive term than *indigenous.* Technically, anyone born in a particular area is indigenous to that area, though in practical usage, indigenous groups are descendants of those that resided in a region before Eurasian colonization and the worldwide creation of nation-states.

Many indigenous groups besides Australian Aborigines can be said to be the first inhabitants of a given region. Native Americans, for example, are descendants of the first human groups to live in the Americas and thus could be said to have been there "from the beginning." Why is it, then, that indigenous Australians have a monopoly on the term *aborigine*?

There from the Earlier Beginning

Human populations first existed in Africa and from there walked north to the sprawling Eurasian continent. Indigenous Australians separated from these populations far earlier than did Native Americans. Evidence suggests that humans arrived in Australia 50,000 years ago, probably by boat from southern Asia.

From that time onward until colonization, the population of Australia was completely isolated from the rest of the world. The same can probably be said for Native Americans, but the difference is that the first humans arrived in the Americas at a much later date, approximately 11,500 to 12,000 years ago. When Europeans first met the indigenous Australians in the 17th century, they had stumbled upon a population that had existed in its own geographic bubble for 50,000 years. The colonizers immediately used the term *aborigine*, "there from the beginning," to describe the indigenous Australians.

Modern Aborigines

A common misconception about Aborigines is that they live in small hunter-gatherer groups in the wild Australian Outback. Although this was very much the case in 1788 when England declared Australia a colony, today most Aborigines are urban and live in poverty. Between 1788 and the 1880s, more than 90 percent of the Aborigine population died of communicable diseases brought over by colonists. Many others were victims to acts of violence and massacre, and much of the remaining population was thrown into isolated shantytowns and excluded from the Australian economy in a situation analogous to that of Native American reservations.

Because of the institutionalized racial hatred shown toward Aborigines over time, the term *Aborigine*—itself a colonial artifact—has negative connotations in Australia. For this reason, many Aborigines prefer to be called indigenous Australians.

THE BEAR TRUTHS

*Although bearlike in appearance, with their rounded ears,
plush fur, and black noses, koalas aren't actual bruins.
Pandas, on the other hand, are true to form.*

Cute as an Opossum?

There are few animals on Earth cuter than the cuddly koala.
They're sometimes called Australia's teddy bears, but koalas are in
fact related more closely to the ratlike American opossum than the
impressive American grizzly.

Koalas are marsupials, which means they raise their young in
special pouches, just like kangaroos, wallabies, and wombats (which
are also indigenous to Australia). Their young, called joeys, are
about the size of a large jelly bean when born and must make their
way through their mother's fur to the protection of the pouch if
they are to survive. As a baby grows, it starts making trips outside
the pouch, clinging to its mother's stomach or back but returning to
the pouch when scared, sleepy, or hungry. When a koala reaches a
year old, it's usually large enough to live on its own.

Unlike real bears, koalas spend almost their entire lives roost-
ing in trees, traveling on the ground only to find a new tree to call
home. Koalas dine exclusively on eucalyptus leaves, of which there
are more than 600 varieties in Australia. Eucalyptus leaves are
poisonous to most other animals, but koalas have special bacteria
in their stomachs that break down dangerous oils in the leaves.

The Case for Pandas

Until recently, the giant panda, despite its appearance, was also
considered a non-bear. Some scientists believed pandas were more
closely related to the raccoon, whereas others speculated that they
were in a group all their own. However, by studying the animals'
DNA, scientists were able to confirm that the giant panda is a
closer relative to Yogi Bear than it is to Rocky Raccoon.

SPACE GHOSTS

Shortly after the Soviet Union successfully launched Sputnik 1 *on October 4, 1957, rumors swirled that several cosmonauts had died during missions gone horribly wrong, and their spacecraft had drifted out of Earth's orbit and into the vast reaches of the universe.*

It was easy to believe such stories at the time. After all, the United States was facing off against the Soviet Union in the Cold War, and the thought that the ruthless Russians would do anything to win the space race—including sending cosmonauts to their doom— seemed plausible.

However, numerous researchers have investigated the stories and concluded that, though the Soviet space program was far from perfect and some cosmonauts had in fact died, there are no dead cosmonauts floating in space.

According to authors Hal Morgan and Kerry Tucker, the earliest rumors of deceased cosmonauts even mentioned their names and the dates of their doomed missions: Aleksei Ledovsky in 1957, Serenti Shiborin in 1958, and Mirya Gromova in 1959. In fact, by the time Yuri Gagarin became the first human in space in April 1961, the alleged body count exceeded a dozen.

Space Spies

So prevalent were these stories that no less an "authority" than *Reader's Digest* reported on them in its April 1965 issue. Key to the mystery were two brothers in Italy, Achille and Giovanni Battista Judica-Cordiglia, who operated a homemade listening post with a huge dish antenna. Over a seven-month period, the brothers claimed to have overheard radio signals from three troubled Soviet spacecraft:

- On November 28, 1960, a Soviet spacecraft supposedly radioed three times, in Morse code and in English, "SOS to the entire world."

- In early February 1961, the brothers are alleged to have picked up the sound of a rapidly beating heart and labored breathing, which they interpreted to be the final throes of a dying cosmonaut.

- On May 17, 1961, two men and a woman were allegedly overheard saying, in Russian, "Conditions growing worse. Why don't you answer? We are going slower...the world will never know about us."

The Black Hole of Soviet PR

One reason rumors of dead cosmonauts were so believable was the extremely secretive nature of the early Soviet space program. Whereas the United States touted its program as a major advance in science and its astronauts as public heroes, the Soviet Union revealed little about its program or the people involved.

It's not surprising, then, that the Soviet Union did not report to the world the death of Valentin Bondarenko, a cosmonaut who died tragically in a fire after he tossed an alcohol-soaked cotton ball on a hot plate and ignited the oxygen-rich chamber in which he was training. He died in 1961, but it wasn't revealed publicly until 1986.

Adding to the rumors was the fact that other cosmonauts had been mysteriously airbrushed out of official government photographs. However, most had been removed because they had been dropped from the space program for academic, disciplinary, or medical reasons—not because they had died during a mission. One cosmonaut, Grigoriy Nelyubov, was booted from the program in 1961 for engaging in a drunken brawl at a rail station (he died five years later when he stepped in front of a train). Nelyubov's story, like so many others, was not made public until the mid-1980s.

Only one Soviet cosmonaut is known to have died during an actual space mission. In 1967, Vladimir Komarov was killed when the parachute on his *Soyuz 1* spacecraft failed to open properly during reentry. A Russian engineer later acknowledged that Komarov's mission had been ordered before the spacecraft had been fully debugged, likely for political reasons.

NO STRANGERS TO FICTION

※ ※ ※

*Here are two bloody blockbuster movies supposedly
based on real-life events. In both cases, Hollywood didn't
let facts get in the way of profitable fiction.*

The Texas Chain Saw Massacre

The myth that Tobe Hooper's 1974 bloodbath has any semblance
to real-life events can be dispelled by the movie's opening narrative, which states that the "real" events took place on August 18,
1973. But the movie was in the can by August 14, 1973, so the
actual events on which it was allegedly based hadn't even happened yet. There is speculation that the movie is loosely based on
the life of Wisconsin serial killer Ed Gein, who, like his cinematic
cohort, wore a mask made of human skin and left behind a cornu-
copia of corpses.

Fargo

In Joel and Ethan Coen's masterpiece of modern film noir, two
wayward kidnappers/murderers wreak havoc on the citizens of
Brainerd and Minneapolis, Minnesota. Again, the real events
depicted onscreen are fictitious, despite claims to the contrary.
The plot does, however, contain references that are similar to
a pair of well-known Minnesota crimes. The first occurred in
1962 and involved an attorney, T. Eugene Thompson, who contracted a man to kill his wife. That man contracted another man
to do the deed, and in the confusion that followed, calamity and
chaos converged. Mrs. Thompson died, Mr. Thompson lied, and
the feebleminded felons were fried, legally speaking. Ten years
later, another crime took place, this one involving the kidnapping
of Virginia Piper, the wife of a wealthy banker. A million-dollar
ransom was paid, and Mrs. Piper was found alive, tied to a tree in
a park. The two men convicted of the crime were later acquitted,
and only $4,000 of the ransom money was recovered.

HARD AS NAILS

❀ ❀ ❀

*You may be soft at heart, but you want your nails
to be as hard as . . . well, nails.*

Gelatin can turn a liquid into a solid—think Jell-O after it sets. So perhaps it makes sense to think that ingesting it or soaking your fingertips in it would strengthen your nails and make them more resistant to chipping and cracking.

The logic may be flawed, but millions of people fell for a marketing scheme that connected gelatin with strong nails. And it's a tribute to that wildly successful advertising campaign that millions of people still believe it today.

In 1890, Charles Knox developed gelatin, a product made from slaughterhouse waste. He sold the public on it by touting its nail-enhancing benefits. The animals (cows and pigs) used to produce gelatin had strong hooves, Knox reasoned, so eating their by-products would give people nails just as strong. Consumers fell for it, lock, livestock, and barrel.

But no matter how many people swear by it, there is no scientific proof that gelatin hardens nails. Gelatin is made from the skin, connective tissue, and bones of cattle and pigs, and so it is full of protein and collagen. The protein is not, however, in a form that's usable by humans. And unless your diet is deficient in protein, which is unlikely, eating more protein is not going to solve your nail problems. The best thing you can do for your nails is to pick up some petroleum jelly and use it to moisturize them.

❀ ❀ ❀

- *Gelatin is used in three major industries: food, pharmaceutical, and photographic. In the food industry, gelatin is used in desserts, marshmallows, gummy candies, and other sweets. It can be used as a gelling agent, a thickener, an emulsifier, or a stabilizer. Gelatin is also used to make the shells of hard and soft capsules for medicines and to make photographic film.*

THE ANASAZI

*There is a prevalent belief that the prehistoric
Native American culture referred to as the Anasazi
mysteriously disappeared from the southwestern
United States. Here are the facts.*

Who Were the Anasazi?

Across the deserts and mesas of the region known as the Four
Corners, where Arizona, New Mexico, Colorado, and Utah meet,
backcountry hikers and motoring tourists can easily spot remind-
ers of an ancient people. From the towering stone structures at
Chaco Culture National Historical Park to cliff dwellings at Mesa
Verde National Park to the ubiquitous scatters of broken pottery
and stone tools, these remains tell the story of a culture that spread
out across the arid Southwest during ancient times. The Anasazi
are believed to have lived in the region from about A.D. 1 through
A.D. 1300 (though the exact beginning of the culture is difficult to
determine because there is no particular defining event). In their
everyday lives, they created black-on-white pottery styles that
distinguish subregions within the culture, traded with neighbor-
ing cultures (including those to the south in Central America),
and built ceremonial structures called kivas, which were used for
religious or communal purposes.

The Exodus Explained

Spanish conquistadors exploring the Southwest noted the abandoned cliff dwellings and ruined plazas, and archaeologists today
still try to understand what might have caused the Anasazi to move
from their homes and villages throughout the region. Over time,
researchers have posed a number of theories, including the idea
that the Anasazi were driven from their villages by hostile nomads,
such as those from the Apache or Ute tribes. Others believe that
the Anasazi fought among themselves, causing a drastic reduction
in their populations, and a few extraterrestrial-minded theorists

have suggested that the Anasazi civilization was destroyed by aliens. Today, the prevalent hypothesis among scientists is that a long-term drought affected the area, destroying agricultural fields and forcing people to abandon their largest villages. Scientists and archaeologists have worked together to reconstruct the region's climate data and compare it with material that has been excavated. Based on their findings, many agree that some combination of environmental and cultural factors caused the dispersal of the Anasazi from the large-scale ruins seen throughout the landscape today.

Their Journey

Although many writers—of fiction and nonfiction alike—romanticize the Anasazi as a people who mysteriously disappeared from the region, they did not actually disappear. Those living in large ancient villages and cultural centers did indeed disperse, but the people themselves did not simply disappear. Today, descendents of the Anasazi can be found living throughout New Mexico and Arizona. The Hopi tribe in northern Arizona, as well as those living in approximately 20 pueblos in New Mexico, are the modern-day descendants of the Anasazi. The Pueblos in New Mexico whose modern inhabitants consider the Anasazi their ancestors include: Acoma, Cochiti, Isleta, Jemez, Laguna, Nambe, Picuris, Pojoaque, San Felipe, San Ildefonso, Ohkay Owingeh (formerly referred to as San Juan), Sandia, Santa Ana, Santa Clara, Santo Domingo, Taos, Tesuque, Zia, and Zuni.

What's in a Name?

The term *Anasazi* is actually a misleading moniker, as it is a Navajo word meaning "enemy ancestors"—which is obviously offensive to the Anasazi's descendants. Today, Native Americans and archaeologists prefer to use "pre-Puebloan" to refer to the ancient inhabitants of the Four Corners.

FEED A COLD, STARVE A FEVER

Don't worry if you can't remember whether you're supposed to feed a cold and starve a fever, or the other way around. Neither approach will cure you—but one could make you feel better.

No one knows for sure where this oft-repeated advice originally came from. But some myth busters have traced the adage back to the Middle Ages, when people believed illnesses were caused either by low temperatures or high temperatures. Those caused by low temperatures, including the common cold, needed fuel in the form of food, so eating was the treatment of choice. To the medieval mind, fever—or any other illnesses that caused a high temperature—was fueled by food, so the recommended treatment was to eat nothing or very little to help the body cool down.

Some evidence of this line of thought can be found in the writings of a dictionary maker named Withals, who in 1574 wrote, "Fasting is a great remedie of fever." But if it actually worked for people back then, it was probably a placebo effect.

Today, most medical experts (except for practitioners who promote fasting for healing) totally disagree with the notion of overeating or fasting to treat viral infections that cause colds and flu. When you have a cold or the flu, you actually need more fluids than usual. Drink plenty of water, juice, soup, and tea, and eat enough food to satisfy your appetite. Hot fluids will soothe a cough, ease a sore throat, and open clogged nasal passages. Food will supply nutrients that help bolster your immune system.

So stock up on chicken soup and tea and honey when the inevitable cold or fever strikes. And if a pint of mint chocolate chip ice cream helps you endure the aches and sniffles, why not indulge?

MISQUOTE GAINS MOMENTUM

*According to bumper stickers and T-shirts worldwide,
Thomas Jefferson believed that "Dissent is the highest form
of patriotism." The problem is that this quote didn't exist
ten years ago, let alone in the 18th century.*

Thomas Jefferson would be impressed by the wildfire spread of his latest alleged sound bite. Tracing this misquote's proliferation is like watching somebody trip in slow motion—you see it happening but aren't sure if the person's reflexes are a match for the inevitability of gravity.

During an interview on July 3, 2002, American historian and social scientist Howard Zinn defended his opposition to the war on terror by arguing that "Dissent is the highest form of patriotism. In fact, if patriotism means being true to the principles for which your country is supposed to stand, then certainly the right to dissent is one of those principles." Zinn appears to be the originator of this quote, and it quickly popped up in political speeches and newspaper articles as a defense for opposition to the war in Iraq.

That would have been the end of it, had the quote not become a nexus for Republican versus Democrat warfare. Republican bloggers picked up on the quote's false source and attacked Senator John Kerry for misattributing it to Jefferson in a 2006 antiwar speech. Since then, so many journalists have debunked the misquote that it just may eventually be salvaged and properly sourced as a Zinn quote. As for Jefferson, he would have wanted nothing to do with the affair, as he explained in a letter he wrote in 1797: "So many persons have of late found an interest or a passion gratified by imputing to me sayings and writings which I never said or wrote...that I have found it necessary for my quiet and my other pursuits to leave them in full possession of the field."

COLOR BLIND

*Some of the media scribes who stumble into
the Super Bowl toss out questions with the decorum
of a caffeine-fueled drunken sailor. But did one of them
really ask Washington Redskins pivot Doug Williams
how long he had been a black quarterback?*

For years, it has been one of the most-discussed and hotly debated topics on Super Bowl Sunday. But despite the annual enthusiastic and comedic rants among sports columnists and cronies, Doug Williams was in fact *never* asked how long he had been a black quarterback. As the first African American quarterback to pilot a team in the Super Bowl and the only black quarterback to lead his team to victory, Williams was thrown a barrage of silly, stupid, and sometimes off-color questions when he faced the media throng before Super Bowl XXII in 1988. These are some of the more ridiculous:

- "Would it be easier if you were the second black quarterback to play in the Super Bowl?"

- "Will America be pulling for the Redskins or rooting against them because of you?"

- "Do you feel like Jackie Robinson?"

- "Why haven't you used being the first black quarterback as a personal forum?"

To Williams's credit, he answered each and every query with propriety and patience. Under that intense cloud of scrutiny, it's a testament to the man and his ability that he went out and led his club to a resounding 42–10 victory over the Denver Broncos and earned the nod as MVP, perhaps as much for his off-field sensibility as his on-field accomplishments.

ONE BAD APPLE

*If there ever was a piece of fruit with
an undeserved reputation, it is the apple.
In the biblical story, it's wrongly cited
as the forbidden emblem of temptation.*

Eve picks a piece of fruit, eats it, and then—well, all hell breaks loose. But did you know that the fruit she bit into was probably not an apple? Apples aren't mentioned anywhere in this popular Bible story. Only the word *fruit* is given in the biblical text. You won't even find the phrase *forbidden fruit* in the book of Genesis.

So if it wasn't an apple, what kind of fruit was growing on that infamous tree? Pears? Cherries? Did Eve reach up and pick a lemon? Genesis describes rivers that include the Tigris and Euphrates in a region that approximates modern-day Iraq. Fruits that would have grown in this area during biblical times include figs, apricots, and pomegranates, but not apples.

The idea that the fruit Eve ate was an apple most likely stemmed from a bit of fifth-century wordplay. The monks who translated the Bible from Hebrew to Latin probably got a kick out of the fact that the Latin word for apple is *malum* and the Latin word for evil is *malus*. Using the word *malum* to mean "fruit," they could emphasize the evil of Eve's actions.

European painters are probably most responsible for placing an apple in Eve's hand. In the Middle Ages, painters tried to relate biblical stories to the masses. The apple was a common fruit—in fact, the word *apple* was used to refer to any fruit. Artists often depicted biblical stories in medieval villages and biblical figures in period clothing. In the same way, apple trees in the Garden of Eden were something that people would recognize and understand.

THE LINCOLN–KENNEDY DEBATES

※ ※※ ※

After President John F. Kennedy's assassination in 1963, history buffs began finding peculiar parallels between Kennedy and President Abraham Lincoln. These lists of Lincoln–Kennedy coincidences are a strange mix of truth, fiction, and folks with too much free time.

Honest-Abe Truths

Fact: Lincoln and Kennedy were elected to Congress 100 years apart (1846, 1946), elected to the presidency 100 years apart (1860, 1960), and had successors who were born 100 years apart (1808, 1908).

Fact: Both men were shot in the head.

Fact: Both had successors with the last name Johnson (Andrew and Lyndon).

Fact: The names Lincoln and Kennedy both contain seven letters.

None of these common facts are particularly remarkable. The head is a logical target for a would-be assassin; Johnson is a common last name. Some people get excited about numeric coincidences while conveniently ignoring countless differences, such as the men's ages at the time of death, years of their births, and the fact that their first names have different numbers of characters (and Lincoln didn't even have a middle name). If the 100-year connection seems uncanny, perhaps it's because round numbers are given undue importance (think of the excitement and foreboding that accompany the end of a decade, century, or millennium).

※ ※ ※

Semi-Truths

Coincidence: Both first ladies lost children while in the White House.
Fact: Although this is technically true, the situations were quite different. The Kennedys' child died a few days after a premature

birth, and two older children (a boy and a girl) survived to adulthood. The Lincolns lost an 11-year-old son to typhoid while they were in the White House. They had three other sons, two of whom died before they reached adulthood.

Coincidence: Lincoln and Kennedy were both assassinated by and succeeded by Southerners.

Fact: Both men chose Southern running mates to help balance their tickets (Lincoln was from Illinois and Kennedy was from Massachusetts). That their assassins were both Southerners is debatable. Although Lincoln's assassin, John Wilkes Booth, sympathized with the South, he spent most of his life in the North and thought of himself as a Northerner. Kennedy's assassin, Lee Harvey Oswald, was born in New Orleans but moved around so much that he didn't identify as Northern or Southern.

Coincidence: Both assassins were known by three names.

Fact: Booth used the names "J. Wilkes Booth" and "John Wilkes" equally, whereas Oswald went primarily by "Lee Oswald" when he was not using one of his many false names. Only after the assassination did police and the media use his full name to ensure proper identification.

Coincidence: Booth and Oswald were both assassinated before their trials.

Fact: Although both men were killed before going to trial, the details of their deaths were different. Two days after Oswald was captured by police, nightclub owner Jack Ruby shot him in the abdomen while he was in transit under police custody. A lawfully armed federal officer named Boston Corbett shot Booth in the neck as he was attempting to evade arrest (hardly an assassination).

Coincidence: Lincoln and Kennedy were both assassinated on a Friday before a holiday.

Fact: Lincoln was shot on April 14, the Friday before Easter, also known as Good Friday. Kennedy was shot on November 22, the Friday before Thanksgiving. Lincoln lived until the next day, whereas Kennedy was declared dead shortly after he was shot.

Coincidence: Both presidents had a special concern for civil rights. **Fact:** It is accurate to say that monumental events in civil rights occurred during each presidency—for example, Lincoln signed the Emancipation Proclamation in 1863, and the March on Washington took place in 1963, during Kennedy's term. But Lincoln was actually not a proponent of civil rights in the modern sense. In fact, during one of his famous debates with Stephen Douglas, he said, "I will say that I am not, nor ever have been, in favor of bringing about in any way the social and political equality of the white and black races." He maintained that blacks should not hold office, intermarry, vote, or sit on juries—rights we now consider inalienable.

❀❀❀

Flat-Out Fibs

Myth: Lincoln's secretary, Kennedy, warned him not to go to Ford's Theatre; Kennedy's secretary, Lincoln, warned him not to go to Dallas.
Fact: Kennedy did have a secretary named Evelyn Lincoln, but there is no evidence that she warned him not to go to Dallas (he was, however, frequently informed of assassination plots). Lincoln, the subject of as many as 80 known plots, was also used to these warnings. But he never had a secretary by the name of Kennedy; his secretaries' surnames were Nicolay and Hay.

Myth: John Wilkes Booth and Lee Harvey Oswald were born 100 years apart, in 1839 and 1939, respectively.
Fact: Even if it were true, it would simply be another instance of giving false meaning to a round number. But it's not true: Booth was born in 1838.

Myth: Booth ran from a theater and was caught in a warehouse; Oswald ran from a warehouse and was caught in a theater.

Fact: Booth shot Lincoln in a theater during a performance of a play. He evaded police for 12 days, during which time he left the state and was captured in a tobacco shed on a farm—not what most would consider a warehouse. Oswald (allegedly) shot Kennedy from the window of a book depository and was captured in a movie theater a few hours later.

Myth: A month before Lincoln was assassinated, he visited Monroe, Maryland; a month before Kennedy was assassinated, he visited Marilyn Monroe.

Fact: Tee-hee. Marilyn Monroe, one of Kennedy's supposed lovers, died more than a year before his death. In addition, there is no Monroe in Maryland, unless one counts the 217 feet of Monroe Street that connects Commerce Street to Clay Street in the town of Point of Rocks.

Common Connections

The violent and untimely deaths of two popular presidents is certainly tragic. It's human nature to make meaning out of tragedy, and drawing these tenuous connections is an attempt at assigning order to a chaotic world. In 1992, the magazine *Skeptical Inquirer* asked for submissions of similar lists of coincidences between presidents. One of the winners found connections between 21 different pairs of U.S. presidents, while another winner found 16 shocking connections between Kennedy and former Mexican President Alvaro Obregón. However, connections can be found between almost any two people, given enough data and research. Comb through and compare siblings, parents, teachers, likes, dislikes, ages, employers, cars, pets, etc., and you'll eventually find a sufficient number of matches. Don't have time for that? Good for you.

MEMORABLE MOVIE MISQUOTES

※ ◈ ※

*People love to recite memorable lines from their favorite
movies, TV shows, and books. But many of the most famous
lines are misquoted or attributed to the wrong character.
In some cases they were never uttered by anyone.*

"Play it again, Sam," from the classic 1942 movie *Casablanca,* is perhaps the most frequently misquoted movie line of all time. In fact, it was never spoken by anyone in the film. Ingrid Bergman's character comes closest when she says, "Play it, Sam." The nearest Humphrey Bogart's character gets is when he says, "If she can stand it, I can. Play it!" The line "Play it again, Sam" was used in the Marx Brothers' 1946 movie *A Night in Casablanca,* however, and Woody Allen used it as the title for his 1972 comedy.

"I think this is the start of a beautiful friendship" is the famous last line of *Casablanca*—and it's a misquote. As Rick and Renault walk off together into the night, Rick's final line is, "Louis, I think this is the beginning of a beautiful friendship."

"You dirty rat!" Cagney never uttered this line in a movie or in any recorded interview. The closest he came was in the 1931 movie *Blonde Crazy,* when he said, "Mmm, that dirty, double-crossin' rat." It is believed that one of Cagney's professional impersonators coined the phrase, and others went on to copy it.

"Elementary, my dear Watson!" is surely the most famous line attributed to the world's greatest detective, Sherlock Holmes. The problem is that at no point in any of the Sherlock Holmes novels from Sir Arthur Conan Doyle does the sleuth utter the line. The phrase first appeared in a *New York Times* film review and was then coined in the 1929 movie *The Return of Sherlock Holmes.*

THE ELEVATOR INCIDENT

*In most urban legends, the story being told
never happened to the person telling the story.
Instead, it's usually traced to "the second cousin
of my great-uncle's pool-cleaning guy."
Here's the basic version of one such tale.*

Three elderly women are visiting the imposing metropolis of New York City for the first time. They have been warned to "not mess around with muggers—do whatever they say." Entering the elevator of their hotel, they are joined by an African American man and his dog on a leash. When the man shouts, "Sit!" the paranoid and terrified women quickly sit down on the floor of the elevator. The man offers his apologies, telling the ladies he was addressing his pet. He leaves with his dog when the car reaches the main floor. Later, as the women dine, they are offered a bottle of champagne from their waitperson, who tells them, "This is compliments of Mr. (famous black celebrity) who, along with his dog, completely enjoyed meeting you in the elevator today."

This story has origins in the early 1980s, when newspaper reporters told the story and named Baseball Hall of Fame slugger Reggie Jackson as the protagonist of the tale (despite his repeated denials.) Over the years, the characters have changed—they have included hoops icon Michael Jordan, boxing champ Larry Holmes, the Reverend Jesse Jackson, Sr., and actor Eddie Murphy. The locations have also been noted as Las Vegas and Los Angeles.

The real source of the story may be the 1970s sitcom *The Bob Newhart Show*. In one episode, a black man tries to control his unruly white dog in a dentist's office. When the man says, "Sit, Whitey!" the dentist obediently plops down on his desk. Of course, what may have happened is that the urban legend served as inspiration for the sitcom script. In the end, though, the versions of the central story are limited only by the tellers' imaginations.

A TORNADO RUNS THROUGH IT

*Residents in communities across the United States
believe they are safe from the threat of tornadoes
because of their proximity to a river.*

Unfortunately, this local legend has done more damage than good
when tornadoes have hit. A Native American belief long held by
residents of Waco, Texas, was that the area was protected from tornadoes by the bluffs of the nearby Brazos River. In 1953, however,
the community was forced to reevaluate its disaster-preparedness
plans when a tornado tore through the city, killing 114 people.

Tornadoes cross rivers, lakes, ravines, and all manner of water.
The deadliest tornado in history—the 1925 Tri-State tornado that
ripped through Missouri, Illinois, and Indiana—killed 695 people
and crossed the Mississippi River. In some cases, tornadoes can
become even stronger when they come in contact with water. A
tornado twisting through a narrow gully or canyon wall will spin
increasingly faster, regardless of the rivers and streams that flow
through these corridors.

Types of Tornadoes

A specific type of tornado known as a waterspout forms on water
and is typically less powerful than a land-based tornado. Waterspouts
occasionally move from water to land, but they are usually fairly weak
when they make this transition. There is also evidence that thunder-
storms, which can spawn tornadoes, weaken as they cross larger
bodies of water, such as lakes. Yet even in this case, a tornado can
form once the storm reaches shore. Rivers appear to have no effect
on the strength of tornadoes that form on land. Weather records
reveal that tornadoes have crossed every major river east of the Rock-
ies. When it comes to surviving a tornado, the safety of a basement
beats the false security of a nearby river.

THE NEVER-ENDING STORY OF THE HIBERNATING BEAR

It's a myth that bears hibernate. It's a myth that bears don't hibernate. Where does this story end?

Once Upon a Time

In the United States circa 1950, the story of the hibernating bear was told with confidence and abandon. Schoolchildren from coast to coast knew of the sleepy bear that, come cold temperatures and snow, escaped into a cave for months of deep respite. With the arrival of spring and warmer weather, the bear would emerge from the cave to search for food and frolic in a nearby stream.

And then came the scientists with their sophisticated shiny metal objects, which they used to measure metabolism, temperature, and oxidation. In the 1960s, '70s, and '80s, many such scientists concluded that bears do not hibernate. The logic went something like this: When animals hibernate, their body temperature drops. Smaller mammals that hibernate can drop their body temperature below freezing. Bears, however, drop their body temperature by only 10 to 15 degrees. Further, whereas some smaller mammals cannot be easily awakened during hibernation, a hibernating bear can be stirred from its sleep with relatively little effort. The conclusion was that bears do not hibernate.

Catastrophes of Classification

This created quite a stir in the scientific community. If bears aren't hibernating, what exactly are they doing? A replacement theory was the concept of "torpor," a biological state in which animals lower their metabolic rates, but generally for shorter periods of time. Torpor is considered to be less of a "deep sleep" than hibernation and is seen in birds, rodents, insectivores, and marsupials.

Yet the torpor argument came with its own set of problems. In many respects, the hibernation period of a bear is actually deeper than that of other hibernating species. Although rodents and other small mammals drastically reduce their body temperatures during hibernation, they wake every few days in order to eat and urinate. Some species of bears are able to go six to eight months without eating, urinating, defecating, or fully waking. Further, it is because of their large size that bears do not drastically reduce their body temperatures during hibernation. In the face of this confusion, words such as *denning* and *dormancy* were coined to describe the habits of bears.

The Essence of Hibernation

Whether the physical inactivity of an animal is labeled hibernation, torpor, or denning, the purpose of these prolonged states is to conserve energy in the face of food scarcity or uncomfortable temperatures. Metabolism is reduced when an animal lowers its body temperature, slows its breathing and heart rate, and reduces its movements. The particular strategy a species takes in these endeavors varies greatly and depends on its environment. In the colder northern regions of North America, where food is unavailable for the long stretch of winter, black bears hibernate for several months. In the Arctic, where food supplies are unpredictable, polar bears can go into hibernation at any time of year. Only female polar bears hibernate, no doubt because of the elevated energy requirements of pregnancy, birth, and feeding the young.

The Shift in Consensus

Scientists moved back into the "pro-hibernation" camp after the discovery of a lemur that hibernates in the tropics, apparently to save energy in the face of heat and food scarcity (the word *estivation* refers to species that hibernate in warm temperatures). It was traditionally thought that hibernation served as an "escape" from the cold, but the energy-saving behavior of the lemur's hibernation demonstrated that the process is about lowering metabolism in the face of environmental stressors that vary from species to species. "Hibernate" is now accepted as a broader phrase that refers to a reduction in metabolism for prolonged periods of time—meaning it is once again safe to tell the tale of the hibernating bear.

FALLACIES & FACTS: MUSIC

Fallacy: *The Beatles smoked marijuana in the queen's loo.*
Fact: *In 1965, the Fab Four went to Buckingham Palace to receive Members of the Most Excellent Order of the British Empire (MBEs) from Queen Elizabeth II. Afterward, Lennon boasted they had shared a joint in one of the palace bathrooms—though McCartney claims it was just a nerve-calming cigarette.*

Fallacy: *Peter, Paul and Mary's "Puff, the Magic Dragon" is about smoking pot.*
Fact: *The songs lyrics include references to Little Jackie Paper and the "land called Honah Lee"—thought by many to be code for rolling papers and a pot-growing Mecca in Hawaii (the village of Hanalei). Alas, the lyrics, written as a poem in 1959 by Cornell University student Lenny Lipton, are simply about the sad end to his carefree childhood. Lipton shared the poem with his friend Peter Yarrow, who made it into a song for his folk-singing trio.*

Fallacy: *Gene Simmons had a cow's tongue grafted to his.*
Fact: *Medical science can do amazing things, but surgically joining bovine and human tongues isn't one of them. The KISS vocalist and bassist does have a freakishly long lapper—and, in keeping with his shrewd marketing mind, he has gone to great lengths to exploit it.*

Fallacy: *Musician Marilyn Manson was a regular on* The Wonder Years.
Fact: *It's rumored that before he became the scourge of America's Bible Belt, the goth shock rocker played dweeb braniac Paul Pfeiffer on the hit TV series. Sorry to disappoint, but that part was actually played by Josh Saviano, who went on to graduate from Yale and is now a lawyer.*

Fallacy: *Keith Richards underwent a full blood transfusion to kick his heroin addiction.*
Fact: *Rumor spread in 1973 that Richards, desperate to end his debilitating heroin habit before a Rolling Stones concert tour, checked into a clinic in Switzerland, where his smack-poisoned blood was drained and replaced with a clean supply. Actually, Richards underwent a form of hemodialysis in order to filter impurities from his blood. He later said he concocted the transfusion story to placate people who kept asking how he'd cleaned up so fast.*

Fallacy: *Deborah Harry was nearly kidnapped by serial killer Ted Bundy.*
Fact: *In 1989, the Blondie singer recalled to a newspaper reporter a night in New York City in the early 1970s when a man lured her into his car, which had no inside door handles. Freaked out, she reached through a partially rolled-down window, opened the door with the outside handle, and then ran away. She said she realized 15 years later that the creepy dude was actually Ted Bundy. Quite the tale, considering the fact that Bundy had never stepped foot in the Big Apple.*

Fallacy: *Bob Dylan didn't write "Blowin' in the Wind."*
Fact: *When Dylan released "Blowin' in the Wind" in May 1963, people in Millburn, New Jersey, claimed they had heard local teen Lorre Wyatt sing the tune months before. This led many to speculate that Dylan bought or even stole the song from the kid. Wyatt eventually admitted that he'd copped the tune (which Dylan wrote in April 1962) from a folk music magazine in September 1962, sang it at a band rehearsal a month later and, after wowing his audience, claimed the song as his own.*

TALE OF A FATEFUL TRIP

❋❋❋

Robinson Crusoe, that classic tale of shipwreck and survival on a deserted island, is widely thought to be purely fictional. In fact, the story is based on the real-life adventures of Scotsman Alexander Selkirk.

Daniel Defoe's *Robinson Crusoe,* frequently cited as the first novel published in English (1719), remains one of the world's most enduring adventure stories, having spawned books, TV shows, and movies that include *The Swiss Family Robinson, Gilligan's Island,* and *Castaway.* The book is a fictional autobiography of an Englishman who is stranded on a remote tropical island for 28 years. The real-life Scottish sailor who inspired the classic tale was born in 1676 as Alexander Selcraig, later to become Alexander Selkirk.

In 1704, Selkirk was part of an English pirate expedition that set out to plunder Spanish vessels in the Pacific Ocean. Before returning to England, Selkirk quarreled with his captain, insisting that the ship be repaired before they attempted to sail around the treacherous Cape Horn. The captain refused to delay the trip, so Selkirk deserted the ship and wound up marooned on the most western of the Juan Fernandez Islands, approximately 400 miles off the coast of Chile.

It turns out that Selkirk's desertion was wise, because the ship soon sank and most of those onboard died. At the time, though, he had no way of knowing this, as he had been stranded on the island for nearly four and a half years before being picked up by a passing ship captained by English privateer Woodes Rogers.

Some claim that Defoe actually met Selkirk in person, heard his tales firsthand, and even gained access to his personal papers. Others believe that Defoe simply read Rogers's published account of Selkirk's adventures. Either way, the link between the two was cemented in 1966 when the Chilean government changed the name of Selkirk's island home to "Robinson Crusoe Island."

TWAIN'S TYPEWRITER

Most sources will tell you that the first novel written on a typewriter was The Adventures of Tom Sawyer, *by Mark Twain. Strangely, Twain himself is the source of this persistent near-falsehood.*

The Adventures of Tom Sawyer wasn't the first novel written on a typewriter, but another of Mark Twain's books, *Life on the Mississippi,* most likely was. The typewriter was invented in 1868 and first sold in 1874 by the gun makers E. Remington & Sons. The early models were clunky and difficult to work with, but Twain was enthusiastic about publishing innovations, so he bought one of the first upon their debut. Twain was working on *The Adventures of Huckleberry Finn* in 1874, but he wasn't sure which of his books was the first to be tapped out on that particular typewriter.

In a letter Twain wrote in 1904, he said, "I will now claim—until dispossessed—that I was the first person in the world to apply the type-machine to literature. That book must have been *The Adventures of Tom Sawyer.* I wrote the first half of it in 1872, the rest of it in 1874. My machinist type-copied a book for me in '74, so I concluded it was that one." Although Twain sounds fairly sure of himself in that statement, one of his biographers later investigated the claim and determined that Twain's machinist had actually typed *Life on the Mississippi,* which was submitted to publishing companies in 1883 as a typewritten manuscript.

Newfangled Nonsense

Twain had a difficult time learning to use his new typewriter, so he pawned it off on his friend William Dean Howells. In a 1904 biographical piece, Twain confesses that the machine "was full of caprices, full of defects–devilish ones. It had as many immoralities as the machine of today has virtues. After a year or so, I found it was degrading my character, so I thought I would give it to Howells. He took it home to Boston, and my morals began to improve, but his have never recovered."

THE MYTH OF THE 24-HOUR FLU

*If you're sitting on or kneeling in front of the porcelain throne,
what you're suffering from is not the flu.*

Every flu season, millions of people who get their flu shots still come down with a nasty stomach bug that puts them in bed for up to 48 hours. The cause of their suffering is not the flu, which is a respiratory disease transmitted by air-borne viruses that can survive up to a month and cause severe or even life-threatening illness. Chances are it's a case of gastroenteritis, an inflammation of the stomach and intestines caused by ingesting a virus or microbe. The associated nausea, vomiting, diarrhea, and stomach cramps often subside within a day.

The likely culprit is the highly contagious novovirus, which accounts for half of food-borne diseases, according to the Centers for Disease Control. Novovirus infection often causes large outbreaks and on occasion has sent the majority of passengers on cruise ships to their sick beds for a day or two. The vomit and stools of those infected are highly contagious, and the virus can linger on the surface of objects for weeks. Approximately 30 percent of stomach bugs are caused by two similar viruses, the rotavirus and the astrovirus.

Other stomach bugs are triggered by bacteria, including *salmonella, shigella, staphylococcus, clostridium,* and *E. coli.* Exposure usually occurs through the consumption of contaminated food or water. Most people don't associate their illness with something they ate or drank, though, because 24 to 72 hours usually pass before they feel sick.

Quiet Killer

Worldwide, inadequate treatment of gastroenteritis kills 5 million to 8 million people per year, and it is a leading cause of death among infants and children under the age of five.

DON'T EVEN ASK

When Civil War general William Tecumseh Sherman was mentioned as a possible Republican nominee for president in 1884, it is said that he rejected the notion, stating, "If nominated, I will not run. If elected, I will not serve." Although the intent of the quote is accurate, the words are wrong.

On March 31, 1968, when President Lyndon B. Johnson announced that he would not seek his party's nomination for a second full term as the nation's chief executive, his impending resignation was referred to a "Shermanesque statement." President Johnson's words on that fateful evening, "I shall not seek, and I will not accept, the nomination of my party for another term as your president," were similar in intent to those used by William Tecumseh Sherman 84 years earlier. But what exactly did Sherman say when he turned down an invitation to run for the country's highest office? In addition to the dozen words inscribed above, some historians claim that Sherman was more concise and more adamant in his refusal to seek public office, declaring, "If nominated, I will not accept; if drafted, I will not run; if elected, I will not serve."

So where does the truth lie? According to the fourth edition of Sherman's memoirs, published in 1891, the general drafted a telegram to a colleague on June 5, 1884, in which he stated, "I will not accept if nominated and will not serve if elected." However, as early as 1871, Sherman had made his intent of not pursuing a political post perfectly clear. In an interview with *Harper's Magazine* on June 24 of that year, he said, "I never have been and never will be a candidate for president; that if nominated by either party I should peremptorily decline; and even if unanimously elected I should decline to serve."

BABE RUTH'S "CALLED" SHOT

*Most of Babe Ruth's achievements can
be appraised by statistics, but a prominent one is
stuck in the vortex between fact and fantasy.*

Like the conundrum about whether those flailing arms in the
distant ocean signal waving or drowning, Babe Ruth's finger to the
sky in Game 3 of the 1932 World Series must be interpreted by
the eye of the beholder.

The Bambino hated the Chicago Cubs, whose fans had been
pelting him with trash and whose players' taunts infuriated him.
So when Ruth came to the plate in the fifth inning with the score
tied 4–4, he seemed to mock his nemeses when he lifted his index
finger and pointed…somewhere.

Although conventional wisdom credits the great slugger with
indicating that Charlie Root's next pitch was destined for Wrigley
Field's centerfield bleachers, most onlookers later recounted that
Ruth appeared to point to the pitcher…or to the Cubs' dugout…
or perhaps that he was simply indicating the count.

There's no debating what happened next: Ruth hammered
a 440-foot laser over the wall, getting his Yankees back into the
game and propelling them to an eventual four-game sweep.

Subsequent news stories nurtured the notion that the Babe
"called" his shot. Many of the principals begged to differ. "He
[just] indicated he had one more strike remaining," assessed Frank
Crosetti, Babe's teammate. Former major leaguer Babe Herman
even claimed to have overheard a conversation between Root and
Ruth years later in which the hitter said, "I know I didn't [call it].
But it made a hell of a story, didn't it?"

In 2000, ESPN aired a newly unearthed 16 mm film of the
episode, which, though not definitive, indicated that Ruth was
merely gesturing to Chicago's bench.

Whether called or merely mauled, the shot was the last of the
Sultan of Swat's 15 World Series home runs.

JIVE TURKEY

Did the Pilgrims start a tradition by eating turkey at the first Thanksgiving—or was that Tiny Tim's doing?

Which came first, the turkey or Thanksgiving? Governor William Bradley's journal from around that time indicates that "besides waterfowl there was great store of wild turkeys, of which they took many." Another record notes that "our governor sent four men on fowling…they four in one day killed as much fowl, as with a little help beside, served the company almost a week."

Of course, "fowl" doesn't necessarily mean turkey, so the best we can say is that the Pilgrims may have eaten it. The only food we know for certain they ate was venison, and that was provided by their guests, the Native Americans (who may have been a little surprised by the meager spread their hosts had laid out). They probably also ate codfish, goose, and lobster, but not a lot of vegetables—you can catch fish and fowl, but it takes time to grow crops. And mashed potatoes? Nope—potatoes hadn't yet been introduced to New England.

So how did the gobbler become the centerpiece of Thanksgiving celebrations? It may have had something to do with the prevalent diet at the time the national holiday was founded in 1863. Beef and chicken were too expensive to serve to a crowd, and even if you had your own farm, you needed the animals' continuous supply of milk and eggs. Venison was an option, but you couldn't always count on bagging a deer in time for the holiday. Turkey was readily available, not too expensive— and very popular, perhaps in part due to the scene at the end of Charles Dickens's *A Christmas Carol* in which Scrooge buys "the prize turkey" for Bob Cratchit's family. The novel, published in 1843, was immensely popular in America and may have secured the humble fowl's center-stage spot on the Thanksgiving table.

PAUL REVERE:
THE TRUTH IS COMING!

*It's hard to get the straight story on Paul Revere,
thanks in large part to Henry Wadsworth Longfellow's
poem about the allegedly lone midnight rider.
Let's sort through some of the misconceptions.*

Revere was half French. True. His mother was a Bostonian, and his father was a French immigrant named Apollos Rivoire, Anglicized to "Revere."

Revere was a brilliant silversmith. Not quite. He was certainly competent, and a good metalworking businessman, but he was no Michelangelo of silver. When history started venerating Paul Revere, it was a package deal: All his activities were magnified, logic and proportion aside.

Revere hung signal lanterns in a church tower. False. He had others hang them. Paul excelled at getting people to help his underground communications network. By the way, the actual signal was two dimly lit lanterns, which meant that the British army would take the Charles River route.

Revere yelled, "The British are coming!" False. That would be like someone from Pittsburgh yelling, "The Americans are coming!" Like nearly all colonists, Revere considered himself British. His warning specified that the "regulars" (i.e., the regular British army) were on the march—which they were. Furthermore, it's unlikely that Revere "yelled" anything, because British army patrols were everywhere.

Revere rode directly to Lexington and Concord. False. Revere was a key organizer of many riders in an informal, early-warning network (much like a primitive phone tree), and he often carried news from point A to point B for the colonial cause. On April 18, 1775, Revere was first in the chain of many riders who went forth to mobilize the militia and protect colonial munitions stores and leaders from surprise seizure. Fellow rider William Dawes soon joined him, and they later picked up Samuel Prescott.

In Lexington, they warned Samuel Adams and John Hancock that the two were about to be arrested, but the men just thanked them and began arguing about what they should do next. Then the riders headed for Concord, but a regular who was stationed at a checkpoint captured Revere. In the subsequent commotion, Dawes and Prescott escaped—Dawes fell off his horse and decided to call it a night, and Prescott was able to warn Concord. (Okay, but how many people have heard of the midnight ride of Sam Prescott?)

Revere fought at Lexington. False. You can't fight while helping another guy lug a chest of documents around town. Revere was close to the fighting, though, with muskets being fired around him. Plus, he was doing more preserving a trunk of secrets than he might have with a musket, especially since the colonial militia broke and ran for it.

Revere was convicted of cowardice in the 1779 Penobscot Expedition. False. Commanding the expedition's artillery, Revere stood accused of disobeying orders. Rightfully offended, after the war he demanded a court-martial—and it exonerated him. Although his military career was underwhelming, the evidence of Revere's life hurls any hint of cowardice out the window.

Revere has always been considered a national hero. False. He was always a regional hero in Massachusetts, but it was Longfellow's poem that got him into history texts and the memories of schoolchildren everywhere. The poem overstates Revere's role at the expense of many others', but its mid–Civil War timing was impeccable in capturing public emotion. As often happens, history's heroes can be either forgotten or exaggerated, but they're rarely remembered as they truly were.

LOCK-PICKING KNOW-HOW

*Regardless of what is portrayed in cops-and-robbers flicks,
you need at least two tools to pick a lock.*

Whether you're a wannabe ruffian or a forgetful homeowner, you should know that it is nearly impossible to pick a lock with only one paper clip, one bobby pin, or one of anything else. Although you can certainly accomplish the task with simple tools, you will need two of them—one to act as a pick and a second one to serve as a tension wrench.

The simple pin-and-tumbler locks on most doors contain a cylinder and several small pins attached to springs. When the door is locked, the cylinder is kept in place by the pins, which protrude into the cylinder. When a matching key is inserted into the lock, the pins are pushed back and the cylinder turns. The key to lock-picking, then, is to push the pins back while simultaneously turning the cylinder. This is why two items are required—a pick to push the pins and a tension wrench to turn the cylinder. Professional locksmiths often use simple lock-picking techniques to avoid damaging the offending lock.

Common household items that can serve as tension wrenches include small screwdrivers and bent paper clips. Items you can use as picks include safety pins, hair fasteners, and paper clips. The determined apprentice may be happy to learn that there is a situation in which one paper clip may suffice in picking a lock: Small, inexpensive padlocks sometimes succumb to large paper clips that are bent in such a way that one end is the pick and the other end is the tension wrench. Even so, the process involves more than just jamming something into the lock and turning the doorknob. Seasoned lock-pickers rely on their senses of hearing and touch to finish the job successfully. They're anticipating a vibration accompanied by a distinct "click" that means each pin is in alignment.

ANCIENT EGYPT—
A WOMAN'S WORLD

꙳ ꙮ ꙳

When feminists today talk about women's rights and equality
with men, they may do well to look to the good old days
of ancient Egypt to see how it was really done.

ERA (Equal Rights, Ancient)

Although the women of ancient Greece could not leave their
homes without a spouse or male relative, ancient Egyptian women
enjoyed equal privileges with men on many fronts, including the
right to buy, sell, and inherit property; to marry and divorce; and
to practice an occupation outside the home. In fact, ancient Egyptian women had more rights than many women do today.

How do we know this? As they did with everything else, the
Egyptians recorded their legal and economic lives in art and historical inscriptions. And it seems that legal rights and social privileges were different between social classes rather than between
genders. In other words, women and men in the same social class
enjoyed fairly equal rights.

An Egyptian girl became universally acknowledged as a wife
after she physically left the protection of her father's house and
entered her new home. Before the marital home was established,
the couple would hire the services of a scribe, who would record
their individual assets.

A Woman's Pyramid Is Her Castle

The ancient Egyptian woman had full control of property, including the right to buy and sell land, goods, livestock, and servants,
and she could free slaves. A woman could, without the guidance
of a man, manage her own property. She could appear in court on
her own behalf and sue a party who wronged her—all without a
male representative. In fact, there are many recorded instances of
women winning lawsuits, particularly in land disputes.

When an ancient Egyptian woman acquired property on her own—through inheritance, gifts, or with money she earned through employment—it was hers to keep before, during, and after her marriage, whether that marriage ended through widowhood or divorce. If her husband requested, she could grant him rights to use or borrow the property.

One of the best examples of women's rights is in the area of wills and estates. An ancient Egyptian woman could inherit one-third of all the community property she acquired through marriage (the remaining estate was divided among the children and siblings of the deceased), and she was free to bequeath property from her husband to her children.

Employment Opportunities

In terms of careers, the work of the upper-class woman was often limited to the home because of her customary role as mother. But ancient art and texts show women as middle-class housekeepers, skilled laborers in household workshops, paid priestesses, and entertainers (dancers, musicians, and acrobats). All professions were open to educated women and men, including clergy, administrators (there was a woman named Nebet during the Sixth Dynasty who was titled vizier, judge, and magistrate), business owners, and doctors. Records mention Lady Peseshet, who is considered the first female physician in Africa, perhaps even in world history.

Fight Like a (Wo)man

Some of Egypt's greatest rulers and heroes were women. The best example is Hatshepsut, who reigned as pharaoh of Egypt rather than as queen. Ancient reports during a military campaign in Nubia tell of the homage she received from rebels defeated on the battlefield. Queen Ahhotep, of the early Eighteenth Dynasty, was granted Egypt's highest military decoration—the Order of the Fly—at least three times for saving Egypt during the wars of liberation against the Hyksos invaders from the north.

COLOR ME TOXIC

❀ ❀ ❀

Mares eat oats, and does eat oats, and little kids eat crayons.
But should Junior wear a HAZMAT suit as
he munches on Burnt Sienna or Cadet Blue?

On May 23, 2003, the *Seattle Post-Intelligencer* fired a shot heard by parents around the world. In independent tests of eight brands of coloring crayons, three brands (Crayola, Prang, and Rose Art) had colors that contained more than trace levels of asbestos.

The three manufacturers immediately dismissed the findings as wrong, citing their own industry tests. Despite the denials, this report set off a firestorm of fear, criticism, and consumer panic.

"Asbestos" is a general term for several minerals that break easily into fibrous threads, and it has been linked to various forms of cancer, especially when inhaled. In these cases, asbestos is likely mixed with the mineral talc, which was used as a binding agent in crayons. Talc and asbestos are found together in rock formations and frequently are combined in the mining process.

In follow-up tests, the Consumer Product Safety Commission (CPSC) found traces of asbestos in Crayola and Prang crayons, but it assured the public that the amount was insignificant. Similar but non-hazardous "transitional fibers" also appeared in the tests. Although the CPSC wasn't concerned about children ingesting any of these materials and found no airborne fibers even after 30 minutes of simulated scribbling, it requested that the manufacturers reformulate their products. All three companies agreed, and later tests showed all of the crayons to be asbestos-free.

Kids Love Crayons

Kids and crayons go together. Crayola claims that the average ten-year-old has already used up 723 crayons, not counting the ones he or she has eaten. A study by Yale University shows that the familiar "crayon scent" is one of the 20 most recognizable smells in the United States.

FALLACIES & FACTS: REDWOODS

Fallacy: *A redwood is the same as a sequoia.*
Fact: *In North America, there are just two native species of cone-bearing redwoods: the coast redwood and the giant sequoia. Thus, sequoias are redwoods, but not all redwoods are sequoias. Other parts of the world have leaf-bearing redwoods, but none so mighty as California's.*

Fallacy: *Redwoods are the oldest trees.*
Fact: *Not even close. Compared to Methuselah, a spry little California bristlecone pine more than 4,700 years old, the oldest living redwood is a relative youngster. Seven other tree types in the United States can outlive redwoods.*

General Sherman, in California's Sequoia National Park, is the biggest—and thus probably the oldest— sequoia. The National Park Service estimates that the General is between 1,800 and 2,700 years old (sprouted between 700 B.C. and A.D. 200). Put another way: When Methuselah was a sapling, Egyptians were just getting the bright idea to pile up stones into big pointy tombs. By the time General Sherman began to grow, Egypt's days of might and grandeur were long over.

Fallacy: *Redwoods require dense fog to thrive.*
Fact: *If that were the case, they wouldn't survive in such fog-poor places as Rotorua, New Zealand, where the tallest redwoods reach 200 feet. Nor would they grow well in areas where summer heat can hit triple digits. Excessive wind will stunt their growth, and they drink literally tons of groundwater, but irrigation can supply this when nature will not. It's just a question of how badly one wants a redwood tree.*

Fallacy: *Redwoods grow at a snail's pace.*
Fact: *In fact, the things grow like weeds in the right conditions (moist, well-drained soil; moderate cold). Timber companies love them, of course, because redwoods can gain an inch of diameter and a yard of height per year in ideal conditions. Redwoods aren't an endangered species; they're just immense evergreens.*

Fallacy: *Redwoods won't grow tall in the eastern United States.*
Fact: *It's true that eastern climates are rough on redwoods. The trees do not like high winds, so it stands to reason that they like twisters and hurricanes even less. Their height makes them targets for Dixie's vicious lightning storms. But those are outside factors. If nature doesn't batter or stunt a redwood, it'll have no trouble growing 100 feet tall in eastern soils.*

Fallacy: *Redwoods aren't found above altitudes of 3,000 feet.*
Fact: *A redwood grove on Maui extends to 6,000 feet above sea level. The myth persists because California redwoods can't thrive above 3,000 feet, but that's because California winters can be punishingly inhospitable at those altitudes.*

Fallacy: *"Bonsai giant sequoia" is a contradictory term.*
Fact: *People actually grow these, but remember that "giant sequoia" is a species name, and every tree begins as a tiny sprout.*

Fallacy: *There is one redwood tree so big, someone has carved an opening so you can drive your car through it.*
Fact: *There are actually three such trees, all in northern California. If you think the privilege is worth three bucks, drive carefully.*

SWEATING LIKE A DOG

❋ ❁ ❋

*It's hot out, and you and your dog are taking
a midday run. As your shirt becomes soaked with perspiration,
Rover breaks a sweat in his own way—by panting.
That's what you've always thought, anyway.*

Dogs don't sweat by panting, but they do regulate their body temperature that way. They release excess heat through their tongues while taking short, rapid breaths—sometimes as many as 300 to 400 per minute. This process expels hot air from their lungs and body cavities. But because such breathing is quick and shallow, it doesn't use up much energy, so the dog doesn't risk overheating more.

It's widely thought that dogs don't sweat at all, but that's not true, either. Although humans perspire through our skin, a dog's fur prevents the release of moisture and heat. Our canine companions lack the extensive sweat glands that we have, but they do have some—and they're located in their foot pads. That's why you can see pad prints on wood floors and outdoor decks in warm weather. That's also why your pet's paws can smell kind of funky, like armpits. As humans do, dogs perspire when they get overheated or anxious. We get sweaty pits, they get sweaty paws.

However, the paws of a dog are too small to release the excessive body heat generated during a vigorous romp in the middle of summer. That's when the tongue flops out. With both cooling systems in operation, a dog is so efficient at lowering its body temperature that it can endure prolonged, high-speed chases—in pursuit of a rabbit, say—without the need to stop. The rabbit, on the other hand, has no such means to cool down. Sure, it'll keep running to evade the dog, but it'll likely drop dead from heat exhaustion in the process.

NO ROOM AT THE INN?

❀ ❖ ❀

*In the traditional Christmas story, an innkeeper turns
Mary and Joseph away from his at-capacity establishment
but offers them the use of his stable. It's a nice tale,
but there are problems with the details.*

No Vacancy

In describing the event, the gospel writer Luke says, "And she
brought forth her firstborn son, and wrapped him in swaddling
clothes, and laid him in a manger; because there was no room for
them in the inn."

To modern readers, the word *inn* conjures up images of a cozy
bed-and-breakfast. But in Luke's original Greek, the word for inn
is *kataluma,* which can also be translated as "lodging place." He
uses the same word later, when referring to the guest room in
which Jesus ate the Passover meal with his disciples just before
his death. At the time, most houses had such rooms, usually on
an upper level and often with a separate entrance, which could
be used by visiting guests. It may be that Mary and Joseph were
headed to such a guest room at the house in Bethlehem, but they
arrived too late and the room was already occupied.

Away in a What?

The word *kataluma* can also refer to a large, covered shelter with
open cooking fires where travelers gathered with all their family members and animals—a hot, crowded, noisy place that Mary
and Joseph might have wanted to avoid at the time. In any event,
there was no room, so they went to a stable, correct? Sorry—the
gospels don't mention a stable, either. After Jesus was born, Mary
laid him in a manger, or feeding trough. If the *kataluma* was in a
private house, the manger may have been in the lower level where
the family's animals were kept. Or the manger may have been in
a nearby cave where animals could stay out of the elements—not
exactly the three-sided wooden shelter of nativity scenes, but at
least a more private place in which to give birth.

HITLER'S SYMBOL OF HATE

※ ※ ※

In 1920, Hitler's Nazi Party adopted the swastika as its official emblem. It soon became—and remains—a powerful symbol of hate, anti-Semitism, and death. Contrary to popular belief, however, Hitler didn't invent it.

The Swastika's Symbolism

For 3,000 years before the rise of fascism, the swastika was in many cultures a symbol of power, life, good luck, and the sun, and the earliest known examples date to 3000 B.C. The word *swastika*, which dates back thousands of years, comes from the Sanskrit *svastika*, meaning "to be good." The symbol was found on artifacts exhumed from the ancient city of Troy, appeared frequently in early Mayan art, and continues to be used today as a positive image in religions such as Buddhism, Hinduism, and Jainism. Historically, Native Americans have used the swastika as a symbol of good luck. During World War I, a swastika even appeared on the patches of the American 45th Infantry Division, which proudly displayed the four-armed symbol to represent the Spanish Heritage of the four southwestern states that made up its membership.

Nazi Negativity

The swastika was also used by the ancient Aryan people of Iran and India, who believed themselves to be a pure race. It was this attribute the Nazis wished to emulate when they adopted the swastika as their own emblem. In his book *Mein Kampf,* Hitler described the symbolic meaning of the Nazi swastika as "the mission of the struggle for the victory of the Aryan man, and, by the same token, the victory of the idea of creative work, which as such always has been and always will be anti-Semitic."

Once the swastika was adopted by the Nazis, of course, its symbolism changed drastically. One way of distinguishing a Nazi swastika from the symbol used in many ancient cultures is by noting the angle at which it's positioned. A Nazi swastika is positioned at a slant, while the ancient swastika usually rests flat.

NO TWO FINGERPRINT READERS ARE ALIKE

❊ ❈ ❊

Even if you're innocent, you may get fingered falsely by a fingerprint. They're not as reliable as people think.

- Until DNA testing came along, fingerprint identification was considered the gold standard of evidence. But it turns out that fingerprint identification is far from foolproof.

- A *Chicago Tribune* investigative study on forensics found that fingerprint analysis is subjective and that even the most experienced examiners make egregious mistakes. *Tribune* reporters reviewed 200 cases of DNA and death row exonerations nationwide over a 20-year period and found that more than 25 percent had been based on flawed forensic testing or testimony.

- Another *Tribune* study examined the "science" of fingerprinting. When researchers sifted through the findings culled by an independent proficiency tester, they learned that crime lab examiners often got things wrong. In fact, nearly a quarter of the U.S. labs cited in the study returned false positives.

- Fingerprint identification is far from an exact "science." Analysts look for points of similarity, but there are no universal standards, and no research dictates the number of points that establish a match with certainty. A complete fingerprint is rarely lifted from a crime scene, and yet no research determines how much of a latent (partial) fingerprint is sufficient to create a match.

- A study published in the *Journal of Forensic Sciences* found error rates at or above 2 percent, while another study found the rate could be as low as 0.8 percent or as high as 4 percent. Obviously, there's more than perception and numbers at stake. A false positive at the 2 percent rate would mean that there are approximately 4,800 false convictions or guilty pleas every year.

BRA BURNING—FROM MEDIA MYTH TO REVOLUTIONARY REALITY

In the late 1960s, the media reported that feminists were burning their bras at organized protests. The initial reports weren't true, but the label "bra-burning feminists" stuck.

Firey Feminists

In 1968, Robin Morgan and other influential feminist activists organized a protest of that year's Miss America beauty pageant. The demonstrators had considered burning bras and other symbols of the female beauty culture, but they decided this would be a fire hazard. Instead, they threw bras, girdles, handbags, and cosmetics into trash cans.

The mainstream media, however, got wind of the initial plan and inaccurately portrayed the hypothetical bra-burning incident as though it had actually happened. Doubtlessly titillated by the word *bra* and all it brings to mind, the male-dominated media began to report on bra burnings as though they were central to the feminist movement. Before long, "bra burners" became a catchphrase for radical feminists.

A Sterotype Goes Down in Flames

Historians and researchers have gone to great lengths to prove that there were no bra burnings at the famed protests. Many have interpreted the obsession with the idea as an attempt to reduce feminist politics into snide remarks about silly girls who torch their unmentionables. Although such bra-burning reductionism is sure to be found in many reports on the feminist movement, recent feminists have since taken up the media's reports and burned their own bras as the radical symbolic statement it was meant to be. Thus, though the famous bra burnings that the media reported never occurred, the spirit of creative destruction as a form of protest is not a myth.

THINGS THAT GET MADE UP IN THE NIGHT: THE AMITYVILLE HOAX

※ ◈ ※

The famous haunted house that has inspired books, movies, sequels, and remakes was nothing more than a famous fraud.

The story behind the myth of *The Amityville Horror* is as fascinating as the supposedly "true" events that spawned a best-selling book, a hit horror movie (and its sequels), and a 2005 remake. The adage "Never let the truth get in the way of a good story" could have been coined specifically for *The Amityville Horror.*

On November 13, 1974, six members of the DeFeo family were shot in their home in Amityville, New York. The sole remaining family member, Ronald "Butch" DeFeo, Jr., later confessed to killing his parents and siblings and was sentenced to 25 years to life. A year after the murders, George and Kathy Lutz, along with their three children, moved into the DeFeo house but stayed only 28 days, alleging the residence was possessed by demonic forces.

A New York TV station employed the services of a team of psychics and ghost hunters who duly confirmed the Lutzes' claims: The house was haunted. *The Amityville Horror: A True Story,* written by Jay Anson, was published in 1977 and became a national best seller; the movie was released in 1979.

Eventually, though, the truth began to emerge. Anson confessed that his book was based on tape-recorded recollections from the Lutzes and that he hadn't verified any facts. Furthermore, the Lutzes had never contacted the Amityville police department about mysterious activity. Weather records show that there was no snowfall on the day the family claimed to have discovered cloven hoofprints in the snow. Most damning of all was Butch DeFeo's attorney, who admitted that he and the Lutzes, inspired in part by the popular movie *The Exorcist,* had created the stories while drinking several bottles of wine.

THE REMARKABLE ERICH REMARQUE

Despite claims by Nazi propagandists, Erich Remarque,
celebrated author of All Quiet on the Western Front,
never tried to hide his heritage.

All Quiet on the Western Front is considered one of the greatest
anti-war novels ever written. The fictional story of German soldiers in World War I was published in 1929 and has sold millions
of copies worldwide. In 1930, it was made into a movie, which
won an Academy Award for Best Picture.

Over the years, however, there have been rumors about the
book's author, Erich Remarque. Chief among them is that his real
surname was Kramer and that he spelled it backward and added a
French flourish to conceal the fact that he was Jewish.

The truth is that Remarque was not Jewish—his family was
Roman Catholic—but he did change his name. He was born Eric
Paul Remark in Germany in 1898, and he legally changed his
name to Erich Maria Remarque after he served in World War I.
His new middle name was in honor of his mother, and Remarque
had been the family name until his grandfather changed it in the
mid-1800s.

When he was 18 years old, Remarque was drafted into the
army and sent to the western front. After he was wounded in combat, he was transferred to a military hospital where he spent the
rest of the war. But his time on the front lines affected him deeply,
and he used the experience as the basis for his best-selling novel.

The Nazi Party banned both the book and the movie, and in
an effort to discredit Remarque's name, it spread the rumor that
he was Jewish and that his real name was Kramer.

Remarque fled to Switzerland in 1931 and moved to the
United States in 1939. He later returned to Switzerland, where he
lived until his death in 1970.

CLARIFICATIONS ON COLUMBUS

Aside from the Pilgrims, Christopher Columbus is one of the most misunderstood figures in U.S. history—in fact, there's question as to whether he was even a notable part of it.

Columbus was not Spanish. He was likely born in Genoa, Italy, of mixed Mediterranean heritages (including Greek). Scholars of medieval Spanish are quick to tell us that Spanish wasn't even his first language.

Columbus did not prove the world was round. This presupposes that any educated person still believed the earth was flat, and by 1492, few did. Of course, most people were uneducated, and because they seldom traveled farther than ten miles from the place they called home, few of them cared.

Columbus did not discover America. Native Americans were already well aware of the continents they had inhabited for millennia. But Columbus didn't even discover America for Europe. West African, Afro-Phoenician, and Viking explorers all show evidence that they'd visited the Americas centuries earlier.

What's more, Columbus never landed in the continental United States or even Mexico. His four voyages took him through the Caribbean islands and to the coasts of South and Central America. In the United States, we make a great fuss over someone whose only sighting of future American soil was Puerto Rico and the U.S. Virgin Islands.

Columbus was never hopelessly lost. Mariners of his day could easily determine latitude but not longitude. It was thus difficult to make accurate landfalls, but Columbus consistently did. Columbus was among the few European navigators who possessed the geographical aptitude of the Polynesians, Arabs, and Chinese. He did believe that he was near India, China, and Japan, but only because he misjudged Earth's circumference.

TRUE COLORS OF
THE WHITE HOUSE

*Legend claims that the residence of the U.S. president
acquired its name—and hue—after an arson attack by British
soldiers during the War of 1812. Here's the real story.*

The "President's House," as it was originally named, is situated
at 1600 Pennsylvania Avenue NW in Washington, D.C. It was
designed by Irish architect James Hoban under the direction of
George Washington. The cornerstone was laid in the fall of 1792,
but Washington left office before construction was completed. In
1800, the home's first occupants, President John Adams and his
wife, Abigail, moved in. By that time, though, the gray quarried-
sandstone exterior of the building had started to look weathered
and was therefore given a coat of whitewash to protect it from
harsh winter conditions. A year later, Thomas Jefferson moved
into the residence as the third U.S. president, and from that point
on, the famous home was given a fresh application of white paint
whenever it was needed.

At the Battle of York during the War of 1812, Canadian Parliament buildings were felled as a result of arson. In a retaliatory act,
British troops set fire to many structures in Washington, including
the residence of President James Madison and his wife, Dolley.
And while Madison ordered the charred and blackened limestone
walls to be repainted in the familiar white, the designation of the
building as "the White House" pre-dates the attack. Sometime
in 1811, a British ambassador referred to the residence as "the
White House at Washington." In March 1812, a congressman by
the name of Bigelow reported that "there is much trouble at the
White House, as we call it—I mean the President's House." Yet
the familiar nickname would not become official until September
1901, when President Theodore Roosevelt signed an executive
order that designated the building "the White House."

OVERKILL: A MATTER OF DEGREES

Boiling water kills bacteria, but it also wastes energy. Here's how you can have your clean water and save the environment, too.

When in doubt about the potability of your water supply, you can ensure its cleanliness (well, at least its "antimicrobialness") by boiling it. But if you don't have an updated wilderness manual, you may not know that boiling water for extended period of time doesn't make it any cleaner, and in fact, boiling isn't even necessary.

It's a misconception that water must reach the boiling point—212 degrees Fahrenheit—to kill pathogens. The temperature needed to knock off most critters (excluding extreme varieties such as bacteria living in volcanoes) is just 185 degrees Fahrenheit. Bacteria, microbes, viruses, and parasites are killed off after just a few minutes at that temperature. Disease-causing pathogens, then, are already dead by the time the water begins to boil.

In developing countries where firewood is scarce and water is filled with bacteria, it is imperative to adhere to recommended boiling times. Since you're unlikely to have a cooking thermometer handy, the prudent route is simply to wait for the water to boil.

Yet various safety guides recommend boiling water for 5, 10, even 20 minutes. At this point much of the water will evaporate, and fuel will have been wasted. In light of criticism about wasting energy to boil water, the Centers for Disease Control and the Environmental Protection Agency recently lowered their suggested boiling times. Both now recommend heating water to a rolling boil for only one minute.

❄❄❄

- *In survival situations when fuel and water supplies are limited, waiting too long for water to boil can have dangerous repercussions. When all you have are a few pieces of firewood and water from a murky stream, sitting idly by as the water boils away may result in a long, cold, thirsty night.*

HE STOLE MY LINE!

❋ ❋ ❋

*"That government is best which governs least" is commonly
attributed to not one but three superstars of history: Thomas
Jefferson, Thomas Paine, and Henry David Thoreau.
Who in this grab bag of greats is the quote's true source?*

That would be Henry David Thoreau, who wrote the words in *Civil
Disobedience* (1849), his renowned essay about the necessity of
individual resistance to unjust government. Thoreau wrote, "I heart-
ily accept the motto—'That government is best which governs least';
and I should like to see it acted up to more rapidly and systematically." Thoreau was actually referencing another source, which
is almost certainly the *United States Magazine and Democratic
Review,* a political and literary journal that contained the words
"The best government is that which governs least" in its first issue.

The quote is often attributed to Thomas Paine or Thomas
Jefferson, who were both, like Thoreau, outspoken in defense of
individual rights and limited government. The quote is not found
in the writings of either man, and it is not clear why they are both
reputed to be the progenitors. It is possible that these words, or
something similar to them, were often spoken in conversations
among the group of intellectuals to which both Paine and Jefferson belonged. If that's the case, Thoreau picked them up and
wrote them down, thus ensuring their place in the towering tomes
of famed quotes.

In *Civil Disobedience,* side by side with the "governs least"
quote, is the first appearance of a similar yet more provocative
passage that has also survived the test of time. Thoreau said, "It
finally amounts to this, which I also believe—'That government is
best which governs not at all'—and when men are prepared for it,
that will be the government which they will have."

THE PIRATES OF PITTSBURGH

While watching a Pittsburgh Pirates baseball game,
it's easy for fans to conjure up romantic images
of Captain Kidd, Blackbeard, or Peg Leg.
Here's the real connection between the team
and those swaggering swashbucklers.

The club logo features a pirate's head over crossed bats (in lieu of a skull and crossbones), so fans might be excused for yelling "Aye!" every time a player throws a strike, scores a run, or steals a base. Yet few people realize that the team's "Pirate" moniker was originally intended as a slur. In fact, calling a Pirate a pirate in 1890 was akin to a mutiny, and use of the epithet might brand the speaker a "dungbie" ("ass" in pirate-speak) by team loyalists. Here's how it came to pass.

The "Alleghenys" (with no reference to Pittsburgh whatsoever) originally formed in 1882 as charter members of the American Association. In 1887, the team transferred to the National League and changed its name to "Pittsburgh." In 1890, baseball was rocked by a players' revolt. Taking on established leagues of the day, the newly formed Players' League would last only one year but would bring forth many changes. After the league dissolved, most players went back to their original teams, provided the organizations had "reserved" them.

As a result of this peculiar loophole, one unattached star player—second baseman Lou Bierbauer, previously of the Philadelphia Athletics—ended up on Pittsburgh's roster. Like a shot fired across the bow, accusations of theft were immediately levied at these "pirates" by the Athletics. The put-down stuck. Eventually, in a classic "If you can't beat 'em, join 'em" move, the Pittsburgh squad adopted the name as its own. Since that day, baseball's pillagers have never looked back. So when you plunk down your doubloons to watch the Pirates play, understand that you are seeing the real deal.

THE COLA CLAUS

Although the Coca-Cola Company helped popularize Santa Claus, it cannot take credit for creating the ubiquitous Christmas image.

Nothing says "Christmas" like the image of a white-whiskered fat man in a red suit squeezing down a chimney with a sack full of toys. But Santa Claus hasn't always looked that way. When the Coca-Cola Company used the red-robed figure in the 1930s to promote its soft drinks, the classic image of Santa was cemented in the public consciousness.

Sorting Out the Santas

Santa Claus evolved from two religious figures, St. Nicholas and Christkindlein. St. Nicholas was a real person, a monk who became a bishop in the early fourth century and was renowned as a generous gift-giver. Christkindlein (meaning "Christ child") was assisted by elfin helpers and would leave gifts for children while they slept.

Santa Claus originated from a Dutch poem, *"Sinterklaas,"* and the legend was added to over time by different writers. Until the early 20th century, though, Santa Claus was portrayed in many different ways. He could be tall and clad in long robes like St. Nicholas, or small with whiskers like the elves who helped Christkindlein.

Have Yourself a Corporate Christmas

In 1881, Thomas Nast, a caricaturist for *Harper's Weekly,* first drew Santa as a merry figure in red with flowing whiskers, an image close to the one we know today. Printer Louis Prang used a similar image in 1885 when he introduced Christmas cards to America. In 1931, the Coca-Cola Company first employed Haddon Sundblom to illustrate its annual advertisements, choosing a Santa dressed in red and white to match the corporate colors. By then, however, this was already the most popular image of Santa Claus, one that was described in detail in a *New York Times* article in 1927. If Coca-Cola had really invented Santa Claus, children would likely be saving the milk and leaving him soda and cookies on Christmas Eve.

RUMORS OF WAR

❋ ❖ ❋

*Plenty of myths have come out of World War II,
but few are as unfounded as the claim that President Franklin
Delano Roosevelt allowed the Japanese to attack Pearl Harbor
so the United States could enter the conflict.*

Unfortunately, this rumor has followed FDR's legacy almost from the moment the attack occurred, and many people continue to believe it today. But countless investigations and studies have failed to uncover a "smoking gun" that proves the president could have engineered such a monumental act of treason.

Coded Knowledge

Conspiracy theorists frequently note that the U.S. military had successfully broken Japanese codes and thus knew in advance of the attack. This is partially true—Japanese codes had been broken, but they were diplomatic codes, not military ones. The military *had* received notice from other sources, including the British, that an attack was pending. What wasn't known was where the attack would take place. Almost everyone assumed it would be against the Philippines or some other Pacific territory, and no one had reason to believe that the target would be the military base at Pearl Harbor.

Another common assumption is that Roosevelt had the Pacific Fleet moved from San Diego to Pearl Harbor to lure the Japanese into attacking. However, it wasn't Roosevelt who made that decision. Rather, it was the State Department, which hoped to deter Japanese aggression with a show of naval force.

Ships at Sea

Many conspiracy theorists also like to claim that the American aircraft carriers based at Pearl Harbor had been sent on maneuvers prior to the attack as a precaution, so the attack wouldn't be as damaging as it could have been. In fact, the Japanese devastated the Pacific Fleet, sinking four U.S. battleships and severely damaging four others. In addition, three light cruisers, three destroyers, and four smaller vessels were demolished or heavily damaged, and 75 percent of the island's military air fleet was annihilated before the planes could take to the sky. The value of the aircraft carriers that survived because they were on maneuvers wouldn't be realized until months later, at the Battle of Midway.

An Excuse to Fight

Perhaps most important is that Roosevelt didn't need a Japanese attack to bring the United States into the war. Though officially neutral at the time, the country was actively engaged in fighting the Axis by providing war materials to Great Britain and other Allied nations via the Lend-Lease Act. Furthermore, antiwar sentiment was waning dramatically as Americans grew increasingly angered by Japanese and German aggression. It was just a matter of time before the United States took off the gloves and waded into the war that was engulfing the world.

In FDR's Defense

It's a huge disservice to one of the nation's greatest presidents to assume that FDR would intentionally sacrifice the lives of thousands of troops and civilians, as well as cripple the country's most vital Pacific naval base, just for the opportunity to enter a war that a growing number of Americans and political leaders were starting to see as inevitable. Japan was intent on aggressively expanding its sphere of influence in the Pacific—territories that included American allies and interests. But as the drumbeat of war grew louder around the world, there was no way the United States could let that happen, despite the country's publicly stated neutrality. What's more, Roosevelt already had the required number of congressional votes for war when the time came.

It's important to note that several major investigations were conducted to determine what went wrong at Pearl Harbor, including an inquiry ordered by Roosevelt just 11 days after the attack. None found cause to suspect the president of any wrongdoing.

D. B. COOPER:
MAN OF MYSTERY

❀ ❖ ❀

D. B. Cooper is perhaps the most famous criminal alias
since Jack the Ripper. Although the fate of the infamous hijacker
remains a mystery, the origins of the nom de crime
"D. B. Cooper" is a matter that's easier to solve.

The Crime

At Portland (Oregon) International Airport the night before
Thanksgiving in 1971, a man in a business suit, reportedly in his
mid-40s, boarded Northwest Orient Airlines flight 305 bound for
Seattle, Washington. He had booked his seat under the name **Dan
Cooper**. Once the flight was airborne, Cooper informed a flight
attendant that his briefcase contained an explosive device. In the
days before thorough baggage inspection was standard procedure
at airports, this was a viable threat. The flight attendant relayed
the information to the pilots, who immediately put the plane into a
holding pattern so that Cooper could communicate his demands to
FBI agents on the ground.

When the Boeing 727 landed at Seattle–Tacoma Airport,
the other passengers were released in exchange for $200,000 in
unmarked $20 bills and two sets of parachutes. FBI agents pho-
tographed each bill before handing over the ransom and then
scrambled a fighter plane to follow the passenger craft when Cooper demanded that it take off for Mexico City via Reno, Nevada.
At 10,000 feet, Cooper lowered the aft stairs of the aircraft and,
with the ransom money strapped to his chest, parachuted into the
night, still dressed in his business suit. The pilot noted the area
as being near the Lewis River, 25 miles north of Portland, somewhere over the Cascade Mountains.

The mysterious hijacker was never seen again. The FBI found
a number of fingerprints on the plane that didn't match those of
the other passengers or members of the crew, but the only real

clue that Cooper left behind was his necktie. On February 10, 1980, an eight-year-old boy found $5,800 in decaying $20 bills along the Columbia River, just a few miles northwest of Vancouver, Washington. The serial numbers matched those included in the ransom. Other than that, not a single note of the ransom money has turned up in circulation.

Origins of the Name

The FBI launched a massive hunt for the man who had hijacked Flight 305. This included checking the rap sheets of every known felon with the name Dan Cooper, just in case the hijacker had been stupid enough to use his real name. When Portland agents interviewed a man by the name of D. B. Cooper, the story was picked up by a local reporter. This D. B. Cooper was cleared of any involvement in the case, but the alias stuck and was adopted by the national media.

Who was Dan Cooper?

Countless books, TV shows, and even a movie have attempted to answer this question. The FBI has investigated some 10,000 people, dozens of whom had at some point confessed to family or friends that they were the real D. B. Cooper. In October 2007, the FBI announced that it had finally obtained a partial DNA profile of Cooper with evidence lifted from the tie he left on the plane. This has helped rule out many of those suspected of (or who have confessed to) the hijacking.

The author of one book about the case, a retired FBI agent, offered a $100,000 reward for just one of the bills from the ransom money. He's never had to pay out. Officially, the FBI does not believe that Cooper survived the jump. However, no evidence of his body or the bright yellow and red parachute he used to make the jump has ever been found. On December 31, 2007, more than 36 years after the man forever known as D. B. Cooper disappeared into the night sky, the FBI revived the case by publishing never-before-seen sketches of the hijacker and appealing for new witnesses.

THE LOST CITY OF ATLANTIS

Ever since Plato first mentioned the ancient civilization of Atlantis in his dialogues Timaeus *and* Critias, *academic analysts have debated the existence of the lost continent. Was the prophetic philosopher fabricating a tale or indicating valuable information?*

According to Plato, the ancient civilization of Atlantis was a colossal naval power that conquered many parts of Western Europe and Africa more than 9,000 years before the time of Solon, or approximately 9500 B.C. After a failed attempt to invade Athens, the entire continent collapsed into the ocean "in a single day and night of misfortune." Since Plato never bothered to divulge the manner of demise, historians have been left to argue over the authenticity of the alleged Atlantis. The skeptical side of the ledger contends that Plato was using his creative leverage to force his readers to both examine and question the limitations and logistics of greed, government, and power. Simply put, Plato's message was that power corrupts and the price paid is high.

Identifying Atlantis

In 2004, Robert Sarmast, a U.S. author, architect, and explorer, announced that he had found circumstantial evidence of the existence of Atlantis 1,500 meters deep in the Mediterranean Sea between Cyprus and Syria. But Sarmast also admitted that he "cannot yet provide tangible proof in the form of bricks and mortar, as the artifacts are still buried under several meters of sediment. We hope that future expeditions will be able to uncover the sediment and bring back physical proof." Until that happens, however, the evidence of Atlantis is inconclusive.

PENNIES ARE HARMLESS

*Pedestrians nationwide halt in their tracks at
the cautionary tale of the penny that, if dropped from the top
of the Empire State Building, kills on impact. However,
a few exercises in reason neatly dispel this myth.*

The Physics

When a penny free-falls from any great height, it gains speed due
to the force of gravity. But it is also slowed by air resistance. To
determine how hard a penny would hit a pedestrian at the base of
the Empire State Building, its terminal velocity, or maximum downward speed (which factors in air resistance), must be calculated.

Myth-busting amateurs everywhere have unanimously
declared that by the time the proverbial penny hits the proverbial
pedestrian's head, the most damage it could cause would be a
small cut. The variables in determining terminal velocity, such as
air density and surface area of the object, are difficult to pin down.
The surface area depends on whether the penny falls flat—which
would slow it down more—or turns on its edge. But regardless of
the specifics of the calculation, the penny would certainly be going
slower than 100 miles per hour as it approached the base of the
building—probably a lot slower.

The Logistics

Even without the weapon of fancy math, the Empire State Building has falling-penny-prevention tricks up its sleeve. Trick number
one is the 83rd floor, which juts out and "catches" pennies and
other debris before they make it to the ground. Trick number two
is the unique updraft created by the building's massive structure.
Wind travels up the side of the building with such power that
things thrown off the top are often thrown right back up, usually
landing on the 81st floor. So paranoid pedestrians can rest assured
that a flung penny wouldn't do much damage—in fact, it would
probably never reach the ground.

SIMPLE TWIST OF FATE

*Is it possible that screenwriters scripted
the special effects that accompanied the movie
Twister when it made the rounds on the
drive-in-movie circuit in Ontario, Canada?*

In 1974, Hollywood introduced the innovative but ultimately ineffective concept of Sensurround to promote the movie *Earthquake*. Featuring a sonic sound explosion that actually shook the seats to create the sensation of an earthquake, the gimmick was dismissed by both cinematic critics and finicky fans. Tinseltown championed other innovations, such as THX sound and IMAX, to get couch potatoes out of the house and into theaters. In 1996, Sensurround made a dramatic return to the screens, scripted with not-so-subtle substance by nature itself.

All myths worth their weight in mystery must be built on a basic foundation of truth, and in the case of the movie *Twister*, the facts are as fascinating as fiction. On May 20, 1996, a tornado tore through the community of Thorold, Ontario, a sleepy little hamlet in the Niagara region of southern Ontario. Most of the city escaped major damage, but the same could not be said of the local drive-in theater, which saw all of its four screens ripped and ravaged by the tempest. Like the whirling winds, rumors were soon flying that the tornado had touched down just as spectators at the drive-in were fueling themselves with popcorn and watching the blockbuster movie *Twister*. The cars-only cinema was indeed showing the disaster flick, but the tornado actually hit during the day, not at night when the movie was being played.

❊❊❊

- *A further and more far-fetched twist on the story is that the tornado hit during a scene in* Twister *when a tornado rips through a drive-in theater that's showing* The Shining.

MYTHICAL SEA MONSTERS

✳ ❈ ✳

*Seafarers of old were respectful and wary of the strange
creatures that lurked below the surface. The reflection
of sunlight upon water, overwhelming homesickness,
or too much drink caused many sailors to see monsters.*

Kraken

The kraken was one of the most horrifying creatures a sailor
could encounter. It was believed to be a many-armed monster—
described by one 14th-century writer as resembling an uprooted
tree—that would wrap itself around a ship, pull down its masts,
and drag it to the bottom of the ocean. The creature was so large
that it could be mistaken for a small island. Early whalers often
saw tentacle and suction marks on the bodies of sperm whales,
which served to cement the kraken's terrifying reputation. Modern
sailors recognize the kraken as a giant squid, which is an enormous, octopuslike mollusk. The giant squid has a long, torpedo-
shaped body, even longer tentacles, and eyes that are more than
18 inches in diameter. They grow to lengths of 60 feet (sometimes
more) and weigh nearly a ton. Although not often seen by humans,
these deep-sea dwellers have been known to attack whales and
tanker ships.

Sea Serpents

Some of the most famous sea monsters, such as Loch Ness's
"Nessie" and Chesapeake Bay's "Chessie," are of the serpent
persuasion. Whether in saltwater or freshwater, a sea serpent
looks similar to a snake or dragon and usually has several "humps."
Although cryptozoologists hold out hope that these creatures are
some sort of surviving dinosaur, that's not likely the case. It is
theorized that freshwater sea serpents, such as Lake Champlain's
"Champ," are actually snakes—perhaps giant anacondas—that
escaped from a passing boat. Naysayers point out that tropical
anacondas don't do well in upstate New York winters.

Ocean-dwelling sea serpents are easier to explain. For centuries, witnesses have mistaken basking sharks, rows of diving dolphins, clumps of sargassum seaweed, seals, and even undulating waves for the head and humps of a sea serpent. Perhaps the most common explanation, however, is the oarfish, which resembles an eel and grows to 26 feet in length (and has been reported at three times that size).

Mermaids

Mermaids—aquatic creatures with a woman's torso and the tail of a fish—have been spotted in oceans and lakes around the world since 1000 B.C. In the past few centuries, several supposedly authentic mermaid specimens have been displayed, but all of them have proved to be hoaxes. These include P. T. Barnum's famous "Feejee Mermaid"; taxidermic creations consisting of sewn parts of monkeys and fish; and "Jenny Hannivers," which are carcasses of rays, skates, or cuttlefish carved and varnished to resemble a winged sea monster with a hideous human head. The name is likely an Anglicization of *jeune de Anvers,* or "girl of Antwerp," in reference to the Belgian port where 16th- and 17th-century sailors made and sold these popular souvenirs.

Seals and sea otters, both known for their playful interaction with humans, have likely been mistaken for mermaids. The legendary selkie—a mythical seal that sheds its skin on land and resumes it while in the sea—derives from mermaid folklore. The dugong and manatee are both cow-like, sea-dwelling mammals that nurse their young above water. In fact, the word *manatee* comes from the Carib word for breasts, which could explain why mermaids are said to be naked from the waist up. Of course, it's also possible that mermaid stories were made up by hapless sailors or fishermen who needed an excuse for spying on skinny-dipping women.

FRANKLIN FLIES A KITE

*As it turns out, Benjamin Franklin did not discover electricity.
What's more, the kite he famously flew in 1752 while
conducting an experiment was not struck by lightning.
If it had been, Franklin would be remembered as a colonial
publisher and assemblyman killed by his own curiosity.*

Before Ben

Blessed with one of the keenest minds in history, Benjamin Franklin was a scientific genius who made groundbreaking discoveries in the basic nature and properties of electricity. Electrical science, however, dates to 1600, when Dr. William Gilbert, physician to Queen Elizabeth, published a treatise about his research on electricity and magnetism. European inventors who later expanded on Gilbert's knowledge included Otto von Guericke of Germany, Charles Francois Du Fay of France, and Stephen Gray of England.

The Science of Electricity

Franklin became fascinated with electricity after seeing a demonstration by an itinerant showman (and doctor) named Archibald Spencer in Boston in 1743. Two years later, he bought a Leyden jar—a contraption invented by a Dutch scientist that used a glass container wrapped in foil to create a crude battery. Other researchers had demonstrated the properties of the device, and Franklin set about to increase its capacity to generate electricity while testing his own scientific hypotheses. Among the principles he established was the conservation of charge, one of the most important laws of physics. In a paper published in 1750, he announced the discovery of the induced charge and broadly outlined the existence of the electron. His experiments led him to coin many of the terms currently used in the science of electricity, such as battery, conductor, condenser, charge, discharge, uncharged, negative, minus, plus, electric shock, and electrician.

As Franklin came to understand the nature of electricity, he began to theorize about the electrical nature of lightning. In 1751, he outlined in a British scientific journal his idea for an experiment that involved placing a long metal rod on a high tower or steeple to draw an electric charge from passing thunder clouds, which would throw off visible electric sparks. A year later, French scientist Georges-Louis Leclerc successfully conducted such an experiment.

The Kite Runner

Franklin had not heard of Leclerc's success when he undertook his own experiment in June 1752. Instead of a church spire, he affixed his kite to a sharp, pointed wire. To the end of his kite string he tied a key, and to the key a ribbon made of silk (for insulation). While flying his kite on a cloudy day as a thunderstorm approached, Franklin noticed that loose threads on the kite string stood erect, as if they had been suspended from a common conductor. The key sparked when he touched it, showing it was charged with electricity. But had the kite actually been struck by lightning, Franklin would likely have been killed, as was Professor Georg Wilhelm Richmann of St. Petersburg, Russia, when he attempted the same experiment a few months later.

The Lightning Rod

Although Franklin did not discover electricity, he did uncover many of its fundamental principles and proved that lightning is, in fact, electricity. He used his knowledge to create the lightning rod, an invention that today protects land structures and ships at sea. He never patented the lightning rod but instead generously promoted it as a boon to humankind. In 21st-century classrooms, the lightning rod is still cited as a classic example of the way fundamental science can produce practical inventions.

MONKEE BUSINESS

*He now sits in a cage at Corcoran State Prison,
but is it possible that Charles Manson, the wild-eyed cult
leader who ruled over a posse of deranged, drug-addled
followers, almost became a member of the Monkees?*

In the mid-1960s, perceptive TV producers Bob Rafelson and
Bert Schneider decided to cash in on the Beatles' onscreen success in *A Hard Day's Night* by formulating their own recipe for a
boy-band bonanza. Borrowing from the Liverpool lads' madcap
antics and animalistic moniker, Rafelson and Schneider concocted
a half-hour comedy show that featured music, skits, and general
goofiness. They called it *The Monkees.* In September 1965, an
open audition attracted 437 musicians, actors, acrobats, hippies,
has-beens, and wannabes, including future Buffalo Springfield
guitarist Steven Stills, Lovin' Spoonful founder John Sebastian,
and Three Dog Night vocalist Danny Hutton.

Another member of the Tinseltown music fraternity rumored
to have staked a claim to fame in front of the producers was a
scruffy mite named Charles Manson, who would gain infamy
for masterminding a bizarre, ritualistic murder spree in August
1969. That event eventually put the diminutive former felon back
into prison for a lifetime stay, but a popular myth placed Manson
among the throng of Hollywood hopefuls trying out for a part in
the show. Although the tale has some credibility—Manson did
have musical ability and befriended Beach Boys drummer Den-
nis Wilson, who helped the maniac record demo tapes—he could
not have attended the audition. At the time, he was strumming
his guitar in a prison at McNeil Island, Washington, and wasn't
released until March 1967. Even if he had somehow wrangled a
weekend pass, Manson was 30 years old at the time, making him
ineligible to be one of the "4 Insane Boys, Age 17–21," as the job
posting indicated. In the end, though, it appears he did meet one
of those requirements.

WHO'S THAT LADY?

The Mona Lisa *has long been the subject
of speculation, admiration, and controversy.
The portrait is adored by millions and possibly worth
billions, but who exactly was da Vinci's subject?*

The Mysterious Florentine

For centuries, the identity of the model who posed for Leonardo da Vinci's masterpiece prompted heated debate. There were no records among da Vinci's papers pertaining to the painting, and the artwork itself was unnamed, unsigned, and undated. What's more, the finished portrait was never delivered to the man who commissioned it. Da Vinci started work on his seminal piece in 1503 and kept it in his possession until his death in 1519. For decades, the image was known simply as "a certain Florentine lady," and it wasn't until the historian Giorgio Vasari published a biography of da Vinci's life and work in 1550 that the painting became known as *Mona Lisa.* Vasari claimed the lady in question was Madam Lisa Gherardini del Giocondo, the 24-year-old wife of a wealthy Florentine. But Vasari was known to use literal license in many of his writings, and skeptical historians discounted many of his claims.

In the Running

Over the years, half a dozen names were mentioned as possible sitters for da Vinci's greatest work. Some scholars suggested that the muse was Cecilia Gallerani, one of the many mistresses of Ludovico Sforza, Duke of Milan. Gallerani was the subject of da Vinci's *The Lady with an Ermine,* which he completed in 1490. But because her image had already been committed to canvas, most researchers discounted her. Other art analysts believed that the person in the portrait was Isabella of Naples, the granddaughter of King Ferdinand I and daughter of King Alphonse II and his wife, Ippolita Sforza. The rumor mill even generated a story that Isabella and da Vinci were a contracted couple, inked and linked together to produce outstanding offspring. The most vocal supporter of Isabella as da Vinci's subject was historian Maike Vogt-Luerssen, who wrote a book titled *Who is Mona Lisa? In Search of her Identity.* Vogt-Luerssen's theory was dismissed, primarily because she claimed that the portrait was painted as early as 1489. Other pretenders to the *Mona Lisa* throne included Costanza d'Avalos, Duchess of Amalfi and a noted poet, and da Vinci's own mother, Caterina.

And the Winner Is...

Despite such speculation, the truth was right there all along. In 2005, it was ascertained that Vasari's information was accurate. Armin Schlechter, a manuscript expert at the University of Heidelberg, discovered a margin note in a text that was once owned by Agostino Vespucci, a friend and confidante of da Vinci's. The note explains that while da Vinci was working on *The Battle of Anghiari* in the Great Council Hall of the Palazzo Vecchio in Florence, Italy, in 1503, he was also working on a pet project—a portrait of Lisa Gherardini, the wife of a local merchant, Franceso del Giocondo. Today, we call her Mona Lisa.

Those Lips, Those Eyes

Ever since the *Mona Lisa* was first glimpsed by an adoring public, admirers have maintained that the subject's eyes are alive and follow their every move. How did da Vinci do it?

The artist used a delicate mixture of light, color, and tone to create a masterpiece that has perplexed art lovers for centuries. Employing a technique called *sfumato* (in Italian, it means "smoky"), da Vinci blended color and tones into subtle shadows that created depth and deception. At the time, it was uncommon to use soft, extremely fine shading instead of lines to delineate forms and features, and da Vinci described the technique as "without lines or borders, in the manner of smoke or beyond the focus plane." Depending on how the light falls upon the portrait and the angle from which the observer views it, Mona Lisa's smile can be perceived to be either a grin or a grimace, and her eyes seem to shift and sway.

SUSPICIOUS SPELL

When the bewitched women in Shakespeare's Scottish tragedy Macbeth *gathered around the cauldron to summon up a spell or two, they did not dispatch their dirge with the phrase, "Bubble, bubble, toil and trouble."*

No one should ever confuse the musings of quirky quacker Scrooge McDuck with the wise and witty writings of William Shakespeare, but that's exactly what occurred when the peculiar pen of Walt Disney and his stable of scribes met the beautiful balladry of the Bard. In the opening scene of Act 4 of Shakespeare's play *Macbeth,* three witches stand around a steaming kettle and warble the famous phrase, "Double, double, toil and trouble, Fire burn and cauldron bubble." The poetic punch of that couplet remained untainted until we were presented with Disney's classic cartoon "Much Ado About Scrooge," a jocular jaunt that parodies Shakespeare's classic tragedy. In the wonderful world of Disney, the trio of ducks reverses the words in Will's rhyming scheme, declaring, "Bubble, bubble, toil and trouble, Leave this island on the double." From that moment on, things were never the same in Stratford-upon-Avon, as countless schoolchildren were convinced that McDuck's verse was right and the *Macbeth* rhyme was wrong. English teachers around the country could only wring their hands and hang their heads.

The trend continued into the modern age of television when, in 1991, the comedy series *Home Improvement,* which would later become a number-one-rated program, presented an episode titled, you guessed it, "Bubble, Bubble, Toil and Trouble." The plot revolved around a whirlpool and a botched bathroom renovation. It goes without saying that *Tool Time* in prime time didn't do Shakespeare any favors.

SNAKES ALIVE!

*If you're bitten by a poisonous snake, leave your pocketknife
alone and use your mouth to call for help.*

It's a dramatic scene in many old Westerns: After a cowboy is bitten by a rattlesnake, he bravely carves an "X" into the wound and
sucks out the venom. This first-aid approach has become so common in popular culture that most people assume it's the right thing
to do. But here's why it doesn't work:

Cutting into the site of a snakebite can damage underlying
tissue and increase the possibility of infection. Sucking the wound
is unlikely to remove any venom—and it puts the person at risk of
absorbing the poison through mucous membranes. Instead, the bite
should be washed thoroughly with soap and water, if it's available.

A Snake Primer

There are four types of venomous snakes in the United States:
rattlesnakes, copperheads, cottonmouth water moccasins, and coral
snakes. Each can be deadly, but whether the snake injects venom
with its bite depends on its mood and its precision. About 50 percent
of the time, snakes deliver a venomless "dry bite." Either it figures the
prey is too large to consume and chooses not to release the venom,
or it doesn't release the poison at the right time. However, even a
venomless snakebite can cause serious—even life-threatening—injury
and infection if not treated.

There are three types of snake venom, and each has a different effect
on the body: Cytotoxic venom attacks the cells, neurotoxic venom
attacks the nerves, and hemotoxic venom affects the blood-clotting
process. Venomous snakes use their fangs to deliver venom directly
into the bloodstream (much like a hypodermic needle), and the victim
often feels the effects quickly. Anyone bitten by a poisonous snake
should seek immediate medical attention, which could involve the
administration of an antivenin. Time is of the essence.

A ROYAL FLUSH

❋❖❋

Every year at the end of January, rumors begin to swirl that the sewer systems in several major cities fail due to the number of toilets that are flushed during halftime of the Super Bowl.

A Mad Dash

During Super Bowl XVIII in 1984, a water main in Salt Lake City ruptured, dampening the sporting spirit in that community. The next day, conversations around office water coolers were rife with rumors that toilet trauma, prompted by a flood of beverage-logged football fans all using the facilities at the same time, had caused the sewer systems of numerous cities to clog up. Such a myth would almost make sense if it were applied to the final of the World Cup of Soccer, where there is continuous action without stoppages of any kind until the halftime break. But anyone who has sat through the six-plus-hour spectacle known as the Super Bowl realizes that there is no merit to this tall tale. The North American brand of football—especially the game played on that particular Sunday—has numerous breaks, pauses, and lapses throughout. So to suggest there is a simultaneous dash to the latrine at any time during this all-day marathon is silly.

Can't-Miss TV

The quality of Super Bowl TV commercials (which cost $2.7 million for a 30-second spot during Super Bowl XLII) usually keeps even disinterested viewers glued to their seats. Although the ads aired on Super Bowl Sunday are among the most highly anticipated events in that day's lineup, most of them are shown during the pre-game, halftime, and post-game spectacles, leaving valuable lulls during football action for human nature's pause for the cause.

❋❋❋

- *The roots of the flushing fabrication can be traced as far back as the 1930s, when audiences supposedly made a mass mad dash for the can only during breaks in the popular* Amos 'n Andy *radio program.*

MISREMEMBERING MEMORIAL DAY

*On Memorial Day, people in the United States
remember the nation's war dead. But how well do they
remember the history of the day itself?*

Ask the average person when Memorial Day began, and you'll
probably get an answer as vague as "after World War I or II." But
the origins of Memorial Day stretch back to an earlier century in a
conflict that divided the country before serving to unite it.

In the years following the Civil War, people in the North and
South often decorated the graves of loved ones lost in battle. These
informal remembrances evolved into celebrations called Decoration
Day in dozens of cities north and south of the Mason-Dixon Line.

The first national Decoration Day took place on May 30,
1868 (when flowers were likely to be in bloom across the nation),
by order of the commander of the Grand Army of the Republic,
General John Logan. In his General Order No. 11, Logan decreed
that May 30 be set aside for "decorating the graves of comrades
who died in defense of their country during the late rebellion."

Of course, language like that didn't make the new holiday very
popular with the southern states. They refused to acknowledge
it until after World War I, when it was expanded to include those
who had died in *all* American wars. By that time, many people had
begun calling it Memorial Day, but it didn't become an official
federal holiday until 1971. At that time, the holiday was moved to
the last Monday in May—to the chagrin of many who felt that the
solemnity of the celebration was not enhanced by making it part of
a "long holiday weekend."

Memorial Day Today

Memorial Day is still sometimes referred to as Decoration Day, and
many people lay flowers on the graves of all of their loved ones, not
just those who had fallen in war.

STARS & STRIPES SEAMSTRESS

*Schoolchildren are taught numerous things about
the American Revolution that aren't necessarily supported
by history. Among the debated stories is the "fact"
that Betsy Ross stitched the first American flag.*

Who was Betsy Ross? Elizabeth (Betsy) Griscom was born in
1752 to a Quaker family, the eighth of 17 children. When she turned
21 in 1773, she eloped with an Episcopalian named John Ross, and
because of their union she was expelled from her congregation.
Before they met, John and Betsy had both worked as apprentice
upholsterers, so they decided to start their own business. Sadly
for young Betsy, John died in January 1776 while serving with the
Pennsylvania militia. The patriotic seamstress continued to run the
business, and she soon expanded her efforts, making and mending
gear for the Continental Army (a receipt exists that shows she made
flags for the Pennsylvania State Navy in 1777).

So she *could* have sewn the first flag. Yes, but there's no
proof that she actually did. In 1870, at a meeting of the Historical
Society of Pennsylvania, Betsy's grandson, William Canby, insisted
that George Washington had sought out Betsy and asked her to
design and create a flag for the new country. Other Canby relatives
swore out affidavits in agreement.

Suppose Washington had indeed asked her to make the first
flag. When he became the first president, why didn't he do something to honor her? Why did her contribution never come up
during her lifetime? Betsy Ross died in 1836, yet her family waited
34 years to announce her accomplishment. It could be that the
family legend embellishes a grain of truth. Betsy Ross did make
flags for the war effort, so she could have lived her life believing
she had made the first American flag.

SLIPSTREAMING FOR SAVINGS

When the price of gasoline is sky high, everyone looks for ways to save money at the pump. But will opening a truck's tailgate really save fuel? The penny-wise want to know.

While talking with his pal Phil at the local service station, frugal Frank suggests a way to save money on gas. "When driving our pickup trucks, we should always keep our tailgates down," proclaims the thrifty man. "That way, drag will be reduced and we'll get more miles to the gallon." Phil glances at his own truck, scratches his head, and says, "Maybe so, but how will I keep my dog from sliding out?"

On paper, opening one's tailgate to save fuel certainly looks plausible. Even a rudimentary understanding of aerodynamics suggests that swirling air trapped in an open box (the truck bed) will introduce drag, thereby increasing fuel consumption. Yet this notion doesn't quite jibe with the facts.

Kind of a Drag

Car companies put a lot of effort into designing their trucks so that air flows just above the tailgate, which will decrease drag. Other efficiency-boosting innovations include "skirts" on the sides of truck trailers and smaller gaps between the truck and trailer. Researcher Kevin Cooper has spent more than 35 years exploring vehicle aerodynamics for Canada's National Research Council, and his studies have shown that an open tailgate often *increases* drag. Here's why:

Backward-facing surfaces create much of a vehicle's drag. When a tailgate is left open or is removed completely, it increases the drag on the back of the truck's cab. The cab has a greater surface area than the tailgate, which erases any potential gains. Furthermore, "gate-droppers" can also experience increased rearward lift at higher speeds. A truly effective way to reduce fuel consumption is to install a tonneau or hard bed cover, which will increase aerodynamics and result in better gas mileage.

THE WORLD'S FIRST CIVILIZATION

The fame of the ancient Egyptians—pyramids, pharaohs, eye makeup!—has led to the common misconception that ancient Egypt was the world's first civilization.

Most Western scholars agree that the Sumerian civilization in Mesopotamia, located between the Tigris and Euphrates rivers in modern-day Iraq, was the first. Yet a deeper look reveals that there is a whole pageant of contenders for that coveted prize.

The Contestants

1. Ancient Sumer. The first civilization is believed to have begun around 4000 B.C. The great city of Ur, associated with Sumer, is possibly the world's first city. Archaeological evidence suggests that "pre-civilized" cultures lived in the Tigris and Euphrates river valleys long before the emergence of Sumer.

2. The Harappan. Next in line are the ancient Indus Valley civilizations, located in the Indus and Ghaggar-Hakra river valleys in modern-day Pakistan and western India. The first mature civilization associated with this area is called the Harappan, generally cited as beginning around 3500 B.C., thus placing it in time after Sumer. However, it is clear that agricultural communities had inhabited the area since at least 9000 B.C.

3. Ancient Egypt. Located in Africa's Nile Valley, it is generally cited as beginning in 3200 B.C. But as with the Indus Valley civilization, it is difficult to establish a firm beginning date because agricultural societies had settled in the Nile River Valley since the tenth millennium B.C.

4. and 5. Ancient China and Elam. The final two, and least known, contestants (from the Western perspective) are the ancient Chinese civilizations and the Elam civilization of modern-day Iran. The Elamite kingdom began around 2700 B.C., though recent evidence suggests that a city existed in this area at a far earlier date—perhaps early enough to rival Sumer. Meanwhile, the ancient Chinese civilizations, located in the Yangtze and Yellow river valleys, are said to have begun around 2200 B.C.

The Criteria

The most salient feature of a civilization is a city, which, unlike a village, should have large religious and government buildings, evidence of social stratification (mansions for the rich and shacks for the poor), and complex infrastructure such as roads and irrigation. Civilizations are also defined by elaborate social systems, organized trade relations with outside groups, and the development of writing.

Marking a "civilization" is difficult because in all five possible cradles of civilization described above, complex societies lived in the same areas long before true civilization emerged. In fact, this is surely why civilizations first developed in these regions—human groups lived in the areas before the development of agriculture. Human populations have roamed the sprawling Eurasian continent for at least 100,000 years.

The emergence of civilization can be seen as the result of culture after culture living in one geographic area for countless generations until something happened that set these seminomadic groups on the path to civilization.

That Certain Something

Historians agree that the development of agriculture around 10,000 B.C. was the "something" that led to civilization. There is a strong correlation between agriculture, population size and density, and social complexity. Once agriculture began, human populations were increasingly tied to the land. They could no longer be nomadic, moving around at different times of the year and setting up temporary villages. As people continued to stay in one place and social relationships became more hierarchical, permanent villages developed into cities.

ZAPPA'S PAPPY

Frank Zappa was the father of four kids—Moon Unit, Dweezil, Ahmet Rodan, and Diva—but he was not the son of Mr. Greenjeans from the Captain Kangaroo *television show.*

Rock music has seen its share of off-the-wall characters over the years, including Alice Cooper, Ozzy Osbourne, and Marilyn Manson. But few have enjoyed the notoriety of Frank Zappa, who, independently and with the band Mothers of Invention, created some of the most outrageous—and influential—music of the 1960s and '70s.

Zappa courted controversy and delighted in challenging the status quo, so his fans were stunned to learn that the legendary rocker was the son of actor Hugh Brannum, better known to children's television viewers as Captain Kangaroo's mild-mannered sidekick, Mr. Greenjeans.

The story isn't true, but the rumor has been rolling since 1969, when Zappa released his independent album *Hot Rats*. The record includes a track titled "Son of Mr. Green Genes," a sarcastic little ditty that encourages listeners to eat their vegetables—along with their shoes and the box they came in. That's so Zappa, but it has nothing to do with the man who fathered him.

Zappa's fans were amused by the idea that the social iconoclast was the spawn of one of television's most staid personalities, but he set the record straight in his autobiography *The Real Frank Zappa:* "Because I recorded a song called 'Son of Mr. Green Genes' on the *Hot Rats* album in 1969, people have believed for years that the character with that name on the *Captain Kangaroo* TV show was my 'real' dad. No, he was not." Actually, Zappa's father was a Sicilian immigrant named Francis Vincent Zappa, Sr.

❈❈❈

- *Another version of the urban legend is even more absurd: This time, the son of meek Mr. Greenjeans is none other than the gun-loving heavy-metal rocker Ted Nugent.*

THE MYTH OF THE BIG EASY

*After Hurricane Katrina, lawmakers and media commentators
questioned the wisdom of reconstructing New Orleans, a city that
they claimed was "built ten feet below sea level."*

According to recent geographical surveys, about 50 percent of New
Orleans rests at or above sea level, and the other half rarely drops
lower than minus six feet. Of the few points that lay ten feet below
sea level—approximately 50 acres of the 181 total square miles of
the city—none have been developed for commercial use or habita-
tion, serving instead as culverts, canals, and highway underpasses.

A Precarious Edge of Disaster

Geography, nature, and economics have conspired over the centuries to make New Orleans particularly vulnerable to floods. The
location that became "the inevitable city on an impossible site"
was chosen by French settlers in 1718 because it offered an easy
portage between the Mississippi River—the main water artery for
the interior of North America—and Lake Ponchartrain, an outlet
into the Gulf of Mexico for trading ships. (It was well into the 19th
century before the mouth of the Mississippi became readily navi-
gable for oceangoing ships.)

Isle d'Orleans

Although that land consisted mostly of cypress swamps, silt
deposits left by seasonal floods over thousands of years created
high ground along the banks of the river. The famous French
Quarter—the original core of the city—was laid out on part of
this elevated ground, some 15 feet above sea level. Over decades,
the higher ground along the bending curve of the Mississippi was
also settled, as the Crescent City grew behind an expanding system of levees. Because it was surrounded by a river, a lake, and
swamps, the French referred to New Orleans as *Isle d'Orleans*,
and for a century the city was a physical and cultural island, an
outpost of the Caribbean on U.S. soil.

Developing the Land

The jewel of Jefferson's Louisiana Purchase, New Orleans grew faster than any other American city between 1810 and 1840, becoming the country's third largest after New York and Baltimore. But New Orleans's improbable geography limited its growth. The lower-lying land remained undeveloped until the early 1900s, when engineer A. Baldwin Wood invented an industrial-size screw pump for an ambitious drainage system that was built to protect the city from floods.

It's Sinking...

With nature seemingly under control, New Orleans expanded greatly during the 20th century. The shores of Lake Pontchartrain, which represent some of the lowest-lying land, were filled in and new levees were built. But the levee system also stopped the seasonal deposits of silt that created most of the land in southern Louisiana. As a result, the city and much of its surrounding landscape is sinking as the loose soil settles without replenishment. Scientists estimate that the current rate of subsidence ranges from one-third to one and a half inches per year, with the possibility that 15,000 square miles will fall at or below sea level within 70 years.

Although the flooding of New Orleans after Hurricane Katrina was definitely a manmade disaster—the levee system designed by the U.S. Army Corps of Engineers failed to perform to its design specifications—the leveed "bowl" in which the city rests is inevitably subject to flooding.

Not So Easy

So New Orleans was not "built ten feet below sea level," but the future of the Big Easy is precarious. A recent study by the National Oceanic and Atmospheric Administration estimates that areas around coastal Mississippi and Louisiana may sink as much as one foot over the next decade, and scientists predict that world sea levels may rise as much as three feet in the next century because of global warming.

DO REAL CATS HATE WATER?

One of humankind's most beloved creatures is mysterious in many ways, and a popular feline myth is that cats hate water.

Some cats may fear water because of how we use it around them: Many a noisy tomcat has had a bucket of water thrown its way, and mischievous kids might tease Mittens with a spray from the garden hose. Forcing a bath on a cat is a sure way to get it to loathe water, but that's no different for any other animal. There's actually a lot of evidence that cats love water. Many cats don't hesitate to jump into a filled sink or running shower and actually seem amused as water from a faucet drips over their heads. One reason for the positive reaction is that cats are attracted to the motion and sound of water.

Among the larger cats, climate makes a difference. Tigers, lions, jaguars, and ocelots from the hot savannas are likely to fancy a plunge into cool, refreshing streams and ponds to get a break from the heat. Logically, cats that live in cold environments—including snow leopards, lynx, bobcats, and cougars—show little interest in getting wet.

Cats are, of course, creatures of habit, so a pet that has been exposed to water since it was young will tolerate a bath much better than one whose human companion shielded it from water out of fear for its safety.

Star Swimmers

Although many people believe that cats can't swim, they're actually naturals in the water. The fishing cat (*Prionailurus viverrinus*) is a non-domestic breed from Malaysia and parts of Indonesia. It dives headfirst into the water to grab fish with its jaws. Another water-loving cat is the Turkish Van, a domesticated cat that lives near Lake Van in Turkey. You don't have to coach this cat into the water; it will swim in a small pond or pool and has even been spotted swimming into the harbor to greet fishing boats!

FASTER, AND SLOWER, THAN THE SPEED OF LIGHT

*Albert Einstein taught us that the speed of light
is constant at 186,282 miles per second. An unbending,
iron law of nature, right? Wrong.*

For years, diligent laboratory scientists have sped up, and greatly slowed down, the components of light. They have actually made light travel many times faster than the "speed of light." And they've decelerated light to a plodding pace that wouldn't merit a speeding ticket.

Speed it Up!

At New York's University of Rochester in 2006, scientists led by optics professor Robert W. Boyd fired a laser into an optical glass fiber. The fiber had been laced with the rare metal erbium, which amplified the signal it produced—by a lot. Before the entire pulse even entered the fiber, part of it appeared at the fiber's end and then raced backward faster than the speed of light. The process was attributed to the erbium, which gave extra energy to the light. Professor Boyd said, with some understatement, "I find it nifty."

Slow it Down!

The University of Rochester team has also taken the opposite tack and slowed down light. In 2003, Boyd's crew shone a green laser through a tiny ruby in an attempt to saturate the chromium atoms that give the gem its reddish tint. When a second green laser zapped the jewel, its light slowed to 127 miles per hour, which is 5.3 million times slower than the light of the first laser. In 1999, scientists at Harvard University slowed laser light to 38 mph, a speed slower than the legal vehicular limit on most interstates. They did this by shooting a laser through matter that was supercooled to 459 degrees below zero—a temperature at which atoms, or particles of light, practically freeze in their tracks.

THREE MEN, A BABY, AND A GHOST

Pause your copy of the comedy hit Three Men and a Baby
*in the right place, and you'll spot the ghost of
a boy who committed suicide in the apartment
where the movie was filmed. Scary, but is it true?*

Although there is nothing supernatural about *Three Men and a
Baby*—beyond, perhaps, how it managed to gross more than any
other movie in 1987—rumors persist that the movie was inadvertently the first to capture a bonafide ghost on film. As with similar
movie myths, the rumor about *Three Men and a Baby* began when
the film was released on home video. In one scene, Ted Danson's
character, Jack, paces around the apartment he shares with his two
roommates, played by Tom Selleck and Steve Guttenberg. Pause
at the right moment, and in the background of the shot you'll see
the ghostly image of a boy in a window. Pause at a later point in
the scene, and the boy has been replaced by the image of what
looks like a rifle. According to rumors, a nine-year-old boy committed suicide with a shotgun in the apartment before it was used
as a set in the movie.

Fortunately, the real explanation is far more mundane. There
was no haunted apartment. The interior scenes of the movie were
shot on a set that was built on a soundstage. In the movie, the Jack
character is an actor, and an earlier scene features a cardboard-
cutout prop of him from a film in which he had recently starred.
If you look carefully at the "ghost boy" and the alleged rifle, you'll
see that they are simply different shots of that cutout.

❈ ❈ ❈

- *So it's now official: The scariest thing about* Three Men and
  a Baby *is Tom Selleck's mustache, not the ghost of a boy in
  the window.*

"I WILL HEAR IN HEAVEN"

Beethoven's musical accomplishments should be enough to secure his place in history. His legacy has been embellished, however, by the misconception that he was totally deaf when he composed his major works.

Ludwig van Beethoven, the most famous composer of his era, was born in Bonn, Germany, in 1770. When he was in his early 20s, he moved to Vienna to study with Joseph Haydn, just after the death of his idol, Wolfgang Amadeus Mozart. In a letter to a friend in 1801, Beethoven admitted that his hearing had been deteriorating for at least three years and he was beginning to show signs of deafness.

Beethoven didn't become completely deaf until 1817. At that point, he had already composed his most celebrated works, including the second through eighth symphonies, the *Appassionata* Sonata, the *Emperor* Concerto, and his only opera, *Fidelio*. This is not to say that Beethoven didn't overcome huge obstacles. His poor hearing inevitably ended his career as a virtuoso pianist, but with the use of rudimentary hearing aids, he continued composing.

Beethoven died in 1827, having been totally deaf for ten years. His final words were allegedly, "I will hear in heaven."

An Appreciative Audience

Once he was completely deaf, his primary work was limited to the completion of the Ninth Symphony. When the work debuted in concert, Beethoven, despite his deafness, insisted on conducting the orchestra. Unknown to him, a second conductor, kept hidden, was also employed to beat out time. At the end of the performance, Beethoven was unable to hear any applause, and he began to weep. It wasn't until someone took his arm and turned him around that he was able to see the audience applauding wildly.

ALL OF YOUR GRAY MATTER MATTERS

*If you think about it—using your whole brain,
of course—the theory that humans use only
10 percent of their brains is 100 percent wrong.*

The persistent and widespread misconception that we use only 10 percent of our brains falls apart when logic is applied. As it turns out, we need all of our gray matter. Here's why:

• The brain is not made of muscle, though many people think it is. But if it were, and we used only 10 percent of it, it would quickly degenerate. The adage "Use it or lose it" applies to muscle. The unused 90 percent of the brain would shrink to nothingness, giving new meaning to the term "airhead."

• What about brain cancer and gunshot wounds to the head? Victims would have a 90 percent chance that the tumor or bullet would lodge in the useless part of the brain. What a relief if that were true.

• An organ that requires so much energy to maintain would not have evolved if it were mostly useless. The brain consumes 20 percent of the body's oxygen and glucose. The time and energy required to develop the brain is responsible for the vulnerability of human infants and the remarkable length and difficulty of human pregnancy and childbirth.

• If seeing is believing, look no further than PET, CAT, or MRI scans of the brain. All reveal there is activity throughout the brain, even during sleep.

Formulating a Falsehood
The 10 percent myth began with some confusing information exchanged among scientists, and it gained traction with the false claims of advertisers, psychics, and questionable "healers."

Throughout the 1800s, it was understood that different parts of the brain were responsible for different functions. Scientists just weren't sure which part matched which function—and that's still partially true today. The idea that different parts perform discrete activities makes the idea of a "functionless" brain area inconceivable.

In the early 1900s, scientists used electricity to zap small parts of the brain to observe what it made people do (e.g., scream, blink, or lift an arm). The subjects appeared to do nothing when certain areas of the brain were zapped. These parts, called the "silent cortex," were considered by some to be functionless. They are now known to be responsible for language and abstract thought.

Others pointed to the rare cases of lobotomy patients who appeared to act normally. Of course, no one had anywhere near 90 percent of their brain lobotomized, and lobotomy patients who functioned "normally" were usually those who had been operated on as children. Young brains, we now know, are able to rewire neural pathways to compensate for damage.

Perpetuating the Same Falsehood

In the first half of the 20th century, scientists made vague claims about unused parts of the brain. This was taken up by psychics, mystics, cultists, and various religious leaders as evidence that their particular creed was the conduit to the brain's untapped powers. The 10 percent claim became popular somewhere around mid-century in advertisements for healing centers and self-help lectures. The myth is still popular in promotional ads for everything from airline companies to television series.

A Brain Primer

There are 100 billion neurons in the human brain, and these specialized cells enable us to do everything from breathing to reading. Although different parts of the brain specialize in certain functions, most activities require a complex synchronization of different areas. At any given moment, neurons all over the brain are active, even if not every one is in use.

BIG SIGNATURE. BIG TALK.
TALL TALE?

*As he put his oversize signature on the Declaration
of Independence, did John Hancock really do some
big talking to fire up the document's other signers?*

Take a look at the Declaration of Independence—specifically, the
56 signatures affixed on the document that formally kicked off the
American Revolution. You'll notice that one name stands out from
the rest. It's written in large, flamboyant script in the center of the
page directly below the main body of text.

That signature, of course, belongs to John Hancock, and it is
the most readily recognized autograph on one of the most revered
pieces of paper in American history. Hancock's inscription is so
well known that his name has become synonymous with the word
signature, as in "put your John Hancock on the dotted line."

John Hancock's John Hancock is big, bold, and symbolic of the
stout defiance of America's founders toward England's tyrannical
King George III. Adding to the aura of Hancock's in-your-face signature was the verbal bravado that history says he used to impress
his fellow signers. Some accounts say that Hancock brashly stated,
"There, I guess King George will be able to read that!"

Hancock's audacious declaration is indeed rousing—too
bad he never actually made it. Hancock was the first to sign the
Declaration of Independence and, aside from a colleague named
Charles Thomson, no one was around when he did (the other
signatories didn't begin signing the document until August 1776).
Thomson never attributed any such statement to Hancock, and
unless Hancock was in the habit of making loud, bold assertions to
himself, he very likely signed the document in silence.

PUTTING THE "C" IN "PANACEA"

❋ ❋ ❋

Vitamin C is an essential vitamin. It plays a critical role
in the formation and repair of collagen, the connective tissue
that holds the body's cells and tissues together. It promotes the
normal development of bones and teeth, and it is a
potent antioxidant. But it is not a cure-all.

Vitamin C was catapulted into the limelight in the 1960s when
Nobel Prize–winning scientist Linus Pauling began touting
vitamin C megatherapy, claiming high doses could reduce the
frequency and severity of colds. Sales of vitamin C exploded after
Pauling's book *Vitamin C and the Common Cold* was published in
1970. Pauling went on to claim that megadoses of vitamin C could
also prevent or slow the growth of cancer, among other diseases.
Even though Pauling's methods (and findings) have been soundly
debunked, the myth that vitamin C is a cure-all persists.

Found especially in uncooked fruits and vegetables, vitamin C
is a water-soluble substance that humans don't produce naturally.
The body's tissues can't absorb more than 100 milligrams a day, so
it's a waste of money to take megadoses. High doses are not known
to be toxic, but too much vitamin C (more than 2,000 mg/day)
can cause gas, diarrhea, and kidney stones, as well as impede the
absorption of other vitamins.

However, there is still debate over vitamin C's role in disease
prevention and treatment. Some studies show a positive impact on
heart disease, cancer, and other illnesses, while others do not—a
few even indicate that it can be harmful. More medical research is
needed for definitive answers.

❋ ❋ ❋

- *In the mid-1700s, a British surgeon discovered that citrus fruit*
  could ward off scurvy, "the scourge of the navy." Vitamin C–rich
  lime juice was added to sailors' diets to prevent the debilitating
  disease—hence the nickname "Limeys" for the British.

PROCESSED FOOD IS JUNK FOOD

Processed food hasn't always been synonymous with junk food. In earlier eras, processed food was actually the safest kind to eat.

These days, "processed food" usually means junk food—something with little (if any) nutritional value, because the healthful parts have been removed or unhealthful ingredients have been added. Fresh, unprocessed food is considered superior—especially if it's organic. Despite its negative connotation, however, processed food is not always devoid of nutrition or bad for you. Processed foods are not all alike and fresh food is not always safe. Myths about food abound!

Processing in the Good Old Days

Processed food isn't a contemporary phenomenon. Food processing, in the form of salting and pickling, had been going on for millennia to keep larders full between harvests. It was unprocessed foods that could be dangerous or even deadly, because they were subject to spoiling and rotting. From the ancient Egyptians, who used yeast to make bread and brew beer, to the French confectioner who invented canning circa 1800 to keep Napoleon's troops supplied during their march across Europe, civilization invented ways to feed itself by preserving (processing) food.

Modern Manipulation

In the 20th century, technology created a mass market for processed foods with previously unheard-of shelf lives. But these foods came at a cost: Large amounts of trans fats, sodium, and sugar were added, and manufacturing techniques often removed nutritional components such as vitamins and fiber. Many snack foods and fast foods are exceptionally high in calories and low in nutritional value. And nitrites added as preservatives to cold cuts and hot dogs may cause cancer. That's how processed food got a bad name and became synonymous with junk food.

FALLACIES & FACTS: JUNK FOOD

Fallacy: *Fresh food is more healthful than processed food.*
Fact: *Food poisoning from such deadly bacteria as* E. coli *and* salmonella *(and transmission of some parasites) most often occurs when you eat fresh meat, poultry, or dairy products that are spoiled or undercooked. Heat treatments used in canning not only give canned goods long shelf lives, but they make them safe to eat without refrigeration. Irradiation kills bacteria in packaged meats, while pasteurization does the same for milk and fruit juices.*

Fallacy: *Processed foods are never as nutritious as fresh foods.*
Fact: *Some are just as nutritious, and some are even more so. Frozen vegetables are processed within hours of harvest, which preserves vitamins and minerals that can be lost in the days or weeks before fresh vegetables are eaten. Some processing techniques actually add nutrition to food. Vitamin D added to milk enhances calcium absorption and helps build strong bones. Separating bran from grain removes phytic acid, which improves iron absorption, and processing tomatoes into paste or sauce increases the amount of the antioxidant lycopene. New trends in "functional foods" add healthful vitamins, minerals, cholesterol-lowering fiber, and antioxidants to foods.*

Fallacy: *Additives and preservatives are artificial and largely unnecessary.*
Fact: *Many processors use laboratory-produced additives such as colors and sweeteners, but many other additives are derived from fruits and vegetables. Salt, sugar, and lemon juice are among the best-known food additives. Tartaric acid from fruit is used to give some foods a longer shelf life. Thickening agents extracted from seeds and seaweed add texture to foods. Vegetable oils and organic acids are used as emulsifiers in spreads such as jams and peanut butter.*

PINSTRIPES AND BABE RUTH

*Did the New York Yankees add pinstripes to conceal
Babe Ruth's expanding barrel gut? The truth is that the Bronx
Bomber's stripes long predated his belt-line bloat.*

Pinstripes
The Yankees first wore pinstriped uniforms on Opening Day 1912,
when George Herman Ruth was 17 years old. Baseball has its own
fashion trends, and other teams were copying the flashy new look,
so the Yanks abandoned the design for a couple of years. Only in
1915 did Yankee pinstripes return for good, by which time about
half the teams in both leagues had tried some variation of them.

Babe's Career
Nineteen-year-old Babe broke into the bigs in 1914 with the Boston Red Sox. Until 1918, he was simply a great pitcher who could
also hit. But pitchers didn't play every day, and Babe's bat was too
helpful to keep on the rack three games out of four. In 1918–19,
the Sox increasingly put him in the outfield or at first base. When
Boston sold Ruth to the Yanks before the 1920 season, New York
made him a full-time outfielder, and he became the most feared
slugger in the game.

Weighty Issues
Ruth undoubtedly lived large, but his gut didn't become large
until he was about washed up. This is best revealed in reliably
dated photographs. In 1914, he hadn't yet filled out. By 1918, the
6'2" Babe just looked like a big, strong guy. In 1923, he was still
looking solidly fit, but by 1930, he probably should have been cutting back on the beer. When he finished with the Boston Braves in
1935, Babe was pretty chubby. His statistics bear out the visuals:
From 1920 to 1930, he stole an average of nine bases per season,
sometimes ranking among the team leaders. Fat guys don't do
that. From 1931 to 1935, he swiped just over two per year. Fat
guys do that.

UNHAPPY BIRTHDAY

❋ ❈ ❋

*Many people believe that the most sung song in the English
language is a traditional folk melody that rests comfortably
in the public domain. In fact, "Happy Birthday to You"
is protected by strict copyright laws.*

That four-line ditty is as synonymous with birthday celebrations as
a cake full of candles. According to the *Guinness Book of World
Records,* the most popular song in the English language is "Happy
Birthday to You." What is less well known, however, is that it is not
a simple tune in the public domain, free for the singing by anyone
who chooses. It's actually protected by a stringent copyright that
is owned and actively enforced by the media conglomerate AOL
Time Warner. You are legally safe singing the song at home, but
doing so in public is technically a breach of copyright, unless you
have obtained a license from the copyright holder or the American
Society of Composers, Authors, and Publishers.

The popular seven-note melody was penned in 1893 by two
sisters, Mildred J. Hill and Patty Smith Hill, as a song titled "Good
Morning to All." It remains unclear who revised the words, but
a third Hill sister, Jessica, secured copyright to the song in 1935.
This copyright should have expired in 1991, but through a number
of revisions to copyright law, it has been extended until at least
2030 and now lies in the hands of AOL Time Warner. The company earns more than $2 million a year from the song, primarily
for its use in movies and TV shows. Because licensing the rights
to the song is a costly endeavor, low-budget movies have to cut
around birthday scenes, and many popular
chain restaurants insist that their employees sing alternate songs to celebrate their
customers' birthdays. Unless you license
the rights, singing the song in public could
result in something decidedly unhappy.

LIDS IN LIMBO

❋ ❋ ❋

*When John F. Kennedy took the presidential oath of office
in 1961, he did so without wearing a hat. This brazen
bareheaded business caused the nation's fashion-conscious male
population to stroll the streets lidless. Or so the story goes...*

The truth is easily exposed when one examines the photographic
evidence of Kennedy's activities during the Inauguration Day
events. The new president was not wearing a hat when he took the
pledge, but he did sport a silk topper throughout most of the day.

At the time of Kennedy's inauguration, hat-wearing was considered a sartorial custom. Nonetheless, Kennedy simply did not
like hats and avoided wearing them when he could. He felt they
made him look too old, and being the youngest man to be elected
to the highest office in the land, he liked to look the part. Dwight
D. Eisenhower did not brandish a bowler for the majority of his
first inauguration ceremony, and it didn't seem to cause any kind
of a fracas. If politicians had that sort of influence on fashion,
President Barack Obama, who often appears in public wearing an
open-neck shirt, could single-handedly trash the tie industry.

There is an entire book dedicated to debunking the myth that
President Kennedy caused the downfall of the derby. In his book
Hatless Jack, journalist Neil Steinberg carefully examines the
evolution and eventual obsolescence of the hat, confirming that
fashion is indeed fickle. Some people assert that hats are cumber-
some, expensive, and a nuisance, and anyone who has ever had
"hat hair" can relate. Critics of that viewpoint are quick to point
out that these factors have not curtailed the wild popularity of the
baseball cap among people of all ages and both genders.

❋ ❋ ❋

- *A similar rumor circulated in the 1930s after Clark Gable
  appeared sans undershirt in the film* It Happened One Night. *But
  that bold move had little if any impact on men's underwear sales.*

RUSSIAN REVELATION

❋ ❖❖ ❋

*Karl Marx was a philosopher, political thinker,
and the father of communism. But he was not Russian.
In fact, he was never known to set foot in the country
whose history he would so indelibly influence.*

Karl Marx was born a Jew in Germany, but his father had the family convert to Christianity so he could keep his job as a lawyer. As an adult, however, Marx maintained no religious beliefs, famously saying, "Religion is the opium of the people" (frequently misquoted as "Religion is the opiate of the masses"). At the age of 25, Marx left Germany for Paris, where he met his lifelong collaborator, Friedrich Engels. Just a year later, he was expelled from the French capital. He lived in Brussels for three years before finally settling in London, where he lived until his death on March 14, 1883.

In 1848, Marx penned *The Communist Manifesto* with the opening line, "The history of all hitherto existing society is the history of class struggles." The first volume of his most famous work, *Das Kapital,* was published in 1867, but Marx lived much of his life in poverty and relative obscurity. He even supplemented his income during the 1850s by serving as a foreign correspondent for the *New York Herald Tribune.*

Marx's Influence

Marx believed that wealth should be distributed "from each according to his abilities, to each according to his needs" and that communism was the inevitable next evolutionary step after capitalism. More than three decades after his death, these ideas formed the basis of the 1917 Bolshevik Revolution in Russia. A wave of communism followed, and in the early 1980s, at its peak, almost one-third of the world's population lived under communist rule. However, these oppressive regimes have badly misrepresented much of Marx's philosophy. There remain as many misconceptions about his work as there are about his life.

THE EARL OF SANDWICH'S FAVORITE SNACK

The famed English statesman John Montagu named,
but did not invent, the sandwich.

Legend holds that Montagu, the Fourth Earl of Sandwich, invented the tasty foodstuff that is his namesake. Montagu was a popular member of England's peerage in the 18th century, and it seems he had a knack for converting nouns into homage to his rank. The Hawaiian Islands were once known as the Sandwich Islands, thanks to explorer James Cook's admiration for the earl, who was the acting First Lord of Admirality at the time. And although it does seem likely that Montagu is responsible for dubbing the popular food item a "sandwich," he certainly was not the first to squash some grub between slices of bread.

A Sandwich by Any Other Name

It seems likely that sandwiches of one sort or another were eaten whenever and wherever bread was made. When utensils weren't available, bread was often used to scoop up other foods. Arabs stuffed pita bread with meats, and medieval European peasants lunched on bread and cheese while working in the fields. The first officially recorded sandwich inventor was Rabbi Hillel the Elder of the first century B.C. The rabbi sandwiched chopped nuts, apples, spices, and wine between two pieces of matzoh, creating the popular Passover food known as charoset.

In medieval times, food piled on bread was the norm—prior to the fork, it was common to scoop meat and other food onto pieces of bread and spread it around with a knife. The leftover pieces of bread, called "trenchers," were often fed to pets when the meal was complete. Primary sources from the 16th and 17th centuries refer to handheld snacks as "bread and meat" or "bread and cheese." People often ate sandwiches; they simply didn't call them that.

It Is Named...Therefore it Is?

Regardless of the sandwichlike foods that were eaten prior to the 18th century, it appears that the Fourth Earl of Sandwich is responsible for the emergence of the sandwich as a distinct food category—but how this happened is unclear. The most popular story relates to Montagu's fondness for eating salted beef between pieces of toasted bread. Montagu was also known for his gambling habit and would apparently eat this proto-sandwich one-handed during his endless hours at a famous London gambling club. His comrades began to request "the same as Sandwich," and eventually the snack acquired its name.

The source that supports this story is *Tour to London,* a travel book that was popular at the time among the upper echelons of society. In one passage, the author of the book, Pierre Jean Grosley, claimed that in 1765, "a minister of state passed four and twenty hours at a public gaming-table, so absorpt in play that, during the whole time, he had no subsistence but a bit of beef between two slices of toasted bread. This new dish grew highly in vogue...it was called by the name of the minister who invented it." According to this scenario, "sandwich" initially referred to Montagu's preferred beef-and-bread meal and was subsequently used as an umbrella phrase for a variety of sandwich types.

Hard Work and Hunger

John Montagu's biographer, N.A.M. Rodger, offers an alternate explanation for the rise of the sandwich. He argues that during the 1760s, when the sandwich  was first called a sandwich, the earl was actually busy with government responsibilities and didn't have time to gamble much. He did, however, spend many nights working at his desk, during which time he liked to munch on beef and bread. It is possible, Rodger argues, that the sandwich came to be as a reference to the earl's tireless work ethic and general fondness for late-night snacking.

PASS THE SALT

When tourists float in the curative waters of the Dead Sea,
they likely believe they are relaxing in the world's saltiest body
of water. This is understandable, because just about every
travel guidebook makes this claim—erroneously.

Are you determined to soak in the world's saltiest lake? If so,
you should skip the Dead Sea and head to Lake Asal in the tiny
East African country of Djibouti. Lake Asal's salinity measures
400 grams per liter—more than the Dead Sea's 340 grams per liter.

Why is Lake Asal so salty? Salt lakes form in locations where
water cannot flow away to the sea and is lost only through
evaporation. Lake Asal was formed somewhere between 1 million
and 4 million years ago, likely the result of volcanic activity and the
resulting shift of Earth's surface. A crater lake 500 feet below sea
level, Asal is fed only by underwater springs and is depleted only
by evaporation. Consequently, the mineral salts have nowhere to
go. Saline levels are so high that crusts of salt up to 13 inches thick
accumulate at the lake's edge and are strong enough to withstand
the weight of a car. There is no plant or animal life in the lake—
nor on the land surrounding it.

Is that much salt a good thing? Lake Asal is not only extraordinarily salty but has the added distinction of being one of
the least hospitable places on the planet. While the Dead Sea's
buoyant, mineral-rich waters attract thousands of visitors annually,
it is unlikely that Lake Asal will ever be a tourist destination.
The air temperatures there are said to be unbearable and the
glare from the salt blinding, and the lake itself emits a sulfurous
stench. If you still want to take a plunge, do so with your shoes on,
because the salt-crystal crusts can rip bare feet to shreds. What's
more, you'll come out of the water coated in a thick, salty film.
Lake Asal is surrounded by a salt pan that is mined, and the salt is
exported by caravan to Ethiopia.

20 MYTHICAL CREATURES

✳ ⬥ ✳

*To the best of our knowledge, none of the animals
listed below is real, so please don't get taken in
by a huckster who wants to sell you one.*

1. Dragon: This legendary monster was thought to be a giant, winged, fire-breathing snake or lizard. Oddly, most ancient cultures that believed in dragons didn't know about dinosaurs.

2. Griffin: Originating in the Middle East around 2000 B.C., the griffin was said to have the body of a lion and the head of a bird (most often an eagle).

3. Phoenix: This ancient Egyptian bird was believed to live for 500 years or more before setting itself on fire. A new phoenix was supposed to have been born from the ashes of the previous bird.

4. Chupacabra: This vampiric creature, whose name means "goat sucker," has allegedly been spotted in the Americas from Maine to Chile. It has been described as a panther, dog, spined lizard, or large rodent that walks upright and smells ghastly.

5. Yeti/Bigfoot/Sasquatch: If these creatures existed, they would likely be the same animal, as they are all bearlike or apelike hominids that live in remote mountainous areas. (The Yeti has been reported in the Tibetan Himalayas, while Bigfoot and Sasquatch are rumored to live in the northwestern United States and Canada.)

6. Skunk Ape: This hairy seven-foot critter weighs in at 300 pounds, smells like a garbage-covered skunk, inhabits the Florida Everglades, and is thought to be a relative of Bigfoot.

7. Vegetable Lamb of Tartary: Mythical animal or vegetable? Eleventh-century travelers told tales of a Middle Eastern plant that grew sheep as fruit. Although the tales were false, the plant is real: It's the fern *Cibotium barometz,* which produces a tuft of woolly fiber.

8. Rukh/Roc: Marco Polo returned from Madagascar claiming to have seen this enormous, horned bird of prey carry off elephants and other large creatures.

9. Jackalope: Sometimes called a "warrior rabbit," the jackalope is a legendary critter of the American West. Described as an aggressive, antlered rabbit, it appears to be related to the German *wolperdinger* and Swedish *skvader*.

10. Adjule: It's reported to be a ghostly North African wolf dog but is likely just a Cape hunting dog, horned jackal, or ordinary wild dog.

11. Andean Wolf/Hagenbeck's Wolf: In 1927, a traveler to Buenos Aires bought a pelt belonging to what he was told was a mysterious wild dog from the Andes. This tale encouraged other crypto-enthusiasts to purchase skulls and pelts from the same market until DNA testing in 1995 revealed that the original sample came from a domestic dog.

12. Fur-Bearing Trout (or Beaver Trout): The rumor of a fur-covered fish dates back to Scottish visitors to the New World who regaled their countrymen with tales of "furried animals and fish" and photographs of pelt-wrapped trout. Occasional sightings of fish with saprolegnia (a fungal infection that causes a white, woolly growth) serve to perpetuate the tall tales.

13. Gilled Antelope (or Gilled Deer): This Cambodian deer or antelope is rumored to have gills on its neck or muzzle that enable it to breathe underwater. In reality, it is the rare Saola or Vu Quang ox, whose distinctive white facial markings only look like gills.

14. Hodag: In lumberjack circles, the hodag was believed to be a fetid-smelling, fanged, hairy lizard that rose from the ashes of cremated lumber oxen. In 1893, a prankster from Rhinelander, Wisconsin, led a successful "hunt" for the fearsome beast, which resulted in its capture and subsequent display at the county fair. It was later revealed that the hodag was actually a wooden statue covered in oxhide, but by then it had earned its place in Rhinelander lore.

15. Sea Monk/Sea Bishop: Reports and illustrations of strange fish that looked like clergymen were common from the 10th through 16th centuries, likely due to socioreligious struggles and the idea that all land creatures had a nautical counterpart. Sea monks were likely angel sharks, often called "monkfish."

16. Unicorn: The unicorn's appearance varies by culture—in some it's a pure white horse and in others it's a bull or an ox-tailed deer—but the single horn in the middle of the forehead remains a constant. Unicorns have reportedly been seen by such luminaries as Genghis Khan and Julius Caesar, but it's likely that such reports were based on sightings of rhinoceroses, types of antelopes, or discarded narwhal horns.

17. Cameleopard: Thirteenth-century Romans described the cameleopard as the offspring of a camel and leopard, with a leopard's spots and horns on the top of its head. The legendary creature in question was actually a giraffe, whose modern name stems from the Arabic for "tallest" or "creature of grace."

18. Basilisk/Cockatrice: Pliny the Elder described this fearsome snake as having a golden crown, though others described it as having the head of a human or fowl. In fact, no one would have been able to describe it at all, because it was believed to be so terrifying that a glimpse would kill the viewer instantly.

19. Mokele-mbembe: Since 1776 in the Congo rainforests, there have been reports of this elephant-size creature with a long tail and a muscular neck. Its name translates as "one that stops the flow of rivers." Hopeful believers—who point out that the okapi was also thought to be mythical until the early 1900s—suggest that it may be a surviving sauropod dinosaur.

20. Lake Ainslie Monster: Lake Ainslie in Cape Breton, Nova Scotia, is frequently said to be home to a sea monster, usually described as having a snakelike head and long neck (similar in appearance to the Loch Ness Monster). Recently, these sightings have been attributed to "eel balls," a large group of eels that knot themselves together in clumps as large as six feet in diameter.

BUNSEN'S BURNER: SCIENTIFIC ERROR

※ ❖ ※

A staple in chemistry classes for generations,
this gas burner's hot blue flame has heated up
the experiments of countless budding scientists.
But the so-called "Bunsen burner" is actually a misnomer.

Among the achievements of 19th-century scientist Robert Wilhelm Bunsen are the co-discovery of chemical spectroscopy—the use of an electromagnetic light spectrum to analyze the chemical composition of materials—and the discovery of two new elements, cesium and rubidium. Bunsen is best known, however, for his invention of several pieces of laboratory equipment, including the grease-spot thermometer, the ice calorimeter, and a gas burner that became the standard for chemical laboratories the world over.

In 1852, Bunsen was hired as a lecturer at the University of Heidelberg and insisted on a new state-of-the-art laboratory with built-in gas piping. Although already in use, gas burners at the time were excessively smoky and produced flickering flames of low heat intensity. Bunsen had the idea of improving a burner invented by Scottish scientist Michael Faraday by pre-mixing gas with air before combustion, giving the device a hotter-burning and non-luminous flame. He took his concept to the university mechanic, Peter Desaga, who then designed and built the burner according to Bunsen's specifications, adding a control valve that regulated the amount of oxygen mixed with gas.

Bunsen gave Desaga the right to manufacture and sell the burner, and Desaga's son, Carl, started a company to fill the orders that began arriving from around the world. Bunsen and Desaga, however, did not apply for a patent, and soon other manufacturers were selling their versions. Competitors applied for their own patents, and Bunsen and Desaga spent decades refuting these claims. The court of history seems to have judged Bunsen the winner.

THE REALITY OF REALITY TV

Reality television has been around as long as the old Candid Camera, *but it experienced a sensational explosion in the 2000s. It may not have much scripting, but it does have a lot of fiction.*

Faking is big Hollywood business. Production crews are professional hoaxers who can produce flying garter snakes, imitate the bellow of a water buffalo in rut, and make up Oprah Winfrey as E.T. They can then make E.T./Oprah seem to emit that bellow while marveling at the reptiles. Just a day at the office for Hollywood—but it means anything we see *might* be fake.

Meet Dr. Frankenbite. A "frankenbite" is a deceptive clip. It may be several out-of-context bits welded together; it may even be one moment's sound matched to another moment's video. If Hollywood wants a contestant to utter something ridiculous, it'll create the necessary frankenbite. Imagine writing a history paper and being allowed to lift and commingle any sentences from your sources, regardless of context. Think of how clever you'd appear— until you got caught, that is.

They only showed the contestants' mean/dumb/weird side. Suppose that a reality TV show has, on average, four film-worthy group activities happening at a given time. Because they also film nighttime activities, sleeping hours count, so that's 672 hours of footage per filming week. Distilling those 672 hours into 42 minutes of TV means you see no more than a fraction of what occurs. If they chose the boring parts, would you watch?

Don't be fooled by that soundstage. The *Big Brother* "house" is a soundstage. Donald Trump's boardroom is a TV set; so are the apartments on *The Apprentice.* How did the *Amazing Race* dolly grip ride along to get that shot of the contestant on the back of a yak? No matter how real it looks, all the Hollywood apparatus is just off camera.

Many contestants are actors. More reality contestants have acting backgrounds than the producers would like to admit. People who have done some acting know how to play the showbiz game, and many would like to play more of it and may be more easily manipulated. That contestant who's constantly singing copyrighted lyrics to spoil the live Internet feeds gives producers headaches.

Reality shows have draconian nondisclosure agreements. These alone reveal how much there is to hide. Reality show participants are required to sign nondisclosure agreements ("snitch, and our lawyers will visit"). Contestants on *Kid Nation* had to sign agreements that extended three years beyond the end of the 13-episode cycle. On other shows, between their elimination and the program's wrap, participants are sequestered at resorts. *The Amazing Race* contestants even made "red herring" appearances around the world to throw off viewers.

Kudos to the Contestants

Not that reality TV producers fake or control everything. They may nudge the process toward a gripping final showdown, but the contestants still have to engage in competition. An *American Idol* finalist always gets a chance to wow the judges and the voting public. Contestants suffer real accidents and injuries. Stagehands didn't push Michael Skupin into the fire on *Survivor IV: The Australian Outback,* nor were his third-degree burns merely makeup. Who doubts that *Fear Factor* contestants authentically vomited the genuine horse rectum, sow uterus, giant cockroaches, and other disgusting things they consumed?

What drives this reality craze? Profit. Reality contestants cost less than big stars. What's more, most show formats offer golden product-placement revenue options. Suppose *Big Brother* contestants win soda in a food competition. Why not make a promotional deal with a top-brand beverage company? The excited contestants produce a free commercial—and all the revenue goes to the network! In the end, the dollar sign makes reality TV.

THE VANDALS' BAD RAP

It is generally believed that the word vandalism *derives from the barbarian Vandals who sacked Rome in* A.D. *455. In reality, the word has a more civilized origin.*

The Vandals were a Germanic barbarian tribe that made quite a name for themselves in the Mediterranean during the fifth century. Over 30 years, the Vandals romped from Poland westward through Europe, the Iberian peninsula, and North Africa, eventually establishing the Kingdom of the Vandals in modern-day Tunisia and Algeria after vanquishing Carthage in A.D. 439.

Have Pity for the Vandals

Why? Because their reputation as conquering warriors is not the one they have today. Instead, thanks to their plundering of Rome in A.D. 455, the Vandals are credited with inspiring the term that describes an act of malicious destruction.

The Vandals were only one of many barbarian hordes during the Dark Ages that ravaged the Western Roman Empire until its fall in A.D. 476. But they weren't any more barbaric than others, nor were they even the first to pillage Rome. Their German cousins, the Visigoths, had turned that trick 45 years earlier.

After a diplomatic falling-out between the two Mediterranean powers, the Vandals headed to Rome, where they plundered the city for two weeks. But even that was considered to be a relatively civilized affair, because the Vandals graciously refrained from wanton burning and violence.

A Bad Rap

So if the Vandals weren't all that vandalistic, where did the word *vandalism* originate? The answer is France, during the French Revolution. As that great experiment in civil liberty and equality began to descend into chaos, the bishop of Blois, Henri Grégoire, denounced what he termed the *vandalisme* of unruly mobs that went around destroying churches and private property.

TURKEY TRACKING

*Exactly how this Thanksgiving favorite got its name
is frequently debated, but one thing is certain: Turkeys
are not so called because they originated in Turkey.*

Turkeys are native to North America. Spanish settlers originally brought the bird back from Mexico in the early 16th century. English merchants picked up the birds in Eastern Mediterranean trading ports, which were then part of the Ottoman Empire, an area that included modern-day Turkey. Believing that the bird originated in this part of the world, the English dubbed it a "turkey bird" or "turkey cock." The turkey was domesticated and bred specifically for its meat and plumage and was then taken by the British to its colonies in America. Of course, the bird was already living there and had been hunted for centuries by Native Americans. The name stuck nonetheless, and eventually "turkey bird" was shortened to plain old "turkey."

Strangely, it was only the English who believed the bird originated in Turkey. Most other Europeans, including the Turks, believed the bird came from India and so dubbed it some variation of "bird of India." This confusion is most likely due to the fact that the Spanish referred to the newly discovered territories of the New World as the Spanish Indies or the New Indies, believing that Mexico was part of Asia.

For the Love of Turkey

According to USDA statistics, between 260 million and 300 million turkeys are consumed each year in the United States. As well as being the long-standing centerpiece at holiday dinners, roast turkey was one of the meals that Neil Armstrong and Buzz Aldrin ate on the moon (it was a "wetpack" dinner that included cranberry sauce and stuffing, heated with the assistance of hot water). For a bird that's unable to fly, the domesticated turkey is certainly well traveled.

EXPOSING THE SUNDANCE KID

Butch Cassidy and the Sundance Kid, released in 1969, is considered one of the most charming and entertaining Westerns ever made. The movie depicts Sundance as a ruthless, though charismatic, gunfighter. But was he a good shot?

The film, of course, features Paul Newman and Robert Redford in the title roles, and as the Sundance Kid, Redford displayed exceptional skill in handling six-guns. William Goldman's screenplay describes the outlaw's pistol prowess during the climax of the movie this way: "[He is] firing with both guns, turning around and around, firing as he spins, and maybe he wasn't the greatest gunman that ever lived but then again, maybe he was…"

A Relatively Sedate Sundance

The immensely popular motion picture established the Sundance Kid as a deadly fast-draw shooter to be hailed alongside Wild Bill Hickok, Billy the Kid, and Wyatt Earp. But facts reveal that during his career of outlawry, the Sundance Kid rarely fired his guns and never killed anyone. From August 1887 to February 1889, young Harry Longabaugh was incarcerated for horse theft in the county jail at Sundance, Wyoming, an experience that produced his famous nickname. The Sundance Kid became a member of Butch Cassidy's Wild Bunch, but most of the gang's bank and train robberies were pulled off without bloodshed.

Following a train robbery in 1899, the Sundance Kid and three other gang members had to shoot their way past a posse, but the only casualty was Sheriff Joe Hazen, who was killed by Harvey Logan. Sundance and Butch then fled to South America.

Hot Shot…Not!

The next year, Butch and Sundance were jumped by Bolivian soldiers, and the Kid apparently was killed in the first volley. It seems that screenwriter Goldman was right about one thing: "Maybe he wasn't the greatest gunman that ever lived…"

A TIRED MISCONCEPTION

❋ ❋ ❋

Most people associate yawning with sleepiness,
but the cause of the open-mouthed reflex remains a mystery.
According to researchers, humans (and many other animals)
yawn for a variety of reasons—fatigue is just one of them.

Scientists have tried for decades to figure out the physical mechanism behind yawning, and they still don't have a definitive answer. A popular older theory held that yawning was a way to bring more oxygen into the bloodstream and move carbon dioxide out. That theory was shot down, however, after experiments showed that increased oxygen intake didn't decrease the rate of yawning.

Another theory suggests that yawning is the body's way of boosting heart rate and blood pressure in anticipation of an energetic or strenuous activity. There may be something to this concept, because it's well documented that Olympic athletes often yawn before a competition and paratroopers yawn before a jump. But that doesn't explain the millions of other times we yawn.

We may not yet know why we yawn, but we do know when. Yes, we yawn when we're tired. We also yawn when we're bored or nervous, and sometimes we yawn for no reason at all. In fact, just thinking about yawning can bring one on.

So the next time someone yawns in your presence, make no assumptions about his or her state of mind or degree of fatigue. Go ahead and yawn right back—yawning, after all, is contagious. Or is it?

❋ ❋ ❋

- *Yawning is also common in the animal world. Dogs, for example, yawn when tired, just like their owners. But they also yawn when excited or tense, and they do it as a way to tell other dogs that they're stressed and need to take a break.*

ALL THAT GLITTERS

*If there was ever an adage for the ages, it is
"All that glitters is not gold." This phrase is commonly
attributed to Shakespeare, but he wasn't the first to write it.*

As far back as 600 B.C., Aesop was warning against the danger of being distracted by shiny outward appearances. In his fable *The Hen and the Golden Eggs,* a farmer has a hen that lays—you guessed it— golden eggs. Thinking that the hen must be filled with gold, he slaughters it, only to find that it's just an ordinary hen. The 12th-century philosopher Alain de l'Isle advised: "Do not hold everything that shines like gold." Two hundred years later, Chaucer introduced this proverb in *The Canterbury Tales:* "But all thing which that schyneth as the gold Ne is no gold, as I have herd it told."

Shakespeare knew a good line when he saw one and adapted the expression for his play *The Merchant of Venice.* The heroine, Portia, instructs her suitors that they must choose which of three caskets contains her picture. One of the caskets is made of lead, one of silver, and one of gold. The first suitor makes the mistake of choosing the one that appears the most valuable—the golden casket. Instead of finding the prize of Portia's picture, he finds a scroll with a poem that begins, "All that glisters is not gold" (and he loses the bid for Portia's hand). The word *glister* comes from the German *glistern,* which translates to "sparkle." In modern English, "glitter" has the same meaning.

Shakespeare's version of this saying has been misquoted countless times. Even the venerated rock band Led Zeppelin put its own twist on the proverb: "There's a lady who's sure all that glitters is gold, and she's buying a stairway to heaven."

GIRLS GONE GOLFING

❋ ❈ ❋

When encountering a female foursome on the links, many a male golfer has muttered that GOLF is an acronym for Gentlemen Only, Ladies Forbidden. Only in your dreams, guys!

No one is completely sure about the origin of the name for the game that involves whacking a small orb across a manicured field. It is speculated that the sport's odd moniker comes from the Dutch words *kolf* and *kolve,* which mean "club." By the time those words had crossed the channel and entered the Scottish lexicon, they had been transformed into *golve, gowl,* and *gouf.*

Mary on the Links

Regarding the game's exclusion of ladies, history tells us that women have been playing almost as long as men have. Mary, Queen of Scots, was an avid golfer in the 16th century—before she was beheaded for treason, that is. Her fondness for the sport became evident when she squeezed in a quick 18 just days after the murder of her second husband. This seemed to cause great consternation among her followers, who felt she should be praying instead of putting. In fact, Mary may have been responsible for introducing the term *caddy* into the vocabulary of golf. When she played the game growing up in France, military cadets often carried her clubs as she took "a good walk wasted." When she returned to Scotland in 1561, she introduced the practice to her subjects, and the club-touting cadets were dubbed "caddies."

Only at Augusta

The mythical acronym does ring true at one famous locale. Since it opened in 1933, Augusta National Golf Club, home of the Masters Tournament, has never allowed women to be a part of its exclusive membership.

WHICH PRESIDENT'S DAY?

Making big plans to celebrate Presidents' Day?
Be careful—the U.S. government says there's no such holiday.

It all began in 1885, when the federal government made George Washington's birthday, February 22, a national holiday—at the same time making Washington the first person to have a federal holiday named after him. This was fine until 1968, when Congress passed the Uniform Monday Holidays Act, which moved Washington's birthday to the third Monday in February. Several other holidays were also moved, supposedly so that families could spend more recreational time together. Cynics have long suspected that the real reason had to do with boosting both tourism and holiday retail sales.

During discussions of the Monday holiday law, some members of Congress lobbied to change "Washington's Birthday" to "Presidents' Day," thereby including Abraham Lincoln in the honors. They figured Lincoln deserved equal billing, and besides, the third Monday in February always falls between Washington's birthday and Lincoln's birthday. But the effort failed and the federal holiday remained Washington's Birthday.

At least, officially. That's because there is no law that says states have to play by the fed's holiday rules. So while some states went along with the government, a few decided to rename the holiday Presidents' Day. Other states celebrate Washington's and Lincoln's birthdays separately, and some went so far as to move the dates to completely different months. For example, Georgia celebrates Washington's birthday in December.

If that weren't bad enough, there's apparently no agreement on the spelling of the day, which can be Presidents' Day, Presidents Day, or President's Day, depending on where you live. The official name of the holiday is Washington's Birthday, regardless of what all the retail ads that weekend say.

DID CUSTER MAKE A STAND?

*"Custer's Last Stand" evokes notions of a war hero
fearlessly advancing in a doomed battle.
What really happened remains unclear.*

The Wild, Wild West

Custer's Last Stand, the legendary designation for the Battle of
Little Bighorn, occurred during the climax of the Indian Wars
of the 1860s and '70s, when the U.S. government corralled the
western Native American tribes onto small reservations. In 1874,
when gold was discovered in the Black Hills of South Dakota, the
government sent troops to make sure Native Americans steered
clear of the jackpot.

Such was the backdrop for the Battle of Little Bighorn. In
June 1876, word spread that a large number of Native Americans had gathered under the auspices of Lakota (Sioux) leader
Chief Sitting Bull. Army units throughout the Montana Territory
planned to converge on and attack the gatherers, and General
George Armstrong Custer led the Seventh Cavalry in this effort.
At the time, Custer was already a Civil War hero known for his
reckless yet successful military campaigns. On June 25, he and
his cavalry stumbled upon the encampment. Fearing that Native
American scouts were aware of his movements, he decided to
attack before waiting for reinforcements.

A Story With No One to Tell It

The truth of Custer's Last Stand remains unclear because everyone under his direct command died in battle. With the intention
of surrounding the native encampment, Custer divided his approximately 600 men into four battalions. Custer's doomed group
numbered around 260 men.

Historical evidence suggests that when Custer's battalion attacked, they thought there were mostly women and children in the village. The plan may have been to take them hostage or use them as a shield. Lakota, Cheyenne, and Arapaho warriors had been fighting with another Seventh Cavalry battalion but quickly moved on to Custer's when they learned it had gotten closer to the women and children. The number of Indians involved in the attack is uncertain, but estimates range from 900 to 1,800. It is likely that the encounter lasted less than an hour; all of Custer's men were killed. Estimates of Native American deaths range from 36 to 300. The remaining battalions of the Seventh Cavalry fought into the following day, though they did not suffer in the same numbers and were shocked to learn of Custer's crushing defeat.

The Evolution of a Myth

The Battle of Little Bighorn created a popular sensation. At this stage in the war, a devastating rout at the hands of Native Americans was unexpected. Despite scattered calls of criticism against Custer's tactics, he was eulogized as a hero. Books, plays, paintings, and eventually movies depicted Custer as the last to die, surrounded by the remaining soldiers who, in the final moments of combat, organized an epic "last stand."

The reality of this scenario is contested. Based on the positions of bullet shells and fallen soldiers, it is likely that Custer's men quickly and unexpectedly realized they were in a hopeless situation. The last men to die possibly gathered for a final effort at the top of Custer Hill, where they'd retreated.

In recent decades, the saga of the Battle of Little Bighorn has slowly replaced the myth of Custer's Last Stand. Native Americans and others have sought to revise the battle's legacy, which at the time was used to fuel anti-Indian sentiment. A multicultural history of the United States would not see the Battle of Little Bighorn as simply a devastating defeat epitomized by the heroic "last stand" of a fallen national hero—it was most certainly a fleeting victory for Native Americans.

ON THE AUTOBAHN

*Owners of high-performance cars dream of pushing
their vehicles to maximum speeds, and the road of their
dreams is the German autobahn. But this expressway
isn't entirely a pedal-pusher's playground.*

Go, Speed Racer!

Most people agree that if you like to speed, Germany is the place to
be. The autobahn has long stretches where you can legally drive as
fast as you want, and it is not uncommon for cars to top 150 miles
per hour. But driver, beware: The autobahn does have speed limits.
In fact, almost half of the system is under some sort of speed control. As you approach major interchanges, cities, or difficult terrain,
you'll start to see speed-limit signs. And even though you will rarely
encounter any *autobahnpolizei* (highway patrols), if you speed and
get caught, it will be expensive. Radar-linked cameras positioned
over interchanges photograph the license plates of all speeders,
who then receive considerable traffic fines in the mail.

Green Concerns

The era of high-speed driving in Germany may actually be coming
to an end. Concerns about fuel consumption and global warming have increased pressure from environmental groups to bring
Germany's traffic laws in line with the rest of Europe—that is
to say, a maximum speed limit of 130 kilometers (81 miles) per
hour. Studies have shown that CO_2 emissions would be cut by 15
percent in the long term once more fuel-efficient cars are on the
roads. But German car companies are working to keep this from
happening, arguing that high-speed driving is an integral part of
the "German brand." The Germans themselves are passionate
about driving—and driving fast—and it is doubtful they will give
up their speedy ways without a fight. In the meantime, if you have
the opportunity to drive through Germany on its famous freeway,
do so with a lightened foot and a cautious eye.

NAPOLEON AND THE SPHINX

As one of the world's biggest riddles, the Sphinx has a mystery of its own: What happened to its nose? Despite evidence to the contrary, many people believe that Napoleon's soldiers used the Sphinx as target practice. Here's why that can't be true.

When Napoleon Bonaparte conquered Egypt, he took along his artists, historians, civilian scholars, and a group of scientists known as savants. Although Napoleon was not an archaeologist, he is considered an early Egyptologist: He was one of the first world leaders to recognize the treasures of ancient Egypt and the need to preserve not only the artwork but the culture itself.

The Battle of the Pyramids took place in July 1798 between the French army and the local Mamluk forces in Egypt. Six months before Napoleon entered Egypt, he sent ahead many of his savants, who contributed to the *Description de L'Egypte* (Description of Egypt)—a comprehensive report of ancient and modern Egypt. These chronicles and sketches clearly show that the damage to the Sphinx had been done well before Napoleon arrived. Even if there were no other proof to debunk the myth that Napoleon was responsible for defacing the Sphinx, his devotion to Egypt would be enough to dispute the idea.

So what happened to the famous statue? The most likely explanation is simple erosion from the sands of time. The Sphinx was carved from a solid piece of limestone, a material that is soft and wears easily. Besides the missing nose, there are several cracks in the face. If you observe statues of all sizes from ancient Egypt, you'll notice that the nose is the one common feature missing from most of them. This explanation is, perhaps, not as exciting as that of Napoleon's soldiers, but it's certainly more plausible.

McURBAN LEGENDS

If you're one of the more than 100 billion served at McDonald's restaurants, you've probably heard at least one shocking (but ultimately untrue) rumor about the fast-food giant.

In the 1980s, word began circulating that McDonald's had implemented an interesting recycling program at its restaurants. Employees secretly rifled through the garbage to reclaim still-intact food-serving packages, which were then reused for subsequent orders. Those "in the know" who ate at McDonald's made sure to crumple their packages to thwart the company's nefarious money-saving scheme.

This garbage-picking anecdote is one of the many outrageous urban legends about McDonald's. Why are the Golden Arches the subject of such scandalous stories? To start, there's the ever-present public suspicion of unscrupulous corporations that seek to maximize profits at the expense of quality and safety. And as a high-profile multinational company perceived as spearheading the globalization movement, McDonald's is a favorite target of antiglobalization Davids looking to slay McGoliath.

Here's a brief look at some of the tastier McDonald's myths that have been served up over the years.

Mmm…worm burgers. A long-standing rumor in the 1970s and '80s was that McDonald's used ground worms as filler in its hamburgers. McDonald's has always maintained that its burgers are 100 percent beef and has gone to great lengths to prove it, including procuring a letter from the U.S. Secretary of Agriculture backing the claim. Besides, McDonald's officials are quick to add, worm "meat" costs a lot more than beef, making its use in patties economically unfeasible. A similar tale was circulated in the 1990s. This time the filler ingredient was cow eyeballs, which are actually in high demand for scientific research. Consequently, their use in Big Macs would be even more cost prohibitive than worms.

What's in the shakes? It has long been alleged that McDonald's calls its milkshakes simply "shakes" because there isn't any milk or dairy products in them. The fact that they can be safely consumed by lactose-intolerant persons, say myth mongers, proves it.

Among the ingredients that McDonald's has purportedly substituted for milk over the years are styrofoam balls, pig fat, and the fluid from cow eyeballs (that way, nothing is wasted!). But according to McDonald's ingredient lists, its shakes do contain milk—specifically, whole milk and nonfat milk solids.

Near-death by bird feathers. One of the more bizarre legends ever conjured up involves an unnamed girl in an unnamed location who had a near-death experience after eating a McFlurry (an ice-cream concoction with fruit, candy, or cookie bits whipped in). The girl, according to the story, almost died from a violent allergic reaction to bird feathers. Doctors traced her dietary consumption leading to the reaction and pinpointed the McFlurry. It seems that they discovered through someone at McDonald's headquarters that one of the ingredients in the frozen treat is indeed bird feathers. In all versions of the tale, the girl and her whereabouts are unnamed because she doesn't exist, and the "feather" reference likely derives from the airy consistency of the product, not the mix-ins.

I'll have a hot choko pie! Another McDonald's falsity perpetrated by e-mailers is that McDonald's apple pies lack one key ingredient—apples. Rumor spreaders in the United States claim that potatoes, pears, and crackers are substituted for apples, while their Australian counterparts offer even more imaginative surrogates, such as ostrich eggs and something called chokos—a cucumberlike fruit that costs significantly more to import to Australia than the Granny Smith apples that are actually used in the handheld dessert.

From a health standpoint, there are plenty of reasons to watch what you eat at fast-food chains such as McDonald's, but an aversion to worm meat, cow eyeballs, or feathers needn't be among them.

GET SAVVY ON THE SEAS

*Many people fall (overboard) for some of the most enduring
myths about the largest area of our world—the oceans.*

Myth: Oceans don't freeze solid because of deep currents.
Fact: Although the water around the Arctic and Antarctica is
freezing cold, oceans don't freeze solid for several reasons. Oceans
contain a lot of water, which circulates around the world. Water
from warmer oceans and from underground volcanoes flows into
the Arctic, which warms it up a bit. But the main reason oceans
don't go into a deep freeze is the salt in the water. The freezing
point of saltwater is lower than that of freshwater, and as ocean
water reaches the freezing point, the salt crystals interfere with the
formation of ice crystals. This water is also more dense and therefore sinks, allowing warmer water to come up to the top—below
the surface ice. The surface ice actually insulates the warmer
water in the same way an igloo insulates the air inside it. The ice
also reflects the sun's rays, and this helps warm the surface and
prevents the ice from thickening further. Nearly all the ice in the
Antarctic is "seasonal," which means it melts and reforms annually.

Myth: Icebergs are made of frozen seawater.
Fact: This seems like common sense because icebergs float in
seawater, but many natural phenomena defy common sense.
Oceanographers agree that icebergs are made of freshwater—in
the form of snow—that has compacted over hundreds or thousands of years. True icebergs are huge pieces of ice that have
broken off from the glaciers that make up the continental ice
sheets (as found in Antarctica or Greenland). Seawater, with its
salt content, doesn't mix with the freshwater of the iceberg. To test
this theory at home, put saltwater and freshwater in the freezer at
the same time—and see which solidifies faster.

MILK FOR CATS

❋ ❖ ❋

It's an image straight out of a Norman Rockwell painting:
a kitty lapping up a saucer of milk as happy children look on.
But now we know better—cats and milk don't mix.

- Cats may like milk—chances are they even crave it. But just as people should avoid certain things that we enjoy, cats are better off without milk (especially cow's milk).

- The notion that Fluffy favors dairy products could have originated on farms, where cats roam freely and help themselves to a quick lap out of the pails when cows are being milked. The question is, are the cats coveting a special source of moo juice or just quenching their thirst when water isn't readily available? Hard to say. But because it's a common behavior, people assume that cats prefer, and perhaps even need, milk.

- Once kittens are weaned, they no longer need milk in their diets. What's more, most grown cats are lactose intolerant. In the same way humans do, cats can experience stomach pain and diarrhea when they drink milk. Because cats don't know to stop drinking something that actually tastes good, they can have continuous diarrhea, which leads to a loss of fluids and nutrients and can endanger their health.

- Can you ever give your cat milk? As always, your veterinarian can tell you what's best for your particular pet. To be on the safe side, consider one of the latest products at pet-supply stores: milk-free milk—for cats! At the same time, though, remember that milk and milk substitutes are really a form of food rather than a beverage. The best way to quench your cat's thirst is with a handy source of fresh, cool water.

YOU SAY URANUS,
I SAY GEORGE

❊ ❊ ❊

*Its name has been the butt of countless bad jokes,
but was the planet Uranus—the dimmest bulb
in our solar system and nothing more
than a celestial conglomeration of hydrogen,
helium, and ice—first known as George?*

There's actually more truth than rumor in this story, but the lines of historical fact and fiction are blurred just enough to make the discovery and naming of the seventh planet fascinating. The heavenly globe that eventually was saddled with the name Uranus had been seen for years before it was given its just rewards. For decades, it was thought to be simply another star and was even cataloged as such under the name 34 Tauri (it was initially detected in the constellation Taurus). Astronomer William Herschel first determined that the circulating specimen was actually a planet. On the evening of March 13, 1791, while scanning the sky for the odd and unusual, Herschel spotted what he first assumed was a comet.

After months of scrutiny, Herschel announced his discovery to a higher power, in this case the Royal Society of London for the Improvement of Natural Knowledge, which agreed that the scientist had indeed plucked a planet out of the night sky. King George III was duly impressed and rewarded Herschel with a tidy bursary to continue his research. To honor his monarch, Herschel named his discovery Georgium Sidus, or George's Star, referred to simply as George. This caused some consternation among Herschel's contemporaries, who felt the planet should be given a more appropriate—and scientific—appellation. It was therefore decided to name the new planet for Uranus, the Greek god of the sky. Let the mispronunciations begin!

TRUTH OR BLAIR?

Although legend says that the town of Burkittsville, Maryland, has suffered from a vengeful witch's curse since 1785, residents say the curse began in 1999— with the production of The Blair Witch Project.

"In October of 1994, three student filmmakers disappeared in the woods near Burkittsville, Maryland, while shooting a documentary called *The Blair Witch Project*. A year later their footage was found." These stark words began the movie *The Blair Witch Project* and touched off one of the biggest fact/fiction controversies since the 1938 radio broadcast of *War of the Worlds*.

The Myth

Local legend tells the tale of Elly Kedward, who lived in Blair Township, Maryland, in 1785. Accused of preying upon neighborhood children, she was tried as a witch and banished. Over the next 150 years, the cursed town (later renamed Burkittsville) was the site of numerous murders, mutilations, and disappearances, all of which were blamed on the so-called "Blair Witch."

Hearing these tales, film students Heather Donahue, Joshua Leonard, and Michael Williams went to Burkittsville in 1994 to film a documentary about the Blair Witch. They entered the woods on October 21 and never came out. A year later, a duffel bag containing their cameras, film, and journals was found buried under the foundation of a 100-year-old cabin.

The Movie

The Blair Witch Project opened to general release on July 16, 1999, and was purported to be a compilation of the missing students' footage. The completely fictional work was the brainchild of struggling filmmakers Daniel Myrick and Eduardo Sánchez, who created the backstory, wrote the 35-page script, and directed the mostly improvisational film. They hired three previously unknown actors and told them only that they would be involved in a movie project about fear and that "safety is our concern...your comfort is not." They took the actors to Maryland's Black Hills State Park, gave them cameras to record their actions and reactions, and used GPS navigators to guide the trio through the movie's narrative, gradually depriving them of food, sleep, and comfortable shelter.

Unlike other contemporary horror movies, *The Blair Witch Project* has no onscreen bogeyman but instead relies on piles of rocks, the infamous "stickman" figures, and babies' cries to strike fear in the hearts of its protagonists (and audiences). The film's video vérité style and the actors' seemingly real fear and frustration heighten the movie's tension. What really snagged imaginations, however, was the overlap between the movie and the real world, helped by its documentary style, extensive mythology, and familiar locations. The preponderance of "evidence" forced even savvy viewers to question their assumptions of fact and fiction.

The Mess

Myrick and Sánchez didn't foresee the problems that they would create with their crossover into reality. Even the Internet Movie Database had, rather ominously, listed the three actors as "missing, presumed dead" prior to the film's release. The statement was changed when post-release media interviews showed the trio to be alive and thriving, a fact that still didn't convince everyone.

Gawkers and vandals besieged Burkittsville, looking for truth about the Blair Witch. A group of townspeople posted an online statement that refuted the legend, the film's geography, and other "facts." When locals started to harass the sheriff's department about the purported 33,000-hour search that was instituted to find the filmmakers, it also published an online rebuttal.

The Reality

To be clear, Myrick and Sánchez made up *The Blair Witch Project* and readily admit it. There is no legend of the Blair Witch; Elly Kedward is a fictional character. Blair Township, Maryland, never existed. Despite these facts, there are some who continue to insist that the story is true.

SNOOPY'S OPUS

※ ❖ ※

In 1965, Charles M. Schulz's comic strip Peanuts *featured Snoopy writing his first line as a novelist: "It was a dark and stormy night." Although Snoopy made the phrase famous, it's a misconception that it had never been used before.*

The line became famous as the worst possible way to open a novel and epitomized an amateur style of writing. That said, a number of published novels have actually opened with that very line. English novelist Edward George Bulwer-Lytton's 1830 novel *Paul Clifford* contains this startling first line: "It was a dark and stormy night; the rain fell in torrents, except at occasional intervals, when it was checked by a violent gust of wind which swept up the streets (for it is in London that our scene lies), rattling along the housetops, and fiercely agitating the scanty flame of the lamps that struggled against the darkness." Whoa. Type that into Microsoft Word, and the Office Assistant will immediately draw your attention to the fact that the line is "too long…and may be hard to follow." No kidding.

In 1982, the English department at San Jose State University began the Bulwer-Lytton Fiction Contest to "celebrate" decidedly bad opening lines. Each year, it "challenges entrants to compose the opening sentence to the worst of all possible novels." (Another of Bulwer-Lytton's lines is "The pen is mightier than the sword.")

Popular Prose

The *Paul Clifford* author wasn't the only person to begin a novel with those same seven words. Madeleine L'Engle's 1962 science-fantasy novel, *A Wrinkle in Time,* opens with the line, and Ray Bradbury used it for comic effect in his 2004 mystery, *Let's All Kill Constance* (he followed it with "Is that one way to catch your reader?"). Even Snoopy himself tapped out variations on the line, including "It was a dark and stormy noon" and this opener for another would-be novel: "He was a dark and stormy knight."

IF THE SHOE FITS...

*Contrary to what manufacturers claim,
costly sneakers aren't always your best bet.*

In the United States alone, people buy some 400 million athletic shoes every year, and their price creeps ever higher. Although manufacturers attribute the rising costs to advanced technological features, they also reflect the price of celebrity endorsements and advertising.

Save Your Money

Despite conventional wisdom and manufacturers' claims, a higher number on the price tag does not guarantee a better athletic shoe. In fact, more expensive shoes could be a waste of money. A study in the *British Journal of Sports Medicine* concluded that low- and medium-price shoes provided the same—if not better—shock absorption and cushioning as the more expensive ones. Study participants who tested the shoes by walking or running on treadmills did not find the pricier models to be more comfortable, either.

Shoe Shopping

Finding the right workout shoe is important. The wrong footwear can cause discomfort and even injury. You should shop in a store with knowledgeable employees who are trained to properly evaluate your gait. And buying a shoe designed for your specific sport makes sense, since those designed for, say, basketball, have different features than those for aerobics or running.

The best time to try on shoes is within an hour of exercising, when your feet are still expanded. Even if you know your size, get measured, because feet change over time.

❋❋❋

- *Be sure to retire your favorite sneakers when they wear out. Experts advise replacing exercise shoes after 300 to 500 miles of use. For most people, this means getting a new pair at least every six months—another reason to check out lower-price sneakers.*

THE HUNDRED YEARS WAR LASTED HOW LONG?

The answer is complicated—the Hundred Years War lasted both more and less than 100 years, depending on how you look at it.

The Hundred Years War was an extraordinarily complicated conflict with far-reaching effects. Piecing together its history requires tracing the tangled genealogy of the royal houses of England and France, not to mention sorting out shifting allegiances, territorial rights, and interspersed civil wars.

The conflict's name is a confusing misnomer. If you tally time from the day war was declared in 1337 to the date of the final treaty that ended it in 1453, the war lasted 116 years. The actual conflict was not continuous, however. There were several periods of declared peace when there were years between active campaigns. If you add up the times of actual fighting, the war lasted only 81 years.

The Fight Explained

This time the two nations weren't fighting over just territory; the prize was the throne of France itself. The last king who ruled France's House of Capet died without a son, and two royal families vied for the open crown.

The House of Valois was a junior line of the royal Capets—it descended from the younger brother of King Philip IV. The House of Plantagenet, the ruling family of England, held its primary claim to the French throne through English King Edward II's queen, Isabella of France, who was Philip IV's only daughter. When she married Edward, a clause in her marriage contract stated that her sons would be in line to inherit both the French and English crowns. When her last brother, Charles IV, died without a son, Isabella claimed France for her son, Edward III, by right of this contract—as Philip IV's grandson, he was the only male directly descended from the House of Capet's senior line. The French weren't keen on a foreign king, however, and they resisted, citing ancient Salic law, which prohibited women from inheriting the throne or anyone from inheriting the crown *through* a female. Instead of accepting Edward, they crowned Philip of Valois, Charles's cousin through his father's younger brother.

A War in Phases

The first phase of the war was initiated in 1337 by England's Edward III, who invaded after the French refused him the throne. Edward's campaigns were interrupted several times by delays and the intervening Breton War of Succession, but they were able to deal the French several devastating defeats. At Poiters, the French king was captured and the country fell into chaos, but Edward was unable to take Paris and negotiated the Treaty of Bretigny in 1360.

Nine years later, France's Charles V resumed hostilities. Over the next 20 years, the French managed to regain much of their lost territory before making peace with Richard II in 1389. England was kept busy with civil strife until 1415, when Henry V invaded, determined to take the French crown. He was stunningly success-ful, especially at the Battle of Agincourt, and he forced a treaty that gained him significant territory and the French king's daughter. Although they officially named their future sons as heirs to the French throne, Henry's gains didn't last long after his death.

France finally gained the upper hand in 1429, when Joan of Arc, supposedly following the word of God, led a relief force that helped the French defeat the English during the siege of Orleans. Over the next quarter century, France continued to see victory after victory, until the English were finally forced to abandon all of France except for the region around Calais.

Changing the Face of War—and Society

So what impact did the war have? It definitely advanced the concept of French and English nationality—and rivalry. New weapons and military tactics were introduced that changed the face of warfare, such as fixed defensive positions and the use of longbows. The need to employ standing armies forever altered the peasant's role in society, and the declining use of heavy cavalry greatly lessened the role of knights.

GUM MAKES YOU HUNGRY

When hunger pangs strike, does chewing a piece of gum stave them off or stoke them? Scientists are still chewing on the answer, but prevailing research gives some clues.

To Chew or Not to Chew?

Dieters sometimes shun gum because they fear it will exacerbate their feelings of deprivation and emptiness. They think—or feel—that chewing gum starts the gastric juices flowing by stimulating saliva in anticipation of some real food. When the juices find nothing to digest, it makes the person feel like devouring something.

Scientists have found evidence to the contrary, however. Stimulating saliva by chewing gum has not been shown to increase hunger. In fact, recent studies indicate that gum can *decrease* one's appetite. A study presented at the 2007 Annual Scientific Meeting of the Obesity Society found that chewing gum before an afternoon snack helped reduce hunger, diminish cravings, and promote fullness among people who were trying to limit their calorie intake.

That Adds Up!

The people who chewed gum before a snack consumed 25 fewer calories from that snack than the non-chewers. The study even touted the benefits of chewing gum for appetite control, saying that it is an easy, practical tool for weight management. If you think 25 calories is insignificant, here's a little weight-loss math: 25×7 equals 175 calories per week; $25 \times 7 \times 52$ equals 9,100 calories (or 2.6 pounds) per year.

Other research studies have shown that hunger and the desire to eat are significantly suppressed by chewing gum at one-, two-, and three-hour intervals after a meal.

If you're still convinced that chewing gum makes you hungry, consider whether boredom, habit, or stress are responsible instead. Until science discovers otherwise, chewing gum is a tasty alternative to an "unnecessary" meal.

DUNKIN' THE DOUGHNUT MYTH

*It's well known that President John F. Kennedy had an affinity
for sweet things (ahem). What isn't true is that he
referred to himself as a jelly doughnut in a landmark speech.*

When JFK journeyed to Berlin in the summer of 1963, his administration had already survived the debacle of the Bay of Pigs and withstood the anxiety of the Cuban Missile Crisis—all while maneuvering through the frigid waters of the Cold War. His trip to West Germany was seen as an endorsement of both democracy and détente, and the speech he was scheduled to deliver to the German people was expected to be one of the most influential of his presidency. When he concluded his commentary with the words "I am a Berliner" in the native language of his listeners, it was regarded as a key moment in his thousand days in office.

The text of Kennedy's speech was a plea for the freedom of all people, and he used Berlin as a symbol of that freedom. To emphasize the point, he used the phrase *"Ich bin ein Berliner"* in an attempt to convey his unity with the people of Berlin. What he didn't realize is that the word *Berliner* could also be used as the word for *jelly doughnut.* By using the phrase the way he did, Kennedy could be accused of indicating that he was a jam-filled pastry rather than a participant in the city's struggle for freedom.

The words were scripted for Kennedy by a respected interpreter, Robert H. Lochner, who was carefully tutored on the proper phrasing. Lochner was informed that while a citizen of Berlin would say, *"Ich bin Berliner,"* that would not be the correct terminology for Kennedy—a non-citizen—to use. This is why the preposition *"ein"* was added to the text, even though it could be loosely construed as a denotation of a doughy delicacy.

BRAINS AND BRAWN

*The Olympic Games haven't always featured athletics alone.
Relive the era when pens carried as much weight as
the pentathlon and a gold-medal performance was
measured in both breaststrokes and brushstrokes.*

Today's Olympic Games feature sports exclusively, but there was
a time when artists competed for gold medals alongside runners,
swimmers, and discus throwers. Cultural events ran side-by-side
with athletics during both the ancient and modern Olympics. But
because the most recent edition of these "brain" games took place
just prior to the television era, knowledge of them is limited.

Herodotus the Hurtler?
Records are scarce, but it appears that the first competitor in
this artistic free-for-all was the writer Herodotus. Competing in
444 B.C. at Olympia, Greece, the athlete participated in both writing and sporting contests. His pairing of brains and brawn would
represent the ideal throughout much of the ancient era.

After a 1,500-plus-year hiatus, the Olympics made a comeback
in 1896. International Olympic Committee founder Pierre de Cou-
bertin lobbied to reinstate the cultural element into the modern
games. His wish became reality at the 1912 Stockholm Olympics.

A Slow Start
The roster of events at that meet included architecture, painting,
sculpture, music, and literature. Despite its historic nature, turn-
out was disappointing—only 35 artists entered the competition.

The 1928 Amsterdam Olympics represented the height of
artistic participation. More than 1,000 works were entered, and
organizers permitted artists to sell them at the competition's end.
This move, though well intended, violated the IOC's stance on
amateurism. Following the 1948 games, an IOC report concluded
that most artistic contestants were receiving money for their works
and recommended that such competition be abolished.

FALLACIES & FACTS: SNAKES

❊ ◈ ❊

Fallacy: *You can identify poisonous snakes by their triangular heads.*
Fact: *Many non-poisonous snakes have triangular heads, and many poisonous snakes don't. You would not enjoy testing this theory on a coral snake, whose head is not triangular. It's not the kind of test you can retake if you flunk. Boa constrictors and some species of water snakes have triangular heads, but they aren't poisonous.*

Fallacy: *A coral snake is too little to cause much harm.*
Fact: *Coral snakes are indeed small and lack long viper fangs, but their mouths can open wider than you might imagine—wide enough to grab an ankle or wrist. If they get ahold of you, they can inject an extremely potent venom.*

Fallacy: *A snake will not cross a hemp rope.*
Fact: *Snakes couldn't care less about a rope or its formative material, and they will readily cross not only a rope but a live electrical wire.*

Fallacy: *Some snakes, including the common garter snake, protect their young by swallowing them temporarily in the face of danger.*
Fact: *The maternal instinct just isn't that strong for a mother snake. If a snake has another snake in its mouth, the former is the diner and the latter is dinner.*

Fallacy: *When threatened, a hoop snake will grab its tail with its mouth, form a "hoop" with its body, and roll away. In another version of the myth, the snake forms a hoop in order to chase prey and people!*
Fact: *There's actually no such thing as a hoop snake. But even if there were, unless the supposed snake were rolling*

itself downhill, it wouldn't necessarily go any faster than it would with its usual slither.

Fallacy: *A snake must be coiled in order to strike.*
Fact: *A snake can strike at half its length from any stable position. It can also swivel swiftly to bite anything that grabs it—even, on occasion, professional snake handlers. Anyone born with a "must grab snake" gene should consider the dangers.*

Fallacy: *The puff adder can kill you with its venom-laced breath.*
Fact: *"Puff adder" refers to a number of snakes, from a common and dangerous African variety to the less aggressive hog-nosed snakes of North America. You can't defeat any of them with a breath mint, because they aren't in the habit of breathing on people, nor is their breath poisonous.*

Fallacy: *Snakes do more harm than good.*
Fact: *How fond are you of rats and mice? Anyone who despises such varmints should love snakes, which dine on rodents and keep their numbers down.*

Fallacy: *Snakes travel in pairs to protect each other.*
Fact: *Most snakes are solitary except during breeding season, when (go figure) male snakes follow potential mates closely. Otherwise, snakes aren't particularly social and are clueless about the buddy system.*

LIZZIE BORDEN DID WHAT?

*Despite the famous playground verse that leaves little
doubt about her guilt, Lizzie Borden was never
convicted of murdering her father and stepmother.*

It was a sensational crime that captured the public imagination of
late-19th-century America. On the morning of August 4, 1892, in
Fall River, Massachusetts, the bodies of Andrew Borden and his
second wife, Abby, were found slaughtered in the home they shared
with an Irish maid and Andrew's 32-year-old daughter, Lizzie. A
second daughter, Emma, was away from home at the time.

Rumors and Rhymes
Although Lizzie was a devout, church-going Sunday school teacher,
she was charged with the horrific murders and was immortalized
in this popular rhyme: "Lizzie Borden took an ax and gave her
mother 40 whacks. When she saw what she had done, she gave her
father 41." In reality, her stepmother was struck 19 times, killed in
an upstairs bedroom with the same ax that crushed her husband's
skull while he slept on a couch downstairs. In that gruesome attack,
his face took 11 blows, one of which cut his eye in two and another
that severed his nose.

Andrew was one of the wealthiest men in Fall River. By reputation, he was also one of the meanest. The prosecution alleged that
Lizzie's motivation for the murders was financial: She had hoped to
inherit her father's estate. Despite the large quantity of blood at the
crime scene, the police were unable to find any blood-soaked clothing worn by Lizzie when she allegedly committed the crimes.

Ultimately Innocent
Lizzie's defense counsel successfully had their client's contradictory inquest testimony ruled inadmissible, along with all evidence
relating to her earlier attempts to purchase poison from a local
drugstore. On June 19, 1893, the jury in the case returned its verdict of not guilty.

MEDIEVALLY EXECUTED

In contrast to popular belief and medieval myth, crime and punishment in the days of yore wasn't all guts and gore.

Although executions may be uncommon these days, they were regular events until the late 20th century. Humankind even invented "humane" ways of sending a convicted criminal to the eternal prison, methods that include the gas chamber, electric chair, and lethal injection. Culprits from medieval times were escorted off this mortal coil by more macabre methods, none of which could be considered morally acceptable by today's standards. Here's the story behind the history.

Lightweight Laws

Common criminals weren't drawn and quartered for petty insults, nor were they sentenced for their transgressions by mob justice without the benefit of a formal inquiry. There were judges and there were trials, and though justice was swift, it was rarely sudden. Hearings lasted less than half an hour, and judges often deliberated and delivered the verdict themselves. In today's system, prison terms are handed out like traffic tickets, but offenders in medieval times were subjected to a "three strikes" policy. If a person was caught committing a crime for a third time, he or she was ushered out of town, which kept the jails uncluttered and the streets safe. The malcontent was sent elsewhere to transgress in a new location. Banishment, not beheading, was the rule of the day. Considering that most common people spent their entire lives within 10 to 15 miles of where they'd been born, being sent away from everything they'd ever known was serious punishment.

Sentences Fit the Crimes

Significant offenses such as murder and arson were treated seriously, often resulting in capital punishment. Most of these wrongdoers met their fate at the end of a rope, which was the preferred method of execution.

Being burned at the stake was the designated demise for pagans and heretics. It was a common punishment in the earlier years of the Protestant Reformation, and the definition of a heretic changed depending on who was in power. In England, Henry VIII split from the Catholic Church, but he still burned Protestants such as Anne Askew. His son, Edward VI, was a devout Protestant, however, and being Catholic during his reign could lead one to the stake. This Catholic/Protestant persecution switched once more after Mary I was crowned, and then back again with Elizabeth I.

The rack was one of the stake's partners in criminal justice. It was used to extract confessions and to "persuade" those already judged guilty to accuse others. Being put to the rack was a torment for commoners only, since it was considered uncouth to torture a member of the nobility. However, jailers had few compunctions about racking a commoner in order to get him to implicate a noble.

Nobles convicted of high treason were spared the traditional drawing and quartering. Instead, they were beheaded—having one's head lopped off with a swift swipe of the blade was considered a "privileged" way to die. The honor was dubious, though, since the ax was usually dull, and it often took several swings before the head was severed.

Treason Wasn't Tolerated

The crime of treason was considered the most momentous transgression of its day. People found guilty of disloyalty to their monarch, spouse, or country were often hanged, drawn, and quartered—not necessarily in that order—in a trilogy of torture techniques that went on until the 1800s. The criminal was dragged to his place of execution on a wooden rack, hanged until he was "almost" dead, then dumped on a table where his entrails and genitals were extracted and his frame pruned into four quarters. Only men were subjected to such sectioning. Women found guilty of treason were hanged or burned. In 1814, an effort was made to reduce the barbaric nature of the proceedings, but the offender who led that charge was hanged until dead before his corpse was filleted into fourths. He got off easy: At least he wasn't breathing when he was butchered.

CROP CIRCLES: HILARIOUS HUMAN HOAXES?

※ ◈ ※

Cereology is the study of crop circles.
It's not a new endeavor, but there is plenty of disagreement
over who or what creates these formations.

The History

A 1678 English woodcut describes the "Mowing-Devil of Hertfordshire," history's first known crop circle. Those were simpler days, when one could blame any weird happenstance on Satan. The demonic hordes seem to have taken a two-century break, as the next recorded mention dates to 1880, this time in Surrey, England. No one understood what or who made these crop circles, but the finger was once again pointed downward.

In the 1970s, crop circles made a big comeback in the English countryside and soon began showing up all over the world. At first, people thought aliens had landed (some still do). The basic disc shape of yore gave way to intricate designs that could be described as crop spirograms, crop mandalas, or perhaps crop snowflakes. Whatever they were called, they were obviously manmade, and paranormal explanations became a tough sell.

The Hullabaloo

Let's apply forensics, like detectives at a crime scene. Suppose your wheat-farming friend Bob calls about a big circular patch of crushed wheat in his field. Because Bob keeps screaming about crop damage as opposed to alien intrusion, you figure this isn't his attempt at a rural practical joke. There are no tractor tracks or boot prints, except where Bob obviously clod-hopped through the site. The wheat is crushed and matted, not cut. You and Bob put your minds to what might have possibly caused it.

A cyclone? It would have had to be a mighty precise one, not to mention stealthy. An alien starship? Maybe one that wasn't big enough to torch the entire wheat field. A sign from Earth spirits? Looks like their alphabet only has one letter. Secret intelligence projects? An intelligence agency that drew such attention to a secret project would be a stupidity agency. You can see why such mysteries created controversy.

When the patterns went beyond discs, someone was obviously just doing crop art. In September 1991, two merry Englishmen, Dave Chorley and Doug Bower, finally admitted that they had created many crop circles. Their method made a perfect circle: Dave stood in the middle and held a rope attached to a board, while Doug stomped the board down in a fixed radius. Or vice versa. Cereologists were embarrassed and felt they'd been played. Meanwhile, Farmer Bob learned that he could charge the curious a nice fee to view the damaged crops, so he stopped cussing and paid off his tractor loan with the proceeds.

But not all crop circles have been positively identified as hoaxes, and some have been quite complex.

The Hypotheses

The fact is that no one has a definitive explanation for the crop circles that can't be traced to hoaxers. Many of the delicate plants in these formations have been manipulated in ways deemed too complex for the average person. So does that point back to space creatures? If alien ships made the crop circles, you'd think someone would have a credible photo of one, or that they'd show up on air-defense radar. Then again, some people report having seen precisely these things. Compared to aliens who could make the trip here, Earthlings would be technological Neanderthals. Surely, such advanced beings could manage to sculpt away at some crops without Bob shooing them away with a shotgun or jet fighters intercepting them. But why in the world would aliens even want to doodle in our dirt? That's a harder question to answer, because alien thought and logic could well be alien to ours.

BELLES IN BATTLE

※ ※※ ※

In the American Civil War, which raged from 1861 to 1865, Union and Confederate armies forbade the enlistment of women. But it is a mistake to think that there were no female soldiers in action.

For many years after the Civil War, the U.S. Army flatly denied that women had played any part in the conflict, making it difficult to know for certain just how many women had served on each side. The best estimates indicate that the number was at least 750. It's hard for people today to imagine that women could have passed themselves off as men and served undetected, but life in the military was very different back then. Army recruiters for both the North and South never asked for proof of identity, and they conducted only farcical physical examinations. Because there were so many under-age boys in the ranks, it was possible for a woman to adopt a male name, cut her hair short, bind her breasts, and pass as a young man.

Most of the male soldiers who served in the war were former civilians who had never fired a gun before enlisting and were therefore just as ignorant of army life as a similarly oriented woman. Soldiers always slept in their clothes, and many refused to use the massive communal latrines, so many of the women soldiers were detected only by accident.

Loreta Velazquez

Loreta Velazquez joined the Confederate army in order to be close to her fiancé. She served under the name Harry T. Buford, wore a false mustache, smoked cigars, and padded her uniform to make herself look more masculine. It wasn't until she was wounded at the Battle of Shiloh and an army doctor examined her that her gender was finally revealed. She was discharged from the military and then wrote a book about her experiences titled *The Woman in Battle*. In it, Velazquez also claims to have worked as a double agent for the Confederacy, usually dressed as a woman.

ELEPHANT GRAVEYARD

Do dying elephants actually separate themselves from their herd to meet their maker among the bones of their predecessors?

Just as searching for the Holy Grail was a popular pastime for crusading medieval knights, 19th-century adventurers felt the call to seek out a mythical elephant graveyard. According to legend, when elephants sense their impending deaths, they leave their herds and travel to a barren, bone-filled wasteland. Although explorers have spent centuries searching for proof of these elephant ossuaries, not one has ever been found, and the elephant graveyard has been relegated to the realm of metaphor and legend.

Elephants Never Forget
Unlike most mammals, elephants have a special relationship with their dead. Researchers from the United Kingdom and Kenya have revealed that elephants show marked emotion—from actual crying to profound agitation—when they encounter the remains of other elephants, particularly the skulls and tusks. They treat the bones with unusual tenderness and will cradle and carry them for long periods of time and over great distances. When they come across the bones of other animals, they show no interest whatsoever. Not only can elephants distinguish the bones of other elephants from those of rhinoceroses or buffalo, but they appear to recognize the bones of elephants they were once familiar with. An elephant graveyard, though a good way to ensure that surviving elephants wouldn't be upset by walking among their dead on a daily basis, does not fit with the elephants' seeming sentiment toward their ancestors.

Honor Your Elders
The biggest argument against an elephant burial ground can be found in elephants' treatment of their elders. An elephant would not want to separate itself from the comfort and protection of its herd during illness or infirmity, nor would a herd allow such behavior. Elephants accord great respect to older members of a

herd, turning to them as guiding leaders. They usually refuse to leave sick or dying older elephants alone, even if it means risking their own health and safety.

But What About the Bones?

Although there is no foundation for the idea that the elephant graveyard is a preordained site that animals voluntarily enter, the legend likely began as a way to explain the occasional discovery of large groupings of elephant carcasses. These have been found near water sources, where older and sickly elephants live and die in close proximity. Elephants are also quite susceptible to fatal malnutrition, which progresses quickly from extreme lethargy to death. When an entire herd is wiped out by drought or disease, the remaining bones are often found en masse at the herd's final watering hole.

There are other explanations for large collections of elephant bones. Pits of quicksand or bogs can trap a number of elephants; flash floods often wash all debris (not just elephant bones) from the valley floor into a common area; and poachers have been known to slay entire herds of elephants for their ivory, leaving the carcasses behind.

In parts of East Africa, however, groups of elephant corpses are thought to be the work of the *mazuku,* the Swahili word for "evil wind." Scientists have found volcanic vents in the earth's crust that emit carbon monoxide and other toxic gases. The noxious air released from these vents is forceful enough to blow out a candle's flame, and the remains of small mammals and birds are frequently found nearby. Although these vents have not proved to be powerful enough to kill groups of elephants, tales of the *mazuku* persist.

The Term Trudges On

Although no longer considered a destination for elephants, the elephant graveyard still exists as a geologic term and as a figure of speech that refers to a repository of useless or outdated items. Given how prominent the legend remains in popular culture, it will be a long time before the elephant graveyard joins other such myths in a burial ground of its own.

THE PHILADELPHIA EXPERIMENT

In 1943, the Navy destroyer USS Eldridge *reportedly vanished, teleported from a dock in Pennsylvania to one in Virginia, and then rematerialized—all as part of a top-secret military experiment. Is there any fact to this fiction?*

The Genesis of a Myth

The story of the Philadelphia Experiment began with the scribbled annotations of a crazed genius, Carlos Allende, who in 1956 read *The Case for the UFO*, by science enthusiast Morris K. Jessup. Allende wrote chaotic annotations in his copy of the book, claiming, among other things, to know the answers to all the scientific and mathematical questions that Jessup's book touched upon. Jessup's interests included the possible military applications of electromagnetism, antigravity, and Einstein's Unified Field Theory.

Allende wrote two letters to Jessup, warning him that the government had already put Einstein's ideas to dangerous use. According to Allende, at some unspecified date in October 1943, he was serving aboard a merchant ship when he witnessed a disturbing naval experiment. The USS *Eldridge* disappeared, teleported from Philadelphia, Pennsylvania, to Norfolk, Virginia, and then reappeared in a matter of minutes. The men onboard the ship allegedly phased in and out of visibility or lost their minds and jumped overboard, and a few of them disappeared forever. This strange activity was part of an apparently successful military experiment to render ships invisible.

The Navy Gets Involved

Allende could not provide Jessup with any evidence for these claims, so Jessup stopped the correspondence. But in 1956, Jessup was summoned to Washington, D.C., by the Office of Naval Research, which had received Allende's annotated copy of Jessup's book and wanted to know about Allende's claims and his written comments. Shortly thereafter, Varo Corporation, a private group that does research for the military, published the annotated book, along with the letters Allende had sent to Jessup. The Navy has consistently denied Allende's claims about teleporting ships, and the impetus for publishing Allende's annotations is unclear. Morris Jessup committed suicide in 1959, leading some conspiracy theorists to claim that the government had him murdered for knowing too much about the experiments.

The Fact Within the Fiction

It is not certain when Allende's story was deemed the "Philadelphia Experiment," but over time, sensationalist books and movies have touted it as such. The date of the ship's disappearance is usually cited as October 28, though Allende himself cannot verify the date nor identify other witnesses. However, the inspiration behind Allende's claims is not a complete mystery.

In 1943, the Navy was in fact conducting experiments, some of which were surely top secret, and sometimes they involved research into the applications of some of Einstein's theories. The Navy had no idea how to make ships invisible, but it *did* want to make ships "invisible"—i.e., undetectable—to enemy magnetic torpedoes. Experiments such as these involved wrapping large cables around Navy vessels and pumping them with electricity in order to descramble their magnetic signatures.

Questionable Witness

According to a man named Edward Dudgeon, invisibility experiments of the questionable kind took place in Philadelphia in August 1943 on both the USS *Eldridge* and USS *Engstrom.* Dudgeon, one of the crew members on the *Engstrom,* claims that after the ships had vanished and rematerialized, some of the sailors themselves mysteriously disappeared from a local bar. However, subsequent investigations revealed that the missing crew members had merely slipped out the backdoor of the bar to avoid punishment for underage drinking. And it's true that the USS *Eldridge* disappeared that night—it went to Norfolk to pick up ammunition but was back in Philadelphia by morning.

MYSTERIOUS MARILYN

Marilyn Monroe's life story has been exposed and analyzed countless times. The problem is that each version seems to contradict the others, making it difficult to sort out even the simplest details of her complicated life.

The iconic film star whose work includes classics such as *How to Marry a Millionaire* and *Some Like it Hot* continues to be the subject of intense scrutiny. But despite all of the books and movies made about Marilyn Monroe, misconceptions about her life abound, including the following:

Myth: Marilyn was illegitimate.
Fact: According to Marilyn's birth certificate, her mother's estranged husband, Martin Edward Mortensen, was her father, but Marilyn never believed this. Her mother, Gladys, left Mortensen after several months of marriage and proceeded to have a series of affairs, most notably with Stanley Gifford, an employee at the film lab where she worked. Mortensen, who had never met Marilyn, always claimed he was her real father. After his death in 1981, a copy of Marilyn's birth certificate was found in his effects, and it is now widely believed that he was telling the truth.

Myth: Marilyn was born blonde.
Fact: Marilyn Monroe's natural hair color was brown. In 1946, she was offered a job modeling for a series of Lustre Cream shampoo ads on the condition that she trade her flowing brunette curls for a straightened blonde hairstyle. It is said that she strongly resisted coloring her hair but ultimately relented under pressure. She was 20 years old at the time and would remain a blonde for the rest of her life.

Myth: Marilyn personified the dumb blonde.
Fact: Marilyn Monroe rose to stardom playing the "dumb blonde" and was considered a master of this Hollywood archetype. But was

she actually featherbrained? She definitely played up that image for the public, but her private pursuits were surprisingly intellectual. She wasn't interested in vapid romance novels; instead, she was often observed on her movie sets absorbed in classic works such as Thomas Payne's *The Rights of Man.* Her library was filled with titles by Willa Cather, Dorothy Parker, and Carson McCullers, among many other notable authors. In one famous photograph, she is sitting in front of her book collection reading a copy of *Poetry and Prose: Heinrich Heine.*

Marilyn also took her work as an actress very seriously and insisted that every take be perfect, which often resulted in her being perceived as difficult to work with. Her 1955 departure from Hollywood to study with Lee Strasberg at the Actors Studio in New York City was a bold attempt to take control of her career. She even went so far as to start her own production company, which enabled her to reject any director or script of which she did not approve.

Myth: Marilyn committed suicide.
Fact: On August 5, 1962, Marilyn was found dead in her home in Brentwood, California. The Los Angeles County coroner's office classified her death as "probable suicide," but many people, especially those closest to her, never believed it. During the summer of 1962, things were looking up for Marilyn. She had just achieved a publicity coup with a cover story in *Life* magazine. Her contract with 20th Century Fox studios had been successfully renegotiated, and several projects were in the works, including a film version of the Broadway musical *A Tree Grows in Brooklyn.* She was busy planning renovations of her new house, the first she had ever purchased (albeit with the help of her ex-husband Joe DiMaggio). To those who knew her well, it did not make sense that she would take her own life, and there are even conspiracy theorists who claim that President John F. Kennedy had a hand in her death. But given the fact that her long-term addiction to sleeping pills had led to near-overdoses in the past, the most logical explanation is that her death was an accident.

CLARIFICATIONS ON KONG

As the most famous inhabitant of Skull Island,
King Kong has long elicited both screams
and sympathy from moviegoers the world over.
But contrary to a popular rumor, Kong was never
portrayed by a man in an ape suit.

We've all heard the term "800-pound gorilla" in reference to something considered big and bad, and in Hollywood, they don't get any bigger or badder than King Kong. Standing a whopping 50 feet tall and weighing in excess of 800 pounds, Kong has captured the imaginations of millions since his premiere in 1933.

Much has been written and said about how Kong was brought to life, and for decades many believed that in some of his scenes, Kong was simply a man in a monkey suit. But such claims are patently false. With the exception of a few scenes that featured a life-size bust or a giant mechanical hand, Kong was made real through a meticulous and time-consuming process known as stop-motion animation. Despite his towering onscreen presence, the mighty Kong was nothing more than an 18-inch articulated metal skeleton (referred to as an armature) covered with rubber and rabbit fur.

Birth of a King

When *King Kong* first hit theaters, moviegoers were awestruck. They watched in amazement as vicious dinosaurs came to life and a huge gorilla ravaged the streets of New York City until biplanes blasted him off the top of the Empire State Building. It was unlike anything they had seen before, and the movie raked in several times the $650,000 it cost to produce.

The myth that King Kong was a man in an ape suit was started by an inaccurate article in an issue of *Modern Mechanix and Inventions,* which featured illustrations showing how a stuntman was used for the scenes in which Kong scaled the Empire State Building.

The Mighty Myth Grows

Thirty years later, a poorly researched Associated Press wire story added to the myth by reporting that King Kong had been portrayed by a Hollywood stuntman named Carmen Nigro. In the article, Nigro made a number of outrageous claims, including the "fact" that Fay Wray was an animated doll and that Nigro had worn "fur-covered ballet slippers with suction pads" to help him stay atop the skyscraper. Nigro also falsely claimed to have starred in *Mighty Joe Young* (1949) as another supersize cinematic simian created through the artistry of stop-motion animation. (Both apes were animated by the gifted Willis O'Brien, who won an Academy Award for his special-effects work on *Mighty Joe Young*.)

Although the original King Kong was only a model, he has been portrayed by a man in a suit in many other movies over the years. The Japanese monster smash *King Kong vs. Godzilla* (1962), for example, featured an embarrassingly bad gorilla suit and a storyline that had the famous ape duking it out with Japan's favorite superlizard. The movie is notable for having two endings: In the version shown in Japan, Godzilla wins. In the version seen by people in the United States, Kong is the victor.

Kong Takes a Beating

In 1976, producer Dino DeLaurentiis promised that audiences would weep over his more sympathetic version of *King Kong*. Audiences cried all right—but only because this peculiar remake was so bad. In addition to special-effects wizard Rick Baker in an ape suit, the movie featured a 40-foot robotic Kong that cost more than $1 million to create and required dozens of technicians to operate. Unfortunately, it broke down so often that it was worthless, and it was ultimately used in only a couple of scenes toward the end of the film. A man in an ape suit was used for the equally goofy 1986 follow-up, *King Kong Lives*, which had the monstrous monkey brought back from the brink of death via a giant artificial heart.

THE FAST-DRAW MYTH

*A deeply ingrained image of the Wild West is that of two
men approaching each other with hands on their gun butts,
determined to prove who can draw and fire faster.
Exciting stuff, but it seldom happened that way.*

In this classic showdown, usually outside the town saloon, the two
scowling scoundrels stand motionless. After a blur of movement
and two nearly simultaneous gunshots, one man drops, hit by the
first bullet. Variations of this scenario include one gunman shooting his adversary in the hand or, with even greater sportsmanship,
letting his opponent draw first.

In 1865, Wild Bill Hickok and Dave Tutt met in front of an
expectant crowd for a prearranged pistol duel in Springfield,
Missouri. At a distance of 75 yards, Tutt fired and missed. Hickok
steadied his revolver with his left hand and triggered a slug into
Tutt's heart. It's a stereotypical depiction, but this sort of face-off
was actually uncommon.

In Western gunfights, the primary consideration was accuracy,
not speed. Gunfighters usually didn't even carry their weapons in
holsters. Pistols were shoved into hip pockets or waistbands, and a
rifle or shotgun was usually preferred over a handgun. A study of
almost 600 shootouts indicates that in one gunfight after another,
men emptied their weapons at their adversaries without hitting
anyone (except, perhaps, for a luckless bystander) or inflicting only
minor wounds.

❊❊❊

- *During the first decade of the 20th century, Westerns became
  a staple of the burgeoning film industry. Hollywood pounced
  on the handful of duels such as Hickok versus Tutt, and soon
  the fast-draw contest became an integral part of the genre. Like
  modern detective films without car chases, Westerns were incom-
  plete without fast-draw duels.*

CHOLESTEROL CONFUSION!

You know the old saying, "You can't judge a book by its cover"?
Well, you can't judge your cholesterol level by your cover, either.

You've probably heard about someone who runs daily and eats a lean, healthful diet but is suddenly struck by a heart attack. The culprit: undiagnosed clogged arteries because of high blood cholesterol. But it's a common misconception that high cholesterol is always the result of poor diet. Although diet can play a significant role in boosting (and lowering) cholesterol levels, other factors may also be involved.

Our genes partly determine how much cholesterol our bodies make, so high blood cholesterol often runs in families. Other potential causes include:

- **Excess weight.** Being overweight boosts cholesterol levels; losing weight can bring down bad LDL cholesterol and increase good HDL cholesterol.

- **A sedentary lifestyle.** Being inactive is a major risk factor for high cholesterol. Increasing physical activity will help lower LDL cholesterol and raise HDL levels.

- **Age and gender.** Cholesterol levels tend to rise naturally as we get older. Before menopause, most women have lower total cholesterol levels than men of the same age. But after menopause, women's LDL levels frequently rise.

Check Your Cholesterol!

Cholesterol is an important health issue, and cholesterol levels should be monitored on a regular basis. Levels that are too high can lead to serious medical problems, including high blood pressure, heart disease, and stroke. Cholesterol levels often can be reduced simply by eating better and getting more exercise. If lifestyle changes aren't successful, drug therapy may be necessary.

THE QUOTABLE NATHAN HALE

In 1776, Revolutionary War hero Nathan Hale
was hanged by the British for espionage.
Is it true that his last words were "I only regret
that I have but one life to lose for my country"?

Those are noble words worthy of a brave Continental officer. No knowledgeable historian would call them inconsistent with Nathan Hale's character: He was a volunteer who dared a dangerous task, conducted himself like a gentleman after capture, and went bravely to the noose. His character isn't being questioned, but did he actually utter the immortal words?

The evidence for the traditional quote comes from a British officer, Captain John Montresor, who told it to Hale's friend William Hull. The quote sounds paraphrased from Act IV of Joseph Addison's inspirational play *Cato,* one of Hale's favorites: "What pity is it, that we can die but once to serve our country!" (In addition to this quote, Patrick Henry's popular proclamation "Give me liberty or give me death" derives from Addison's play.)

Hale may have said the words, or something like them. Or Hull may have revised or misheard them, or Montresor may have gotten them wrong in the first place. There were only a few eyewitnesses, and versions didn't take long to begin wandering. Revolutionary-era media printed several variants on the theme, all of which make Hale sound like a valiant martyr.

What is beyond doubt: Hale was captured and legally executed as a spy. Before he died, he gave a rousing oration befitting a Yalie and a die-hard Continental patriot. This didn't stop his captors from putting him to death, but it did inspire them to tell the story, speak his name with respect (which British officers did not often do of their colonial counterparts), and describe him as a hero.

HOCKEY'S HAT TRICK

*One might logically assume that NHL great
Gordie Howe invented the "Gordie Howe Hat Trick."
Then again, when you assume...*

Mr. Hockey did not invent the three-pronged feat that bears his name. In fact, the term used to describe the art of recording a goal, an assist, and a fight in a single hockey match didn't enter the sport's lexicon until 1991. That's a full ten years after the game's longest-serving veteran hung up his blades.

Honoring a Hockey Great

Make no mistake: Gordie Howe was more than capable of achieving all three elements necessary to complete the celebrated triple play. He was a wizard at putting the biscuit in the basket, a magician at deftly slipping a pass through myriad sticks and skates and putting the disc on the tape of a teammate's stick, and he wasn't opposed to delivering a knuckle sandwich to a deserving adversary. However, the tattered pages of the NHL record books show that he recorded only one Howe Hat Trick in his 32-year career in the NHL and the World Hockey Association. On December 22, 1955, in a game against the Boston Bruins, Howe (playing for the Detroit Red Wings) scored the tying goal, set up the winning 3–2 tally, and bested Beantown left winger Lionel Heinrich in a spirited tussle.

The Record Holder

The Gordie Howe Hat Trick isn't an official statistic—in fact, the San Jose Sharks is the only franchise that lists the achievement in its media guide—but it is a widely acknowledged measurement of a skater's ability to play the game with both physical skill and artistic grace. The New York Rangers' Brendan Shanahan is the NHL's all-time leader in "Howe Hats." According to *The Hockey News,* Shanny scored a goal, recorded an assist, and had a fight nine times in the same game.

HAPPY BIRTHDAY, DEAR VALENTINE?

*Why do we celebrate St. Valentine's birthday? We don't.
Instead, we commemorate his martyrdom.*

Who was St. Valentine? The Catholic Church says there were actually three St. Valentines, and all were martyrs. So which one does Valentine's Day honor? The most likely candidate was a Roman priest during the reign of Claudius II, emperor of Rome from A.D. 268 to 270. Desperate for men to fight his wars, Claudius forbade soldiers to marry. According to the legend, young lovers came to Valentine to be married, and these unauthorized marriages led to his imprisonment. While awaiting his execution, he fell in love with his jailer's daughter. Shortly before his death on February 14, he wrote her a letter and signed it "From Your Valentine."

The problem is that there's no proof any of this actually happened. Valentine's name is not on the earliest list of Roman martyrs, and there's no evidence that he was put to death on February 14. In fact, in 1969, the Catholic Church removed Valentine's Day from the list of official holy days.

How did Valentine become associated with a celebration of love? It may be that February 14 was chosen by the early Church to replace a Roman fertility festival called Lupercalia, which fell on the same date. Another explanation is that the sentimentality of Valentine's Day can be traced to the Middle Ages, an era fixated on romantic love. It was popularly believed that birds chose their mates on February 14, a legend Geoffrey Chaucer referenced in his poem "Parliament of Foules": "For this was on St. Valentine's Day, when every fowl cometh there to chooses his mate."

What about all the flowers and chocolates? These fairly recent additions to the Valentine story have more to do with the power of retailers than the passion of romance.

REMEMBER THE ALAMO

*The famous quote attributed to Edward Burleson,
"Thermopylae had her messenger of defeat;
the Alamo had none," only reinforces the
misconception that there were no survivors
from the defense of the Alamo.*

A Desperate Situation

The siege of the Alamo began on February 23, 1836, when the army of General Antonio Lopez de Santa Anna surrounded the San Antonio mission. It proved to be a key event in the Texas struggle for independence from Mexico. Fewer than 200 volunteers defended the Alamo for 13 days against Santa Anna's estimated 6,100 troops. They were led by William B. Travis and included such famous names as knife man Jim Bowie and adventurer and former congressman Davy Crockett. By sunrise on March 6, 1836, though, the Alamo had fallen, and virtually all the Texans bearing arms lay dead or dying.

The Survivors

Although the exact number of survivors is not entirely clear, documents indicate that as many as 20 women, children, and slaves survived the famous battle. Some of the defenders had brought family members into the Alamo, and a number of them were spared by the conquering Mexican army. For example, Susanna Dickinson, the 22-year-old wife of Almeron Dickinson, was spared along with her baby daughter. Santa Anna sent her to Gonzales to warn other Texans that they faced the same fate as the Alamo defenders if they continued their pursuit of independence.

Several slaves owned by members of the volunteer army also survived the siege—pointedly, two were owned by the aforementioned leaders William Travis and Jim Bowie. One member of the Alamo rebels, a former Mexican soldier, survived the battle by claiming to have been a prisoner of the Texan volunteers.

DUI NONSENSE

※ ◈ ※

*People drink and people drive, and then there are those who mix
the two. Because that's against the law, the act of disguising
the deed has become an art. But putting a penny under your
tongue to pass a breath-analysis test will get you nowhere.*

Despite the fact that some people put an amazing amount of effort
into it, there is no successful way to beat the breath alcohol testing
devices that police officers use in field sobriety tests. Still, some
genius at some point in time decided that placing a penny under
the tongue would do the trick. Supposedly, when the copper in the
penny combines with saliva, it sets off a chemical reaction powerful enough to disguise the smell of alcohol. But this preposterous
proposition doesn't even have potential. The modern U.S. one-
cent piece is composed of 97.5 percent zinc and only 2.5 percent
copper. And zinc doesn't mask stink.

Not to be deterred from comitting their felo-
nies, those who drink and drive have developed
other ways to slip the sheriff. Some amusing but
equally ineffective methods include mixing a table-
spoon of mustard in some milk and drinking it (you'd
have to be booze-addled to drive around with a supply of mustard
and milk) and chewing on a wad of cotton (worse than nails on a
chalkboard!) to absorb the offending "mouth alcohol."

A Mythical Origin

In ancient Greek mythology, Charon was the ferryman of Hades who
transported dead bodies across the river Styx, which divided the
world of the living from that of the dead. A coin to pay Charon was
placed under the tongues of the deceased, and those who couldn't
afford to pay were doomed to wander the shores for 100 years.
These days, placing a coin under your tongue while drinking and driving can only speed up your encounter with the mythical Charon.

CLEOPATRA'S DEATH

*Cleopatra is one of history's most exotic and mystifying rulers,
but perhaps more intriguing than her life is her death.
Here is why Cleopatra really committed suicide.*

Remember the illustrious movie *Cleopatra*? Let's revisit the death
scene: Roman general Mark Antony (Richard Burton) falls on his
sword and dies in the arms of Cleopatra (Elizabeth Taylor). With
her lover dead, Cleopatra allows an asp to bite and kill her. How
intense, how romantic, how…untrue.

Antony and Cleopatra were indeed lovers. But the greatest
love of her life was Egypt, and she took tremendous pride in being
its ruler. If Antony had died but Egypt had survived, it's doubtful
that Cleopatra would have killed herself.

For one thing, she had three children by Antony (and one son
by Julius Caesar). Cleopatra persuaded Antony to part ways with
his Roman partner-turned-nemesis Octavian, and he then agreed
to her request that Egypt remain independent rather than become
a Roman province. Under her influence, Antony also declared
Cleopatra Queen of Kings and Queen of Egypt, to rule with her
son by Caesar. He also distributed the kingdoms of Armenia, Par-
thia, Libya, and Syria among their three children.

Rome considered these acts treasonous, and in 31 B.C., Octavian destroyed Cleopatra's and Antony's navy in the Battle of
Actium. In 30 B.C., Octavian refused Antony's resignation and
attacked Egypt. Antony, who had no means of escape and possibly
believed that Cleopatra was already dead, killed himself. However,
Cleopatra did not consider suicide yet.

Instead she locked herself in her mausoleum and refused
food. Octavian threatened to harm her children if she died, so she
began to eat again. Octavian then planned to send her to Rome to
be led as a captive in the procession celebrating his triumph, and it
was at this point that she reached for the snake. The fear of public
humiliation was the determining factor in Cleopatra's suicide.

SATANIC MARKETING

What's behind the vicious rumor that put mega-corporation Procter & Gamble on many churches' hit lists?

Procter & Gamble, one of the largest corporations in the world, manufactures a plethora of products that range from pet food to potato chips. The company takes pride in its reputation as a business that can be trusted, so it came as a huge shock when, starting in the 1960s, Christian churches and individuals around the country spread the rumor that P&G was dedicated to the service of Satan.

The Devil Is in the Details

How the rumor got started remains a mystery. According to one of the most popular versions of the story, the president of P&G appeared on *The Phil Donahue Show* in March 1994 and announced that, because of society's new openness, he finally felt comfortable revealing that he was a member of the Church of Satan and that much of his company's profits went toward the advancement of that organization. When Donahue supposedly asked him whether such an announcement would have a negative impact on P&G, the CEO replied, "There aren't enough Christians in the United States to make a difference."

There's one problem with this story—and with the variations that place the company president on *The Sally Jessy Raphael Show, The Merv Griffin Show,* and *60 Minutes:* It didn't happen.

Lose the Logo

Adding fuel to the fable was the company's logo, which featured the image of a "man in the moon" and 13 stars. Many interpreted this rather innocuous design to be Satanic, and some even claimed that the curlicues in the man's beard looked like the number 666—the biblical "mark of the Beast" referred to in the Book of Revelation. By 1985, the company had become so frustrated by the allegations that it had no choice but to retire the logo, which had graced P&G products for more than 100 years.

Speaking Out

Procter & Gamble did all it could to quell the rumors, which resulted in more than 200,000 phone calls and letters from concerned consumers. Company spokespeople vehemently denied the story, explaining in a press release: "The president of P&G has never discussed Satanism on any national televised talk show, nor has any other P&G executive. The moon-and-stars trademark dates back to the mid-1800s, when the "man in the moon" was simply a popular design. The 13 stars in the design honor the original 13 colonies."

In addition, the company turned to several prominent religious leaders, including evangelist Billy Graham, to help clear its name, and when that didn't work, it even sued a handful of clergy members who continued to spread the offending story.

Talk show host Sally Jessy Raphael also denied the allegations, noting, "The rumors going around that the president of Procter & Gamble appeared on [my] show and announced he was a member of the Church of Satan are not true. The president of Procter & Gamble has never appeared on *The Sally Jessy Raphael Show*."

Senseless Allegations

Of course, like most urban legends, this story falls apart under the slightest scrutiny. Foremost, one must ask why the CEO of an international conglomerate (especially one that must answer to stockholders) would risk decades of consumer goodwill—not to mention billions of dollars in sales—to announce to the world that his company was run by and catered to Satanists. And even if that were the case, he needn't bother announcing it, since any deals made with the devil would be a matter of public record.

❀❀❀

- *In 2007, a jury awarded Procter & Gamble $19.25 million in a civil lawsuit filed against four former Amway distributors accused of spreading false rumors about the company's ties to the Church of Satan. The distributors were found guilty of using a voicemail system to inform customers that P&G's profits were used to support Satanic cults.*

SEARCHING FOR
THE GREAT WALL

※ ※※ ※

An old Ripley's Believe It or Not *cartoon claims
that the Great Wall of China is the only man-made
object visible from the moon. Well, you can't see it,
so there's no reason to believe it.*

This myth actually originated with Richard Halliburton's *Second
Book of Marvels* (1938). But as any astronaut can tell you, there
are many artificial creations that can be spied from space—if
by "space" you mean low-Earth orbit, approximately 100 miles
up. These include the lines of major highways and railroads; the
sprawl of large cities; and giant, individual constructions such as
the Pentagon and the manufactured islands of Dubai. During the
flight of *Gemini V* in 1965, space jockeys Charles Conrad and Gor-
don Cooper detected the network of roads around the Nile River,
as well as the aircraft carrier that was scheduled to pick up their
returning capsule.

But from orbit, you can barely see the Great Wall. Often, you
can't make it out at all. China's first astronaut, Colonel Yang Liwei,
confirmed this on returning to Earth in 2003. "Earth looked very
beautiful in space, but I did not see our Great Wall," Liwei said.
United States astronaut William Pogue thought he saw it from
Skylab, until he realized he was looking at the ancient Grand
Canal outside Beijing. And a space station scientist remarked that
the Great Wall is less visible than many other objects; you really
have to know where to look.

The wall is difficult to see because large parts of it have
crumbled away or have been buried by dirt and sand. It also is
rather narrow, less than 20 feet across in many places—a mere
microdot from space. In addition, the wall is hard to spot because
it is made from materials that are the same color and texture as its
surroundings.

THE PURPOSE OF PURRING

*Felines are forever mysterious to mere humans.
One of our favorite ponderings is the act of purring.*

Don't cats purr because they're content? When cats purr, people are happy. But cats aren't always happy when they purr. There are actually several reasons why cats purr, and happiness is only one of them. Purring begins at birth and is a vital form of communication between mother and kitten. The kitten purrs to let its mother know it's getting enough milk, and the mother cat purrs back to reassure her kitten.

What's the significance of purring? Cats purr throughout their lives and often at times you wouldn't expect. Cats purr when they are frightened, ill, or injured, and they even purr while giving birth. Animal behaviorists believe that cats purr under stressful conditions to comfort themselves and to signal their feelings to other cats. A frightened cat may purr to indicate that it is being submissive or non-threatening, and an aggressive cat may purr to let other cats know that it will not attack. Some cats purr even when they're dying.

Interestingly, domestic cats aren't the only felines that purr. Some of the big cats—lions, cougars, and cheetahs—also exhibit this endearing behavior. But it's much more soothing—not to mention safer—to stroke a purring pet cat than the king of the jungle.

Self-Soothing

At the Fauna Communications Research Institute in North Carolina, founder Elizabeth Vonmuggenthaler has studied feline purring under a grant from the National Science Foundation. She reports that cats often purr to heal themselves from illness or injury. A particular frequency of purring, which has been shown to lower the blood pressure of humans in close proximity to a cat, apparently has the same soothing effect on the cat itself.

THE HOLE TRUTH

❋ ❋ ❋

How do we know something is there
if we can't see it? With apologies
to the often discussed and dubiously sighted
Loch Ness Monster and Sasquatch,
the mystical black holes that populate
the great beyond do exist—but they're invisible.

The scientific jargon needed to properly explain the principles behind the concept of black holes would put the average person to sleep faster than a heavy meal on a warm afternoon. Let's describe them this way: Black holes are so dense that not even light can escape their gravity. If an object does not emit any kind of light, it cannot be seen. Because nothing can travel faster than light, nothing can escape from inside a black hole. What we do know is that black holes absorb and suck up all sorts of matter, gases, and outer-space junk into their mysterious confines. That activity allows scientists to determine exactly where the black holes are. What you are seeing is not the black hole itself but the elements that define its shape.

If you're seeking a black hole that is actually visible, you should visit the library at Warner Bros. Cartoons, Inc., where you'll find one of the most clever and comedic caricatures in the animators' vaults. "The Hole Idea" tells the story of meek and mild inventor Calvin Q. Calculus, who designs a "portable hole," presumably to revolutionize the storage of dog bones and other debris and to bring immense and instant gratification to putt-weary golfers. In a classic case of life-meets-art, Mr. Calculus actually conceived the idea of the hole as a hatch to escape the hostilities perpetrated by his loud and loquacious wife, who feels that all of his inventions are worthless. Calamity ensues with a comedic conclusion: Calvin's wife falls into the hole, only to be thrown back out. It seems she's not wanted there, either.

CALIGULA AND INCITATUS

*Caligula (A.D. 37–41) is the poster child for depraved
Roman emperors, and not without reason. An oft-repeated story
about his life says that he appointed his horse a consul of Rome.
It makes a great tale, but there's no evidence that it's true.*

Both surviving ancient accounts, Suetonius's *Lives of the Twelve
Caesars* and the papers of historian Cassius Dio, were written long
after Caligula's death. These chroniclers agreed that "Little Boot"
(in Latin, "Caligula"; his proper name was Gaius) was touchy,
boorish, unpredictable, dangerous—and particularly fond of his
horse Incitatus. It's said that Caligula went so far as to handpick
and purchase a "wife" for Incitatus, a mare named Penelope.

For the Love of a Horse
According to Dio, Caligula had Incitatus over for dinner, toasted
his health, fed him gold-flecked grain, appointed him a priest, and
promised to make him a consul. Dio believed it was a serious vow.
Suetonius wrote that Caligula gave Incitatus a luxurious stable
with an ivory feed trough, lavish purple blankets, jeweled collars,
and many attendants. On evenings before races, the emperor forbade any noisemaking that might agitate Incitatus. Suetonius also
mentioned the plans of consular promotion.

Not Out of the Question
No ancient source says the horse was ever actually consul. Priest,
maybe, if you believe Dio. We have the consular list from 37–41,
and Incitatus isn't on it. Both Dio and Suetonius convincingly
describe him as a pampered pet; only one feels Rome might have
had a neigh-saying consul had Caligula lived longer. Both describe
Caligula as someone descending into lunacy, capable of any number of mad deeds. Had he lived, we might today gaze upon Roman
coins bearing Incitatus's horsey countenance. Perhaps, near the
end of the sordid Caligula reign, Incitatus was the only creature
his master truly liked and trusted.

Hey, I Never Said That!

LINCOLN DEFENDS GRANT

※ ❖ ※

*During the Civil War (1861–65), after hearing complaints
of General Ulysses S. Grant's hard-drinking ways, did
Abraham Lincoln really say, "For heaven's sake, find out
what he drinks, and make the rest drink it, too"?*

Lincoln certainly had reason to make such a
comment, and not the obvious one. His generals
frustrated him, and he was always trying to kick
their butts toward battle (preferably against the
rebels rather than one another). Despite many
Union advantages, the Confederacy habitually
paddled the bluecoats until fighters such as Grant
and Sherman put steel into the Union army's spine. What if jealous rivals were simply feeding a rumor mill?

There's an assumption that Grant was a drunkard to begin
with. As a junior officer (1854), he did have a drinking problem and
left the service because of it. In his Civil War return, he seemed
to have learned his limits. Brigadier Grant made rapid gains in
reputation, rank—and enemies. Numerous credible eyewitness
accounts describe Grant as a moderate drinker, never intoxicated
on the battlefield—something that can't be said of other leaders.

King George, the Joker

Don and Virginia Fehrenbacher, in *The Recollected Words of Abraham Lincoln,* write that the quote can be traced to an 1864 Democratic joke book and is likely a recycled witticism from King George II (1683–1760). When he received complaints from the British Court that General James Wolfe was a madman, the king replied, "Mad? Then I only hope he bites my other generals!"

GIVE ME AN "H"!

*There's widespread belief that the "H" in the center
of the Montreal Canadiens' logo stands for* Habitants.
In fact, it stands for "hockey"—go figure.

The logo for the Montreal Canadiens consists of a stylized "C"
with the letter "H" situated in its middle. The "CH" actually
stands for *Club de Hockey Canadien* (Canadian Hockey Club).
Yet, to this day, some of the most ardent Montreal Canadiens sup-
porters believe that the "H" in the center of their favorite team's
logo stands for *Habitants.*

This much is true: For the majority of its existence, the most
successful hockey team in the history of the game has been known
by its nickname, *Les Habitants,* or simply the Habs. Of course,
the team has also been called *Les Glorieux* (the Glorious) and
Les Bleu, Blanc, et Rouge (the Blue, White, and Red). Mostly
the Canadiens have been called victorious—the club has won an
astonishing 24 Stanley Cup championships since first hitting the
ice on January 5, 1910.

The origin of the nickname *Les Habitants* comes from the
earliest days of the franchise. Originally formed in 1909, the team
was organized as an exclusive French hockey club that awarded
negotiation rights to any French-speaking player born in the province of Quebec. Natives of the province were often referred to as
Habitants, a French word that means settler or inhabitant. Since
every member of the initial team was of French origin, the players
and their team were called *Habitants* by their fanatic followers.
Although the team has always been known as the Canadiens,
the franchise was initially owned by an organization called the
Canadian Athletic Club. The team's original club logo was a "C"
interlocked with the letter "A." In 1917, the corporation became
known by its present name and the "CH" logo was adopted for the
first time.

KISS AND MAKEUP

*Why were protective parents around the globe convinced
that the name of the rock band KISS was really
an acronym for Knights in Service of Satan?*

Branding a Band

Onstage, they looked like they'd come straight from the gates of
hell, dressed head-to-toe in black, their faces adorned with macabre makeup. When KISS hit the concert circuit in 1973—the
group drew a sitting-room-only crowd of three people to their first
gig—rock and roll was undergoing an image transformation. The
emergence of androgynous rockers such as David Bowie and Marc
Bolan, along with the popularity of glam groups such as Mott the
Hoople and the New York Dolls, forced bands to find new, exciting, and controversial methods to market their product. When
four young rockers from New York City decided to combine comic
book characters and colorful costumes with a morbid mentality,
they needed an appropriate handle to describe themselves, one
that was easy to spell and mysterious enough to keep their fans
confused. Drummer Peter Criss had been in a group called Lips,
which prompted the crew to dub themselves KISS.

What's in a Name?

According to the boys in the band, the name was spelled in capital
letters to make it stand out and was never meant to be an acronym
for anything. But that revelation didn't stop members of religious
flocks, who considered rock and roll to be synonymous with the
sounds of Satan, from claiming that the group's moniker was a
devilish derivation. In fact, the KISS name has spawned several
acronymic identities, including Keep it Simple, Stupid; Kids in
Satan's Service; and Korean Intelligence Support System. Judging
from the millions of records they've sold in their 35 years in the
business, as well as their relentless licensing of KISS-related merchandise, a more appropriate name for the band might be CASH.

SOME OF MY BEST FRIENDS ARE DIRTY RATS

When logic fails us in the heat of an argument,
we often attempt to insult our opponents by insinuating
that their looks, behavior, or smell is more suited to an animal.
But the real insult is to the poor critter.

"Blind as a bat." Actually, bats' vision isn't all that bad. They are color-blind (as are many humans), but they also have supersharp night vision and can find their way around very well by using echolocation, a form of natural sonar. While in flight, bats emit sounds that bounce off nearby surfaces, and they use those echoes to judge distances.

"Sweaty as a pig." When humans get too hot, we sweat. We release perspiration through approximately 2.6 million (give or take a few) sweat glands in our skin, and that perspiration evaporates and cools us down. Pigs, however, have no sweat glands and can't sweat at all, which is why they attempt to lower their body temperature by wallowing in mud.

"Slimy as a snake." Although a snake's scales are shiny and often appear slimy, the reptile's body is dry to the touch. People may confuse snakes with amphibians such as frogs and salamanders, which have thin skins that are moist to the touch. And worms are definitely slimy.

"Dirty as a rat." Even before the Black Death in the 14th century, rats had a reputation for being filthy. Due to their lack of an assertive PR department, they haven't been able to point out that fleas were actually the responsible party. Rats, in fact, are quite clean and tidy. They spend 40 percent of their time washing themselves (more than the average house cat), searching out water for grooming, and compulsively cleaning and de-cluttering their habitats.

BRAIN POWER

*Mental gymnastics are not the only way to keep
your brain sharp. Physical gymnastics—or any form
of exercise—are just as important.*

Looking to roll back the cognitive clock? Or maybe just remember
where you put your car keys? Cognitive "training"—that is, doing
mentally challenging activities such as crossword puzzles and
sudoku—has been all the rage lately because it's been shown to
help preserve brain function. But there's another kind of workout
that could be the real ticket to keeping your brain young.

Stay Sharp and in Shape

Studies show that regular, moderate exercise helps our brains stay
sharp. Researchers have found that one hour of aerobic exercise
three times a week can increase brain volume, which in turn may
delay some age-related changes. It takes only a few months to start
seeing results, suggesting that it's never too late to start exercising.
Other studies done on animals concur that more exercise equals
better brain function. Even the dormant neural stem cells in
elderly mice "wake up" once the critters hit the running wheel.

In one study that examined older men and women with
memory problems, mental workouts (in the form of brain teasers
and puzzles) produced encouraging results when combined with
physical exercise and a heart-healthy diet. What's good for the
cardiovascular system appears to also be good for our gray matter,
giving us another reason to lower our blood pressure, weight, and
cholesterol levels.

Experts caution not to waste money on dietary supplements
and vitamins that claim to have "anti-aging" benefits, and we don't
need to buy special "brain fitness" computer programs. Engaging in a pleasurable activity, such as studying a foreign language,
reading, or playing a musical instrument, is a great way to keep us
thinking and learning.

"OH, THE HUMANITY!"

※ ❈ ※

On May 6, 1937, when the luxury German airship
Hindenburg *burst into flames midair, 36 people lost their lives.*
But it's wrong to assume that no one survived the disaster.

When the Zeppelin Company completed the 242-ton *Hindenburg*
in 1936, the airship had the distinction of being the largest ever
made. At 804 feet long and 135 feet wide, the dirigible was approximately four times larger than modern Goodyear blimps and managed a top speed of more than 80 miles per hour. On May 3, 1937,
36 passengers and a crew of 61 boarded the airship in Frankfurt,
Germany, for the first transatlantic flight of the season. The craft's
landing on May 6 at New Jersey's Lakehurst Naval Air Station
was delayed for several hours because of a storm. When weather
conditions finally improved, the *Hindenburg* began its widely publicized and highly anticipated approach for landing.

When the craft was about 200 feet above the ground, horrified
onlookers noticed a small burst of flame on the ship's upper fin.
Less than half a minute later, the flame had ignited the *Hindenburg's* 7 million cubic feet of hydrogen. Some passengers jumped
from the windows, others fell, and the rest were trapped in the
burning craft. Herbert Morrison, reporting for radio station WLS
in Chicago, uttered the words "Oh, the humanity!" as he watched
the fiery vessel hit the ground. The recording remains one of the
most famous in broadcast history.

Despite the speed at which the airship incinerated, only 35 of
the 97 passengers and crew onboard died in the disaster, along
with one member of the 200-strong ground crew. The cause of the
fire has never been explained with certainty, though it is believed
to have been a result of the highly combustible varnish used to
treat the fabric on the outside of the *Hindenburg*. Other theories
have cited foreign sabotage, sparks from static electricity, and
lightning strikes.

FUGU ABOUT IT

*People who love sushi and sashimi say these Far Eastern delicacies
are to die for. Although they don't mean that literally,
consuming some raw fish truly is dangerous.*

Beware the Pufferfish

The most notorious and celebrated of the Japanese sashimi selec-
tions is the pufferfish, called fugu in Japan. The flesh of the pufferfish can be lethal if prepared incorrectly, and only specially licensed
chefs are allowed to sell it. Even so, a number of people die every
year from eating it (often, they are untrained enthusiasts who catch,
prepare, and consume their own pufferfish and accidentally kill
themselves). The poison paralyzes the person, who stays fully conscious before dying from asphyxiation.

Most Japanese cities have several fugu restaurants, which are
usually clustered together because regulations once placed limits
on where they could operate. And though closely monitored, not all
fugu restaurants are equal. People seek out the best-quality fugu,
which supposedly still has nonlethal amounts of the poison remaining in its flesh and produces a tingling sensation on the tongue.

Sushi Safety

Although fugu remains an almost exclusively Japanese delicacy,
sushi ranks among the most wildly popular "exports" from Japan. If
you've hesitated to try it, you may have good reason. Raw fish can
be infected with parasites, and every year there are hundreds of
cases of illness caused by them. In the United States, however, you
are more likely to become ill from eating cooked beef or chicken
than raw fish. That's because commercial fish intended for raw
consumption must be frozen for at least 72 hours at –4 degrees
Fahrenheit in order to kill dangerous parasites and their larvae.

A Wormy Problem

You won't care about the odds of getting sick, however, if you
encounter a bad piece of sushi. The most common infection is

the tapeworm, a relatively benign parasite that many people don't realize they have until they pass it. Tapeworms, as well as flukes or "flatworms," can cause abdominal cramps, diarrhea, nausea, fatigue, and weight loss, but they are usually easy to treat with anthelmintics. Of much greater concern is the roundworm, also known as *anisakis*, which can bore into the lining of a person's stomach or intestines and cause severe abdominal inflammation and pain, often within an hour of eating. Surgery may be required to remove it. The worm can taint the flesh of a fish with toxins, and eating it could cause a severe allergic reaction.

A Food and Drug Administration study of Seattle-area restaurants found that one in ten samples of salmon contained roundworm. Fortunately, virtually all were dead because the fish had been flash frozen. As in the United States, most countries now require that all types of commercial fish intended for raw consumption be deep frozen. However, researchers with California Health Services (CHS) continue to place raw fresh fish on its list of seven risky foods that can carry infection-causing viruses, bacteria, and parasites (other foods on  the list include rare-cooked ground beef, uncooked egg yolks, unpasteurized milk, and alfalfa sprouts). According to CHS, properly prepared, handled, and frozen sushi-grade fish is safer than other raw fish, but it still is not as safe as cooked fish.

The Case for Dining Out

The bottom line is that it is safest to eat cooked seafood. But if you can't resist sushi, make sure it is prepared by trained, experienced chefs who know what they're doing. The FDA suspects most illness is caused by the consumption of homemade sushi. Satiate your sushi cravings at reputable restaurants and ask whether the fish has been deep frozen. The safest bet is to order sushi dishes made with cooked fish, such as California rolls. And if you go to Japan, get your fugu fix only from a reliable dealer.

FAMOUS GIANTS

*Sir Isaac Newton saw further by standing on
the shoulders of giants. Most attribute this apt image
to the famed physicist himself, but Newton was quoting
the less famous giants who came before him.*

In February 1676, Sir Isaac Newton wrote in a letter to his friend Robert Hooke, "If I have seen further it is by standing on ye shoulders of giants." Since then, the line has been quoted and re-quoted as prized testament to the modesty inherent in the scientific method: Even Newton knows he's nothing without the accumulated knowledge of yesteryear.

Yet Newton's quote is an adaptation of past pronouncements, all delivered by scholars of old. One of the earliest known references to the metaphor comes from scholar John of Salisbury, who wrote in 1159 that fellow scholar Bernard of Chartres "used to say we are like dwarfs on the shoulders of giants." The quote became better known in the early 17th century, when famous scholar Robert Burton re-quoted less famous scholar Didacus Stella: "I say with Didacus Stella, a dwarf standing on the shoulders of a giant may see farther than the giant himself."

It was not until Newton became associated with the phrase that it gained fame outside of scholarly circles. His version is actually relatively immodest, as he takes out the bit about the dwarf. Yet he never actually claimed to be the quote's originator. Rather, the credit to Newton perfectly demonstrates how quotes become memorable in the first place: by being attributed to famous people. Sociologist Robert Merton, who wrote an entire book on the quote's history, sagely observes that it "became Newton's own, not because he deliberately made it so but because admirers of Newton made it so."

NOT IN HALL AT ALL

*Their "Who's on First?" routine has forever tied them
to America's pastime, but Abbott and Costello were
never inducted into the Baseball Hall of Fame.*

Who's in Cooperstown?

The compelling comedy of William (Bud) Abbott and Louis Francis Cristillo (Lou Costello) combines rapier-sharp repartee, witty word play, and confounding confusion with the speed of a heater and the twists and twirls of a forkball, making "Who's on First?" the most famous comedy routine about baseball. In 1956, a recording of the skit was prominently placed in the Baseball Hall of Fame in Cooperstown, New York, leading many to believe that the performers were also given the honor. Sadly, such was not the case. Abbott and Costello do, however, make a daily appearance in the hallowed hall, courtesy of modern technology. A video of the skit is shown continuously, and an audio version is frequently used to greet visitors when the baseball shrine takes its vast collection on the road.

The skit—a staple of Abbott and Costello's live act throughout their career—was first performed in 1937 and reached a national audience in February 1938, when the duo debuted the ditty on the widely syndicated radio program *The Kate Smith Hour.* The shtick is based on a series of old-time burlesque routines, including "Who Dyed?" and "Cracked Nuts" (the latter features a town named What, which is next to Which, which is…well, you get the drift).

The daffy duo's comedic classic involves a conversation between a peanut vendor, Sebastian Dinwiddle (played by Costello), and Dexter Broadhurst, manager of the mythical St. Louis Wolves (voiced by Abbott), in which Broadhurst informs Dinwiddle of the names of the players on his team. Complications and calamity ensue. One rumor about the skit is actually true: The right fielder is never named.

Fallacy: *Pilgrims left England for America because of religious persecution.*
Fact: *Then called Separatists, the Pilgrims did indeed leave England to escape religious persecution. The catch: They first went to the college town of Leiden in the Netherlands, not the wilderness of America.*

After some peaceful years in Leiden, the Separatists grew discontented at the bottom of the commerce-driven Dutch totem pole. Worse still, their children were learning liberal Dutch ideas, including religious tolerance. To keep Satan from gaining an ugly victory through the children, and to preserve their English identity, the Separatists decided to leave.

Fallacy: *Going to (future) Massachusetts was a foregone conclusion for the Pilgrims.*
Fact: *They first considered Guiana (where the Dutch had already established a colony called Essequibo) and the existing settlements in Virginia.*

Fallacy: *They sought religious freedom in America.*
Fact: *Not as most Americans understand it today. By "religious freedom," Pilgrims meant freedom to be a Pilgrim, not something other than a Pilgrim. Native Americans and Quakers would discover that the fine print didn't include a cheerful embrace of pluralistic religious beliefs.*

Fallacy: *Most of the* Mayflower *passengers were Pilgrims.*
Fact: *Not quite half were. It's easy to forget now that the* Mayflower *voyage was in essence a commercial venture, with the Separatists/Pilgrims as homesteaders and cheap labor. The backers jacked the Separatists around, bending or breaking various promises. The secular passengers—who*

would cause some trouble in the New World—were mostly fortune-seekers completely uninterested in a devout lifestyle.

Fallacy: *The Pilgrims first landed at Plymouth.*
Fact: *Actually, they made their first landfall at Provincetown on Cape Cod after a perilous approach. It didn't take them long to see that Provincetown made a crummy site for a colony.*

Fallacy: *Pocahontas, John Smith, and Powhatan were key figures in Pilgrim history.*
Fact: *Don't confuse the colonies: Jamestown (Virginia, 1607) and Plymouth (Massachusetts, 1620) were dissimilar settlements, with little direct contact. John Smith, the Native American princess Pocahontas, and her father Powhatan all figure in the Jamestown story. Miles Standish, Squanto, and Massasoit (leader of the Pokanoket) are part of the Plymouth/Pilgrim saga.*

Fallacy: *Pilgrims were essentially Puritans.*
Fact: *Not at first. The key theological difference between them was their relationship to the Anglican Church. Puritans wanted to reform the Church, Pilgrims abandoned it. However, when the Puritans began to follow the Pilgrims to New England, Puritanism essentially engulfed and absorbed its more tolerant Separatist brethren.*

Fallacy: *The Pilgrims immediately began stealing Indian land.*
Fact: *This isn't even possible. The tribes of the region had already been depleted by a staggering 90 percent because of disease, yet even that hardy, tragic remnant vastly outnumbered the initial Mayflower colonists. Thus, the Indian survivors had plenty of land to sell (or trade for flintlock muskets).*

Most Pilgrim leaders made successful efforts to get along with their Indian neighbors—probably more out of pragmatism than love of diversity. Any other course would have been self-destructive.

PEARLS OF WISDOM

❋ ❈ ❋

Is it true that oysters produce pretty pearls? The answer isn't quite so black and white, round or smooth, say biologists.

- Pearls do come from oysters, which are members of the mollusk family, but not all types of oysters produce pearls. This is especially true of the kind we eat, so don't expect a pretty white surprise the next time you're enjoying oysters on the half shell at your favorite raw bar. To make matters more confusing, oysters are not the only mollusks that produce pearls. Clams and mussels are also known to generate the coveted orbs.

- Oysters are bivalves, which means their shell is made of two parts held together by an elastic ligament. An organ called a mantle manufactures the oyster's shell, which is lined with a substance called nacre—a beautiful iridescent material made of minerals derived from the oyster's food. Pearls are produced when a foreign substance, such as a grain of sand, becomes embedded in the shell and irritates the mantle. To reduce the irritation, the mantle covers the substance with layer upon layer of nacre. Over time, this creates a pearl.

- Natural pearls are most prized, but because of the way they're produced, they're not the most common variety. To meet consumer demand, most pearls used in jewelry are cultivated— which involves making a tiny cut in an oyster's mantle and inserting an irritant. The oyster does the rest of the work.

❋ ❋ ❋

- *Another common myth about oysters is that it's safe to eat them only in months that contain the letter "r"—September through April. It is thought that oysters harvested in the remaining four months are more likely to carry harmful bacteria, which could cause food poisoning. According to the Centers for Disease Control and Prevention, however, oyster-related bacterial illnesses occur year round.*

MACHIAVELLI, THE PARTY GUY

❀ ❀❀ ❀

*It turns out that 16th-century philosopher
Niccolò Machiavelli was much more interested in having
fun than in gaining power through treachery.*

Powerful or Playful?

Based on Machiavelli's name alone, you might expect that he was
quite an unpleasant person. After all, the term "Machiavellian"
is often used to describe craftiness and deceit. The philosopher's
most famous work, *The Prince*—a guidebook on achieving and
maintaining power—justifies evil as a means to an end and advises
leaders that cruelty will get them further than love. In it he writes,
"It must be understood that a prince...cannot observe all of those
vitues for which men are reputed good, because it is often necessary to act against mercy, against faith, against humanity, against
frankness, against religion, in order to preserve the state."

It is then understandable that one would assume that Machiavelli himself was ruthless and power-hungry. In fact, this was not
the case. He was generous, witty, and always ready to play a practical joke. Machiavelli was, by all accounts, the life of the party.

Man of Many Talents

A contemporary of Leonardo da Vinci, Machiavelli was a true
Renaissance man, living his life through the political turmoil of
Florence in the early 1500s. He was a painter, engineer, diplomat,
playwright, philosopher, and poet. In his day, he was not known
for his political treatises. Instead, his lighthearted songs and bawdy
plays were his claim to fame. *La Mandragola* (The Mandrake), a
raunchy comedy that made fun of (among other things) the clergy,
had plenty of off-color humor and was one of his biggest hits. True
to character, Machiavelli wrote the play while in exile for allegedly
plotting against Medici.

Social Butterfly

Between his work as a diplomat, which sent him all over Europe, and his engineering endeavors (he collaborated with da Vinci on a failed attempt to divert the Arno River), Machiavelli somehow managed to find time to relax. He spent most of his evenings with friends in the taverns and alleys of Florence, gambling, drinking, and telling stories. He is known to have fallen in love twice (neither time with his wife) and was a regular customer of the city's brothels. His intellectual stimulation seemed to come from a group that he called his "noontime friends," a collection of writers, poets, and scholars of some repute. Although they most certainly discussed weighty issues of philosophy, it appears that they also spent a good deal of time drinking and making up carnival songs.

Blame *The Prince*

The Prince, which Machiavelli wrote to gain the favor of the ruling Medici family, was poorly received and was not even published during his lifetime. Twenty-five years after its publication, the Catholic Church banned it because of its perceived anti-Christian sentiments. The ban greatly contributed to its author's increasing unpopularity. Soon, the caricature of Machiavelli as evil incarnate began to take hold. It is said that Shakespeare based many of his most villainous characters on Machiavellian traits. Machiavelli's reputation has not been helped by the fact that some of history's most diabolical figures were fans of his work. Hitler, Napoleon, and even organized crime figure John Gotti are said to have studied it. Full of contradictions, and controversial to this day, Machiavelli's political writings seem to have something for everyone. Feminists, communists, and Christians have all found positive aspects in his work.

A Pleasing Personality

Machiavelli spent his lifetime aspiring to please, courting the favor of whomever was in charge of Florence at the time (and landing in exile or even the torture chamber when he happened to end up on the wrong side). Through all of this, poetry interested him much more than politics. He remained lighthearted even on his deathbed, where it is said he entertained his friends by telling jokes.

HELL'S BELLES

❋ ❈ ❋

*Comparing the furor and fires of Hades to the content of
a woman's contempt has long been addressed by the adage
"Hell hath no fury like a woman scorned." Not only is the
message misquoted, but its author has long been mislabeled.*

Few scribes have described the complexities of the female persona
with the delicacy and decorum of William Shakespeare. However,
he did not liken the disdain of man's better half to the luminous
flares of the devil's lair. The credit for that comparison should be
given to English author, playwright, and poet William Congreve,
who scripted the lines "Heaven has no rage like love to hatred
turned, nor hell a fury like a woman scorned" in the lone tragedy
he penned during his career, *The Mourning Bride.* Congreve,
whose comedies are still popularly featured on stages worldwide,
died unaware that a line from a largely unsuccessful work would
live forever in the light of day—albeit in an abridged and inau-
thentic form.

Its inaccurate usage was best exemplified during the 1991 con-
firmation hearings regarding Clarence Thomas's nomination to the
Supreme Court. During the proceedings, Anita Hill, a university
professor and former attorney and advisor to Thomas, accused the
nominee of sexual harassment and sexual impropriety, an imputa-
tion that shocked the nation. Thomas denied any wrongdoing,
pointing the finger at Hill herself. Senate Judiciary Committee
chair Joseph Biden summarized Hill's testimony by saying, "After
being spurned, she took up the role in the way Shakespeare used
the phrase 'hell hath no fury like,' and that's what's being implied
here." Fortunately, Alan Simpson, an obviously literate senator
from Wyoming, stepped forward and corrected his colleague,
informing the assembly of the actual author and the correct quote.

"FIFTEEN WOMEN ON A DEAD WOMAN'S CHEST..."

If Calico Jack had heard the famous pirate song sung this way,
would he have declared it blasphemous? Don't bet your booty.

Women of the Sea

Throughout history, women have received more than their share of omissions, and this certainly was the case during the Golden Age of Piracy. Although it's true that men were the predominant players in this high-seas melodrama, women had important roles. Most people have heard of Captain Kidd, Blackbeard, and Calico Jack, but those same people might scratch their heads while trying to recall Anne Bonny, Lady Mary Killigrew, and Mary Read.

Despite their relative anonymity, female swashbucklers were as much a part of the pirate experience as garish costumes and hand-held telescopes. In fact, the story of female pirates is at least as captivating as buried treasures or mutinous uprisings.

Female pirates date back at least as far as the fifth century, but the most notable figures appeared long after that. Mary Killigrew, a lady under Queen Elizabeth I, operated in the late 16th century. In her most celebrated outing, Killigrew and her shipmates boarded a German vessel off of Falmouth, Cornwall. Once on deck, they killed the crew and stole their cargo. When later brought to trial for the murders, Killigrew was sentenced to death. With some well-placed bribes and a queen sympathetic to her plight, however, she was eventually acquitted. Her bold tale is said to have inspired female pirates yet to come.

The Story of Mary and Anne

The exploits of pirates Mary Read and Anne Bonny rank among those of their male counterparts. Read was born in London in the late 17th century and spent her entire childhood disguised as a boy. The reasons for her unusual dress are lost to time, but Read's thirst for adventure has never been in question.

Working as a "footboy" for a wealthy French woman, "Mark" Read eventually grew tired of such drudgery and signed on for sea duty aboard a man-o'-war. From there, the cross-dressed woman joined the Flemish army, where she served two stints. Eventually, Read booked passage on a ship bound for the West Indies. While on this fateful journey, her vessel was attacked and captured by none other than Captain (Calico) Jack Rackham.

A dashing figure in her male persona, Read drew the amorous gaze of Bonny, who was Calico Jack's mistress and a pirate in her own right. Upon the discovery of Read's gender, the two became friends, and they struck a deal to continue the ruse. The game wouldn't last long. A jealous Calico Jack confronted the pair, and he too learned the truth. Finding appeal in the prospect of having two female pirates on his crew, the captain let things stand.

Adventure-loving Read took well to her life of piracy and soon fell in love with a young sailor. This upset a veteran crewmate, who challenged the would-be Lothario to a duel. Fearful that her man would be killed by the strapping seaman, Read demanded her own showdown. She was granted her wish. After the combatants discharged their pistols, both stood unscathed. When they reached for their swords, Read cunningly ripped her shirt open and exposed her breasts. The stunned seaman hesitated, and Read, in classic pirate fashion, swung her cutlass. It found its mark.

Courageous Buccaneers

Read's victory would be short lived. Charged with piracy after their ship was seized by Jamaican authorities in 1720, Read, Bonny, and Calico Jack were tried and sentenced to hang. When asked in court why a woman might wish to become a pirate and face such a sentence, Read cockily replied, "As to hanging, it is no great hardship, for were it not for that, every cowardly fellow would turn pirate and so unfit the seas, that men of courage must starve." Read could easily have added "women of courage" to her answer. She and other female pirates had pillaged at least that much.

THE MEN ON THE MOON

*On July 20, 1969, millions of people worldwide watched in awe
as U.S. astronauts became the first humans to step on the moon.
However, a considerable number of conspiracy theorists contend
that the men were just actors performing on a soundstage.*

The National Aeronautics and Space Administration (NASA) has
been dealing with this myth for nearly 40 years. In fact, it has a
page on its official Web site that scientifically explains the pieces of
"proof" that supposedly expose the fraud. These are the most common questions raised.

**If the astronauts really did take photographs on the moon,
why aren't the stars visible in them?** The stars are there but
are too faint to be seen in the photos. The reason for this has to do
with the fact that the lunar surface is so brightly lit by the sun. The
astronauts had to adjust their camera settings to accommodate
the brightness, which then rendered the stars in the background
difficult to see.

Why was there no blast crater under the lunar module? The
astronauts had slowed their descent, bringing the rocket on the
lander from a maximum of 10,000 pounds of thrust to just 3,000
pounds. In addition, the lack of atmosphere on the moon spread
the exhaust fairly wide, lowering the pressure and diminishing the
scope of a blast crater.

**If there is no air on the moon, why does the flag planted by
the astronauts appear to be waving?** The flag appears to wave
because the astronauts were rotating the pole on which it was
mounted as they tried to get it to stand upright.

**When the lunar module took off from the moon back into
orbit, why was there no visible flame from the rocket?** The
composition of the fuel used for the takeoff from the surface of
the moon was different in that it produced no flame.

Conspiracy theorists present dozens of "examples" that supposedly prove that the moon landing never happened, and all of them are easily explained. But that hasn't kept naysayers from perpetuating the myth.

❊ ❊ ❊

Twenty-three years after the moon landing, on February 15, 2001, Fox TV stirred the pot yet again with a program titled *Conspiracy Theory: Did We Land on the Moon?* The show trotted out the usual array of conspiracy theorists, who in turn dusted off the usual spurious "proof." And once again, NASA found itself having to answer to a skeptical but persistent few.

Many people theorize that the landing was faked because the United States didn't have the technology to safely send a crew to the moon. Instead, it pretended it did as a way to win the final leg of the space race against the Soviet Union. But consider the situation: Thousands of men and women worked for almost a decade (and three astronauts died) to make the success of *Apollo 11* a reality. With so many people involved, a hoax of that magnitude would be virtually impossible to contain, especially after almost four decades.

For additional proof that the moon landing really happened, consider the hundreds of pounds of moon rocks brought back by the six *Apollo* missions that were able to retrieve them. Moon rocks are unique and aren't easily manufactured, so if they didn't come from the moon, what is their source? Finally, there's no denying the fact that the *Apollo* astronauts left behind a two-foot reflecting panel equipped with dozens of tiny mirrors. Scientists are able to bounce laser pulses off the mirrors to pinpoint the moon's distance from Earth.

The myth of the faked moon landing will probably never go away. But the proof of its reality is irrefutable. In the words of astronaut Charles Duke, who walked on the moon in 1972 as part of the *Apollo 16* mission: "We've been to the moon nine times. Why would we fake it nine times, if we faked it?"

COCKY COCKROACHES

❋ ❖ ❋

Would the cockroach be the sole survivor of a nuclear war? No, but the mightiest of the mighty still looks up to this creepiest of crawlers.

We've all heard the scenario: A swarm of nuclear missiles is launched in unison, aimed at strategic targets throughout the world. The end of humankind is assured. In the span of a few minutes, entire civilizations are obliterated and the vital peoples and creatures that once roamed the planet are left dead or dying. Soon all life forms will succumb to the insidious effects of radiation. All except one, that is.

Blattodea, better known as the common cockroach, is the tough-guy holdout in this nightmarish scene. With the ability to withstand doses of radiation that would easily kill a human, this pesky insect might be forgiven for flaring its chest with pride. But the cockroach shouldn't gloat too much. The insect kingdom boasts tougher players still.

It is generally accepted that a human will perish after receiving a 400- to 1,000-rad dose of radiation. In contrast, the hardy cockroach can withstand a 6,400-rad hit and continue crawling, which suggests that this bothersome bug is champ. This is certainly true when compared with humans, but let's see what happens when *Blattodea* messes with the big, er, *small* boys.

Fruit flies may be tiny, but they sure are resilient. It takes 64,000 rads to deck the average specimen. This figure bests the roach by a factor of ten. The Caribbean fruit fly, the "mighty mite" among these little fellows, takes a 180,000-rad dose like it's nothing.

Conan the Bacterium

The most radiation-resistant organism in the world is the microscopic bacterium *Deinococcus radiodurans*. Named "Conan the Bacterium" by adoring researchers, it can easily handle a 1.5-million-rad dose. Compared with this omnipotent, if infinitesimally small, title holder, the once-swaggering cockroach may want to retreat under a floorboard.

WHO PUT THE PB IN THE PB&J?

What goes equally well with jelly, bacon, marshmallow fluff, chocolate, and banana? Peanut butter, of course. And most schoolkids think that George Washington Carver is the man behind that magic.

The Well-Traveled Peanut

The myth that George Washington Carver invented peanut butter has spread as easily as this spreadable favorite. But by the time Carver was born in 1864, peanuts were being crushed into a paste on five continents. Peanuts have been grown for consumption in South America since 950 B.C., and the Incas used peanut paste in much of their cooking. Fifteenth-century trade ships took peanuts to Africa and Asia, where they were assimilated into local cuisines, often as a paste used for thickening stews. In the 18th century, peanuts traveled back across the Atlantic Ocean to be traded to North American colonists. In 1818, the first commercial peanut crop was produced in North Carolina. Today, there are approximately 50,000 peanut farms in the United States, and 50 percent of the peanuts produced on these farms are turned into peanut butter.

A Popular Nut Paste

So the Incas, not Carver, must be credited with first grinding peanuts into a paste. But the forefather of modern-day peanut butter was an anonymous doctor who, in 1890, put peanuts through a meat grinder to provide a protein source for people with teeth so bad they couldn't chew meat. A food-processing company saw the potential in the doctor's product and started selling the nut paste for $0.06 per pound. Dr. John Harvey Kellogg (the inventor of corn flakes) had been feeding a similar paste made from steamed, ground peanuts to the patients at his sanatorium in Battle Creek, Michigan. In 1895, he patented his "process of preparing nut meal" and began selling it to the general public.

The nut paste caught on, and peanut-grinding gadgets became readily available, along with cookbooks full of recipes for nut meals, pastes, and spreads. In 1904, visitors at the St. Louis World's Fair bought more than $700 worth of peanut butter. In 1908, the Krema Nut Company in Columbus, Ohio, began selling peanut butter, but only within the state because of problems with spoilage.

Carver's Contributions

So how did George Washington Carver get in the middle of this peanutty story? Carver was an agricultural chemist, inventor, and innovator who had a strong interest in peanut production and a firm belief that it could benefit American agriculture. Although born to slaves, Carver worked and studied hard. He earned master's degrees in botany and agriculture from Iowa Agricultural College (now Iowa State University), and he became the director of agriculture at the Tuskegee Normal and Industrial Institute for Negroes in 1897.

At the Tuskegee Institute, Carver researched and developed approximately 290 practical and esoteric uses for peanuts, incorporating them into foods, cosmetics, ink, paper, and lubricants. He didn't patent any of these products, believing that the earth's crops and their by-products were gifts from God. Although he published several works about the benefits of peanuts in agriculture, industry, and cuisine, he became nationally associated with the crop only late in his career.

Influential Nonetheless

The story of Carver's humble beginnings, talents, and professional success took on mythic proportions. A number of articles and biographies generously (and erroneously) credit him with everything from inventing dehydrated foods to rescuing the South from crushing poverty by promoting peanut products. At some point, the invention of peanut butter was attributed to him.

Schoolchildren everywhere are entranced by Carver's personal success story and his contributions to American agriculture. He is a role model despite the fact that he didn't invent peanut butter. Giving credit where it's due—to the Incas—does not diminish the value of Carver's accomplishments.

HOW DID HOUDINI DIE?

*Ehrich Weiss, better remembered as Harry Houdini,
was the master escape artist and illusionist of his time—perhaps
of all time. Contrary to rumor, though, he did not die
at the hands of angry spiritualists.*

Several of Houdini's stunts almost did him in, especially if sabotage or malfunction affected the gear. He finished numerous escapes bleeding, bruised, or otherwise broken. But he was always a "show must go on" performer, and that's ultimately what caused his death.

Houdini was a consummate showman, but he was also a trifle odd. He developed the macho habit of encouraging people to test his stony abs by slugging him in the gut. In 1926, while visiting Houdini backstage before a performance in Montreal, a college student asked to give the famous abs the punch test. The eager recruit hit him before the magician could brace himself for the repeated blows, and a terrible pain shot through Houdini's side. Despite his agony, that night's performance went on.

Later that evening, still in severe pain, Houdini was reading a newspaper while waiting for a train to his next gig, in Detroit. A burly "fan" approached him and drove a fist straight through the paper and into the performer's stomach, worsening matters considerably.

In Detroit, Houdini finished his show by sheer will before finally checking into a hospital. Doctors found that he had an abnormally long appendix that spanned his pelvis, and as a result of the blows, it had ruptured. Rumors began to swirl that the student who had punched Houdini was actually an offended member of a group of spiritualists whom Houdini often spoke against and attempted to expose. The truth isn't quite so sensational. Houdini died of peritonitis six days after he was hospitalized—quite fittingly, on Halloween.

BIRD ON A WIRE

*Few names call to mind a love of birds more than that of John Audubon,
but any bird with a brain would have done well to steer clear of him!*

There is no doubt that 19th-century wildlife illustrator John James
Audubon cared about his feathered friends. He devoted his life to
their study, observing and drawing them from the time he was a
child. However, Audubon's shotgun was as important a tool as his
paintbrush. He may have loved birds, but he had no qualms about
killing them.

In the era before photography, most wildlife illustrators used
stuffed animal carcasses as their models. That's how Audubon,
a self-taught artist, began drawing birds. Frustrated by the lack
of vibrancy in his illustrations, he set out to find new ways to
draw the birds he had shot. His ultimate goal was to "represent
nature…alive and moving!" It was at this time that he began pierc-
ing freshly killed birds, securing them to boards and using wires to
pose them into "lifelike" positions. Eventually, Audubon mastered
the technique of manipulating fresh carcasses like puppets and
was able to draw birds as they had never been rendered before.
His paintings showed animals in lifelike situations—nesting, hunting, and even feeding one another.

On Behalf of Birds

Although the National Audubon Society has no connection to John
Audubon other than the use of his name, would this environmental
group even want him as a member? By contemporary standards,
probably not, but in his day Audubon was as close to a conservation-
ist as you could get. Even though he shot thousands of birds in his
lifetime, he was also one of the first to sound alarms over the destruction and loss of bird habitats. Had he been born a hundred years
later, Audubon probably would have readily traded his gun for an even
better tool with which to capture birds–a camera.

HOW MANY
WORDS FOR SNOW?

❈ ❈❈ ❈

The notion that the Inuit have dozens
of words for snow is widespread, completely false,
and still taught in schools. How did this unfounded
myth gain such momentum?

From Ivory Towers to Pop Culture

Most people have been told at least once that "Eskimos" (explanation to follow) have many words for snow. This pearl of wisdom is usually shot off in an academic setting as an example of how different cultures adapt their language to the specifics of their environment. Few know that this "fact" is not only false but makes no sense, given a basic understanding of Eskimo languages.

The myth got started in 1911 when renowned anthropologist Franz Boas pointed out that Eskimos have four distinct root words for snow, translating as "snow on the ground," "falling snow," "drifting snow," and "snowdrift." It is unclear where Boas collected this linguistic data. Eskimos speak a polysynthetic language, meaning they take a root word, such as *snow*, and then add on to it a potentially endless number of descriptors. For example, Eskimos could take their root word for *snowdrift* and tack on to it their words for *cold, high, insurmountable,* and *frightening,* thus creating one very long and descriptive word. Because the language works in this way, there are, technically, an infinite number of "Eskimo words for snow."

Because Boas was widely read in academic circles, textbooks soon started to make seemingly random claims about the number of ways Eskimos refer to snow. According to Roger Brown's *Words and Things,* Eskimos have just three words for snow. Carol Eastman, in *Aspects of Language and Culture,* claims they have "many words" for snow. Once these academic postulations such as these drifted into the mainstream, the number of Eskimo words for snow inexplicably skyrocketed. A 1984 *New York Times* article put the number at 100, while a 1988 article in the same paper marveled at the "four dozen" different words for snow.

What Is an "Eskimo" Word, Anyway?

The Eskimo-words-for-snow myth becomes even more nonsensical when you consider that there is no such thing as one "Eskimo" language. "Eskimo" has become a popular blanket term for the indigenous peoples of eastern Siberia, Alaska, Canada, and Greenland. Eskimos are generally divided into the Inuit and Yupik. In some regions, the term "Inuit" has come to be used as a replacement term for "Eskimo," but in other regions this is not accepted, as not all Eskimos are Inuit. The groups collectively referred to as Eskimo or Inuit speak many different languages, though there are commonalities among them.

The popularity of the language myth is fueled by an "Oh wow, aren't they strange!" factor that often comes with fast facts about different cultures. Even if some Inuit languages do have more words for snow, that fact in itself isn't terribly provocative. Linguist Geoffrey Pullum points out in his essay *The Great Eskimo Vocabulary Hoax:* "Botanists have names for leaf shapes; interior decorators have names for shades of mauve; printers have many names for different fonts... would anyone think of writing about printers the same kind of slop we find written about Eskimos in bad linguistics textbooks?"

Perhaps at some point in the future, a rumor will spread among the Eskimos that "Americans" have a dizzying number of words for snow, including but not limited to *flurry, blizzard, nieve, neve, slush, schnee, snowball,* and *snowflake.*

What's the Eskimo Word for "House"?

That would be *igloo,* and another misconception is that Eskimos of yore lived in rounded structures made from neatly stacked ice blocks. In fact, basic igloos could be constructed quickly and were typically used only as emergency shelters. Eskimos lived in sod houses in the winter months and tents in the summer.

THE TALL AND SHORT ON COFFEE

*A cup of java may keep kids up at night,
but it won't affect their height.*

In past generations, parents didn't allow their children to drink coffee, believing that it would stunt their growth. But today, kids are consuming coffee in record numbers and at younger ages. In fact, young people are now the fastest-growing coffee-drinking group in the United States.

Does this trend indicate a corresponding shrinkage in the younger generation's adult height? No, say researchers. There is no evidence that drinking coffee affects growth or a person's eventual height.

At one time there seemed to be a link between caffeine consumption and the development of osteoporosis, and that may be how coffee originally got blamed for inhibiting growth. Early studies suggested that drinking lots of caffeinated beverages contributed to reduced bone mass.

More recent studies have debunked that idea. Dr. Robert Heaney of Creighton University found that much of the preliminary research on caffeine and bone loss was done on elderly people whose diets were low in calcium. Other researchers have noted that even if caffeine does affect bone mass, its influence is minimal and can easily be counteracted with a sufficient amount of calcium-rich foods.

The myth that coffee stunts growth was laid to rest by a study that followed 81 adolescents for six years. At the end of the study, there was no difference in bone gain or bone density between those who drank the most coffee and those who drank the least.

In other words, don't worry about letting your kids have an occasional cup of joe, but unless you want to be up all night while they bounce off the walls, make sure they drink it in the morning.

WYATT EARP

*Movies, books, and legends have
surrounded one of the Old West's most famous
names with a cloud of gunsmoke. Was he was
a hardened killer who took advantage of his job title?
On the contrary, Wyatt Earp was a good cop.*

Even in rough towns, most citizens wanted law and order. Only the criminals wanted lawlessness, and they weren't the majority even in Tombstone, Dodge City, or Wichita—three places Wyatt Earp wore a badge.

Earp earned a reputation for firm law enforcement. Everyone made the same claim: If you were breaking the law, Earp would surely make you stop. He didn't care how big the gang was, but he also didn't want innocent civilians getting involved—for their own safety. Most Westerners had heard of Wyatt Earp and didn't want trouble with him. His reputation helped keep things dull, in the best of ways.

Earp avoided excessive force. He preferred using a pistol-barrel crack to the noggin followed by an arrest, and he kept the hammer on an empty chamber. The first time Earp actually killed anyone was during the gunfight at the OK Corral, when he shot Frank McLaury. The incident itself was a lawful arrest resisted by known felons who were using deadly force against legally appointed officers.

When Earp finally cut loose, it was only after serious personal provocation. Within a few months of the OK Corral incident, Wyatt's brothers were brutally ambushed—Virgil was seriously wounded and Morgan died. Wyatt tried to resign from his police position, but his superiors refused the resignation. He then went on a rampage against his brothers' attackers, hunting them down and killing them. Wrong as that was, Earp never undertook the revenge ride under pretense of legal policing.

WOUND CARE CATASTROPHE!

Hydrogen peroxide isn't the miracle cure it's cracked up to be.

You'll find a brown plastic bottle of hydrogen peroxide in most medicine chests, right next to the iodine and calamine lotion. It's been touted for decades as the ideal treatment for cuts, scrapes, and other minor wounds.

There's just one problem, medical experts say: Applying hydrogen peroxide to open wounds may actually do more harm than good.

Hydrogen peroxide became an integral part of most home first-aid kits because people had the mistaken belief that it killed germs and helped wounds heal faster. However, recent studies have found that hydrogen peroxide can actually damage the healthy tissue around a wound, which slows the healing process. Worse, it's a lousy germ fighter. Many other compounds, such as over-the-counter antibacterial salves, work much better.

In recent years, hydrogen peroxide has been touted as a cure for everything from cold sores to foot fungus to arthritis. Few of these claims have been confirmed by the Food and Drug Administration (FDA), which warns that hydrogen peroxide in high concentrations can be dangerous and even deadly if swallowed.

The FDA has approved just one home use for hydrogen peroxide—as a mouthwash. But even then it should be used infrequently. According to researchers at Massachusetts General Hospital, extended use of hydrogen peroxide as a mouth rinse can damage cells and soften tooth enamel.

Hydrogen peroxide comes in a variety of strengths. Most household hydrogen peroxide products are 3 percent solutions. Much higher concentrations are available commercially for disinfectant and other uses.

So when you scrape your skin, don't reach for the hydrogen peroxide. There are better products to use on your wound.

ETHAN ALLEN

✳ ❖ ✳

*In the spring of 1775, when Ethan Allen and Benedict Arnold
seized strategic Fort Ticonderoga at the start of the Revolutionary
War, it's said that Allen claimed to have done so "in the name
of the Great Jehovah and the Continental Congress."*

That's the explanation Allen later alleged he gave British lieutenant
Jocelyn Feltham, who challenged Allen's authority to enter Fort
Ticonderoga. It sounds so red-white-and-blue: The homespun,
religious citizen-soldier cites God and Country as his authorities,
and the rebellious redcoat backs off. There is, alas, good reason to
believe Allen's words were cruder.

By all accounts, Allen was often crude—because he had to be.
No mild-mannered dilettante could possibly have controlled Allen's
Vermont militia, the Green Mountain Boys, who despised New York
and the British alike. It is unlikely Allen would have invoked the
Continental Congress, because he hardly respected its authority; it
is far more likely he would have heaped scorn upon said Congress.

Another problem with the quote is its source—Ethan Allen
himself. Lieutenant Feltham and one of Allen's junior officers
agree, nearly to the word, that Allen actually yelled, "Come out of
there, you damned old rat!"

A Reason for Treason

Allen's command, by the way, lived down to his example. To the Green
Mountain Boys' glee, the surrendering British captain kept a private
stock of 90 gallons of rum. What do you suppose occurred? A party!
When Arnold tried to enforce some discipline among the inebriated
troops, two Green Mountain Boys shot at him. Luckily for Arnold, drunks
aren't good shots, but Allen relieved Arnold of authority—at gunpoint. No
wonder Arnold became disgruntled and eventually committed treason.

YANKEE DOODLE DUDS

※ ※※ ※

*Is it possibly true that television ratings plummet when
the New York Yankees fail to reach the World Series?*

Can't Buy Victories

The acceptance of this myth lies in the belief that bigger is better, and in terms of baseball, no franchise can match the New
York Yankees in bang or bucks. The Yankees' operating budget in
2007 was an astronomical $216 million, more than the combined
totals of the Tampa Bay, Washington, Pittsburgh, and Florida
franchises. Despite the clout wielded by owner George Stein-
brenner's wallet, the Bronx Bombers have bombed on the playing
field, failing to reach the World Series from 2004 through 2007.
It is commonly believed that the Yankees' participation in the
Fall Classic lifts national television ratings to levels that match the
team's salaries. However, the figures that line the bottom line do
not support this argument.

Ordinary Ratings

In 2004, the series between the Boston Red Sox and the St. Louis
Cardinals garnished a 15.8 rating, among the highest in the previous 11 seasons. The 2005 through 2007 Fall Classics did not reach
the peaks of the late 1990s, but they hardly plummeted without
the presence of the Yankees. When New York does make the
Series, the ratings are merely mediocre. The 1998 World Series
between the Yankees and San Diego Padres attracted a 14.1 share
of the viewing public, the worst TV rating in post-season baseball
history up to that time. To further accentuate the
point, the much-anticipated 2000 Subway Series
between the Yankees and cross-town-rival New
York Mets garnished only a 12.4 rating, the worst
television percentage of any Yankee World Series
appearance. The Sultans of Swat may have the
cash, but they don't seem to have the clout.

GROUNDHOG RECKONING DAY

In the midst of our winter woes, we celebrate the groundhog—but is it a meteorological marvel or a marketing gimmick?

A Shadowy Assertion

The world's greatest weather forecaster, according to common belief, is essentially a large squirrel. No, it's not Al Roker—it's a groundhog. As the story goes, if the groundhog sees its shadow on February 2, there will be six more weeks of winter. No shadow means an early spring. How did this myth get started?

Lacking the Weather Channel, our ancestors relied on numerous methods of predicting the weather, and some were better than others. One had to do with animals (such as the groundhog, or "woodchuck") that hibernate in winter. If hibernating animals were out and about in the early part of the year, spring must be near.

The idea makes some sense from a meteorological standpoint as well. To see shadows, you need clear skies, and in winter that means cold weather. An overcast sky provides the earth with a blanket of warmth that could mean the end of winter. And since Groundhog Day falls on February 2—roughly halfway between the winter solstice and spring equinox—it has long been seen as a natural turning point for the weather.

Punxsutawney Phil

How did the lowly woodchuck become the bearer of winter weather reports? The notion seems to have begun with German settlers in Punxsutawney, Pennsylvania, where groundhogs are plentiful. In the late 1800s, a group of friends formed the Punxsutawney Groundhog Club to conduct an annual search for groundhogs. In 1887, the group introduced Punxsutawney Phil and proclaimed him to be the only "official" weather-predicting woodchuck. That title didn't last long. Many other cities and towns have since named their own meteorological rodents, but none have caught on like Punxsutawney Phil.

IT'S OVER THERE—THE REAL BATTLE OF BUNKER HILL

In June 1775, two months after the start of the American Revolution, the vicious Battle of Bunker Hill erupted in Charlestown, Massachusetts, across the Charles River from Boston. But where, exactly, did the fighting take place?

The logical answer is, of course, on Bunker Hill. History books continue to cite that location more than 230 years after the fact—but they actually have it wrong.

Word had gotten around that British troops were planning an attack from Boston, Massachusetts, where they held complete control. On June 16, nearly 1,000 American militiamen led by Colonel William Prescott dug into the highest land in the area—a spot known as Bunker's Hill. But the commander thought better of the location and moved his troops a half mile closer to Boston, a lower elevation referred to as Breed's Hill. The soldiers quickly built a barrier of dirt that was 6 feet high, 80 feet across, and 160 feet long.

The next morning, British major general William Howe led more than 2,200 redcoats from Boston against the militiamen. But they were hampered by a lack of boats, lousy maps, and low tides. While cannons fired against the patriots across the Charles River, Howe struggled to reach Charlestown itself. By mid-afternoon, his soldiers were finally ready to make their assault on Breed's Hill.

As the British advanced, Prescott famously yelled, "Don't fire until you see the whites of their eyes—then shoot low!" It took the Brits three separate charges to eventually overtake the position and capture Charlestown. But they paid a high price, with more than a thousand deaths and injuries among the troops. The militia, which had grown to more than 2,500 soldiers, suffered close to 400 casualties. But the grit and determination of the Americans led Howe to never again fight a battle in Massachusetts.

THE "ROSWELL" INCIDENT

*Whether or not you believe that space aliens
landed in Roswell, New Mexico, you are at least
entitled to know where the real crash site was.*

On July 7, 1947, something strange touched ground in New
Mexico. The two most popular theories are (1) that aliens crash-
landed in the desert—and the military covered up recovery of the
aircraft—and (2) that the wreckage consisted of the remnants of a
military research balloon launched from a nearby airfield.

That morning, rancher Mac Brazel, foreman of the Foster
Ranch near Corona, New Mexico, found strange metal debris and
a gouged-out trench across a portion of the property. After the
mysterious material was discovered, Brazel reported that the sheep
he was herding refused to cross the debris field, and from there,
reports of alien crash sites started springing up around the region.

Oddly, not one of the sites was actually in Roswell. On a detailed
map of the southeastern corner of New Mexico, amid the names of
mesas, canyons, and draws, one can find three "alleged UFO debris
sites": the Corona Site, the Jim Ragsdale Site, and a third one on the
Hub Corn Ranch. The third site is the closest to Roswell, but even
that is a good 30 miles north of town, down an isolated dirt road.
In a book about the incident, *Crash at Corona,* the authors note,
"Nothing crashed at Roswell, despite the titles of the books; it was
just the largest city within 75 miles of the crash site."

Alien Exploitation

Roswell city officials realized they could put the rumor to good economic use: Today, the city is home to the International UFO Museum
and Research Center and hosts an annual UFO Festival, which
began in 1996. Despite the fact that the military and UFO believers remain at odds over the Roswell Incident, the city touts its alien
brand with pride.

SEEING DOUBLE

Can't tell which identical twin is which?
Check their fingerprints. Identical twins may look
like carbon copies, but research shows they are not exact
duplicates of each other. Indistinguishable to the eye,
some differences are skin deep—but most are much deeper.

Identical twins result when a zygote (a fertilized egg) divides in half, forming two embryos. The embryos develop in tandem and, at birth, are identical twin siblings. In the past it was largely assumed that identical twins were exact replicas of each other. After all, they formed from the exact same genetic material. But scientists have found that there are variations in identical twins' individual gene segments. Researchers believe these disparities occur in the womb, when dividing cells cause small genetic differences in each twin. This explains why one identical twin can develop a genetic disorder while the other twin remains healthy. It also is the reason one twin may be right-handed and the other left-handed.

In addition to subtle differences in their genetic blueprints, there is another difference in identical twins—their fingerprints. Fingerprints are formed while a fetus is growing and are the result of DNA and environmental influences in the womb. By the second trimester of pregnancy, the ridges and loops in our digits are permanently etched into our skin. Factors such as contact with amniotic fluid and the pressure of bone growth affect the unique patterns. Although no two fingerprints are alike, identical twins often have similar patterns.

The unique fingerprints can also assist confused parents who return home from the hospital with their newborn identical twins, remove the ID bracelets, and then can't figure out who is who. The babies can be identified by refingerprinting them and matching the prints with the originals on file at the hospital.

A CRITICAL MYTH

❋ ❋ ❋

*Contrary to a widespread rumor, famed film critic Gene Siskel
did not insist that he be buried with his thumb pointing up.*

Few in the specialized field of film criticism have been as well-
known or respected as Gene Siskel, who penned countless movie
reviews for the *Chicago Tribune* and later teamed up with fellow
critic Roger Ebert of the *Chicago Sun-Times* on the popular television show *Siskel & Ebert*.

The show was famous for its movie rating system of "thumbs up/
thumbs down," which became the duo's critical trademark. Shortly
after Siskel's death in 1999 from complications following brain surgery, this story started to circulate: Among other provisions, Siskel's
will stipulated that he be buried with his thumb pointing skyward.

Siskel's thumbs had made him internationally renowned, a
legacy that he may have wanted to take to his grave. The rumor
raced through the Internet in the form of a fake UPI news story
that noted Siskel's unusual request. It read, in part: "According
to public records filed in chancery court in Chicago, Gene Siskel
asked that he be buried with his thumb pointing upward. The
'Thumbs Up' was the Siskel-Ebert trademark."

The story continued: "'Gene wanted to be remembered as a
thumbs-up kind of guy,' said Siskel's lawyer. 'It wasn't surprising to
me that he'd ask for that. I informed his family after his death, but
he didn't want it made public until after his will had been read.'"

The faux article carries all of the marks of a typical urban legend. Most telling is its failure to identify Siskel's attorney by name,
which no legitimate news organization would do.

❋ ❋ ❋

- *The magazine* Time Out New York *investigated the rumor and
  reported on July 15, 1999: "A glance at the will, now on file with
  a Chicago court, makes clear that there are no digit-placement
  requests in [Siskel's] last wishes."*

EARTH-SHAKING DEVELOPMENT

*Although it's widely regarded as the preferred
instrument for measuring earthquakes,
the Richter scale has long played second fiddle
to the moment magnitude scale.*

While listening to your car radio, you hear an earthquake bulletin.
The excited newscaster says, "Looks like this is the big one we've
dreaded. You seldom see anything this high on the moment magnitude scale!" The *what*?

The Richter Scale

You were expecting the guy to reference that *other* scale, the one
developed by seismologist Charles Richter in 1935, considered by
many to be the chief method for measuring the intensity of earthquakes. Although most people define a quake by its Richter scale
rating, assumptions of the scale's superiority are patently false.

The Richter scale measures an earthquake's shockwaves with
the use of a logarithmic scale on which each unit represents a
tenfold increase in energy (a 7.0 is ten times more powerful than
a 6.0). This measurement, which gives a general idea of an event's
magnitude, is limited because it cannot completely describe the
impact. This is particularly true of quakes that measure above 6.8,
where the scale saturates and "sees" each earthquake as the same.

The Moment Magnitude Scale

For more than a decade, scientists have used the moment magnitude scale to measure severe earthquakes. Taking into account such
factors as geological properties and ground slippage (displacement),
the moment magnitude scale—devised by seismologists Hiroo
Kanomori and Tom Hanks—expresses a tremor's total energy. Like
the Richter scale, it operates logarithmically. Unlike the Richter
scale, it doesn't saturate in its upper reaches and can more closely
pinpoint real-world effects and overall destruction. Perhaps news-
casters will get on board some day.

CHARMING CHARLATANS

The only thing mystifying about snake charmers is their cunning ability to bamboozle. Here's what's really happening when a cobra "dances" to the music.

Strolling past a bazaar in India, you spot a man sitting cross-legged in front of a basket. After he raises a flute and begins to play, a venomous cobra starts to sway, rhythmically "dancing" to the music. You look on, mesmerized. At times the serpent is mere inches from the snake charmer's face; indeed, the man even fearlessly "kisses" it. The man and his music seem to have a calming effect on the surly serpent.

In truth, it doesn't require much nerve to charm a cobra—and here are the dynamics behind the demonstration. Contrary to folklore, the much-feared cobra is not aggressive. In fact, it will try to scare off potential predators rather than fight them. A cobra accomplishes this by standing erect and flaring its hood. When it sets its sights on a potential threat, it will sway its body along with the motions of the intruder. Sound familiar?

A snake charmer knows this behavior well—and capitalizes on it. To get a cobra to rise from a basket and stand erect, the performer simply lifts the lid. Startled by the sudden light, the serpent emerges. But before the cobra will "dance" along with the flute music, it must first be conditioned to regard the instrument as an enemy (the performer will often tap the snake with it during "training" sessions). Once accomplished, the snake will follow the flute's every move.

What a Charmer!

When a snake charmer performs feats such as kissing or touching a cobra, he isn't risking much, because the snake lacks the ability to attack objects above its head. All of this looks quite perilous for the charmer, of course, and the audience walks away mystified and perhaps a few rupees poorer. How's that for charm?

THE TRUTH ABOUT SPACE TRAVEL

Like nature, humans abhor a vacuum,
and we've been filling the void of scientific knowledge
with near-truths and outright falsehoods ever since
we broke the grip of Earth's gravity. Here are a few.

There is no gravity in space. There is a difference between "weightlessness" and "zero-g" force. Astronauts may effortlessly float inside a space shuttle, but they are still under the grasp of approximately 10 percent of Earth's gravity. Essentially, gravity will decrease as the distance from its source increases—but it never just vanishes.

Gravitational forces are powerful enough to distort a person's features. This popular notion can be traced to the fertile minds of Hollywood filmmakers, who quickly learned the value of "artistic license" when dealing with the subject of outer space. In 1955's *Conquest of Space,* director Byron Haskin portrayed space travelers stunned and frozen by the forces of liftoff, pressed deep into their seats with their faces grotesquely distorted. When humankind actually reached space in 1961, the truth became known: Although gravitational forces press against the astronauts, they are perfectly capable of performing routine tasks, and their faces do not resemble Halloween masks.

An ill-suited astronaut will explode. Filmmakers would have you believe that an astronaut who is exposed to the vacuum of space without the protection of a spacesuit would expand like a parade float. With eyes bulging and the body swelling like a big balloon, the poor soul would soon blow up. It would be a gruesome sight, indeed, but that's not the way it would happen. The human body is too tough to distort in a complete vacuum. The astronaut would double over in pain and eventually suffocate, but that unfortunate occurrence would likely not make the highlight reel.

Stranded space travelers will be asphyxiated. The film world's take on space dangers has occasionally spilled into reality. In movies such as *Marooned,* astronauts are stuck in space as their oxygen supply runs out. Although the danger of being stranded in space is very real *(Apollo 13* comes to mind), astronauts in such a situation would not die from lack of oxygen. Carbon dioxide in a disabled spacecraft could build up to life-threatening levels long before the oxygen ran out.

The world watched as the *Challenger* "exploded." Myth even lies in one of the most tragic spaceflights in U.S. history—the *Challenger* disaster of January 1986. Stories tell of the millions of horrified viewers who watched as the spacecraft and its solid-rocket boosters broke apart on live television. Except for cable network CNN, however, the major networks had ceased their coverage of the launch. Because crew member Christa McAuliffe was to be the first teacher in space, NASA had arranged for public schools to show the launch on live TV. Consequently, many of those who actually saw it happen were schoolchildren. It was only when videotaped replays filled the breaking newscasts that "millions" of people were able to view the catastrophe. Another misconception about the *Challenger* is that it actually "exploded." It didn't, at least not in the way most people assume. The shuttle's fuel tank ripped apart, but there was no blast or detonation.

We even have the quote wrong. History has attributed this famous quote to Neil Armstrong as he stepped from the lunar module and became the first man on the moon in July 1969: "That's one small step for man, one giant leap for mankind." But Armstrong was misquoted. He never intended to speak on behalf of thousands of years of human development by declaring it "one small step for man." An innocent "a" got lost in the clipped electronic transmission of nearly 250,000 miles. According to Armstrong himself (and upon further review of the recording), he said, "That's one small step for a man, one giant leap for mankind," giving a much more humble tone to his statement.

CRIME-BUSTING BEATLES

As more than 74 million people watched the Beatles' first performance on the Ed Sullivan Show *in February 1964, it's said that felons in the United States refrained from thugging long enough to case the Fab Four.*

Missing the Joke

Alas, the Beatles' career as crime-countering crusaders is highly overrated. B. F. Henry, a writer for the *Washington Post,* perpetrated this myth with his poison pen. Henry wrote a sneering and satirical editorial about the Beatles' TV debut, concluding that this was the only good thing about their appearance: "During the hour they were on *Ed Sullivan,* there wasn't a single hubcap stolen in America." As with most scripted sarcasm, the message went soaring over the heads of Henry's readers, who took the comment at face value. The quote gained national prominence when *Newsweek* reprinted it—without the nuanced derision.

Soon, myth mongers were inferring that between eight and nine o'clock on that Sunday evening, crime and time stood still. Even George Harrison believed the hype, stating, "While we were on, there were no reported crimes, or at least very few. When the Beatles were on *Ed Sullivan,* even the criminals had a rest for ten minutes."

Hubcap Hullabaloo

The simple truth is that crime and criminal patterns are not measured by the hour, so there is no way to accurately gauge whether the streets in the United States were safer while the Beatles tossed tunes at their adoring fans. As for the hubcap issue, a guy named Lawrence Fellenz, of Alexandria, Virginia, reported that all four of his were stolen off his vehicle that very same night. Hmm…that's one for each Beatle, so the question becomes: Were John, Paul, George, and Ringo really the ones performing on Sullivan's stage that evening? That's another rumor for another time.

DO UNTO OTHERS

The Golden Rule is one of the world's most widespread moral philosophies. It's also the basis of a series of quotes so often misquoted as to make misquotes irrelevant.

Socrates may never have said, "Do unto others as you would like done to you," but he did say something to the effect of "Do not do unto others what angers you if done to you by others." This translation wins few points for eloquence, but the bottom line is that Socrates, Confucius, or Jesus could all be attributed with stating the Golden Rule in one version or another, and it serves as the moral basis for religion and philosophy the world over.

The Golden Rule is so pervasive that many modern ethicists think it represents some fundamental truth of human morality. Adherence to the rule necessitates empathy and imagination, as it requires one person to imagine how another person would feel in a given situation. So whoever said which version, the essence remains the same: Treat people how you want to be treated.

Variations on the Golden Rule

A comprehensive list of Golden Rule quotes would be epic in length, but here are some examples: "He sought for others the good he desired for himself. Let him pass," from the Egyptian *Book of the Dead*; "And as you wish that men would do to you, so do them," from the Bible; "What is hateful to you, do not to your fellowman. This is the entire Law; all the rest is commentary," from Talmud; "This is the sum of duty: Do naught unto others which would cause you pain if done to you," from the Mahabharata; and, finally, to mix it up with some imagery, the proverb of Nigeria's Yoruba tribe: "One going to take a pointed stick to pinch a baby bird should first try it on himself to feel how it hurts."

SPANISH FLY

❋ ◈ ❋

Although dance is an essential element of the accomplished art of flamenco, it's by no means the most important. And unless they're performing for show, most dancers dress in black.

- The flamenco is often thought of as just a dance, but it's actually a complex musical convolution composed of four harmonious parts: guitar, vocals, dance, and hand clapping.

- Don't be fooled into thinking that the dance is widely performed throughout Spain. The flamenco's origins are rooted in one specific area of the country—Andalusia, a region composed of eight provinces, including Cardoba and Granada. It is generally acknowledged that flamenco grew out of the unique uniting of native Andalusian, Islamic, Sephardic, and Gypsy cultures.

- The central component that gives the flamenco its flavor is the music, a percussive portfolio of rhythm, tempo, and time. It sets the pulse of the spectacle and generates the pace and emotional center that fuel the visual aspect of the performance. The music is propelled and augmented by sweeping strums and rhythmic finger taps on the guitar, accompanied by hand claps and foot stomps, all employed to create and caress the beat. The flamenco dance is an impassioned, powerful performance characterized by grand gesturing with the arms and intricate footwork.

- Many Spanish dancers who perform for crowds of tourists hold castanets or wear them on their fingers to further accent the cadence and tempo of the music; likewise, these dancers are more likely to don elaborate costumes. Women wear long dresses that are adjusted at the waist and complemented by an underskirt that may be colorful, plain, or adorned with polka dots. Flounces or strips of pleated material on the skirt and the sleeves provide the final visual effect.

DISNEY ON ICE

When his family shared only sketchy details
of Walt Disney's death and next-day funeral
with the media, a rumor germinated:
He'd been cryonically frozen and was stashed under
Pirates of the Caribbean *at Disneyland.*

According to records at St. Joseph's Hospital in Burbank, California, Walter Elias Disney died of lung cancer on December 15, 1966. On December 16, his studios announced that the funeral had already taken place at the Little Church of the Flowers in Forest Lawn Memorial Park in Glendale, California. There was a small, private funeral, followed by cremation and entombment on December 17.

The speedy ceremony raised a few eyebrows. Disney's daughter Diane had written years earlier that her father was neurotic about death. But because he hated funerals and didn't want one, his family simply honored his wish with a private burial. Months later, when a California psychologist underwent the first cryonic preservation, rumors began to swirl that Disney himself had been frozen.

Disney, a wealthy technophile, certainly could have afforded the expense of early cryonic preservation, but there is no evidence that he was particularly interested in the procedure. Records reveal that Disney's estate paid $40,000 for his burial plot, and his ashes rest at Forest Lawn—at the ambient temperature.

❋❋❋

- *Another popular myth about Walt Disney is that just before he died, he prepared a videotaped presentation in which he advised top executives on how to keep his namesake business running profitably. However, this rumor presupposes that Disney actually ran his own corporation. In fact, he had little to do with business operations, leaving those details to his brother Roy.*

WHO ARE YOU CALLING A MONKEY?

❉ ❖ ❉

*Everyone knows what a monkey is...or maybe they
just think they do. Is a chimpanzee a monkey?
How about an orangutan or an ape?*

To answer these questions, one must wander into the confusing world of animal taxonomy, where scientists attempt to lump species together, figuring out which ones are closely related and which just look similar. Monkeys, prosimians, tarsiers, chimpanzees, and humans are all examples of the order known as primates, a relatively inclusive taxonomic category. Monkeys represent a suborder of primate that is more closely related to humans, genetically speaking, than to primates such as tarsiers.

All in the Family

After the primate category comes a less inclusive grouping known as a family. This is where apes come in. All apes belong to a family called Hominidae, which includes gibbons, gorillas, chimpanzees, orangutans, and humans. This family is subdivided into the "lesser apes" and the "great apes," and the latter category is reserved for chimpanzees, gorillas, humans, and orangutans (gibbons get chucked). Great apes are unique in that they have no tail, are larger than other primates, have unusually long gestation periods (eight to nine months), and have an extended adolescence.

Of the great apes, humans are most closely related to chimpanzees. To further complicate things, there are actually two main types of chimpanzees: common chimpanzees and bonobos, also known as pygmy chimpanzees. It seems that humans are equally related to both common chimpanzees and bonobos. Chimpanzees are known for their aggressive social relations, while bonobos prefer to make love instead of war. Many have wondered about the fact that humans seem to represent a fusion of the social behaviors of our two closest biological relatives, who most definitely are not monkeys.

THE INTELLIGENCE ON IQ TESTS

*IQ scores are best known as quantitative
representations of a person's intelligence.
Yet the original IQ test was intended to predict
future scholastic achievement, not intelligence.*

Relatively Smart?

The famed dumbbell Forrest Gump had an IQ of 75, but he did
pretty well for himself. He was a military hero, savvy businessman,
exceptional table tennis player, and beloved son, husband, and
father. An IQ test is supposed to measure intelligence, but there is
much debate over what an IQ score actually means.

A person's intelligence quotient is calculated according to
his or her performance on a standardized test. This means that
the score is not derived from how many questions are answered
correctly but on how many the person gets right *relative to others
who have taken the same test.* IQ tests are usually standardized
so that 100 is the mean score, and half of the scores lie within 10
points of the mean—so half the population has an IQ between
90 and 110. "IQ test" actually refers to a number of popular tests
that are standardized in a similar fashion, such as the Wechsler or
Stanford-Binet tests.

The first IQ test was developed in the late 1800s, hand-
in-hand with the appearance of special-education programs in
schools. Administrators needed a reliable way to identify those
who were unable to learn as easily or quickly as others. From the
beginning, then, IQ tests were meant to measure one's ability to
perform academic tasks; this is not necessarily synonymous with
intelligence.

Kinds of Smart

IQ test questions measure such functions as short-term memory,
vocabulary, perceptual speed, and visual-spatial reasoning. These

are all skills that help a person succeed in a school, work, or even social environment. Not surprisingly, high IQ scores are positively correlated with one's future academic success. They are also correlated, though not as strongly, with the socioeconomic status of one's parents, as well as on future income and future job performance.

Many researchers have pointed out that IQ tests neglect to calculate many types of talent that could also fall under the "intelligence" heading. Psychologist Howard Gardner developed his theory of multiple intelligences, which include linguistic, logical-mathematical, spatial, bodily-kinesthetic, musical, interpersonal, intrapersonal, and naturalist. Many multiple-intelligence tests try to include indicators of "books smarts," "street smarts," and "creativity smarts."

Testing IQ Tests

The reliability of IQ tests as meters of intelligence is also suspect because, on average, African American, Native American, and other minority or immigrant populations score lower than populations of Euro-American descent. These minority groups tend to come from areas where there is a high dropout rate and limited access to quality education. IQ tests are administered in standard English, which partly accounts for the low scores (especially in the verbal section) among people who speak other dialects of English or English as a second language.

Understanding Intelligence

IQ tests are reliable indicators of proficiency in cognitive skills that are important in the modern academic system, yet they may not be a measure of an absolute, stable "intelligence." The famed scientist and developmental theorist Jean Piaget envisioned intelligence as an elusive quality that is best summarized as a person's ability to perceive and understand the situation he or she is in and the capacity to act accordingly. The IQ test does measure something, but the wisdom of assuming this "something" is intelligence remains in question.

HOW OLD IS OLD IRONSIDES?

*It is the oldest warship in the U.S. Navy—and it's
still in service. But the 44-gun frigate USS* Constitution,
*the hero of the War of 1812, has survived
only through numerous restoration
efforts and a lot of patriotic passion.*

The Legend's Service Record

Commissioned in 1797, this salty warrior made its name in an
1812 duel with Britain's HMS *Guerriere* off Nova Scotia. As
Guerriere fought for its life, a U.S. sailor watched a British can-
nonball glance off *Constitution* and crowed, "Its sides are made
of iron!" The name ennobled a legend. A few months after *Guerriere* settled beneath the Atlantic waves, *Constitution* wrecked the
speedy HMS *Java* off Brazil. Later, Old Ironsides would pummel
two smaller vessels, HMS *Cyane* and HMS *Levant,* taking *Cyane*
into U.S. service as a prize.

Old Ironsides actively served until 1855. The ship sat out the
Civil War in New England after a quick escape from Annapolis.
When the war ended, the Navy meant to tow it back, but Old
Ironsides returned under its own power ten hours ahead of the
steam tug. However, things were about to get ugly for the brave
old frigate. By 1871, its sea legs were failing, so the Navy sent it to
Philadelphia for repairs.

A Humiliated Hulk

Even given five years' lead time, no one managed to get *Constitution* shipshape for the 1876 Centennial. The job was completed
a year late, with questionable workmanship and materials. On its
last foreign cruise in 1879, Old Ironsides ran aground off Dover,
England, then endured its worst indignity to date: It had to be
hauled to safety by a British tug. The Navy sent it to Portsmouth,
New Hampshire, and built barnlike barracks on its deck to house
new recruits, much like Noah's Ark.

National Change of Heart

By 1900, some felt it was time to use Old Ironsides for target practice, but Congress realized that a national treasure was going to waste. Work finally started in 1906, and the deeper the crews dug, the worse decay they found—especially in the original timbers. A national campaign raised one-fourth of the million dollars needed to gut and restore the ship, which took until 1930. It spent the next four years showing the flag from Puget Sound to Bar Harbor, visited and loved by millions.

Later Restorations

Old Ironsides's home port is Boston, and there it spends most of its time as a beloved monument to the days of a young Republic. It underwent major renovations in the mid-1950s, early 1970s, and early 1990s, and by now even its original cannons have been replaced. Though only the keel and some ribs remain of the proud frigate that watched HMS *Guerriere*'s masts fall, Old Ironsides gets better care entering its third century of service than it ever has. After far too much abuse, it finally has the dignity it is due.

Facts About Old Ironsides

- USS *Constitution* is a Vietnam veteran! In 1845, the West called Vietnam "Cochin-China." *Constitution*'s captain impulsively sent a U.S. Marine force ashore at Da Nang (where many other Marines would serve 120 years later) to demand a French missionary's release from captivity. Vietnamese officials called his bluff, and the captain backed off.

- In 1821, the Navy attempted to fit Old Ironsides with sailor-powered paddlewheels. Its captain took them off before the test was finished but didn't explain why. Reasonable guess: As a conservative old salt, he found the newfangled rig more trouble than it was worth.

- *Constitution* is still a ship of war, with a large enough crew to function as such. Were New England ever invaded, Old Ironsides's captain could theoretically put to sea and run out the guns.

HOLLYWOOD HERESY

*Credit Hollywood, not Notre Dame football coach Knute Rockne,
with the emotional plea "Win one for the Gipper."*

The oft-repeated line is from the movie *Knute Rockne: All American,* which was released in 1940. In the famous football flick, Rockne tells his troops that their teammate George Gipp's dying words were: "Rock, sometime when the team is up against it and the breaks are beating the boys, tell them to go out there with all they've got and win just one for the Gipper." No one really knows what Gipp and his coach talked about in the days before the star player's death. Gipp died in 1920, and Rockne met his own tragic fate in a plane crash in 1931, so neither man was in a position to refute the scriptwriter's soliloquy.

What is known is this: Rockne didn't get around to using Gipp's request as a motivating muscle until 1928, a full eight years after George died. According to Francis Wallace, the newspaper reporter who was responsible for dubbing the team the "Fighting Irish," Rockne made his famous speech to his underdog charges before a game against Army at Yankee Stadium on November 10, 1928. Wallace reported that Rockne rose before the assembled throng and said, "The day before he died, George Gipp asked me to wait until the situation seemed hopeless and then ask a Notre Dame team to go out and beat Army for him. This is the day, and you are the team." Although that does evoke the spirit of "win one for the Gipper," in reality those words are a Hollywood embellishment.

The quote gained new life when Ronald Reagan, who played the role of Gipp in the Hollywood homily about Rockne, used the catchphrase as a rallying cry during the 1988 Republican Convention.

THE LOWDOWN ON HOCKEY FIGHTS

❋ ❋❋ ❋

The old joke is, "I went to a fight and a hockey game broke out."
A typical pro football game has regular skirmishes, and major
league baseball teams clear the benches to brawl over
a hangnail. And people call hockey ultraviolent?

You've heard it before: "I love hockey! It's the only team sport that allows fighting." In fact, it doesn't. Hockey measures penalties in minutes: two-minute minors, five-minute majors, ten-minute misconducts, and ejection for a game misconduct or match penalty. Fighting is a five-minute major penalty.

Can't You Play Nice?
Let's compare some of the other hockey crimes, many of which merit less sin-bin time than fighting. You can't shove with the shaft of the stick, hook someone with it, or slash with it like a broadsword. These minor penalties usually merit only two minutes in the hockey hoosegow. Major penalties besides fighting include stabbing with the stick's blade or butt, ramming someone too hard into the boards (how subjective is that?), and any flagrant version of a minor penalty (e.g., you shove someone aside with the stick shaft in his face).

That's Some Sport
If you join a fight in progress or get your third fighting major in the game, you'll be charged with automatic game misconduct. Breaking your stick in frustration, grossly disrespecting officials, and flipping the bird or a puck at the fans: misconduct. Leaving the penalty box early: game misconduct. Pulling hair: match penalty. You can also get the heave-ho for kicking with your skate blade, spitting on someone, head-butting, throwing the stick like a javelin, face-masking, biting, or any act seen as a deliberate attempt to injure. On second thought, maybe the game *is* ultraviolent.

COPYRIGHT CLARIFICATIONS

What is the link between Jaws, Starlight Express,
and Strawberry Fields? *They are all titles of creative
works—and they cannot be copyrighted.*

Like a patent or a trademark, a copyright gives the creator of an
original work the exclusive right to control and profit from his or
her efforts. Although literary works, movies, songs, paintings, and
video games can all be copyrighted, not all forms of intellectual
property can be protected. Titles of books, plays, songs, and films
are not protected by copyright.

Copy Cats

According to the U.S. Copyright Office, title 17, section 102 of the
copyright code extends only to "original works of authorship" and
clearly states that ideas, concepts, and titles are not subject to copyright protection. The copyright on a novel such as *The Da Vinci
Code*, for example, is designed to restrict others from creating
derivative works based on Dan Brown's story of a Harvard symbol-
ogist deciphering a code hidden in the works of Leonardo da Vinci.
It does not, however, prevent someone from writing a book or a
play or making a movie about codes hidden in famous paintings, as
long as it is not judged to be a copy of Brown's work. There is also
nothing to prevent someone from using *The Da Vinci Code* as a
title for his or her work. This is one reason why there are so many
movies with the same or similar titles. The other reason, of course,
is that Hollywood has never been known for its originality.

In some instances, titles that fall into the category of brand
names may be entitled to protection under trademark laws, but for
the most part there is nothing to stop you from publishing a book
with the same title as a best seller. As long as the actual content
of the book is not copied or closely adapted, no one can claim
infringment. That's not to say someone won't try, though, and
copyright lawyers tend to be a particularly litigious bunch.

LINDBERGH'S HISTORIC FLIGHT

*Acclaimed aviator Charles Augustus Lindbergh became
famous for his historic flight in the* Spirit of St. Louis,
but he was not the first to fly nonstop across the Atlantic.

On May 21, 1927, the airplane *Spirit of St. Louis* touched down in
Paris, France, having just made a nonstop flight from Long Island,
New York. Undertaken by Charles Lindbergh (who was affectionately known by the nicknames "Lucky Lindy" and "The Lone
Eagle"), the 3,610-mile flight was indeed a first in aviation history
and catapulted Lindbergh to international celebrity. But it was not
the first nonstop flight across the Atlantic Ocean. That feat was
accomplished by two British pilots, Captain John William Alcock
and Lieutenant Arthur Whitten Brown. On June 15, 1919, they
successfully flew their modified bomber aircraft from St. John's,
Newfoundland, to Galway, Ireland. Although the aircraft crash-
landed in a bog near the town of Clifden, the flight stands as the
first nonstop transatlantic crossing.

By the time Lindbergh emulated Alcock and Brown's achievement in the *Spirit of St. Louis* nearly eight years later, at least 81
people had already made the trip. What sets Lindbergh apart is
that he was the first to fly *solo* across the Atlantic without stopping.
He took off from the Roosevelt Airfield in Garden City on May 20
and arrived at Le Bourget Airport in Paris 33.5 hours later.

* *Lindbergh's daring solo achievement earned him the
$25,000 Orteig Prize offered by New York hotelier Raymond
Orteig, a ticker-tape parade along New York's 5th Avenue, the
Distinguished Flying Cross, and eventually a Medal of Honor.
The former Minnesota farm boy's accomplishment also boosted
the public's interest in flying, a phenomenon referred to as the
"Lindbergh Boom." For the first time, people began to view air
travel as a safe, reliable means of transportation.*

WITH A WHISTLE
IN HIS HAND

*"The Ballad of Casey Jones" was first sung in 1900,
and more than 40 versions of the catchy tune have been
recorded in the years since. Despite his folkloric status,
however, Casey Jones was a real person.*

John Luther Jones was born in 1863 and grew up in Cayce, Kentucky. While working as a railroad engineer on the Illinois Central Railroad, known as the IC, his fellow railroad men dubbed him Cayce Jones after his hometown. His wife mistakenly spelled it Casey in her letters to him, and the name stuck. Without the popular folk song, however, it's unlikely anyone would remember Casey Jones today.

The ballad tells of Jones's heroic death in April 1900, when he gave his life to save the passengers on the train he was driving. After his death, Jones's friend Wallace Saunders, an engine wiper for the IC, coined the lyrics and set them to the tune of a popular song at the time called "Jimmie Jones." Soon it was sung all along the IC. In 1909, vaudeville performers T. Lawrence Seibert and Eddie Newton had the song published under the title "Casey Jones: The Brave Engineer."

Although the ballad celebrates Jones's heroism, an investigation concluded that he was responsible for the train accident that took his life. In the early morning hours of April 30, Jones drove engine 382 toward the town of Vaughn, Mississippi. A disabled freight train on the same track could not clear the way, and Jones slammed on the airbrakes to slow his train. He was unable to avoid a collision, but because of his quick actions, only the caboose suffered impact. Jones's body was discovered in the wreckage with one hand on the brake lever and the other, as the song correctly suggests, on the whistle chord.

THE SIX WIVES OF HENRY VIII

*A lot of people think that England's King Henry VIII had
a penchant for chopping off the heads of his wives. In truth,
only two of his brides got the ax.*

History has much to say about England's King Henry VIII (1491–1547) and his six wives. Henry was certainly the marrying type, yet he held no qualms about ending a marriage that inconvenienced him. How he ended those marriages is where historical fact blurs into misconceptions. Many people believe that as Henry lost interest in his wives, they lost their heads on the executioner's block.

But Henry wasn't quite the lady killer he's perceived to be. In actuality, two of Henry's wives survived their marriage to him, and only two were beheaded. Here's a brief look at how things really ended between Henry and his brides.

Catherine of Aragon (1485–1536): married 1509, divorced 1533. Catherine of Aragon proved to be the most tormented of Henry's wives. It didn't help that she wasn't considered attractive, but she was doomed by her inability to provide Henry with a male heir (their only surviving child, Mary, would later establish her own blood-stained reign). Catherine suffered through Henry's scorn, neglect, and public infidelities, most notably with her eventual successor in the royal marital bed, Anne Boleyn.

By 1526, desperate for a son and smitten by Anne, Henry began his ultimately unsuccessful petitioning of Pope Clement VII for an annulment from Catherine. In 1533, he denounced Clement's authority and married the now-pregnant Anne. That same year, the Archbishop of Canterbury annulled Henry's marriage to Catherine, who died in prayer-filled exile in dark, damp Kimbolton Castle three years later.

Anne Boleyn (c. 1500–36): married 1533; executed 1536.
Henry truly loved Anne—just not while they were married. She, too, fell out Henry's favor for not producing a son (their only child

would later rule as Queen Elizabeth I). She also had a knack for making enemies among powerful members of Henry's court. Those same enemies, taking advantage of Henry's growing infatuation with Anne's lady-in-waiting, Jane Seymour, pinned trumped-up charges of adultery, witchcraft, and treason on Anne that cost her her head in 1536.

Jane Seymour (1509–37): married 1536, died 1537. Only days after Anne's head rolled, Henry rolled the matrimonial dice with Jane Seymour. Jane produced the male heir Henry longed for (the future Edward VI) in October 1537 but died of complications from childbirth two weeks later. Her reward was to be the only one of Henry's wives to be buried with him in his Windsor Castle tomb.

Anne of Cleves (1515–57): married January 1540, divorced July 1540. Henry agreed to marry Anne of Cleves with the intention of gaining her brother, the Duke of Cleves, as an ally against France. Upon first glance of Anne, Henry called her a "Flanders mare" and declared his dislike. He married her anyway in January 1540, but his gaze quickly turned to the younger and prettier Catherine Howard. Anne, looking to save her neck, agreed to an annulment seven months later. The man who arranged the marriage, Henry's chief minister, Thomas Cromwell, was beheaded shortly after.

Catherine Howard (c. 1522–42): married 1540, executed 1542. Henry fell hard for Catherine Howard, whom he married 19 days after his annulment from Anne of Cleves. But the 49-year-old Henry lacked the sexual oomph to satisfy teenage Catherine, who began to seek satisfaction from men her age. The jilted Henry had her beheaded for adultery in February 1542.

Katherine Parr (1512–48): married 1543, widowed 1547. Henry took his final marital plunge with the twice-widowed Katherine Parr. Their marriage nearly ended over religious differences, but after patching things up they got along swimmingly—until Henry died in 1547 and made Katherine a widow for a third time.

LUNA TICKS

A full moon holds mysterious attractions,
prompting love at first sight, criminal malfeasance,
and boosted birthrates. Does the gleaming globe really
have magical powers, or is it just our state of mind?

For centuries, there have been reports of abnormal human behavior under the whole of the moon. Full moons have been linked to fluctuating rates of birth, death, crime, suicide, mental illness, natural and spiritual disasters, accidents of every description, fertility, and all kinds of indiscriminate howling. People with too much spare cash and not enough common sense have been known to buy and sell stocks according to phases of the moon. The word *lunatic* was coined to describe irrational and maniacal individuals whose conduct is seemingly influenced by the moon; their desolate domicile is dubbed the "loony bin."

Don't Blame it on the Moon

So is there a scientific relationship between the moon and human behavior? In 1996, researchers examined more than 100 studies that looked into the effects of the moon—full or otherwise—on an assortment of everyday events and anomalies, including births and deaths, kidnappings and car-jackings, casino payouts and lottery paydays, aggression exhibited by athletes, assaults and assassinations, suicides and murders, traffic accidents and aircraft crashes.

Dr. Ivan Kelly, a professor of educational psychology and human behavior, found that the "phases of the moon accounted for no more than $\frac{3}{100}$ of 1 percent of the variability in activities usually termed lunacy." This represents a percentage so close to zero that it can't be considered to have any theoretical, practical, or statistical interest. Because there was no significant correlation between the aforementioned occurrences and the periods and phases of the moon, it's safe to assume that the only moonshine that's causing trouble is the kind that's brewed in the Ozarks.

A REAL STRETCH

❀❀❀

During the Cold War, everyone was acutely aware of the Red Scare. But was the Marxist menace really so bad that highways in the United States were built as emergency runways?

The information highway has perpetrated more than its share of misconceptions, including one about highways in the United States. According to rumor mongers, the Federal-Aid Highway Act of 1956, which launched the Interstate Highway System and created a 42,800-mile ribbon of roads across the country, contained a clause that stated that one out of every five miles of newly paved blacktop had to be completely straight. The purpose of this rigid regiment of roads was to supply the U.S. military with a set of highway landing strips in case its aircraft came under attack and needed an emergency runway. These straight stretches were designed to be easily visible from the air, allowing a perplexed or panicked pilot to guide an aircraft to a safe stop.

However, from an aerial standpoint, this proposition makes no sense. Given the rate at which modern aircraft travel, a landing strip every five miles would be both unfeasible and unnecessary.

Although President Dwight D. Eisenhower fully supported the Interstate Highway System as a vital and viable link to secure the country's economy, safety, and defense, he never proposed any kind of one-out-of-five-mile rule, and Congress certainly didn't include such a requirement in the fine print of the Federal-Aid Highway Act. In other words, this myth has no basis in law or fact.

❀❀❀

• *Airplanes have occasionally landed on interstate highways, but that course of action has been taken only in cases of an emergency when no other alternative landing space was available.*

IT'S A DOG'S LIFE

*Ask a proud dog owner about the age
of his or her beloved pooch, and you'll likely hear this
response: "Well, Fido is five in human years,
so multiply that by seven, and he's 35 in canine
years." But doggone it, it's just not that easy.*

Calculating Canine Years

A number of factors are taken into account when one attempts to
equate a dog's developmental level with that of a human being.
Breed, size, heredity, nutrition, and training can affect and influence the development (and therefore the "human age") of a dog.
Generally speaking, human beings experience developmental
stages at these approximate ages: infant, 1 year; toddler, 3 years;
youngster, 6 years; adolescent, 11 years; teen, 15 years; adult,
20 years; mature adult, 65 years; old coot, 85 years. Note that the
rate of development is faster and closer together in the beginning
years and spreads out as time goes on.

Dogs experience similar developmental stages—they just
don't always hit at the same points and in the same time frames
as humans do. For example, an infant gains certain motor and
communications skills, as well as knowledge, in his or her first
year. In the same time period, most dogs—regardless of breed or
size—reach a physical and "emotional" maturity similar to that of a
teenager.

Almost all dogs develop at the same rate in their first 5 years.
Relative to human years, they generally follow this range:

1 human year = 15 dog years
2 human years = 24 dog years
3 human years = 28 dog years
4 human years = 32 dog years
5 human years = 36 dog years

A Breed Apart

Relatively speaking, a larger breed will "age" at a faster rate than a smaller breed. At 7 human years, a Chihuahua is considered 44 in dog years, whereas a Labrador has hit the big 5-0 in dog years. This span will continue to grow as the years go by. At 10 years old, the Chihuahua is 52 in dog years, where the Lab is ready to collect social security at 66.

Part of this growth disparity is due to the fact that larger breeds tend to have a shorter lifespan than smaller breeds. Larger breeds, such as Great Danes, St. Bernards, and Irish Wolfhounds, are susceptible to disabling ailments such as arthritis and hip dysplasia. Other concerns include adequate nutrition and health-care. If the family dog receives a balanced meal, as well as regular checkups and shots, it should live a full life. Also, just as humans do, dogs start to experience problems with sight, hearing, mobility, teeth, gums, and digestion as they near the "senior citizen" status of 60 or 70 dog years—a mere 12 or 13 human years. But the good news, according to veterinarians, is that a dog's average lifespan has increased from 7 to 12 years in the past 8 decades.

More Myths About Dogs

A wagging tail indicates a friendly dog. It depends on the position of the tail when it's wagging. A loose, mid-level wag usually indicates an approachable dog, but tails held high or low could signal an aggressive or defensive demeanor.

A dog is sick if its nose is warm. The assumption is that a warm-nose dog has a fever, but the fact is that a thermometer is the only reliable way to measure a dog's temperature. The normal body temperature for a dog is 100.5 to 102.5 degrees Fahrenheit.

AHEAD OF HIS TIME

It's long been claimed that Dr. Joseph-Ignace Guillotin, the presumed creator of the guillotine, was put to death during the French Revolution by the decapitating contraption that bears his name. It would be the ultimate irony—if the story were true.

Before we take a closer look at this long-lived myth, we should probably clear up a larger misconception: Joseph Guillotin did not invent the guillotine. Mechanical beheading devices had long been used in Germany, Italy, Scotland, and elsewhere, though it was the French who made them (in)famous.

The Good Doctor

Guillotin, a respected physician and member of the French National Assembly, opposed the death penalty. However, he realized that public executions weren't about to go out of style anytime soon, so he sought a more "humane" alternative to being drawn and quartered, which was the usual way that impoverished criminals were put to death.

A quick beheading, Guillotin argued, was far more merciful than being hacked apart by a dull ax. And it had the added benefit of making executions socially equal, since beheading had been, until that time, the method of execution only for aristocratic convicts who could buy themselves a quicker, kinder death.

Guillotin hooked up with a German engineer and harpsichord maker named Tobias Schmidt, who built a prototype of the guillotine as we know it today. For a smoother cut, Schmidt suggested a diagonal blade rather than the traditional round blade.

Heads Will Roll

The guillotine's heyday followed the French Revolution in 1789. After King Louis XVI had been imprisoned, the new civilian assembly rewrote the penal code to make beheading by guillotine the official method of execution for all convicted criminals—and there were a lot of them.

The first person to lose his head was Nicolas Jacques Pelletie, who was guillotined at Place de Greve on April 25, 1792. King Louis XVI felt the blade a year later, and thousands more followed. The last person to be publicly guillotined was convicted murderer Hamida Djandoubi, who died on September 10, 1977, in Marseilles.

Joseph Guillotin survived the French Revolution with his head attached, though he was forever stigmatized by his connection with the notorious killing machine. He died in 1814 from an infected carbuncle on his shoulder, and his children later petitioned the government for the right to change their last name, not wanting to be associated with their father's grisly past.

❋ ❋ ❋

A common belief often associated with the guillotine is that people who are beheaded remain conscious for several agonizing seconds—and even respond to stimulus. Whether or not this is true remains open to debate. Many scientists believe that death is almost instantaneous, while others cite anecdotal evidence that suggests the deceased are well aware of what has happened to them.

Indeed, stories abound of "experiments" during the height of the guillotine boom in which doctors and others made agreements with condemned prisoners to determine once and for all if the head "lived" on for moments after being severed.

One story claims that Charlotte Corday, who was guillotined for killing Jean-Paul Marat, looked indignant when the executioner held her severed head aloft and slapped her across the face. However, it was also claimed that her cheeks reddened as a result of the slap, which seems unlikely given the loss of blood. It's been said that other severed heads have blinked or moved their eyes when spoken to, and some have allegedly bitten their executioners.

Most doctors agree that the brain may remain active for as long as 15 seconds after a beheading. Whether the individual is actually aware of what has transpired remains a medical mystery that likely will never be answered.

"JUDY, JUDY, JUDY"

❈ ❈ ❈

*Hollywood icon Cary Grant appeared in more than 70 movies,
and the utterance most frequently attributed to him is
"Judy, Judy, Judy." The problem is that he didn't say it.*

Born Archibald Alexander Leach in Bristol, England, in 1904,
Cary Grant would grow up to become one of Hollywood's most
popular leading men. His early career included a stint as a stilt
walker in a traveling sideshow that toured the United States,
where he eventually decided to live and work. While performing
in a series of roles in light comedies on Broadway, he signed with
Paramount Pictures and took his stage name. By 1932, Grant was
starring with screen sirens Marlene Dietrich and Mae West, and
he soon became one of Alfred Hitchcock's favorite leads. His films
with such costars as Katherine Hepburn, Rosalind Russell, Ingrid
Bergman, Grace Kelly, and Audrey Hepburn are considered some
of Hollywood's all-time classics.

Along with film icons such as Jimmy Stewart and Humphrey
Bogart, Grant became a favorite subject of impersonators. But the
scripted line he is most often tagged with was never heard by a
movie audience. The closest Grant ever came to uttering the line
was in the 1939 film *Only Angels Have Wings*, with Rita Hayworth
as his ex-girlfriend, Judith. Grant says, "Hello, Judy," "Come on,
Judy," "Now, Judy," but never "Judy, Judy, Judy."

Setting the Record Straight

Grant told one interviewer that he believed the line came from a radio
show in which he may have uttered the phrase during on-air banter about
Judy Garland. "Where is this 'Judy-Judy-Judy' coming from?" Grant wondered. "I don't know anybody named Judy-Judy-Judy. The only Judy I knew
was Judy Garland. And when I saw her, there weren't three of 'em!"

DOUBLE NEGATIVES: NOT (NECESSARILY) UNGRAMMATICAL

Despite the rallying cries of grammarians to banish the double negative, many people see the construction as a logical and vital part of the English language.

The grammar rules enforced by grade-school teachers can stick in the brain as reflexive laws that must be followed: It is incorrect to start a sentence with "but" or end one with "of"; make sure your subjects and verbs agree; double negatives are illogical, etc. But many matters in grammar are not straightforward, and the double negative is a good example.

Not a Mathematical Matter

The common objection to the double negative goes something like this: Using logic analogous to algebra, two negatives make a positive. Therefore, saying, "I am not unhappy" is logically equivalent to saying, "I'm happy." The problem is that words convey meaning, and in most cases this meaning is not simply negative or positive. The double negative is used in languages worldwide to convey the many nuances between "yes" and "no."

There are several types of double negatives, and most respected grammar books accept some grudgingly and reject others outright. One kind uses the double negative to express a weak affirmative, or to stealthily affirm something without coming right out and saying it. Referred to as the rhetorical figure *litotes,* these constructions convey understatement by denying the contrary, and they're often used to avoid an overstrong presentation. Examples include "I don't dislike him" or the aforementioned "I am not unhappy."

Don't Be So Negative!

The double negative that provokes strong negative reactions is the type that uses two or more negatives to convey a nuanced or emphatic negative meaning. Examples include "I'm not going nowhere," "You ain't heard nothing yet," and "We don't need no stinking education."

Using the double negative in this way follows consistent rules of grammar, yet this particular usage has fallen out of favor. In this case, words such as "no" and "nothing" serve as the logical equivalents to "any" and "anything," transforming the previous sentences into "I'm not going anywhere," "You haven't heard anything yet," and "We don't need any stinking education." In most languages, two negatives are preferred to the "negative-plus-any" construction. Yet, according to the "two negatives equals a positive" argument of grammarians, the sentences would translate roughly as "I'm going somewhere," "You've heard something," and "We need a stinking education."

Old and New Opinions

The double negative fell out of favor in the 18th century, when English and American academics attempted to create a standardized language that could be used in writing. Although the double negative had long been treasured as a powerful rhetoric device—Erasmus once deemed it "graceful" and "elegant"—many came to see the double negative as either illogical or vulgar; George Orwell felt it should be "laughed out of existence." The double negative of the "don't need no" variety came to be associated with the lower classes and was condemned as illogical. The "not unhappy" variety, which was still used by many in the upper classes, was permitted.

Double negatives in English are alive and thriving today, and according to linguist Jenny Cheshire, "They're used in all the dialects, whether rural or urban, Southern Hemisphere or Northern Hemisphere; they occur in African American English and in all the English Creoles. It is only in the standard variety of English that double negatives have fallen out of favor." It would probably be a bad idea to use the double negative in a college application essay, but as far as the logic of the double negative is concerned, it's not incorrect to say it's okay.

※ ※ ※

- "Now, correct me if I'm incorrect, but was I not told it's untrue that the people of Springfield have no faith? Was I not misinformed?" —Brother Faith, in The Simpsons *episode "Faith Off"*

STICK AROUND

What happens if you swallow a stick of chewing gum?
Will it stick around for seven years? Twist around your innards?
Form a blockage in your digestive tract?

It's called chewing gum, not swallowing gum. But sometimes, accidentally or on purpose, a piece of gum ends up dropping down the gullet. When that happens, who hasn't wondered what the consequences will be?

No one knows how it got started, but the idea that swallowed chewing gum stays in the digestive system for seven years is a pervasive myth. It seems the misconception dates back thousands of years, as archaeologists have found evidence of ancient wads of chewing gum. Way back when, gum didn't come wrapped in paper and foil, but the concept was the same—it was something pleasant to chew on but *not* to swallow.

No matter how old the myth, you need not worry about swallowed gum taking up long-term residence in your stomach. Gastroenterologists say that inspections of the digestive tract, with exams such as colonoscopies and endoscopies, do not reveal clumps of petrified gum. When gum does show up on such scans, it is most often a recent arrival.

Although it's not intended to be ingested, chewing gum usually is not harmful if it ends up in your stomach instead of a trash bin (or under a desk). Some chewing gum additives, such as sweeteners and flavoring, are broken down by the body, but the bulk of gum is not digestible. Ingredients such as rubbery elastomers and resins remain intact during their slow voyage through the digestive tract. Eventually, the gum moves down and out.

In rare cases, an extremely large clump of swallowed gum could get stuck on its journey out of the body, causing a dangerous blockage. This potential problem can be avoided, however, if you chew just one stick at a time.

BILLY THE KID

✳ ❁ ✳

Henry McCarty, aka William Bonney or Billy the Kid,
was a Western icon romanticized as a fast-shooting outlaw
who killed 21 men—one for each year of his life. However,
the body count proves to have been exaggerated.

In 1877, at Fort Grant in Arizona Territory, Billy the Kid was repeatedly slapped and then thrown to the ground by a burly blacksmith named F. P. Cahill. Because he'd been bullied by Cahill for months, the slightly built 17-year-old pulled out a revolver and fatally wounded him. Then, in a Fort Sumner saloon early in 1880, the Kid was challenged by gunman Joe Grant. When Grant's six-gun misfired, the Kid pumped a slug into the man's head. The following year, the Kid shot his way out of jail in Lincoln, New Mexico, and gunned down guards J. W. Bell and Bob Olinger in the process.

Cahill, Grant, Bell, and Olinger are the four men who are known to have fallen under the revolver fire of Billy the Kid. But the Kid was also a central figure in New Mexico's bloody Lincoln County War. Early in the conflict, the Kid and several comrades, lusting for vengeance, blasted two prisoners, Frank Baker and William Morton. Then the Kid led an ambush on Lincoln's main (and only) street, and the bushwhackers killed Sheriff William Brady and Deputy George Hindman. During the five-day Battle of Lincoln in July 1878, the Kid was blamed for killing Bob Beckwith, though there is a strong case that Beckwith fell to friendly fire.

Doesn't Add Up

During the last four years of his life, Billy the Kid was involved in at least 16 shootouts, ambushes, and running fights, and he was a key player in one major gun battle. He killed four men and helped slay at least four others. So Billy the Kid did not kill 21 men, and there's considerable debate as to whether he even lived to see his 21st birthday.

A QUESTION OF CANINE CLEANLINESS

Smooch your pooch at your own risk.
It's not man's best friend that could kiss and kill.

Most dog owners will tell you that their dog's mouth is much cleaner than a human's. In fact, this old wives' tale has been touted so loudly and for so long that most people assume it's true. Most veterinarians, however, disagree. They'll tell you it's a stalemate—both human and canine mouths are rife with bacteria.

One of the biggest reasons people believe the myth is the fact that dogs lick their wounds, and those wounds tend to heal very quickly. But it's not as though a dog's saliva has amazing antibacterial properties. Dogs' cuts and scrapes get better fast because their tongues help get rid of dead tissue and stimulate circulation, which in turn facilitates the healing process.

You Know Where It's Been

If you still think a dog's tongue is more antiseptic than your own, just take a look at what your pet's tongue touches over the course of a day. Dogs use their tongues for eating and drinking, as well as for activities such as bathing and exploring garbage cans and weird dead things in the yard.

A dog bite, like a human bite, can cause infection if it breaks the skin. But the bacteria transmitted in each are fairly species-specific. In other words, a bug that's harmful to humans likely won't be transmitted to your pooch if you give him a big, slobbery kiss on the mouth, and vice versa.

❋❋❋

- *The one critter you don't want to kiss is the Komodo dragon, which is indigenous to Indonesia. The mouth of this giant, carnivorous lizard is a veritable petri dish of disgusting bacteria, many of which can cause an agonizing, often fatal infection.*

BENEDICT ARNOLD

❋ ❊ ❋

Here's the story: On his deathbed in 1801, Benedict Arnold donned his old Continental Army togs and repented his treason with the words "Let me die in this old uniform in which I fought my battles. May God forgive me for ever having put on another." And here's the truth.

While serving as a general in the Continental Army during the Revolutionary War, Benedict Arnold switched sides when he attempted to surrender the American fort at West Point to the British. Twenty years later, as Arnold lay dying of dropsy at home in England, his wife, Margaret, could do little to relieve his terminal suffering and delirium. When she broke the sad news to his sons in America, she described him as barely able to breathe, suffering from "a very dreadful nervous symptom." The same letter says nothing about a uniform or a dying wish.

Another weakness in the story: It sounds exactly like what later generations of patriotic Americans would like to hear. It also sounds far too noble for Arnold, who had turned his coat seeking opportunity and ended up finding little. If people want a feel-good story about Arnold, they should note that this brave, energetic officer did the colonial cause far more good than harm. By the time he betrayed the colonies, much had gone wrong for the British (thanks in part to Benedict himself). Arnold was in heavy debt and felt slighted in favor of mediocre officers. Most good officers rise above such frustrations, but the temperamental Arnold chose high treason instead.

His unsavory reputation had followed him from Canada to England, making him a tolerated but unpopular figure. His postwar businesses hadn't thrived, and with Napoleon running amok, Arnold's death and burial were relatively insignificant.

DOUBTING THE BIG DIPPER

*There are folks who like to argue that NBA
great Wilt Chamberlain built his statistics against
inferior competition. In fact, he faced some
of basketball's all-time greatest players.*

Proponents of the myth argue that because of his overwhelming
size, Wilt Chamberlain had an unfair advantage over his opponents. Although it's true that Wilt the Stilt stood more than seven
feet tall and weighed nearly 275 pounds, he was still a smooth ball
handler and a crisp and accurate passer. He possessed a deadly
jump shot and was nimble on his feet, attributes not usually associated with an athlete of his size. And he played in an era before the
dunk was a recognized offensive weapon, so the majority of his
points were made the old-fashioned way—he earned them, often
while being double- and even triple-teamed. Height alone is never
enough. Just ask Rik Smits, Shawn Bradley, and Ralph Sampson—
a trio of heralded seven-footers who couldn't manage to translate
size and dominance at the college level into the big-league success
that Chamberlain enjoyed.

Known as "The Big Dipper" (he often had to dip his head
while walking through doorways) and "Chairman of the Boards"
during his playing career, Chamberlain held a number of NBA
records, including the unapproachable mark of 100 points in a
game and 55 rebounds in a game. Chamberlain
had to stand in the paint and go toe-to-toe
with luminaries such as Bill Russell, Kareem
Abdul-Jabbar, Nate Thurmond, and Bob
Cousy, hard-nosed competitors whose talent
was exceeded only by their determination.
In fact, during his 14-year career on the hard
court, Chamberlain faced more than half of
the 50 players named to the NBA All-Time team in 1996.

IN YOUR EOSTRE BONNET

Easter, which celebrates Jesus Christ's resurrection from the dead, is thought by some to be nothing more than a pagan holiday. Despite all the bunnies and bonnets, though, its religious roots hold firm.

Some people think Easter has its origins in paganism because it falls roughly at the time of the spring equinox, when the earth comes back to life from the dead of winter.

It *is* a significant Christian holiday. True, but Easter is actually associated with Passover, the Jewish holiday that celebrates the Hebrews' release from bondage in Egypt. Jesus and his disciples were in Jerusalem to celebrate Passover when he was arrested, tried, and crucified. Following his resurrection, the disciples understood Jesus to be the sacrificial lamb that took away the sins of the world, a fulfillment of the Passover lambs that were sacrificed each year. Hence the original name for Easter was *Pasch,* from the Hebrew word for Passover, *Pesach.*

So where does the word *Easter* come from? It derives from Eostre, the Old English name for the month of April. According to the ancient historian Bede (writing in the eighth century), the month of Eostre was named after a goddess of the same name. Much later, Jacob Grimm (of the Brothers Grimm) speculated that Eostre was named for the ancient German goddess Ostara. The reference could also come from the word *east*—the direction of the sunrise—or from the old Germanic word for "dawn," which makes sense, given that dawn comes earlier in the spring.

As for the date of Easter, which varies from year to year, it's calculated based on the lunar calendar and some complex ecclesiastical rules. These calculations include the spring equinox, when the sun is directly above Earth's equator. But whether the equinox and Easter fall close together is purely a matter of chance.

FUR-LOVING FÜHRER

Did the Third Reich treat "subhumans" subhumanly?
Even as Nazi Germany exterminated millions of people,
it fiercely protected its animal population.

The Holocaust tells the heart-wrenching tale: Nazis, operating
under the decidedly mad precepts of Adolf Hitler and the Third
Reich, systematically and diabolically destroyed the lives of those
it deemed subhuman. By the twisted definition of their steering
organization, this number included people of non-Aryan blood-
lines, such as Jews, Gypsies, and other "racially inferior" groups.
Overlooking the subhuman stipulation entirely, this did not
include members of the animal kingdom. Here's the backstory to
an uneven regime that found beauty and worth in its animals while
it delivered death and destruction to humankind.

Animals' Best Friend

Not many would disagree that Adolf Hitler was the living definition of a monster. Yet in the area of animal rights, he was anything
but. This bizarre dichotomy also applied to Hitler's principal
henchmen, Hermann Goering and Heinrich Himmler. All felt
that defenseless animals deserved better treatment than they were
receiving and took proactive steps to ensure it.

As early as 1927, members of the Nazi party called for actions
against animal cruelty. In particular, they zeroed in on the kosher
butchering that was being practiced throughout the homeland.
(Later, in order to justify his persecution of Jews, Hitler promoted
graphic films that showed them slaughtering lambs.) In early 1933,
just after the Nazi organization had risen to power, its parliament
passed laws regulating the slaughter of animals. Most notably,
Goering started a ban against the act of vivisection (the dissection
of animals for scientific study): "An absolute and permanent ban
on vivisection is not only a necessary law to protect animals and
to show sympathy with their pain, but it is also a law for humanity

itself," said Hitler's right-hand man. "I have therefore announced the immediate prohibition of vivisection and have made the practice a punishable offense in Prussia [the core of the German Empire]. Until such time as punishment is pronounced, the culprit shall be lodged in a concentration camp." Goering would go on to ban commercial animal trapping, and he placed strong restrictions on hunting. He even went so far as to regulate the boiling of crabs and lobsters, allegedly because he felt distressed by their "screams" during the cooking process.

Man's Worst Enemy

It helps to understand the era's political overtones. Even as Nazis were passing groundbreaking legislation on behalf of animals, they were drawing up decrees that would define "lesser" beings, targeting them for eventual extermination. In their demented view, these "subhumans" included anyone descended from non-Aryan parents or grandparents. Even those with one grandparent from the "wrong" bloodline were placed in jeopardy. In the same years that the Nazis passed their sweeping pro-animal laws, they opened the Dachau, Buchenwald, Ravensbruc, and Sachsenhausen concentration camps.

Although Hitler's regime would eventually exterminate an estimated 6 million Jews and untold numbers of other human beings, it would continue its efforts on behalf of animals. In 1934, the government passed a stringent hunting law. By 1936, animal laws were extended to include protections for such "lower-rung" species as fish and crustaceans. Throughout, the systematic killing of humans continued.

It's beyond ironic that this sort of animal-rights model should come from such a diabolical source, but that's how history has played out. The Nazis viewed the issue in simplistic terms and acted accordingly. In their distorted view, Aryans ruled the hierarchy; animals were second; and subhumans, or *untermensch,* dwelled on the bottom. It was the gross misfortune of 6 million living souls that their assigned classification wasn't at least on a par with that of a dog.

ANYONE CAN
BE PRESIDENT...ALMOST!

*With hard work, reasonable intelligence, and a lot of money,
anyone can be president. But what if you weren't born in the
United States? You still have a shot—if you have the right parents.*

When John McCain ran for the presidency in 2000 and 2008,
some argued that his being born in Panama made him ineligible
for the highest office. The opposition had a field day, chiding
McCain for defying the founding fathers' wishes—but they were
wrong: It is possible to have been born on foreign soil and still be
commander in chief.

According to the U.S. Constitution, Section 1, Article II, a
"natural-born citizen, or a citizen of the United States...shall be
eligible for the Office of President." So who is considered to be
a natural-born citizen? In 1790, the first naturalization law stated
that "the children of the citizens of the United States that may be
born beyond sea, or out of the limits of the United States, shall
be considered as natural-born citizens." McCain's parents were
American citizens, so even though he was not born within the
bounds of the United States, he qualifies as being "natural born."

On the other hand, it would require a change in the Constitution to allow California governor Arnold Schwarzenegger to seek
the presidency. Although he has been a naturalized U.S. citizen
since 1983, he was born in Austria to Austrian citizens, which
disqualifies him for the presidency. Schwarzenegger has said he
supports a constitutional amendment that would allow him to run.

President Jerry?

Shock-show host Jerry Springer has expressed presidential aspira-
tions, but he is also ineligible. He was born in England to German
parents. And that's a shame, because who wouldn't want to hear a
primary season filled with chants of "Jerry! Jerry!"?

DID NERO FIDDLE WHILE ROME BURNED?

※ ※※ ※

*Over the ages, the phrase "Nero fiddled while Rome
burned" has become a euphemism for heedless
and irresponsible behavior in the midst of a crisis.
But as a matter of historical fact, legend has it wrong.*

In A.D. 64, much of Rome burned to the ground in what is known as the Great Fire. According to legend, the reigning emperor, Nero, purposely set the blaze to see "how Troy looked when it was in flames." From atop a palace tower, he played his fiddle and sang as the fire raged and consumed two-thirds of the empire's capital.

Nero, a patron of the arts who played the lyre, wrote poetry, and fancied himself a great artist, often performed in public, challenging the beliefs of Rome's political class who believed such displays were beneath the dignity of an emperor. But music was, in fact, the most dignified of Nero's interests. Under the influence of a corrupt adviser who encouraged his excesses, his life became a series of spectacles, orgies, and murders. A few months after his first public performance, the Great Fire ravaged Rome for five days. Roman historian Suetonius, who hadn't even been born at the time of the fire, describes Nero singing from the Tower of Maecenas as he watched the inferno. Dio Cassius, a historian who lived a hundred years later, places him on a palace roof, singing "The Capture of Troy."

However, the historian Tacitus, who actually witnessed the fire, ascertained that the emperor was at his villa in Antium, 30 miles away. Many contemporary historians agree that Nero was not in Rome when the fire broke out (and there's no denying the fact that the fiddle wasn't invented until the 16th century). According to Tacitus, Nero rushed back to Rome to organize a relief effort and, with uncharacteristic discipline and leadership, set about rebuilding and beautifying the city he loved.

STAR POWER

Although he had every right to, Hugh Hefner wasn't bragging about his sexual prowess on the cover of Playboy *magazine.*

In addition to being founder and publisher of the world's largest-circulating men's magazine, Hefner also rightly holds claim to the title of "Playboy of the Western World." It's a reputation he has carefully cultivated from the moment he conceived the magazine that would make him rich and famous.

Hef's Secret Code?

Hef has made no secret of the fact that he has slept with hundreds of beautiful women over the years, so it seemed logical to many *Playboy* readers during the 1960s and '70s that the number of tiny stars that appeared on the cover each month was actually a sort of rating system for how good that issue's centerfold was in bed. In a variation on the story, the stars indicated the number of times Hef had slept with the Playmate. It was also rumored that when the stars appeared outside the "P" in "Playboy," Hef had been unsuccessful in seducing that month's centerfold.

These rumors ran rampant, and until recently the magazine's editors didn't exactly go out of their way to confirm or deny them. After all, such tales played up Hef's image as the ultimate ladies' man and *Playboy* as the lifestyle manual for the wealthy, sophisticated male. However, the truth is far less salacious than the myth: The stars merely indicated the domestic or international advertising region for that particular edition of the magazine.

Playboy Explains

"Except for a six-month period in 1976, the stars appeared on our covers from 1955 until 1979. The star system changed over the years, but it ranged from zero to 12 at its peak."

ALASKAN STORIES

*"The Great Land," as Alaska's name means in Aleut,
spawns stories to match its size. "Sourdough" Alaskans
love to see if cheechakos ("tenderfeet," or non-Alaskans) will
fall for them. But some big Alaska tales don't exaggerate.*

Most of Alaska cannot be reached by roads. True. You can
drive a car to Anchorage, the Kenai Peninsula, Fairbanks, the oil
fields at Prudhoe Bay (if you have official business), the Yukon
border with Canada, and Haines and Hyder in southeastern
Alaska (via Canada). Anything in the western half of the state is
inaccessible by road, so high school sports teams often must fly to
away games.

Surf's not up in Alaska. False. There are plenty of opportunities
to hang ten in Alaska, which has close to 47,000 miles of tidal
shoreline. On Turnagain Arm near Anchorage, surfers put on wet
suits and paddle out to ride the single daily bore tide.

You get paid to live in Alaska. True. The state has invested vast
mineral royalties in the Permanent Fund, which pays each man,
woman, and child roughly $1,100–$1,800 per year. However, to
get the dividend one must live in Alaska for a full calendar year
and have no felony convictions. Before you start packing your
bags, though, remember that the freight expense for goods makes
the Alaskan cost of living higher than that of the lower 48 states.
The dividend doesn't fully compensate.

Alaskans live in igloos. False, of course. Alaskans live in
anything from ritzy condos to trailers to bush cabins. However,
if you go adventuring in the bush, study up. In Alaska, almost
everything is done a little differently, and you're mostly on your
own in the bush. The penalty for ignorance can be death at the
hands of nature, so it would behoove you to learn how to build a
snow shelter.

For fun, Alaskans get tossed into the air on blankets. True. However, this custom is Inupiaq (northwestern Alaska Native, formerly referred to as Eskimo) and originates from the practice of tossing hunters into the air so they could see across the horizon. Now it's mostly part of spring festivities. If you had to spend the winter in Barrow, which goes without sun an average of 84 days per year, you'd be in the mood to celebrate springtime, too.

Moose regularly wander into Anchorage. True. Moose can show up nearly anywhere in Alaska (including most towns) at any time of year. They aren't playthings; they are wild animals that can be very grumpy and dangerous, so don't toy with them. By definition, the worst location in Alaska is between a sow grizzly and her cubs. The second worst is between a cow moose and her calf, and moose are far more numerous than bears.

Everyone huddles inside during Alaskan winters. False. Alaskans know cabin fever in ways few "outsiders" do, but they also make a point of going on with life and having fun all year. Anchorage's outdoor Fur Rendezvous (which everyone calls "FurRondy") in February has ice sculptures, a Miners and Trappers Ball with a prize for the best beard, and FurRondy police who will throw you in a mobile jail if you're caught without a Fur Rendezvous pin. Anywhere else, there'd be lawsuits; in Alaska it's all in the spirit of the festival. FurRondy coincides with the ceremonial start of the famed Iditarod dogsled race to Nome.

Mosquitoes in Alaska are twin-engined. True. They are enormous and voracious in summer, and the blackflies are just as bad. Alaskan lore says that mosquitoes always feast on "sourdough" Alaskans before they resort to *cheechakos.*

Alaskans don't like outsiders. False. Alaskans often feel ignored and misunderstood by outsiders, but they're like any other group: They generally welcome visitors who embrace and respect Alaskan style, culture, and natural beauty. The main thing to pack for a trip to Alaska is an open mind.

BEAST OF BURDEN

❈ ◈ ❈

*The amazingly adaptable camel can plod through
the desert for a week without fluids—but don't attribute
this water-conservation ability to that big hump.*

With an unwieldy body that defies its life's mission and a disposition that often has it spitting at its owner, a camel's value as a "desert horse" seems questionable. Then there's that outsized hump, or humps in the case of the Bactrian camel. Hideous so far as aesthetics go, this natural canteen is the camel's true claim to fame. Because of it, the ungainly beast can travel with impunity in temperatures hot enough to fry an egg or kill a person. Or so many people believe.

In truth, this assertion is all wet. A camel does not store water in its hump. That bulge is composed primarily of fatty tissue that, when metabolized, serves as a source of energy. When this energy supply runs low because of a lack of nourishment, the hump shrinks considerably, sometimes to the point of flopping over to one side. On a healthy camel, however, the hump can weigh as much as 80 pounds.

A camel has a unique way of carrying and storing water—through its bloodstream. For this reason, it can go as many as eight days without a drink and can lose as much as 40 percent of its

body weight before it feels ill effects. The amount it drinks when water is available—as much as 21 gallons in about ten minutes—would cause severe problems in most animals. What's more, a camel isn't too particular about the water it drinks. A muddy puddle that another animal might wrinkle its nose at would be slurped dry by a thirsty camel.

THE NOT-SO-CODED CODE NAME

When rumors emerged that Nazi Germany was developing an atomic bomb during World War II, the United States quickly initiated its own program, the Manhattan Project. Where did this name come from?

The venture culminated in the detonation of the first atomic weapon in the New Mexico desert on July 16, 1945, and then the strikes on Hiroshima and Nagasaki that ended the war. Many people assume that the top-secret plan was given the cover name the Manhattan Project simply to confuse the enemy. In fact, the New York borough played a key part in the development of the bomb.

In 1942, General Leslie R. Groves, deputy chief of construction for the U.S. Army Corps of Engineers, was appointed to direct the top-secret project. The United States needed to build an atomic weapon before Germany or Japan did. Groves established three large engineering and production centers at remote U.S. sites in Oak Ridge, Tennessee; Hanford, Washington; and Los Alamos, New Mexico. The project's headquarters, however, was situated at 270 Broadway, New York City, home to the Army Corps of Engineers' North Atlantic division.

Standard Operating Procedure

The first proposed cover name for the project was the Laboratory for the Development of Substitute Materials. That hardly rolls off the tongue, and Groves also felt that it would draw unwanted attention to the operation. Instead, he opted to follow Corps procedure and name the unit after its geographical area. The initial cover name of Manhattan Engineer District soon was shortened to the Manhattan Project. In 1943, the headquarters moved to Oak Ridge, Tennessee, and while much of Manhattan's early role in the project has been forgotten, there is a poignant reminder on Riverside Drive outside the New York Buddhist Church: It's the statue of a monk that survived the atomic bombing of Hiroshima.

BLIND MAN'S BLUFF

Known for his soaring tenor and eloquent ballads about life's lessons and lost love, Roy Orbison was equally famous for his horn-rimmed dark glasses. Since he was rarely seen sans shades, many people believed the sweet-singing Roy was blind. Was it all a bluff?

When Roy Orbison's flashy falsetto began to fly up the charts, he shared radio time and record sales with two other performers who had similar vocal talents and stage attire. Like Ray Charles and Stevie Wonder, "The Big O" wore dark glasses when he performed onstage. Unlike the aforementioned artists, Orbison was not sightless. Back in the day, it was rare for performers to wear any kind of eyewear onstage, and most people assumed that artists who wore dark glasses did so because they were blind. Although Roy's eyesight was decidedly less than 20/20, he could see relatively well, and there was no devious dupe behind his choice of eye apparel. In 1963, he was asked to tour Europe with a potpourri of artists, including the Beatles. When Orbison arrived in England, he discovered he had left his regular glasses in the United States and was forced to wear his prescription sunglasses. He wore the shades onstage, which garnished a favorable reaction from both fans in the seats and beat writers reviewing the concerts. The popularity of the Fab Four assured that there were plenty of both at every venue.

Made in the Shades

Orbison's personal life was marred by tragedy—in 1966, his wife died as a result of a motorcycle accident, and in 1968, two of his three sons died in a house fire. Offstage, he was a taciturn and humble man who tended to shun the spotlight. But contrary to rumor, Roy did not hide behind his dark shades. Early in his career, he was often photographed without his trademark frames and was noticeably lensless when he starred in the 1967 film *The Fastest Guitar Alive.*

THREE SIDES
TO EVERY STORY

*Few geographical locations on Earth
have been discussed and debated more than
the three-sided chunk of ocean between
the Atlantic coast of Florida and the regions
of San Juan, Puerto Rico, and Bermuda
known as the Bermuda Triangle.*

Over the centuries, hundreds of ships and dozens of airplanes
have mysteriously disappeared while floating in or flying through
the region commonly called the Bermuda Triangle. Myth mongers
propose that alien forces are responsible for these dissipations.
Because little or no wreckage from the vanished vessels has ever
been recovered, paranormal pirating has also been cited as the
culprit. Other theorists suggest that leftover technology from the
lost continent of Atlantis—mainly an underwater rock formation
known as the Bimini Road (situated just off the island of Bimini in
the Bahamas)—exerts a supernatural power that grabs unsuspecting intruders and drags them to the depths.

A Deadly Adjective

Although the theory of the Triangle had been mentioned in publications as early as 1950, it wasn't until the '60s that the region
was anointed with its three-sided appellation. Columnist Vincent
Gaddis wrote an article in the February 1964 edition of *Argosy*
magazine that discussed the various mysterious disappearances
that had occurred over the years and designated the area where
myth and mystery mixed as the "Deadly Bermuda Triangle." The
use of the adjective *deadly* perpetrated the possibility that UFOs,
alien anarchists, supernatural beings, and metaphysical monsters
reigned over the region. The mystery of Flight 19, which involved
the disappearance of five planes in 1945, was first noted in newspaper articles that appeared in 1950, but its fame was secured

when the flight and its fate were fictitiously featured in Steven Spielberg's 1977 alien opus, *Close Encounters of the Third Kind.* In Hollywood's view, the pilots and their planes were plucked from the sky by friendly aliens and later returned safely to terra firma by their abductors.

In 1975, historian, pilot, and researcher Lawrence David Kusche published one of the first definitive studies that dismissed many of the Triangle theories. In his book *The Bermuda Triangle Mystery—Solved,* he concluded that the Triangle was a "manufactured mystery," the result of bad research and reporting and, occasionally, deliberately falsified facts. Before weighing anchor on Kusche's conclusions, however, consider that one of his next major publications was a tome about exotic popcorn recipes.

Explaining Odd Occurrences

Other pragmatists have insisted that a combination of natural forces—a double whammy of waves and rain that create the perfect storm—is most likely the cause for these maritime misfortunes. Other possible "answers" to the mysteries include rogue waves (such as the one that capsized the *Ocean Ranger* oil rig off the coast of Newfoundland in 1982), hurricanes, underwater earthquakes, and human error. The Coast Guard receives almost 20 distress calls every day from amateur sailors attempting to navigate the slippery sides of the Triangle. Modern-day piracy— usually among those involved in drug smuggling—has been mentioned as a probable cause for odd occurrences, as have unusual magnetic anomalies that screw up compass readings. Other possible explanations include the Gulf Stream's uncertain current, the high volume of sea and air traffic in the region, and even methane hydrates (gas bubbles) that produce "mud volcanoes" capable of sucking a ship into the depths.

Other dramatic and disastrous disappearances amid the Bermuda Triangle include the USS *Cyclops,* which descended to its watery repository without a whisper in March 1918 with 309 people aboard. Myth suggests supernatural subterfuge, but the reality is that violent storms or enemy action were the likely culprits. The same deductions had been discussed and similar conclusions reached in 1812 when the sea schooner *Patriot,* a commercial vessel, was swept up by the sea with the daughter of former vice president Aaron Burr onboard.

Flight 19

The incident that nailed the Triangle's notoriety as a map point of the macabre was the disappearance of Flight 19. On December 5, 1945, five TBM Avenger torpedo bombers seemingly dropped off the radar screens while on an authorized overwater training flight from the Naval Air Station in Fort Lauderdale, Florida. Lieutenant Charles Carroll Taylor was supervising the flight but was not out front in the lead position. At some point, and for reasons that are unclear, Taylor assumed the lead, only to become confused and cantankerous. Instead of guiding the bombers back to Fort Lauderdale, he ended up flying as far as 200 miles out to sea, east of the Florida peninsula. In his last transmitted message, Taylor said, "We'll have to ditch...we all go down together." The five planes and 14 crew members were lost without a trace, and despite numerous missions throughout the years to recover remnants of the planes, no missing links to the mission have ever been found.

Although a number of other aircraft had met a similar fate before Flight 19—including four U.S. Navy Lockheed PV-1 Venturas in 1943—the 1945 enigma caught the attention of theorists. Holly- wood cited alien abduction as the answer, but scientists and military officials suggest a far simpler solution. Experts believe that Taylor had become disorientated during the flight and ran out of fuel while trying to find his way home. Like lemmings to the ledge, his squadron flew as he flew, eventually joining him in the brine below.

Further sensationalizing the incident was the disappearance of one of the PBM Mariner rescue seaplanes sent out to search for Flight 19. As the Mariner scoured the area for traces of the lost flight, the tanker SS *Gaines Mills* reported that the plane exploded in midair. All 13 crew members died.

VOLTAIRE'S DEFENSE

※※※※

Voltaire, the infamous 18th-century French Enlightenment
writer, is supposed to have said, "I disapprove of what you
say, but I will defend to the death your right to say it."
Noble as this concept may be, it was actually one of
Voltaire's many biographers who penned the words.

Voltaire, also known as François-Marie Arouet, was an outspoken
and unwavering advocate of free speech. It is difficult to believe
that the most powerful words ever written in support of this
freedom cannot be attributed to the master himself, but the fact
remains that the famous quote comes from Evelyn Beatrice Hall's
1907 book *The Friends of Voltaire*, which was published 129 years
after Voltaire's death.

Hall wrote under the pseudonym Stephen G. Tallentyre at
a time when it was difficult for women to publish nonfiction. At
one point in the book, Hall discusses Voltaire's support of a fellow
writer, Helvetius, who had been censored by the French government. The direct quote from Hall's book is: "The men who had
hated [Helvetius' book] flocked round him now. Voltaire forgave
him all injuries, intentional or unintentional…'I disapprove of
what you say, but I will defend to the death your right to say it,'
was his attitude now."

Thus, through her indulgent dramatization of Voltaire's life,
Hall inadvertently succeeded in summarizing his views on censor-
ship in terms that were more eloquent than anything uttered by
Voltaire himself (Hall later explained that the line was meant as a
paraphrasing of his views). Voltaire did, however, write a similar
line in a 1770 letter, which translates as, "Monsieur l'abbe, I detest
what you write, but I would give my life to make it possible for you
to continue to write."

TAKE A SEAT

❀ ❀ ❀

When your mother told you to sit up straight,
she was off by about 45 degrees.

Mother Usually Knows Best

Mom was right when she admonished you to not slouch. But universal maternal advice about sitting perfectly straight can actually be harmful to your back's long-term health. That's right—when it comes to sitting up straight, you're advised not to listen to your mother.

Until recently, the long-standing conventional wisdom about sitting was that the back should be held ramrod straight, with thighs parallel to the floor. This posture was believed to protect the spine and cause the least amount of strain.

New research appears to have pulled the chair out from under this theory. It turns out that sitting upright for long periods of time can actually trigger chronic back pain. Several studies have found that the once-recommended 90-degree sitting posture puts strain on the lower back. This position causes the disks between each vertebra to shift out of alignment. Over time, this can cause pain, deformity, and damage to the disks. And, as anyone who has tried to sit up straight for an extended period of time will tell you, it's just not very comfortable.

Experts now say it's best to sit with the chair back adjusted at a slight recline—a 135-degree angle—while your feet rest on the floor. This position reduces stress on the spine and causes the least amount of misalignment. Using this optimal position may help prevent back pain as well as treat it.

❀ ❀ ❀

• *Although modern life dictates that we spend a majority of our time seated, our bodies were not built to sit for long stretches. Research shows that getting up periodically and walking around during the day, along with adjusting chairs to the optimal recline, considerably helps reduce—and may even prevent—back strain.*

THE LATE, SEMI-GREAT *TITANIC*

Many believe the sinking of RMS Titanic *to be the champion of all maritime disasters, but history tells a far different tale.*

When the luxury liner *Titanic* slipped beneath the waves in 1912, people of the era witnessed a truly historic spectacle. An estimated 1,500 souls had been snuffed out by the hand of fate. While the death toll was indeed appalling, it was by no means the worst on record. Lesser-known shipwrecks before and since have claimed more lives. Here are a notable few.

The *Sultana*

On April 27, 1865—nearly 44 years before the *Titanic* received its first rivet in an Irish shipyard—the paddle-wheel steamer *Sultana* made its way up the mighty Mississippi River. Onboard were an estimated 2,300 passengers, a group primarily composed of Union soldiers returning home from the Civil War. Just after the ship cleared Memphis, Tennessee, one of its main boilers exploded. In an instant, hundreds of people and a sizable chunk of the superstructure ceased to exist. Seconds later, a raging fire hurled a second volley of mayhem at those who had survived the initial explosion. A horrific tragedy was in the making.

All told, approximately 1,700 perished in the incident. The culprit was determined to be an improperly patched boiler that never stood a chance against such elevated pressures. In the most heartbreaking of ironies, many of *Sultana's* victims were newly released POWs who had survived the notorious Cahawba and Andersonville Confederate prison camps. That they died while on their way to freedom demonstrates how precarious life can be.

The *Provence II*

Less than four years after the *Titanic* met its tragic end, another vessel surpassed the *Sultana* in total lives lost. On February 26, 1916, the French auxiliary cruiser *Provence II* was making its way across the Mediterranean Sea, transporting an enormous contingent of sailors from North Africa to Salonika. A torpedo launched by the German submarine *U-35* struck the craft, mortally wounding it. The damage caused an immediate and pronounced list that rendered most of the ship's lifeboats useless. Of the nearly 4,000 people onboard, 3,130 would follow the ship down to its watery grave. This number trumped *Titanic's* fatalities and nearly doubled *Sultana* in lives lost. A new "champ" had been crowned.

The Goya

Even in such a macabre category as maritime disasters, there always seems to be another tragic event that will displace the "top dog." Consider the *Goya,* a German transport ship that was evacuating some 7,000 refugees and wounded soldiers from the Baltic states of East Prussia and Poland. On April 16, 1945, after setting out for Copenhagen, the ship tragically moved into the crosshairs of the Soviet minelayer submarine *L-3*. Locking on its quarry, the *L-3* fired two torpedoes at the ship. They found their mark, and the *Goya* split in two. The vessel sank in a blisteringly fast four minutes and took nearly everyone with it. Of the 7,000 onboard, 183 survived.

The Dona Paz and the Vector

It doesn't require icebergs or a world war to commit a vessel to the "worst of" category. Sometimes an innocuous ferry crossing can produce disastrous results. Such was the case with the Philippine passenger ferry *Dona Paz*. As the craft negotiated the Tablas Strait on December 20, 1987, it struck the oil tanker *Vector.* Nearly 9,000 barrels of petroleum ignited into a firestorm and spread onto the *Dona Paz*. In minutes, the blazing ship sank, taking nearly everyone onboard with it. Things were almost as bad on the *Vector.* Of the 13 crew members who went to work that fateful day, only two returned home.

So, if not an outright record, what was the death toll on the *Dona Paz*? Here's where things get interesting. The "official" toll was 1,565, but other sources place the number at 4,375. Then again, since the ferry was severely overcrowded, well-reasoned estimates reach as high as 9,000. If that's the case, the *Dona Paz* is the deadliest maritime disaster in history.

JUNK FOOD VERDICT: NOT GUILTY

*Your complexion may be bumpy, but if you eat a lot
of junk food, you can at least have a clear conscience.*

Pimple-prone adolescents are often told to skip the pizza, fries,
and potato chips to keep their faces acne-free. But greasy foods
only affect your appearance if you're a messy eater. Research
shows that breakouts are caused by a surge in hormones, which
stimulates the body's secretion of oils.

When the oil glands in the skin are overactive, pores get
clogged from the secretions and become perfect hosts for a bacterium called *Propionibacterium acnes* that thrives without oxygen.
It's the bacteria's activity that produces pimples.

Chocolate has also been blamed for causing acne, but it's
not at fault either. A University of Pennsylvania study compared
people who ate a bar of chocolate with those who ate a bar with
similar amounts of fat and sugar. The study found no evidence that
chocolate had an effect on producing acne. (Besides, chocolate has
an abundance of antioxidants, which may help prevent wrinkles.)

You might want to think twice about eating dairy, though. A
recent Harvard study found that women who drank two or more
glasses of skim milk a day were 44 percent more likely to report
severe acne as teenagers. Researchers believe that hormones or
whey proteins found in dairy products might be the cause.

Causes and Cures

The most important factors associated with acne include a family
history of the condition, stress, dirty skin, and the use of some drugs,
particularly steroids. Treatments include antibiotics, hormonal therapy,
topical retinoids, and phototherapy. All work in one of four ways: pre-
venting blockage of skin pores, killing bacteria, reducing skin inflammation, or lowering oil secretions in the skin.

HER MALIGNED MAJESTY, MARIE

❀ ❀ ❀

*"Let them eat cake." Most people recognize this dismissive remark
as a slight uttered by the supremely snooty Marie Antoinette.
As it turns out, the queen didn't say it.*

It's 1789, and the French Revolution is under way. Peasants are
rioting in the streets, protesting a shortage of bread. Their queen,
Marie Antoinette, not only ignores their hungry cries but flip-
pantly feeds them a wisecrack. If there's no bread to be found, her
haughtiness reasons, "Let them eat cake."

In French, the original quote is *"Qu'ils mangent de la bri-
oche,"* in reference to a type of bread characterized by a sweet
flavor and flaky texture. Perhaps the queen was simply suggesting
that her subjects not limit themselves to their usual staple and that
they consider other forms of sustenance—like, well, *fancy* bread.

In fact, historians maintain that the line had nothing to do with
the queen. Records show that it had been used in print to highlight
aristocratic abuses since at least 1760. Philosopher Jean-Jacques
Rousseau (who died more than a decade before the French Revolution began) claimed to have heard it as early as 1740.

Even if such evidence didn't exist, the utterance of such a
remark seems out of character for Marie Antoinette. According
to biographer Lady Antonia Fraser, the queen had certain faults,
but she wasn't tactless. "It was a callous and ignorant statement,"
explains Fraser, "and she [Marie Antoinette] was neither." Fraser
believes the remark was actually made by Queen Marie Thérèse
(wife of Louis XIV) nearly a century before the revolution began.

So why is the remark attributed to Marie Antoinette? Most
historians believe propaganda played a big part. During the revolution, turning people against the queen was almost sport, and Marie
endured plenty of scorn until her public beheading in 1793.

WHO'S TOO OLD FOR THE OLYMPICS?

※ ※※ ※

Think of the average Olympic athlete, and the following images
likely come to mind: physical perfection, drive, determination—
and youth? Not necessarily. It could be just a matter of time
before the AARP holds its own Olympic trials.

Hilde Pedersen. When Norway's Pedersen took home the
bronze in the ten-kilometer cross-country-skiing event at the
2006 Turin Winter Olympics, she became the oldest woman
to win a Winter Games Olympic medal. It was an impressive
achievement for the 41-year-old, but as she and other "older"
competitors have proved in the past, age is no barrier to claiming
an Olympic medal.

Oscar Swahn. Swedish shooter Swahn participated in three
Olympic Games. At age 60, he won two gold medals and a bronze
at his first Olympics, which took place in London in 1908. Four
years later, at the Sweden Games, he won a gold in the single shot
running deer team, making him the world's oldest gold medalist.
Swahn returned to the Olympics in 1920 at age 72 and managed to
win a silver medal in the double shot running deer competition.

Anders Haugen. Even at the ripe age of 72, Swahn is not the
oldest person to have won an Olympic medal. At the first Winter
Olympic Games in Chamonix, France (1924), U.S. ski jumper
Anders Haugen placed fourth with a score of 17.916 points. Third-
place winner, Norway's Thorlief Haug, received a score of 18.000
points. Fifty years later, a sports historian determined that Haug's
score had been miscalculated and that he should have finished
behind Haugen. At a special ceremony in Oslo, Haugen was finally
awarded the bronze medal when he was 83 years old, making him
the "eldest" recipient of an Olympic medal and the only American
to ever win a medal in the ski-jump event.

MARX'S WORD CHOICE

✽ ✦ ✽

*Karl Marx said many things, but he didn't say,
"Religion is the opiate of the people." It's odd that
the man who penned* The Communist Manifesto
and Das Kapital *may be best known for writing a single
word—even if people seldom get that word right.*

Opium or opiate? With religious zealots addressing the masses
with overblown rhetoric, it's not surprising that secular sensa-
tionalists often reference the renowned religious diatribe that
Karl Marx authored in February 1843. In the introduction to his
paragraph-by-paragraph critique of Hegel's 1820 book *Elements
of the Philosophy of Right,* Marx remarked: "Religious suffering
is, at one and the same time, the expression of real suffering and a
protest against real suffering. Religion is the sigh of the oppressed
creature, the heart of a heartless world, and the soul of the soulless
conditions. It is the opium of the people."

To some analysts, Marx was saying that religion is a drug that
dulls people's pain but leaves them incapable of or unwilling to
affect change. To others, the erudite economist was of the opinion
that religion provides solace to people in distress and eases whatever pain they may be feeling, much like a drug such as opium.
At the time, opium was a legal pain-reducing product, though
attempts were starting to be made to prohibit its production.

✽ ✽ ✽

• *Marx's most famous statement is continually misquoted and
misprinted to read, "Religion is the opiate of the people." What's
more, "masses" is often substituted for "people," and that misquote is further spread by followers of the Arizona industrial-
metal band Opiate for the Masses.*

TALL TALES ABOUT NAPOLEON

*Napoleon Bonaparte, one of the most successful
and brutal military leaders of all time, had a short
fuse and was often shortsighted. But he was not,
as is popularly believed, short in stature.*

Slighted by History

It turns out that an error in arithmetic contributed to history's
perception of Napoleon as a small man. The only known measurement of Bonaparte came from his autopsy, which reported a height
of 5'2". But it was not taken into account that this measurement
was calculated in French units. Translating to slightly more than
168 centimeters, his height was actually 5'6" by the English Imperial system. This was above average for a 19th-century Frenchman.

Another possible reason for this misconception is the fact that
Napoleon kept himself surrounded by a group of relatively tall
guardsmen. Napoleon was never seen in public without his "imperial guard." These soldiers averaged six feet in height and would
have towered over Napoleon.

A Napoleon Complex

Napoleon wasn't short, but his temper was. Over time, the notion
that the general's irascible, aggressive personality stemmed from
his small size has been applied to any small-statured man who
uses his temper to compensate for his height. This is referred to
as a "Napoleon Complex," and though psychologists regard it as
a negative social stereotype, it also proves to be a myth. In 2007,
researchers at the University of Central Lancashire studied the
effect of height on aggression in men. Using heart monitors to
gauge reactions, scientists found that *taller* men were more likely
to respond to provocation with aggressive behavior.

As Napoleon himself said, "History is the version of past
events that people have decided to agree upon." It turns out that
history cut Napoleon about four inches short.

BILL VEECK

✳ ✦ ✳

*Bill Veeck was the most colorful team owner
in the history of baseball. Was he just a goofball party animal,
or was he a genius ahead of his time?*

The Case for Goofball Party Animal

Personal life: Bill Veeck smoked like an Industrial Revolution chimney. Not only did he close down bars, he kept them in business. He barely maintained contact with his children by his first wife—irresponsible, most would say. He loved to use his wooden leg for gags: He'd suddenly stab it with an ice pick or use it as an ashtray. He sat shirtless in the stands, booing the umpires and chatting with the fans over beer. Any photograph of Veeck wearing a necktie is phonier than a refunded legal fee. He simply didn't look or act like the important baseball executive he was.

Operations: He loved to annoy other owners, especially the Yankees', then managed to look shocked when they voted against him nearly every time. He brought 42-year-old Negro Leagues legend Satchel Paige into the American League, then sent telegrams to the disapproving, ultra-establishment *Sporting News* in which he proposed Paige as Rookie of the Year. He cheated like a riverboat cardshark at grounds maintenance: He watered the basepaths when the visiting team was faster, groomed the infield to help his side and irritate the opponents, and once set up an outfield fence that could be moved in and out between innings. Veeck was chaos theory applied to sports management.

Promotions: Not even the legendary Chris von der Ahe pulled stunts as goofy as Veeck's gags. Veeck used professional clowns to coach bases, and he once sent 3'7" Eddie Gaedel to bat in a big league game. He was always giving away bizarre door prizes, including kegs of nails, live pigeons, and blocks of ice. Traditionalists considered him a moneychanger in the game's venerated temple.

The Case for Foresighted Genius

Finance: Veeck rarely had anywhere near enough money to buy a baseball team, but he had few equals at lining up capital. He had studied accounting but kept that detail secret so that his competition would think he was a business buffoon. He bought several teams with relatively little of his own money, yet sold them for capital gains. In what universe is this buffoonery?

Winning/attendance: Veeck took the Cleveland Indians from 68–86 (1946) to 97–58 and a World Series title (1948). He didn't win with the St. Louis Browns on the diamond, but he got far more people to come watch the most consistently lousy team in baseball history than anyone imagined possible. When he took over the Chicago White Sox, they won their first pennant (1959) since 1919. He tended to shatter attendance records and win ball games, which is pretty much the point.

Promotions: Veeck generated buzz by reflex. He did everything possible to welcome women to his ballparks: decent restrooms, daycare, ladies'-day promotions. He invented the exploding scoreboard. He gave the fireworks contractor extra money and told him to "knock the joint down." He invited St. Louis fans to serve as grandstand managers while his trained pro sat in a recliner wearing a bathrobe and smoking a pipe—and the amateurs managed the team to victory!

※ ※ ※

The Verdict

How you evaluate Bill Veeck's career depends largely on how seriously you take baseball. If you attended ball games for pure fun, no owner gave better value. If baseball was a sacred, dignified, deadly serious game for you, Veeck was likely an offensive travesty.

A PIRATE'S LIFE FOR ME

Time travelers from the Golden Age of Piracy (1650–1725) would be dismayed at the way pirates are portrayed today—as drunken, bloodthirsty, torturous derelicts who talked funny On behalf of pirates everywhere, we'll address the myths.

Pirates were just drunken debauchers. Yes, these guys tended toward drunkenness and debauchery; it's the "just" part that's inaccurate. They were also violent, womanizing scoundrels—but for the most part, they restricted these unseemly behaviors to shore. Rules governing their conduct often stipulated a lifestyle better suited to Boy Scouts than to bloodthirsty thieves. To avoid shipboard violence among the crew, captains frequently banned women and gambling, forbade drunkenness while on duty, and strictly enforced early "lights out."

Pirates made their prisoners walk the plank. Pirates had a number of unpleasant punishments for prisoners and rule breakers, including twisting cords around an offender's head until his eyes popped out, forcing him to eat his own ears, or tying him to a mast and throwing glass at him or burning him with matches. What pirates didn't do was make prisoners walk the plank (how nice of them). Only one reputable, first-hand account of plank walking exists, and it took place 100 years after the peak of piracy. The idea that this was a common practice comes primarily from J. M. Barrie's play *Peter Pan* and old Hollywood movies in which walking the plank was one of the few forms of torture that would get past the censors.

All pirates talked the same way. If for a period in the 1950s it seemed like every movie pirate had the same accent, it's because they did, or rather, they shared an accent with Robert Newton, the actor who portrayed both Blackbeard and Long John Silver several times on big and small screens. Newton was

born in Dorset, England (as were many famous pirates), and his rough accent and trilled "r" fit the public's image of pirates nicely. But pirate ships were melting pots, pulling sailors in from all over Europe, the Caribbean, and the Americas, so there was no "typical" pirate accent. What's more, Ol' Chumbucket and Cap'n Slappy, the aspiring-pirate masterminds behind International Talk Like a Pirate Day, would like to point out that no pirates—fictional or otherwise—ever said, "Arrrgh," though they might have said, "Arrr."

Pirates were lawless criminals. Who says there's no honor among thieves? Pirates had few qualms about liberating a treasure-laden merchant ship of its burden, but they operated under strict codes of conduct on their own ships. Called Articles of Agreement, these pirate codes varied from ship to ship and governed elections and management, division of booty, disability compensation, shipboard safety, ethics, and responsibilities. Each pirate was required to sign the agreement before embarking on a voyage, and those who violated the rules found themselves marooned—that is, left on a remote island with as little as a flask of water and a weapon. Here are a few of the provisions in the Articles of Agreement drawn up by Captain John Phillips for the crew aboard his ship *Revenge*:

- *If any Man shall steal any Thing in the Company, or game, to the Value of a Piece of Eight, he shall be maroon'd or shot.*

- *That Man that shall strike another whilst those Articles are in force shall receive Moses's Law (that is 40 Stripes lacking one) on the bare Back.*

- *If at any time you meet with a Prudent woman, that Man that offers to meddle with her, without her Consent, shall suffer present Death.*

THE REICH STUFF

*Fanta sodas were first produced by the Coca-Cola Company
at its plant in Germany at the start of World War II.
Despite widespread rumors, however, the popular soft
drink was not invented by the Nazis, nor was it
produced under the direction of the Third Reich.*

Coca-Cola was hugely popular in Germany in the 1930s, more so than anywhere else in Europe. When the American-born director of the company's plant in Germany died in 1938, the German-born Max Keith took over. With the outbreak of World War II, Keith was unable to obtain the ingredients to continue producing the drink, but instead of halting production he created a new beverage, christened Fanta by one of his salesmen. To create the beverage, Keith originally used whey, a by-product of cheese, and apple fiber, a by-product of cider. He also used whatever fruits he could obtain at the time, which likely accounts for the number of fruit-flavored Fanta varieties still on the market today.

Plenty of Nazis undoubtedly enjoyed the new drink, but Keith created Fanta for the German market as a whole. He personally refused to join the Nazi party, and instead of making himself or the Third Reich rich from the production of Fanta, he handed the profits back to the Coca-Cola Company at the end of the war. The rumor that the Nazis invented Fanta probably started before the war when, as an international company, Coca-Cola advertised its product in the popular media of the day. In Germany, that would have inevitably included newspapers and magazines sympathetic to the Nazi cause. In 1960, the company bought the recipe for Fanta and began producing the drink in the United States, and people of all political persuasions have been enjoying it ever since.

SHOULD AULD ACQUAINTANCE BE FORGOT?

*Every December 31, as the clock strikes midnight,
English-speaking people all over the world sing
"Auld Lang Syne" to herald in the new year.
Although few people can claim to know all the words,
or indeed what they mean, even fewer know
the history of this New Year's Eve tradition.*

The song itself dates as far back as the 17th century, but the custom of singing it at the start of a new year didn't begin until the 1930s. Scottish poet Robert Burns first published "Auld Lang Syne" in the mid-1790s, though the earliest mention of this traditional Scottish folk tune was more than a hundred years earlier. Translated from the Gaelic, "auld lang syne" literally means "old long since," but in this context it is better translated as "times gone by." The opening verse of the song asks if old friends and old times should be forgotten. The chorus then answers no, that we should take a drink of kindness and remember the times gone by.

The poignant sentiment and old-fashioned tune fit perfectly with the dawn of a new year, but it wasn't Burns who transformed the song into a New Year's Eve anthem. The musician Guy Lombardo first played "Auld Lang Syne" a few minutes before midnight at a New Year's Eve party in New York City in 1929. He and his orchestra were regulars on New Year's Eve radio (and then television) programs for the next 50 years, and in the process he became that generation's version of Dick Clark. Lombardo's New Year's Eve show became so popular that the TV networks CBS and NBC competed over broadcast rights. As a compromise, CBS broadcast the show until midnight, and NBC took over after midnight. This in turn prompted Lombardo to play "Auld Lang Syne" at the stroke of midnight to signal the end of the old year and the start of the new.

HONG KONG:
THE CITY THAT ISN'T

Hong Kong was once a British crown colony.
Now it's a Special Administrative Region of China.
But the one thing it has never been is a city.

Hong Kong is a dynamic Asian metropolis that seemingly rises straight from the waters of the South China Sea. Its main harbor is ringed by a captivating phalanx of skyscrapers and towers that illuminate the night with vivid neon hues.

Unquestionably, Hong Kong would rank with New York, London, and Rome as one of the world's great cities if not for a minor detail: Hong Kong is not a city. It is, officially, the Hong Kong Special Administrative Region (SAR), a territory governed by China that enjoys autonomy in its political and economic affairs (aside from foreign relations and defense). The Hong Kong SAR came into being in 1997 when Great Britain transferred control of Hong Kong to China after ruling the territory as a British crown colony since 1842. Initially, the colony consisted of Hong Kong Island, but in the span of 55 years, its territory expanded to include the Kowloon Peninsula, Lantau Island, and 260 smaller islands.

Within Hong Kong are several cities and towns concentrated mainly on the Kowloon Peninsula and the northern shore of Hong Kong Island. These settlements have no formal boundaries and mesh into one urbanized area crammed with most of Hong Kong's 7 million residents—making Hong Kong look like one big city.

Territory of Trees

Another popular misconception about Hong Kong is that it is a monolithic urban jungle. In reality, Hong Kong is a very green place—less than one-quarter of its 426-square-mile area is developed. The rest is protected parklands, nature reserves, beaches, and lushly forested hillsides and mountains.

RAGING BULL

❋ ◈ ❋

A bullfight brings a certain image to mind: a magnificently attired matador waving a crimson cloak at a snorting, stampeding bull. Most observers would turn red-faced upon learning that the color of the cape does not cause the animal to charge.

If you questioned the average person about what transforms a bull from a passive, pasture-loving bovine into a rip-roaring lethal ton of bolting beef, the answer you'd receive would probably revolve around the rotating red cape brandished by the sartorially splendid matador. If it could offer a retort, the bull would tell you that it isn't the color of the cloak that causes it to snort and stomp; rather, it's the matador's tormenting and provoking mannerisms that raises its ire. The constant furling and unfurling of the red cape by a skilled matador unleashes an aggressive streak in the bull, which has been specially bred and trained to be belligerent and hostile. The exaggerated movements cause the animal to charge at full speed with the intent of doing harm to the manipulator of the muleta. To further anger (and weaken) the bull, a horseman called a picador stabs the animal in the neck and shoulders repeatedly with a sword.

Seeing Red

Cape color has never been a factor, because bulls are colorblind. They are charging at the move-
ment of the matador and his cape, which they perceive to be gray in color. The traditional bullfighter's cape is crimson for two reasons: Red is a color that can be easily seen by the onlookers who enjoy watching this type of spectacle, and it also camouflages the blood that is inevitably spilled by the slowly butchered bull.

THOMAS CRAPPER: WIZARD OR WASHOUT?

❋ ❈ ❋

There are many myths about Englishman
Thomas Crapper swirling around like so much…conjecture.
Some claim he invented the toilet, and others credit his
last name with creating a crude colloquialism.
It's time to flush away the guesswork.

Thomas Crapper was an actual person, a 19th-century London plumber who held several patents in waste-handling systems. But the concept of the flush toilet dates back to the late 1500s, when England and France used a "closet" full of water to wash waste out of the toilet bowl and into a sewer line. Even before that—in the 26th century B.C.—flushlike toilets were used by members of the Indus civilization in what is now Pakistan. By the late 1700s, the practice of keeping water in the bowl served to eliminate odors by sealing off the drain line. Crapper ran a London plumbing business and installed many "water closets" in the late 1800s. And though this was certainly a noble effort to keep the city smelling fresh and clean, Crapper was never knighted by royalty, quelling the rumor that he was given the title "Sir."

Regarding the word attributed to Crapper's last name: The 15th-century Middle English word *crappe* referred to husks of grain on a barn floor (similar to *chaff*). Other meanings of the word *crap* date back to the 1500s, when it referred to anything cast off, or a useless residue. It is reported that U.S. soldiers returning from World War I had encountered toilets overseas sold by Thomas Crapper's company. Seeing the brand name on the side of the tank led them to associate the maker with the device they used, and as often happens, noun becomes verb.

CASTRO STRIKES OUT!

Though an avid fan of the game, Fidel Castro never came close to playing professional baseball. While we're at it, the bearded Cuban was never an aspiring movie star, either.

Former Cuban president Fidel Castro is one of the most controversial and divisive national leaders of the 20th century. He is also one of the longest lasting, ending his almost-50-year political reign when he handed power to his brother, Raul, in February 2008 due to poor health.

Not surprisingly, Castro is the subject of numerous myths, and the most popular is that he was given a pitching tryout in the 1940s by the New York Yankees (or the Washington Senators, depending on which version is told).

A Love of Baseball

Castro was a longtime fan of the great American pastime, which remains equally popular in Cuba, but there is no evidence that he was ever scouted by an American major league team. He never played baseball professionally in his native country, though it's possible he may have played a bit of extracurricular ball during his college years. But even if that's true, the revolutionary leader certainly didn't possess the athletic skills that would have drawn the eye of a major league scout.

It's likely that this myth started as a way to humiliate Castro by portraying his revolutionary ambitions as payback for the fact that he was found lacking by an American baseball team—especially one called the Yankees. Such myths carry great power in trivializing the motivations of one's enemies.

Castro Takes the Mound

That said, there is strong evidence that Castro did have one brief, shining moment on the mound—when he faced third baseman Don Hoak, who would later go on to play for the Brooklyn Dodgers, Pittsburgh Pirates, and other teams.

According to his wife, singer/actress Jill Corey, Hoak played in the Cuban leagues during the winter of 1950–51, just prior to joining the Brooklyn Dodgers. In a game between Cienfuegos and Marianao, a large group of rowdy fans ran onto the playing field in the middle of an inning. Before being chased out of the park by security guards, one of the fans took to the mound and threw several pitches to Hoak, who was at bat at the time. According to Corey, the "pitcher" was none other than a young Fidel Castro. Hoak himself confirmed the bizarre incident in an article he wrote with journalist Myron Cope titled *The Day I Batted Against Castro*.

The Mythical Movie Extra

A shattered dream of baseball glory isn't the only urban legend involving Fidel Castro. It is also commonly reported that he was an extra in several Hollywood movies in the 1940s, including *Two Girls and a Sailor* (1944), *Holiday in Mexico* (1946), and *Easy to Wed* (1946). But like the spurious baseball tryout, this rumor is also untrue. In fact, Castro wasn't even in the United States during the time he allegedly was making Hollywood movie history. Rather, he was a student in Havana.

The rumor apparently started after bandleader Xavier Cugat, who appeared in several of the movies often linked to Castro, made mysterious references in a magazine interview to a dancer he had hired. Cugat refused to give the dancer's name because the man was "a South American general" at the time.

It doesn't help that the Internet Movie Database erroneously lists *Holiday in Mexico* and *Easy to Wed* as two movies in which Castro allegedly appears uncredited. The popular movie Web site identifies the infamous dictator as an extra in the former movie and as "poolside spectator" in the latter.

Fidel Castro was one of the modern era's longest-serving political figures, outlasting nine U.S. presidents. But he was never rejected by the New York Yankees, the Washington Senators, or any other major league team, nor was he a minor league Hollywood hopeful.

IN ENGLISH, *POR FAVOR*

*It may be arrogance on the part of English speakers
the world over or just a common misconception. Is English
the most widely spoken language on Earth?*

There are between 5,000 and 6,000 languages spoken around the world today, depending on the criteria you use to differentiate *language* from *dialect*. Approximately one-third of these languages are spoken by no more than 1,000 people, but 200 are used by more than a million native speakers. Of course, we don't need to concern ourselves too much with most of these languages because, as English speakers, we're already fluent in the most commonly spoken language in the world—or at least that's what many of us mistakenly believe.

Estimates of how many people speak a language tend to be imprecise, but there is no doubt that Mandarin Chinese has the most native speakers—about 1.1 billion people compared with approximately 330 million native English speakers. Mandarin developed from the principal dialect spoken in the Beijing area of China and is now the country's official language. It is also spoken outside of China, in countries such as Brunei, Cambodia, Indonesia, Malaysia, Mongolia, the Philippines, Singapore, Taiwan, and Thailand.

English, on the other hand, is spoken in 115 countries around the world, more than any other language. Many people also speak English as a secondary language, and it is considered the primary language of international diplomacy. However, if we include all the people who speak English as a secondary language, the number of speakers swells to approximately 480 million—still a distant second to Mandarin Chinese.

So if you plan on traveling abroad, we recommend that you master at least the following Mandarin phrase: *"Ni hui jiang yingyu ma?"* ("Do you speak English?").

DON'T HOLD THE PEPPERONI

For years, spicy foods and stress took the rap for causing ulcers.
The real culprit, however, has a Latin name.

You can have an ulcer and eat your pepperoni pizza, too. Research has proved that certain foods—including hot chilies, coffee, and curry—do not cause ulcers. Nor does stress, no matter how much you have to endure on the job or on the home front.

Your lifestyle is not to blame for the gnawing pain in your gut, though it can exacerbate your symptoms. Ulcers are most frequently caused by a bacterial infection. The little bug is called *Helicobacter pylori,* a corkscrew-shape bacterium that commonly lives in the mucous membranes that line the stomach and small intestine. Antibiotics are usually successful in eliminating such an infection.

Ulcers can also be caused by excessive use of nonsteroidal anti-inflammatory drugs (NSAIDs), such as ibuprofen or aspirin. That's because these medications inhibit the production of an enzyme that plays an important role in protecting your sensitive stomach lining.

Drinking alcohol and smoking, once also indicated as ulcer-causing habits, don't have primary responsibility for the development of ulcers, but they can be contributing factors. And they can definitely make an existing ulcer worse. Alcohol is an irritant that increases the amount of stomach acid you produce. The nicotine in cigarettes increases stomach acid, too, and prevents healing.

❋❋❋

Don't confuse heartburn symptoms—burning, pressure, belching, and a bitter taste after eating—with those of an ulcer. Spicy foods *can* aggravate heartburn and gastroesophageal reflux disease (GERD), which are much more common than ulcers.

If you have ulcers, you don't have to worry about spicy foods. But if you have frequent heartburn, stay away from the chicken curry.

THE OPIUM WAR

*Contrary to popular belief, the Anglo-Chinese War,
otherwise known as the Opium War, was not waged
to keep China from exporting opium to Britain.*

Between 1839 and 1842, Britain and China fought the Opium War
to prevent widespread British trafficking of the illegal drug into
China. The war resulted in a decisive defeat for China, which was
forced to import British shipments of the narcotic.

Britain's Drug Trade

In the early 19th century, Britain was the world's largest trafficker of
illegal drugs, dwarfing the activity of any of today's South American
drug cartels. It shipped tons of opium annually from its plantations
in India to Canton, China, in exchange for Chinese goods such as
tea. This was despite the fact that the trade and consumption of
opium was illegal in Britain because of its harmful effects. The trade
had a devastating impact on Chinese society—an estimated 27 percent of the adult male population was addicted to the drug by 1906.

Opposition to Opium

In 1836, the imperial Chinese government made opium illegal and
started closing down the vast number of opium dens that littered
the country. British trade in the drug continued, however, thanks
to widespread bribery and corruption. In 1839, when the morally
resolute Lin Tse-hsu became Imperial Commissioner at Canton,
he had the British stores of opium destroyed and requested that
Britain's Queen Victoria cease trade in the drug. When Chinese
boats attempted to prevent English merchant vessels from entering Canton in November 1839, war broke out and the British
immediately deployed warships to the area. The Chinese suffered
humiliating defeats to the technologically superior British and
were forced to agree to the Treaty of Nanking. This gave Britain
control of Hong Kong, and over the next 30 years, opium trade to
China more than doubled.

UNDRAFTED QUARTERBACKS, TOO, SHALL PASS

*Although NFL teams would have us believe that finding a good
one engenders the complexity of quantum physics, plenty of
would-be quarterback stars tumble into a black hole on draft day.*

In the NFL, "making it as an undrafted free agent is next to
impossible." It says so on page 128 of the *Complete Pro Football
Draft Encyclopedia,* so it must be true, right? Wrong. Almost
one in ten of today's players were not selected in the sport's
extravagantly orchestrated April lottery. That includes a surprising
number of the league's glamour boys—the quarterbacks. Six of the
32 teams' primary quarterback starters in 2007 were not drafted,
and that doesn't include a standout (the Carolina Panthers' Jake
Delhomme) who missed most of the year with an injury and two
others who won jobs in December.

According to Pete Williams, author of *The Draft: A Year Inside
the NFL's Search for Talent,* teams spend, on average, approximately $2 million a year preparing to select the seven or so rookies
they feel will best fortify their rosters. But the tradition of overlooking great passing prospects goes way back. Warren Moon, the
first African American quarterback to make the Hall of Fame, was
not drafted. Nor were four-time Pro Bowler Jim Hart, 20,000-yard
man Jim Zorn, Dallas Cowboys star Tony Romo, or the greatest
still-active sin of omission, Kurt Warner.

Warner went undrafted in 1994, was cut by the Green Bay
Packers, and had to prove himself in NFL Europe and with the
Iowa Barnstormers of the Arena Football League before getting
a shot with the St. Louis Rams. A decade later, the 2008 Arizona
Cardinals' signal-caller was the NFL's second-highest-rated passer
of all time, a two-time MVP, and a Super Bowl champ. So much
for the NFL's complicated scouting radar.

BLOOD, SWEAT, AND TEARS

*When he became prime minister during his
nation's darkest hours of World War II, Winston
Churchill told Parliament: "I would say to the House,
as I said to those who have joined this government:
'I have nothing to offer but blood and toil, tears and sweat.'"
But that's not the first time the phrase had been used.*

Winston poured a defiant dash of mustard on the last part, bracing listeners for the lousy war news to come. Perhaps it was a preemptive strike against the inevitable second-guessing that would surely result; it simply wouldn't do to raise hopes that he knew he could not possibly fulfill. He made good on his offer: Britain got all the blood, toil, tears, and sweat it could want, and Winston's words gained fame.

The error lies not in the quote itself but in denying Churchill credit for having uttered the words. By the same token, however, people are wrong to assume that he invented the phrase. Churchill likely borrowed from Henry James's 1886 novel *The Bostonians,* which contains a similar line. Another source could have been Theodore Roosevelt, who used this reference in at least one oration: "The credit belongs to the man who is actually in the arena, whose face is marred by dust and sweat and blood...."

Borrowed from the Best

Roosevelt may have used it in other contexts as well. If that's where Churchill got it, he at least had an excellent source. The prime minister was a generation younger than Roosevelt and had probably read some of his speeches. Perhaps he remembered the reference when it came time to compose this vital address to Parliament. Maybe Churchill was even hoping the reference would stir the heart of Teddy's younger cousin, Franklin D. Roosevelt, then president of the United States—which is where Britain's greatest hope for victory lay.

PUTTS ARE NOT ENOUGH

※ ※ ※

There's a saying in golf: "Drive for show and putt for dough."
However, none of the top five putters on the PGA tour in
2007 finished among the top 20 money winners.

Golf's most lovable cliché, complete with rhyming couplet and a minds-eye visual presence, unfortunately does not ring true on the bottom line—the line that counts in professional sports. The long bombers elicit the "oohs," "aahs," and cries of "in the hole" from fairway fanatics, and the masters of the putting surface receive the majority of the media coverage. But in 2007, neither group dominated the list that every golfer wants to climb—the money list.

Just Putting Along

The top five putters on the PGA tour in 2007 didn't finish anywhere near the top of the leader board in cash earned. Tim Clark, the tour leader in putts per round, made $2.6 million in 2007, not exactly pocket change but not enough to put him among the top 20 earners. Wallops didn't fill the wallet, either. Bubba Watson, the game's longest hitter, finished 55th on the cash list, while John Daly, the PGA's most popular slugger, barely cracked the top 200, finishing 188th on the dollar dais. Even Tiger Woods, the first person to earn a billion dollars because of his ability to propel a dimpled orb across a manicured cow pasture, was a dismal 48th in putting and a distant 12th in yards off the tee.

※ ※ ※

Improvements in club and ball technology have made driving length a secondary factor. Everyone on the tour is capable of slamming the pill 300 yards down the fairway, but management, accuracy, and the ability to maneuver through the myriad bunkers and brooks have become the keys to victory.

THE BIG BANG? BAH!

*In the late 1970s, the nuclear accident at
Three Mile Island in Pennsylvania gripped the
country and caused panic throughout the region.
It was serious, but it was no Chernobyl.*

Nuclear power has always been controversial. Advocates see it as the answer to our national energy needs, while opponents view it as an environmental disaster just waiting to happen. The latter group almost saw its nightmare come true on March 28, 1979, when a series of events led to a severe core meltdown at the Three Mile Island nuclear power plant near Middletown, Pennsylvania.

Today, three decades after the accident, many people still believe that the area around the power plant was blanketed with radioactive fallout that endangered thousands. The truth, however, is much different. Though the Nuclear Regulatory Commission (NRC) calls the accident "the most serious in the U.S. commercial nuclear power plant operating history," no lives were lost and the amount of radiation released was within safe levels.

How Safe Is "Safe"?

According to an NRC report, which followed numerous studies of and investigations into the accident, the average dose of radiation to approximately 2 million people in the area was only about 1 millirem. "To put that into context," the report explains, "exposure from a full set of chest X-rays is about 6 millirem. Compared to the natural radioactive background dose of about 100–125 millirem per year for the area, the collective dose to the community from the accident was very small. The maximum dose to a person at the site boundary would have been less than 100 millirem."

Multiple Malfunctions

The cause of the accident was a combination of mechanical problems and human error. It started when the main feed-water pumps stopped running in a secondary, non-nuclear section of the plant. This was caused either by a mechanical or an electrical failure, and it prevented the steam generators from removing heat. The turbine automatically shut down, and so did the reactor. Immediately, the pressure in the primary system—the nuclear portion of the plant—began to increase. To prevent that pressure from becoming excessive, a special relief valve opened. The valve should have closed when the pressure decreased by a certain amount, but it failed to do so. Signals to the operator did not show that the valve was still open; as a result, cooling water poured out of the valve and caused the core of the reactor to overheat.

Because the operators did not realize that the plant was experiencing a loss-of-coolant accident, they took a series of actions that made conditions worse by further reducing the flow of coolant through the core. Consequently, the nuclear fuel overheated to the point where the long metal tubes that hold the nuclear fuel pellets ruptured and the fuel pellets began to melt.

The accident at Three Mile Island was a serious cause for concern, and the plant was extremely fortunate to have avoided a catastrophic breach of the containment building and the release of massive amounts of radiation into the environment.

Chernobyl in Comparison

As bad as the Three Mile Island event was, it pales in comparison to the accident at the Chernobyl nuclear power plant just outside the town of Pripyat, Ukraine, on April 26, 1986. Chernobyl remains the largest nuclear power plant disaster in history. That event directly killed 31 people; produced a massive plume of radioactive debris that drifted over parts of the western Soviet Union, Eastern Europe, and Scandinavia; left huge areas dangerously contaminated; and forced the evacuation of more than 200,000 people.

※ ※ ※

- The China Syndrome, *a movie about a fictional nuclear power plant disaster, had been released just 12 days before the Three Mile Island meltdown, which greatly added to the public panic.*

THE BUNNY HYPE

※ ※※ ※

Everyone knows that rabbits do not lay eggs. So how did a colored-egg-toting bunny become associated with Easter?

It is sometimes claimed that rabbits and eggs are fertility symbols associated with springtime, and their connection to Easter is a simple derivation of ancient pagan practices. Not so fast. Rabbits are indeed a symbol of fertility, because they reproduce like—well, rabbits. And it makes sense that ancient pagans associated the advent of spring—the time of rebirth, renewal, and new life—with rabbits and eggs.

Why decorate hard-boiled eggs for Easter? This custom may have originated among Christians in the Middle Ages, when eating eggs was prohibited during Lent, the 40 days leading up to Easter. The faithful broke the Lenten fast with an Easter celebration that included feasting on brightly colored hard-boiled eggs—which were probably plentiful by that time.

Where did the idea of an egg-carrying rabbit come from? One theory points to hares' tendency to overbuild when it comes to home construction. Hares raise their young in hollows in the ground and sometimes separate them into multiple nests for safety's sake. People hunting for eggs may have found them near, or even in, an unused hare's nest—appropriated by some resourceful bird—and came to the mistaken conclusion that the hares had laid eggs.

This confusion may have become the foundation for an old German myth about "Oschter haws" (Easter hare), which laid eggs in gardens for good children to find. German immigrants brought the legend of the Easter hare to America (along with the story about a shadow-sighting groundhog). In the United States, rabbits are more plentiful than hares, and the egg-bearing bunny soon became part of the folklore of Easter.

FEEDING HITLER

*Have you ever seen a photograph of Hitler
enjoying a Bavarian sausage? The answer is likely no,
but it's not because he was a vegetarian.*

Adolf Hitler wanted the world to believe he was a vegetarian. This was propaganda—part of his image as a superhuman "aesthetic." He would publicly abstain from alcohol, tobacco, and womanizing so as to seem above all weaknesses. He often brought up his vegetarian diet in conversations and speeches, touting its virtues and predicting that Germany would eventually be a meat-free society. But Hitler was never a strict vegetarian.

Hitler drank alcohol (he used it to fall asleep), and he kept a mistress (Eva Braun). He also relished sausages and ham, and he had a weakness for caviar. When he began to suffer from an array of digestive problems, he was advised to take breaks from eating meat. Many of his doctors were actually quacks who prescribed a strange assortment of vitamin injections and fasting regimens. This was most likely the real reason for his occasional vegetarian diet.

But the myth of Hitler's vegetarianism has persisted. Tired of that name being included in their ranks, vegetarian activists have done much to unearth actual instances of Hitler eating meat. One of these is an excerpt from a 1960s German cookbook in which the author writes that "roast squab" was Hitler's favorite dish at a hotel where she'd worked. Apparently, he couldn't get enough of it. *Leberknödel* (liver dumplings) were another of his favorites.

※ ※ ※

• *A clear demonstration of Hitler's hypocrisy was the fact that he banned vegetarian societies in Germany. Those who met openly to discuss the philosophy of vegetarianism risked imprisonment or worse. There have been many famous vegetarians throughout history, but Adolf Hitler was not one of them.*

READY, SET, CYCLE!

From the sandbox to the sorority house, gal groups are powerful.
Guys might even say magical. But can women exert a kind of
chemical alchemy over one another?

• A landmark 1971 study of 135 members of an all-female college dormitory showed that women who lived together tended to have menstrual periods within days of one another. In the study, roommates whose periods averaged more than six days apart in October were less than five days apart six months later.

• The theory of menstrual synchrony—called the "McClintock Effect" after the author of the study—was long accepted as established fact, especially among women. McClintock, a graduate student who then became a University of Chicago psychologist, speculated that pheromones (chemical messengers received through the sense of smell) were responsible for the phenomenon.

• Recent studies have cast doubt on the theory of synchrony. In 1992, H. Clyde Wilson published a report accusing a slew of studies—McClintock's included—of faulty research and shoddy methodology. And researchers have pointed out that synchrony is impossible when women have cycles of different lengths.

• In 2007, psychologist Jeffery Schank published a study involving 186 Chinese women who lived together in a college dorm. Though he uncovered some interesting menstruation patterns among the women, he found no evidence that their cycles were in sync. The researchers reviewed McClintock's original study and went so far as to say that the results in 1971 could be chalked up to chance.

• The strongest evidence against menstrual synchrony is that, in all studies, women's cycle lengths continue to vary radically, even if their start dates get closer over a designated period of time.

JULIUS CAESAR: ROME'S GREATEST EMPEROR?

❊ ❊❊ ❊

The question assumes that Caesar was an emperor. He was powerful, illustrious, famous, and Roman to the core, but he was never an emperor. He couldn't have been, because Rome became an empire after his death, and then only gradually.

Gaius Julius Caesar was born around 102 B.C. to one of the Roman Republic's noblest patrician families, and he rose swiftly through the military and political ranks:

75 B.C.: Cilician pirates kidnap Caesar for ransom. Their demand of only 20 talents of gold offends Caesar's colossal ego, so he orders the pirates to increase their demand to a more fitting 50 talents.
60: Caesar joins Pompey and Crassus in the First Triumvirate, which dominates Rome for seven years.
51: He completes his conquest of Gaul (modern France and Belgium) for Rome—and his popularity makes the senate nervous.
46: After pummeling Pompey in civil war and fighting his way back to Rome from Egypt, Caesar is elected dictator. Apparently, the senate didn't feel it had much choice.
45–44: The senate votes Caesar frequent and random honors and powers, fawning over him and making him dictator-for-life.
44: Senators rescind the "life" portion of dictator-for-life, using sharp knives. Messy but effective.

Caesar held great power, of course, including privileges that actual emperors would one day hold—all voted to him by the republican senate. The point is that these powers were the senate's to grant. Rome was in transition from republic to empire, and few historians would call Rome of 44 B.C. an empire. Most consider Caesar's great-nephew and adopted heir, Augustus, the first leader whose powers became imperial—and those powers far exceeded Caesar's former offices.

ALL CHOKED UP

Recollections of Mama Cass Elliot should include million-selling singles, garish garments, and a flamboyant stage presence. Instead, she is often remembered for dying with a hoagie gorged in her gob. Let's satisfy the public's hunger and set her record straight.

As renowned for her prodigious girth as she was for the rich timbre of her singing voice, Ellen Naomi (Mama Cass) Cohen knew no half measures—she lived life to the fullest. Although the musical Mama had an appetite for substances of all quantities and assortments, the details surrounding her untimely demise have been greatly exaggerated, not to mention inaccurate.

Shortly after news of her death in a London apartment was announced to the public, rumors abounded that the corpulent chanteuse had punched her ticket to the great beyond by choking on a ham sandwich. The genesis for the gossip was a notation on the official police report, which stated that a half-eaten sandwich had been found near her expired form. However, the autopsy report, a far more reliable document, revealed that there was no evidence of food particles in her trachea.

The simple truth is that Mama Cass died a rather pedestrian death. The vocalist perished from heart failure, most likely because of her unhealthy habit of alternating periods of food and substance abuse with intervals of crash dieting.

The Cursed Apartment

One measure of the Mama Cass myth is accurate, however. When Keith Moon, drummer for The Who, succumbed to his own personal demons four years later, he did so in the same rented flat where Mama Cass took her last breath. And it is also true that the domicile for the dearly departed duo was owned by singer/songwriter Harry Nilsson, whose own exit took place under similarly dark circumstances in 1994.

SO WHICH WAY IS NORTH?

*If you, like most people, think the topmost symbol
on a compass always points north, take care not
to get lost in the Southern Hemisphere.*

North, south, east, and west: These directions are meant to be set
in stone, the unchangeable points of reference that lead sailors
through treacherous seas and intrepid adventurers through dark
and unknown lands. Yet even these directions, such stalwarts of
clarity and precision, come with a medley of misconceptions.

The North Magnetic Pole

One misconception is that a compass points to the North Pole.
In reality, a compass points toward Earth's North Magnetic Pole,
which is different from the geographic pole that you'll find on a
map. Earth has a magnetic field, which is created by the swirling motion of molten lava that resides in its core. This magnetic
field makes an angle with Earth's spin axis. The geographic poles,
in contrast, are the places that Earth's imaginary spin axis pass
straight through. So while the geographic and magnetic poles
are close to each other, they are never in the exact same place. If
you're heading "due north" as the compass reads, you're heading
to the North Magnetic Pole, not the North Pole. But compasses
don't work close to a magnetic pole, so if you're going to the
North Pole, a compass will take you only so far.

To complicate matters further, the North Magnetic Pole is
always moving, because the motion of the swirling lava changes. In
2005, the North Magnetic Pole was 503 miles from the geographic
North Pole, placing it firmly in the Arctic Ocean, north of Canada.
Meanwhile, the South Magnetic Pole was 1,756 miles from the
geographic South Pole, in Antarctica just south of Australia. The
rates of change of the magnetic poles vary, but lately they've been
moving at approximately 25 miles per year. Scientists project that
in 50 years, the North Magnetic Pole will be in Siberia.

The South Magnetic Pole

That moves us right along to misconception number two, which is that the "N" on a compass always points north. Assuming that the designation "north" always coincides with the notion of "up," the runaway North Magnetic Pole reminds us that "up" is relative. Earth is a sphere, so logically any single point could be  designated as the top, making whatever lies opposite this arbitrary top the arbitrary bottom. It made sense for early mapmakers to draw the North Pole at the top of a map, because this was their approximation of where that handy compass pointed. As the North Magnetic Pole continues to wander from the point cartographers deemed the "North Pole," the designation of this geographic location as due north may eventually become obsolete.

Meanwhile, in the Southern Hemisphere, a compass points toward the South Magnetic Pole and more or less toward the corresponding yet inevitably inaccurate location that is deemed the geographic South Pole. Early mapmakers hailed from the Northern Hemisphere, so the North Pole is logically represented as being at the top of the map and the top of the world. Yet in the Southern Hemisphere, it would be equally logical to place the South Pole at the top of the map.

How Does Santa Manage?

If this exercise in relativity makes your head spin, one tidbit remains that might just make it spin faster: Earth's magnetic field is prone to flipping over, meaning the North and South Magnetic Poles trade places. Usually, a few hundred thousand years pass between these flips, so for now you just have to keep in mind that your compass could lead you to Siberia instead of the Arctic.

HOWLIN' AT THE MOON

One of the most romanticized images of the wild is that of a lone wolf howling against the backdrop of a full moon. The light of the moon usually gets our attention, but it's doubtful that a wolf cares what's happening in the night sky.

When Shakespeare wrote, "Now the hungry lion roars and the wolf behowls the moon," he was referring to the long-held belief that wolves are more likely to howl when the moon is full. In fact, wolves howl at all times, and the moon itself doesn't trigger any special reaction from them. When any animal howls, it extends its neck upward, but this is to project sound rather than to target a specific object.

The notion that wolves howl at the moon is probably common among people because *they* are attracted to a full moon, not because wolves are. Moonlight draws people outdoors, which increases the chances that they will hear the sounds of wildlife at night. Anecdotal reports that wolves howl more during a full moon are not backed by scientific observation.

Wolves howl for a variety of reasons. The alpha wolf will howl to gather pack members for a hunt, and a wolf that has been separated from its pack will howl to try to regain contact. The most haunting sound is when a group of wolves howl in a chorus to claim a stretch of territory. By shifting the pitch of their howls, the pack makes itself sound larger than it is. Wolves will howl in this manner through an entire night and can be heard for miles. These are the scary sounds that punctuate the scenes of countless horror movies, serving to cement in our consciousness the connection between wolves and a full moon.

SURVIVAL OF A QUOTE

❀ ❁ ❀

*"Survival of the fittest," thought to summarize
the theory of evolution, is actually a metaphor for natural
selection that was not coined by Charles Darwin.*

A quote may have an original creator, but its evolution occurs independently of the person who said it first. "Survival of the fittest" has a definite creator: 19th-century economist Herbert Spencer. Yet after Spencer coined the phrase in *Principles of Biology* (1864), it took on a life if its own.

Spencer conjured the phrase as a reference to Charles Darwin's theory of natural selection, which Spencer had read about upon the 1859 release of *On the Origin of Species by Means of Natural Selection.* Darwin's theory was strictly biological: Given the preconditions of variation, replication, and heritability, traits favorable to a given environment are preserved over time (natural selection), and thus change occurs (evolution). By means of analogy, Spencer brought this concept into the economic realm to describe how the "fittest" societies evolve over time.

Despite popularizing the same phrase, Darwin and Spencer didn't use it in the same way. By "fittest" Darwin did not mean "best" but rather whatever trait allows an organism to survive and reproduce in a given environment, thereby increasing the frequency of said trait. Spencer, on the other hand, did intend fittest to mean "best," and he applied the idea to social evolution, not biology.

What Darwin meant by natural selection is best summarized by a quote that actually appeared in *On the Origin of Species,* from the first edition ad infinitum: "Any variation, however slight…if it be in any degree profitable to an individual of any species…will tend to the preservation of that individual, and will generally be inherited by its offspring."

IT'S IRON-IC

✳ ✦ ✳

Popeye credited his trusty can of spinach for his bulging biceps. But his assumptions about spinach were based on a widespread misconception about its iron content.

Popeye didn't start the rumor about the nutritional value of spinach. He simply popularized the widely held belief, based on a scientific study that spinach is a superior source of iron.

Thanks to a Typo

But the leafy greens' reputation wasn't so ironclad. An 1870 German study of spinach claimed it had ten times the iron content of other green leafy vegetables. This claim, uncontested for 70 years, turned out to be based on a misprint—a misplaced decimal point. The iron content of spinach was overestimated by a factor of ten! By the time the error was discovered in 1937, Popeye had already helped spread the myth far and wide—and encouraged several generations of children to tolerate the unappealing vegetable in hopes of developing their hero's brawn.

The hype about spinach didn't end then, however, because the error wasn't publicized. It wasn't until an article on the mistake was published in a 1981 issue of the *British Medical Journal* that the public was informed of the true iron content of spinach.

In the 1990s, spinach received another nutritional blow when it was discovered that its oxalic acid content prevents the body from absorbing more than 90 percent of the vegetable's iron. Oxalic acid binds with iron and renders most of it unavailable for absorption.

Still Packs a Wallop

Luckily for Popeye's legacy, however, the spirited sailor was not wrong to think that spinach has abundant nutritional merit. It's a terrific source of vitamins A, B_1, B_2, B_3, B_6, C, E, and K, as well as magnesium, calcium, and potassium.

If it's muscles you're after, you'll need pump iron rather than consume it.

VIVA THE CHAUVINIST

*Most people today would define a chauvinist as a man who
believes that women are inferior beings. But a look at
the origins of the word reveals a different meaning.*

When people use the word *chauvinist,* it's usually in reference
to an ignorant bigot who believes that women are inferior to
men. Originally, though, the word had nothing to do with gender. Instead, it was used to describe someone who has an ardent
loyalty to a nation or group. The term is derived from a legendary
French soldier, Nicolas Chauvin, who was wounded 17 times and
severely disabled while serving under Napoleon Bonaparte. The
deposed emperor of France was a hugely unpopular figure in that
country after the Napoleonic Wars in the early 19th century, but
Chauvin bucked popular opinion and remained a dedicated supporter of Bonapartism. Like other Bonapartists, Chauvin refused
to acknowledge the French defeat at Waterloo or the Congress
of Vienna, which redrew the political map of Europe following
Napoleon's defeat.

Chauvin's name entered the public lexicon when he was
featured as a character in the satirical French play *La Cocarde
Tricolore* in 1831 and in Emmuska Orczy's 1903 novel *The Scarlet
Pimpernel.* The word *chauvinism* was coined to describe blind
nationalism, and in the French language, at least, it retains that
meaning.

In the English-speaking world, however, "chauvinist" was
adopted by the women's liberation movement of the 1960s and
was used to describe men who view women as being inferior due
to their gender. Initially, the term used was "male chauvinist" or
even "male chauvinist pig." Over time the "male" became obsolete, and the word *chauvinist* was used to describe a bigoted man
who wasn't afraid to express his sexist (rather than patriotic) views
in either word or deed.

DON'T FENCE ME IN

The saying "Good fences make good neighbors"
can be used for a variety of purposes—so many that
few people are clear on its true intention.
Should we be outfitting our property lines with chain
link or picketing our neighbor's pickets?

The line is lifted from Robert Frost's poem *Mending Wall* (1914), in which two men walk their property lines together, repairing the stone wall that separates them. The narrator wonders at the wall's purpose, as neither of them owns livestock, and the wall separates one type of tree from another. The neighbor, repeating what he firmly believes, twice states, "Good fences make good neighbors."

A Matter of Interpretation

Some people use this saying to mean its opposite—that fences make terrible neighbors. The poem's narrator is clearly against his neighbor's belief in boundaries. He points out that the wall keeps nothing in or out, that a wall could give offense, and the yearly damage shows that a wall goes against nature itself. He even compares the neighbor to a "savage." To many, if the narrator said it, then Frost said it, and therefore it must be true. Walls are bad, end of story.

Another use of this phrase emphasizes the quality of the fence, as if that were the issue rather than the existence of the fence. If you're going to have a fence, it should be a good fence. It is not neighborly to allow your wall to fall into disrepair so that your dog ends up soiling your neighbor's yard.

Still others use this phrase to advocate metaphorical distance from other people as a way to be happy. The 1960 musical *The Fantasticks* tells the story of two scheming fathers who build a wall between their properties so that their children will have an obstacle to overcome and, thus, fall in love.

Give Me My Space

Folks in the United States are fond of fences—more than 3 million people live in gated communities. Some towns are entirely surrounded by fences, and there is a fence along portions of the country's southern border. Many people believe that private property is sacrosanct. No flesh-and-blood neighbor could ever be as pleasant as a barrier demarcating Yours and Mine. Just as early pioneers would move when they saw smoke from a neighbor's chimney, Americans love wide open spaces and plenty of room between neighbors. Although the open frontier no longer exists, a fence creates that elbow room, much the same way an invisible line drawn down a car's backseat separates squabbling siblings.

This sentiment is not limited to people in the United States. Proverbs from around the world suggest that a little separation is a good thing. From the medieval Latin *Bonum est erigere dumos cum vicinis* ("It is good to erect hedges with the neighbors") to the Japanese "Build a fence even between intimate friends" to the Norwegian "There must be a fence between good neighbors," variations exist in many cultures and religions.

A recent study by scientists at Brandeis University and the New England Complex Systems Institute show that there is some truth to this idea. In places occupied by more than one cultural group, clearly defined boundaries such as fences can help ease ethnic or cultural tensions. Another study by University of California research economists found that every 10 percent decline in population density results in a 10 percent increase in neighborly communication and a 15 percent increase in community involvement.

Neighborly Returns

Good fences can make good neighbors, if they are indeed good fences that create enough personal space between you and your good neighbors. Although there are multiple, conflicting interpretations of this saying, it usually serves to unite people. Perhaps this is why, when we rebuild damaged relationships and come together the way Frost's narrator and his neighbor do, the act is called "mending fences."

TOO HOT TO HANDLE

*Although the Great Chicago Fire garnered
international headlines, a later inferno
that raged in Peshtigo, Wisconsin, burned
brighter, longer, and deadlier.*

Consider the colorful tale of Mrs. O'Leary's cow—yes, the one
about the celebrated igniter of the Great Chicago Fire of 1871.
Despite historical evidence that attempts to lay this fanciful tale to
rest, many believe that a clumsy bovine tipped over the gas lamp
that started the infamous fire. To go this myth one better, consider
the "great" fire itself. Apparently, many believe that the Chicago
fire was the most disastrous blaze in U.S. history.

To this misinformed if well-intentioned lot, we offer two
words: Peshtigo, Wisconsin. In a bizarre twist of fate, the great
Peshtigo fire happened to erupt precisely when Chicago staged
its little bonfire. In total devastation and number of fatalities, the
Peshtigo blaze leaves Chicago in its embers. To this day, it is considered the worst forest fire in North American history. Here's the
backstory to the backdraft.

From Tinderbox to Tragedy
Unlike many large fires, Peshtigo's was a conglomeration of
smaller blazes that joined into a firestorm. At the time, a prolonged drought had turned the usually lush countryside into a dry
thicket. Slash-and-burn land-clearing practices (the cutting and
burning of woodlands to create agricultural space) were also pre-
senting a potential problem. With a slew of these fires burning on
October 8, 1871, the area around Peshtigo had become a tinder-
box, with conditions ripe for disaster.

According to some accounts, the great blaze began when railroad workers touched off a brush fire. But these reports are about
as reliable as the fable concerning Mrs. O'Leary's cow. No one is
sure of the fire's precise origin, but one thing is certain: Once it

started, the fire took on a life of its own. Survivors would compare its violent winds to those of a tornado. A firestorm had been born.

Extensive Losses

In one hour's time, Peshtigo was completely gone. Eight hundred lives were lost in the town alone. As the fire continued on its hellish mission, 16 other towns would succumb to its deadly, wind-whipped flames. The great blaze would destroy a 2,500-square-mile area (nearly 500 square miles larger than the state of Delaware) and wouldn't relent until its winds changed course, pitting the fire against itself and robbing it of its fuel source.

Damage estimates from the fire reached $169 million, which happens to be identical to the Chicago fire. But what stood out were the fatalities. The Chicago fire had snuffed out the lives of an estimated 250 people—no small number, of course—but the Peshtigo fire had claimed as many as 2,400 lives.

Since the greatest loss of life occurred in Peshtigo itself, the fire became closely associated with the town. Many wondered why the Peshtigo fire department couldn't do more to control the blaze. But the department was staffed about as well as any of that time, which is to say it was woefully understaffed. The fire company had a single horse-drawn steam-pumper designed to fight fires at its sawmill. Beyond that, it didn't have the technology to fight even the simplest structural fires, never mind an unprecedented vortex of flame. Peshtigo's citizens were reduced to "sitting ducks" as they awaited their fate amid dry wooden buildings and sawdust-strewn boulevards.

❋ ❋ ❋

Perhaps the most troubling detail about the Peshtigo Fire is its near-anonymity. Most adults have never heard of it, and despite its well-documented impact, schools seem to overlook it. This undoubtedly speaks to Chicago's fame, which served to magnify the relative significance of its fire. But there's no need for enhancement when the fire being considered is the "Great Peshtigo Fire." Its sobering statistics say it all.

SPREADING FEAR

*Surgery always carries risks,
but spreading cancer is not one of them.*

One of the most unfortunate medical misconceptions—that surgery causes cancer to spread throughout the body—has persisted for years. Specialists in cancer surgery say there is no truth to this misconception, but it sometimes prevents cancer patients from seeking life-saving treatment.

A 2005 survey by the American Cancer Society found that 41 percent of respondents believed cancer spreads throughout the body as a result of surgery. And 37 percent of those responding to a 2003 survey by the Philadelphia Veterans' Affairs Medical Center survey thought cancer spreads when simply exposed to air.

Experts surmise that misconceptions about cancer surgery were launched before the advent of effective diagnostic tools such as magnetic resonance imaging and ultrasound. Back then, the only conclusive way to know if a patient had cancer was through exploratory surgery. In many cases, by the time the patient was opened up in the operating room, the cancer already had metastasized, and there was little doctors could do to stop the advancement of the disease. Ailing patients mistakenly blamed the surgeon for their declining health, believing it was the operation that had caused the cancer to spread.

Today, doctors are able to identify cancer at much earlier stages, when patients have better treatment options. Surgery, often in combination with chemotherapy and radiation, is an important part of the journey back to health. Surgeons are able to safely perform biopsies and remove tumors without introducing cancer cells into other parts of the body.

❋ ❋ ❋

- *Cancer spreads three ways: through the blood, through the lymphatic system, or by invading tissue near the tumor.*

FDR'S FORESIGHT

*There's debate as to whether Franklin Delano Roosevelt
coined the phrase "The only thing we have to fear
is fear itself." Regardless of its origins, though, no one
has uttered the words quite the way he did.*

The full quote is: "So, first of all, let me assert my firm belief that
the only thing we have to fear is fear itself—nameless, unreason-
ing, unjustified terror which paralyzes needed efforts to convert
retreat into advance." Thus said FDR, using his patrician New
York diction, in the opening paragraph of his first inaugural
address on March 4, 1933.

FDR was certainly a well-educated president, having studied
at Groton, Harvard, and Columbia Law School. He was also an
eloquent speaker who surrounded himself with talented speech-
writers. Still, it appears that Roosevelt appropriated the famous
line—and his potential sources include Michel de Montaigne,
Francis Bacon, and Henry David Thoreau.

For his part, Roosevelt had good reason to address public fear.
The United States floundered in the Great Depression. Russia had
gone communist; millions there were dying as the result of famine.
In Germany, defeated at great cost 15 years earlier, Adolf Hitler
had his country's young democracy on the ropes.

On the positive side for the United States, it had recently dedicated Mt. Rushmore, and *King Kong* had just hit movie theaters.
Small comfort, however, as Roosevelt was preparing Americans for
draconian measures. Later in the speech, FDR proclaimed that if
necessary he would put matters right with or without the coopera-
tion of Congress, even if he had to seek a formal declaration of war
upon "the emergency."

Although he was primarily referring to sweeping economic
change, it seems Roosevelt also foresaw war. Most Americans
preferred to let the Old World stew in its own tribal conflicts, but
FDR saw that this might not be possible—and indeed, it was not.

WALLY PIPP'S WHOPPER

*Many a misinformed baseball fan believes that
Lou Gehrig's "ironman" streak began on June 2, 1925,
when he replaced Wally Pipp, who couldn't play because
he had a headache. In fact, Gehrig replaced Pipp when
the incumbent first baseman was benched for poor play.*

Not Today, Dear…

First things first: The Iron Horse's playing streak of 2,130 consecutive games actually began on June 1, 1925, when the slugging collegian pinch-hit for shortstop Paul "Pee Wee" Wanninger. The following afternoon, Yankees manager Miller Huggins penciled in Gehrig to start at first base, supposedly because Pipp had a throbbing migraine. Pipp's cranial crick may have become the most famous headache in baseball folklore, but it's not the reason he was replaced. It wasn't until Gehrig died more than 15 years later that the first stories about Pipp's headache were printed in newspapers, and by that time, the facts had been eroded by the sands of time. In interviews, Pipp reported that he'd been suffering the effects of an errant pitch that bounced off his bugle during batting practice on the day Gehrig began his assault on the record books. Well, Pipp did get plunked, but it didn't happen until a month later.

A Change in the Lineup

By June 1925, the Yankees were immersed in a season-long slump, hovering near the basement of the American League and 11 games on the deficit side of the break-even ledger. Babe Ruth was on the sidelines nursing an assortment of maladies, so to shake up his parade of plummeting pinstripes, manager Huggins sat out four underperforming Yankee regulars—Aaron Ward, Steve O'Neill, Wally Schang, and the far more famous Mr. Pipp. By 1926, Gehrig was a star, Pipp was in Cincinnati, and the team was on the cusp of becoming the Bronx Bombers.

WE THREE (?) KINGS

米 ※ 米

*Tradition tells us that three kings came from
the East to honor Jesus at his birth. But they weren't kings,
and there were probably more than three of them.*

According to the gospel of Matthew, "After Jesus was born in
Bethlehem in Judea, during the time of King Herod, magi from
the east came to Jerusalem." The word *after* is important: Countless Christmas pageants notwithstanding, the magi ("wise men")
were not present at the manger scene with the sheep, goats, and
shepherds. Although it's not known exactly what country the wise
men came from—it could have been Persia or Babylon—the journey must have taken weeks or even months. By the time the men
arrived, Joseph and Mary had been able to find more comfortable
lodging. (Matthew indicates this when he says, "On coming to the
house, they saw the child with his mother, Mary.")

So who were the magi? They appear to have been religious
or governmental officials—maybe both—who were well versed in
astrology. They may have been followers of the Persian prophet
Zoroaster.

The wise men interpreted the mysterious star of Bethlehem as
the birth announcement of an extremely important king, and they
headed off to pay their respects. They took along valuable gifts—
gold, frankincense, and myrrh—just as diplomatic visitors today
might bear gifts representing the best of their country's offerings.

Because Matthew mentions three gifts, early readers assumed
that there were just three magi. They also began to think of them
as kings, probably seeing the visit as a fulfillment of this verse in
the Bible (Psalm 72:11): "All kings will bow down to him and all
nations will serve him." But Matthew is unclear about their job
titles and doesn't say anything about their numbers. So the song
"We Three Kings," written by John H. Hopkins, Jr., in 1857, is
more poetic than accurate.

IT'S NOT TRUE, BY GEORGE!

*George Washington is known for a great many
things, some of which are true (he was the only president
to be elected unanimously) and many others
that are imagined. Here are some of the latter.*

Washington wore wooden dentures. It's common knowledge
that Washington had gnawing dental problems. This brought the
leader much pain and sent him in search of relief. Over time,
each of Washington's teeth had to be extracted and replaced
with dentures. Legend holds that these dental appliances were
fashioned from wood, which (some say) could account for
Washington's "wooden" smile.

In fact, Washington's false teeth were made from hippopota-
mus and elephant ivory, as well as human teeth that were not his
own. During his lifetime, Washington used several sets of falsies.
Most were ill-fitting and therefore contorted his expression, but
none were made from wood.

Washington threw a silver dollar across the Potomac River.
George was a tall (6'2"), athletic man, but he certainly wasn't a
good enough throw to hurl a silver dollar all the way across the
Potomac River, which is close to a mile wide at Mount Vernon,
Maryland (site of the president's home). There is evidence that,
as a boy, he tossed something across the Rappahannock River in
Fredericksburg, Virginia (near his childhood home). If that's the
case, though, that "something" certainly wasn't a silver dollar,
because the coins didn't even exist when Washington was young.

Washington wore a wig. Despite the fact that it was all the rage
for men to sport a powdery hair hat in the late 1700s, George
would go only so far to fit in. He kept his brownish-red hair at a
length that allowed him to tie it back in a braid, and then he'd
ocasionally give it a good dusting of powder just for the sake of
fashion.

JACK THE RIPPER

❊❊❊

Between 1888 and 1891, he brutally murdered at least five women in London's East End. But was there really a connection between Jack the Ripper and the British royal family?

The serial killer known as Jack the Ripper is one of history's most famous murderers. He breathed terror into the gas-lit streets and foggy back alleys of the Whitechapel area of London and became renowned the world over. Despite the countless books and movies detailing his story, however, his identity and motives remain shrouded in mystery. One of the most popular theories, espoused by the 2001 movie *From Hell* (starring Johnny Depp), links the killer to the British royal family.

The Crimes

Five murders are definitively attributed to Jack the Ripper, and he has variously been connected to at least six other unsolved slayings in the London area. The body of the first victim, 43-year-old Mary Ann Nichols, was discovered on the morning of August 31, 1888. Nichols's throat had been cut and her abdomen mutilated. The subsequent murders, which took place over a three-year period, grew in brutality. The killer removed the uterus of his second victim, Annie Chapman; part of the womb and left kidney of Catherine Eddowes; and the heart of Mary Kelly. All of his victims were prostitutes.

The Name

A man claiming to be the murderer sent a letter (dated September 25, 1888) to the Central News Agency, which passed it on to the Metropolitan Police. The letter included the line, "I am down on whores and I shant quit ripping them till I do get buckled." It was signed, "Yours truly, Jack the Ripper." A later postcard included the same sign-off. When police went public with details of the letters, the name "Jack the Ripper" stuck.

The Suspects

Officers from the Metropolitan Police and Scotland Yard had four main suspects: a poor Polish resident of Whitechapel by the name of Kosminski, a barrister who committed suicide in December 1888, a Russian-born thief, and an American doctor who fled to the States in November 1888 while on bail for gross indecency. Since there was little or no evidence against any of these men, the case spawned many conspiracy theories, the most popular of which links the killings to the royal family.

The Royal Conspiracy

The heir to the British throne was Prince Albert Victor, grandson of Queen Victoria and son of the man who would later become King Edward VII. The prince, popularly known as Eddy, had a penchant for hanging around in the East End, and rumors abounded that he had a daughter, Alice, out of wedlock with a shop girl named Annie Crook. To prevent major embarrassment to the Crown, Eddy sought assistance from Queen Victoria's physician, Dr. William Gull, who institutionalized Annie to keep her quiet. However, her friends, including Mary Kelly, also knew the identity of Alice's father, so Dr. Gull created the persona of Jack the Ripper and brutally silenced them one by one. A variation on this theory has Dr. Gull acting without the knowledge of the prince, instead driven by madness resulting from a stroke he suffered in 1887.

Royal involvement would certainly explain why the police were unable to uncover the identity of the Ripper or to even settle on a prime suspect. There *was* a shop girl named Annie Crook who had an illegitimate daughter named Alice, but there is nothing to connect her to either the prince or the murdered prostitutes. In fact, there is no evidence to suggest that the murdered women knew one another. Until the identity of Jack the Ripper is settled beyond doubt, these and other conspiracy theories will likely persist.

A GRAND GESTURE

In ancient Rome, gladiators fought each other in front of thousands of spectators, but the last thing the loser wanted to see from the crowd was a collective "thumbs-up."

In the Roman empire of the first centuries A.D., gladiatorial games that pitted man against man or man against beast were the most popular form of public entertainment. With these games came an involved set of rules, including what a gladiator should do once he had his opponent defeated: go for the kill, or show mercy. Historians have argued that this decision was often left up to the crowd. According to popular belief, a thumbs-down gesture meant instant slaughter, while spectators' thumbs turned up meant the loser would live. In fact, it worked the opposite way.

It is almost certain that the Roman crowds used some sort of thumb gesture to indicate the fate of the vanquished, but the assumption that a "thumbs-up" meant mercy is probably colored by the contemporary Western meaning of the signal. Some historians believe "thumbs-down" actually indicated that the triumphant gladiator should lay down his weapon and spare his foe, while "thumbs-up" indicated that the victor should slash open his opponent's throat. Another theory posits that a "thumbs-sideways" motion symbolized a slash to the neck.

Deathly Decisions

Luckily (or unluckily) for the gladiators, their fate was not always left up to the crowd. Such games were often fixed, or the emperor or another powerful figure had the final say in matters of life and death. Fatal gladiatorial games were actually not as common as is now perceived. Gladiators were expensive to train, so a dead gladiator was usually not in the best interest of anyone. The most gruesome gladiatorial games involved the mass killing of criminals who had already been sentenced to death. In these cases the gladiators were sure to die, regardless of the direction of the crowd's thumbs.

ALL THAT GLITTERS

❋ ❖ ❋

*When the producers of the James Bond film
franchise heard the rumor that Shirley Eaton,
who portrayed the gold-plated woman in*
Goldfinger, *had died from skin suffocation,
they were shaken—and stirred.*

Shortly after the release of *Goldfinger,* the third spool in the James Bond library, rumors spread that the actor who portrayed the damsel Jill Masterson—who dies in the film's opening sequence after being adorned from head to toe in a golden varnish—had passed away from paint poisoning. The actor whose body was used as a human canvas by the sinister smuggler Auric Goldfinger and his parasitic sidekick Oddjob was Shirley Eaton, who was alive then and is still among us today.

In fact, the brass behind Bond were so cognizant of the dangers inherent in dabbing a person from head to toe in gold paint that they instructed Eaton to wear a strategically placed undergarment and left an area of her stomach unpainted to allow her body to "breathe." Although she was exposed in the movie only for a matter of moments, her alleged celluloid demise became legendary, even warranting her placement on the cover of *Life* magazine. Eaton went on to appear in dozens of other movies and played the title character in the notorious (and notoriously awful) *The Million Eyes of Su-Muru* with beach-boy Frankie Avalon before retiring in the late 1960s to raise her family.

In fact, the glistening glamour girl that most people associate with the movie isn't Eaton at all. Margaret Nolan, who is best known as one of the bodacious babes in the *Carry On* gang films, played the gold-fleshed filly in the movie's title sequence, and she was the model prominently featured on the subsequent movie-poster advertising blitz.

A QUICKSAND SHAM

*If you happen to get trapped in one of nature's
suction pits, hang loose. Your moves are the only
things that can drag you down.*

Let's say you're running through the woods and you trip and fall.
As you attempt to right yourself, you realize that the earth below
you isn't really earth at all, and you find it impossible to find purchase. You are wet and covered in a granular grime, but it's not a
body of water or sand pit that you've fallen into. This substance
seems more like a combination of the two. In fact, it is—you have
fallen into a quicksand pit. What you do from this point forth will
determine whether this will be a momentary inconvenience or just
a slightly longer inconvenience.

A Quicksand Primer
Quicksand is a sand, silt, or clay pit that has become hydrated,
which reduces its viscosity. Therefore, when a person is "sucked"
down, they are simply sinking as they would in any body of water.

So why does quicksand make people so nervous? It's probably
due to the fact that it can present resistance to the person who
steps in it. This is particularly true of someone who is wearing
heavy boots or is laden with a backpack or other load. Obviously,
the additional weight will reduce buoyancy and drag one down.

It's All in the Legs
In the human thirst for drama, quicksand has a reputation as a
deadly substance. But the facts show something far different.
Because quicksand is denser than water, it allows for easy floating. If you stumble into a pit, you will sink only up to your chest or
shoulders. If you want to escape, all you need to do is move your
legs slowly. This action will create a space through which water
will flow, thereby loosening the sand's grip. You should then be
able to float on your back until help arrives.

LEAPING LEMMINGS

*A bit of fraudulent filmmaking and a popular
video game have done much to uphold
the long-standing misconception that
lemmings commit mass suicide.*

The image of lemmings hurtling over cliffs to certain doom is
entrenched in our culture to the point where "lemming" has
become a metaphor for any sort of collective self-destruction. But,
come on: Lemmings don't commit suicide. No animal does, with
the exception of human beings. Unlike people, lemmings do not
mindlessly follow crowds at their own peril, but they do engage in
one behavior en masse, and that is mating.

Numbers Are Up, Numbers Are Down

These fuzzy Arctic rodents mate only a few weeks after being born
and birth litters of as many as 13 pups three weeks after mating.
Lemmings can give birth multiple times in one summer, leading to
an exponential boom in population. Every four years, there is what
is known as a "lemming year," when the critters' numbers reach a
critical mass that can no longer be sustained by their surroundings.
Violence among the animals increases, and they begin to disperse
over large distances in search of food. Contrary to popular belief,
they do not move together as one single pack but instead go in all
directions, following one another in randomly formed lines. They
often end up at riverbanks or cliffs and will enter the water and
swim as far as they can in an attempt to reach land or an ice patch.

Of course, some end up drowning—but
that's purely accidental.

Curiously, "lemming years" are followed by a crash in population numbers,
with the next year's crowd dwindling to
practically nothing. What happens to
all of the lemmings after a boom year?

Scientists have settled on increased predation as the explanation. When the lemming population surges, owls, foxes, and seabirds gorge themselves on the rodents, which in turn gives rise to a boom in their own populations. The next summer there are so many more predators that they bring the lemming population down to near extinction. That's where the furious mating comes in handy—in no time, the cycle starts all over again.

Another Disney-Made Myth

So how did the popular theory about lemming mass suicides come to be? Most sources point to the 1958 Disney movie *White Wilderness*. This film depicts a collection of lemmings scurrying across a cliff until they reach the edge of a precipice overlooking the Arctic Ocean. The lemmings then leap over the cliff to sad and certain oblivion. But a bit of creative license was taken to create this shot—it was filmed in Alberta, Canada, which is landlocked. (Lemmings aren't even native to Canada. All of the creatures used in the film were imported.) In order to give the illusion that the lemmings were migrating in large groups, the filmmakers covered a turntable with snow and put a few lemmings on it, filming as the animals went around and around. To show the lemmings landing in the water, the filmmakers herded a group over a riverbank. Once in the water, the little guys had just a short, safe swim to shore.

❊❊❊

- *Those who missed the Disney nature film can witness (and manipulate) a version of a lemming mass suicide in a video game released in 1991.* Lemmings, *one of the most popular video games of all time, has players rescuing lemmings as they follow one another aimlessly off ledges and into a host of treacherous death traps, many involving lava or acid. Suddenly, a plunge into a cool pool of water doesn't look so bad.*

IS THAT A CIGAR IN
YOUR POCKET?

*Did Freud really say, "Sometimes a cigar is just a cigar,"
or does our subconscious just wish he had?*

Thanks to Sigmund Freud, penis envy and Oedipal complexes are common fodder for awkward conversations the world over. The Austrian psychiatrist, considered "the father of psychoanalysis," made popular the idea that your mind can hide its true desires, which are revealed only if you examine dreams and other subconscious thoughts for symbolism.

What a relief to hear that Freud, the ultimate overthinker, might have admitted that sometimes an object has no hidden meaning. In most retellings, this apocryphal anecdote occurs during a lecture on one of his pet topics, such as phallic imagery. An audience member cheekily asks what Freud's omnipresent cigars represent (wink, wink), causing the doctor to pronounce, "Sometimes a cigar is just a cigar."

Although Freud's fondness for cigars is well documented—he smoked 20 a day—there is no record he ever wrote or uttered the phrase. It is not included in his official papers, personal letters, or memoirs, nor is it mentioned in his daughter's biography. Even the curators of the Freud Museum in London can't verify it.

The quotation has a long history in comedy and is often linked with cigar-wagging Groucho Marx doing an imitation of Freud. On the other hand, folklorists relate the saying to Rudyard Kipling's poem *The Betrothed*, which reads, "And a woman is only a woman, but a good cigar is a smoke."

But Freud might have said, if he had been the type to say such things, "Sometimes a pithy saying is just a pithy saying."

NOT JUST FOR NERDS: ROLE-PLAYING GAMES

❋ ❈ ❋

Many myths abound about role-playing games (RPGs), the increasingly popular tabletop adventures in which players create characters whose fates are decided by a roll of the dice.

Gamers are all nerds who live in their moms' basements.
A wide variety of people from all walks of life answer to the siren song of a 20-sided die (d20). Men aren't the only ones playing, either—the number of women gamers is growing rapidly. Gone are the days of the stereotypical geeks dominating the gaming tables as more and more people—from teens to college kids to well-employed adults—discover the fun in gaming.

❋ ❋ ❋

Live-action role-playing (LARP) is sick—people bite each other and hit each other with weapons! There are always a few groups who prefer to play things out with props, but most standard LARP rules don't allow it. In fact, the rules for combat are strict, for the players' safety. A common way to play combat is that the participants have index cards—one for each "weapon" they use—rather than a prop. When they "attack," they tap the target with the card. Physical contact between players is extremely limited, if not strictly forbidden.

❋ ❋ ❋

Dungeons & Dragons (D&D) is satanic. This rumor most likely started because of the large image of a demon on the cover of the original *Dungeon Masters Guide*. If it has a devil on the cover, that must mean it's satanic, right? In fact, the first couple of modules (suggested campaigns) were designed so the players would eventually fight and destroy the devil. So why is there a demon on the cover? The answer is simple: design and marketing.

A big nasty demon presents the possibility of a more interesting challenge than a low level "kobold" or a simple skeleton.

It's obvious that game developers were eager to get away from the satanic stereotype—the second-edition *Monster Manual* is noticeably thinner in the "D" section (all references to demons and devils were removed). However, the use of demonic nasties as villains was popular with players, so the characters made a comeback in the third edition, released in 2000.

Ironically, the co-authors of *D&D*, Dave Arneson and Gary Gygax, were an Evangelical Christian and a non-denominational Christian, respectively (another popular myth is that Gygax was a Jehovah's Witness).

※※※

RPGs teach kids how to cast spells. If you think reading the *D&D Players Handbook* will teach you how to cast a real magic missile, you're in for a surprise. Waving your arms around and saying some variation of "Abracadabra, fireball!" won't accomplish anything but knocking over your Mountain Dew.

The *Harry Potter* books give more details on how to cast a spell than *D&D* does. The rules lay out whether you need special components—such as an identifying spell that requires a pearl worth 100 gold pieces—or if you need to be able to speak and/or make certain motions (since you could be silenced or held immobile and therefore unable to make the required verbal or movement-based parts of the spell). What those specific words or gestures are is not usually mentioned, though a few gestures were included in earlier editions as in-jokes. For instance, to cast a spell that caused small flames to spout from the caster's fingers, the caster had to make a hand gesture that was the same as one would make to light a lighter. To cast a spell in the game, the player would say, "I cast [insert spell name]." No rituals involved.

FALLACIES & FACTS: ANIMALS

❋ ❋❋ ❋

Fallacy: *Giraffes cannot make sounds.*
Fact: *Giraffes actually make a wide variety of sounds to communicate. Although normally taciturn, when inspired they can growl, cough, snort, sneeze, snore, bleat, or bellow.*

Fallacy: *Zebras are white and have black stripes.*
Fact: *It may be a minor quibble, but zebras are actually black and have white stripes—not the other way around. Each zebra has a unique stripe pattern, like a human's fingerprints, that helps other zebras recognize it. And to save you the trouble of shaving one, we'll also tell you that zebras have black skin under their coats.*

Fallacy: *Those creepy vampire bats from Transylvania will suck your blood.*
Fact: *Vampire bats come from South and Central America, not Transylvania, and they don't suck blood. They use their teeth to make small cuts in a sleeping animal's skin, and then they lap up the blood with their tongues. Their "take" amounts to just a few tablespoons, which isn't fatal to the victim—but there's still that gnawing issue of rabies.*

Fallacy: *Opossums sleep hanging upside down by their tails.*
Fact: *Baby opossums can hang by their tails for maybe a few minutes, but adult opossums are far too heavy. They use their prehensile (grasping) tails for balance and to help them climb over limbs and carry small sticks or grasses.*

Fallacy: *Whales expel water from their blowholes.*
Fact: *When a whale surfaces after a dive, it exhales air from its lungs through its blowhole. As the warmed air hits the colder ocean air, it condenses into droplets, making it appear that the whale is spouting water.*

'TIL PORT DO US PART

*The captain of a ship holds wide-ranging legal powers
when that vessel is at sea, but it's a nautical myth that any
ship's captain can perform a legally binding marriage.*

- Unless the captain of a vessel happens to also be an ordained minister, judge, or recognized official such as a notary public, he or she generally doesn't have the authority to perform a legally binding marriage at sea. In fact, a suitably licensed captain is no more qualified to perform marriages than a similarly licensed head chef, deck hand, or galley worker. There are a few specific exceptions: Captains of Japanese vessels can perform marriages at sea, as long as both the bride and groom hold valid Japanese passports. And thanks to a quirk in Bermuda law, captains with Bermuda licenses are also legally authorized to officiate weddings aboard ship.

- The myth that any ship's captain has the power to marry at sea has been propagated by countless romantic movies and is so widely believed, even among sailors, that the U.S. Navy specifically forbids it. Section 700.716 of the U.S. Navy Regulations reads: "The commanding officer shall not perform a marriage ceremony on board his ship or aircraft. He shall not permit a marriage ceremony to be performed on board when the ship or aircraft is outside the territory of the United States, except: (a) In accordance with local laws…and (b) In the presence of a diplomatic official of the United States…"

- As an alternative to a wedding at sea, couples may to want to consider exchanging vows aboard a ship that is docked in a port. Ultimately, though, if you want to avoid a legal battle to validate your cruise-line marriage, you may want to heed the adage displayed on many vessels: "Any marriages performed by the captain of this ship are valid for the duration of the voyage only."

WORLD'S OLDEST PARLIAMENT

※ ※※ ※

*Contrary to popular belief, the world's oldest parliament
is not in Britain. It's not in the United States, either.*

First, a Definition

A parliament is a representative assembly with the power to pass
legislation and most commonly consists of two chambers, or
houses, in which a majority is required to create and amend laws.
Congress became the supreme legislative body of the United
States in 1789. The roots of the British Parliament date back to the
12th century, but it wasn't until 1689 that the Bill of Rights established Parliament's authority over the British monarch and gave it
the responsibility of creating, amending, and repealing laws.

The title of Oldest Functioning Legislature in the World
belongs to the Parliament of Iceland, known as Althing, which
is Icelandic for "general assembly." Althing was established in
A.D. 930 during the Viking age. The legislative assembly met at
Thingvellir (about 30 miles outside of what is now the country's
capital, Reykjavik) and heralded the start of the Icelandic Com-
monwealth, which lasted until 1262. Althing convened annually
and served as both a court and a legislature. One of Althing's earliest pieces of legislation was to ban the Viking explorer Erik the
Red from Iceland in 980 after he was found guilty of murder.

Even after Iceland lost its independence to Norway in 1262,
Althing continued to hold sessions, albeit with reduced powers,
until it was dissolved in 1799. In 1844, Althing was restored as an
advisory body, and in 1874 it became a legislative body again, a
function it maintains to this day. The parliament is now located in
Reykjavik.

※ ※ ※

- *Considering the fact that it was created by a horde of bloodthirsty Vikings, Althing is an amazing testament to democratic
government.*

GASTRIC GEOGRAPHY

*The adage "You are what you eat" may be accurate
in terms of describing the relationship between consumption
and health, but it would be unwise to confuse the foods
we eat with the countries they are named for.*

One of the most popular fast-food staples in the junk-food jungle is the French fry. Poll the average carbohydrate consumer on the country of origin of this particular potato product, and the most likely answer would be France. And that answer would be wrong. French fries were likely first cooked up in Belgium. The verb "to french" refers to the technique of cutting something into long, thin strips.

On a similar note, the popular salad enhancer known as French dressing doesn't come from France, either. In fact, the sugary-sweet substance isn't widely available in that country. Popular folklore tells us that the wife of Lucius French, the man who founded Hazleton, Indiana, created the recipe to "dress up" the vegetables she prepared for her husband.

✳✳✳

Another example of a product that does not share its domicile with its domain is the popular pastry known as the Danish. The idea for the fruit-filled doughy delight was dreamed up in Austria, which is why the sweet supplement is known as *Vienerbrod* (or "Vienna bread") in Denmark. It was, however, introduced to American appetites by a Danish baker named L. C. Kiltteng, who claims to have first baked the buttery biscuit for the wedding of President Woodrow Wilson in December 1915. After introducing the pastry to people in communities as diverse as Galveston, Texas, and Oakland, California, Kiltteng established the Danish Culinary Studio on Fifth Avenue in New York City, where bakers from far and wide were schooled in the fine art of creating the dainty delicacy.

MONUMENTAL MYTHS

Historians and conspiracy theorists have long debated the true meaning and origin of Stonehenge, the prehistoric series of stone monoliths located in England. Were they erected as an altar to aliens, a calendar for cosmic calculations, or a health spa?

No one really knows who built Stonehenge, because it was erected at a time before written language as we know it existed and word of mouth was, at best, unreliable. The ancient rumor mill claims that the Druids—a sect of Celtic priests—built the structures as a site for ceremonial sacrifices. This theory was posited by a couple of 16th-century Stonehenge antiquarians, John Aubrey and William Stukeley. But later archaeologists determined that the monuments predate the Druids by a thousand years, and it's also been noted that the sect worshipped in wooded areas, not stony enclaves.

Skyward Speculations

Because the entire structure has an out-of-this-world mystique, some imaginative analysts suggest it was built as a shrine to extra-terrestrials, or that aliens themselves assembled the monuments. As evidence, these believers point to the fact that crop circles have repeatedly formed near the site. Still others are convinced that the monuments were created to act as a cosmic timepiece, and that the stones are precisely situated so the shadows they cast move like the hands of a clock.

Healing Among the Rocks?

Evidence of an ancient village on the outskirts of the site suggests the area was a place for the living, and that Stonehenge was a cemetery and memorial. Some researchers believe Stonehenge was a haven for wellness. The first stones moved to the site originally came from a bluestone quarry in west Wales that was used as a healing retreat. Archaeologists maintain that these stones were believed to have medicinal powers and were brought to Stonehenge for that purpose.

WHAT WAS THE BLACK DEATH?

❋ ❈ ❋

The Black Death, also called the Great or Black Plague, first swept through Europe in the 1340s, killing nearly 60 percent of the population. It returned periodically, spreading panic and death, and then disappeared into history. Was it bubonic plague, as many people believe, or was something else to blame?

"The Great Mortality"

Brought to Italy in 1347 by Genoese trading ships, the Black Death spread through Europe like wildfire. Contemporaries described scenes of fear and decay—the sick were abandoned and the dead were piled in the streets because no one would bury them. Anyone who touched the infected, the dead, or the infected people's belongings also caught the disease.

It could take as long as a month before symptoms showed, which was plenty of time for the infection to spread. But once the dreaded blackened spots began to appear on a victim's body, death was quick—usually within three days. At least one autopsy recorded that the person's internal organs had almost liquified and that the blood within the body had congealed.

A Theory in Doubt

The symptoms described by people who lived through the Black Plague and the profile of the outbreak don't match up with those of bubonic plague (*Yersinia pestis*). Through analysis of records and writings of the day, scientists have determined that the Plague was likely a viral hemorrhagic fever such as Ebola or Marburg.

Transmission

One major problem with the bubonic plague theory is that bubonic plague doesn't transmit from person to person—it can only be transmitted through the bites of fleas that have left an infected rat after its death. The signature symptom—the black swellings, or *buboe*—begin showing within two or three days. Accounts of the Great Plague often mention people who became infected merely by touching an infected person. Some writings describe the infection as spreading via droplets of body fluid (whether sweat, saliva, or blood), which isn't possible for bubonic plague but is a defining characteristic of hemorrhagic fever.

Incubation and Quarantine

It must be mentioned that it is possible for a bubonic plague infection to spread to the lungs and become pneumonic plague, and this kind of infection *is* transmittable from person to person. However, pneumonic plague is extremely rare—it occurs in only 5 percent of bubonic plague cases. It also isn't easily transmitted, and it certainly isn't virulent enough to have been responsible for the widespread person-to-person infection rates during the Black Death. Like bubonic plague, pneumonic plague also has a very short incubation period, taking only a few days from infection to death. However, historical records show that the Black Plague took as long as a month to do the same thing. It was no coincidence that cities started to mandate a strict 40-day quarantine. Officials had observed from multiple cases that that much time was needed to determine whether someone was infected. If it had been pneumonic plague, such a long period of quarantine would not have been needed. Those infected would have been dead within a single week.

Another anomaly that casts doubt on the bubonic plague theory is how the Plague spread in Iceland. There were no rats in Iceland and there wouldn't be until 300 years later. However, the Plague still ravaged the island, killing nearly 60 percent of the population.

Rapid Spread

The Black Death spread throughout Europe faster than any disease people had ever seen. It made the trip from Italy to the Arctic Circle in less than three years and is recorded as having traveled 150 miles in England within six weeks. Rats can't travel that quickly, but people can. Frightened citizens fled from cities where the epidemic raged, not knowing that they were infected, and they spread the disease as they went. Many parish records indicate that after strangers arrived in town, the Plague emerged there within a few weeks.

In contrast, studies of confirmed bubonic plague outbreaks show that it spreads very slowly. One outbreak in India in 1907 took six weeks to travel only 100 yards, and another in South Africa from 1899 to 1925 moved only eight miles per year.

An Odd Connection

A strange piece of evidence that backs up the hemorrhagic fever theory is the connection between the Black Death and *Human immunodeficiency virus* (HIV). A large percentage of Europe's native population has a genetic mutation known as *CCR5-delta 32* (shortened to Δ32). This mutation prevents *CCR5* receptors in the body's white blood cells from acting as entry ports. Viruses such as HIV cannot enter the white blood cells through those receptors (and aren't able to use the cells to replicate), so people with the Δ32 mutation are partly protected from viruses that work in this manner.

Molecular biologists have traced the increased frequency of the Δ32 mutation to approximately 700 years ago—right around the time of the Great Plague. They conclude that the Plague must have been a disease that used the *CCR5* receptors in the same way that HIV does, which points to a viral culprit.

Interestingly, the Δ32 mutation is found only in people of European descent. It is not found in people from eastern Asia or Africa—places the Plague didn't touch. Being spared the horror of the Black Death in medieval times may have contributed to the rapid spread of HIV infections in those places today.

The mutation could not have been caused by bubonic plague, because bubonic plague is a bacterium that doesn't use *CCR5* receptors as entry points. Bubonic plague also doesn't have the mortality rate necessary to make the mutation so prevalent in the surviving population—another nail in the coffin of the bubonic plague theory.

HOW WELL DO YOU UNDERSTAND SHARKS?

They look frightening and strike fear into the hearts of nearly everyone who dips their toes into the ocean. Unfortunately, sharks are still one of the most misunderstood creatures on Earth. Do you know which rumors are true and which aren't?

Sharks are vicious man-eaters. False! People are not even on their preferred-food list. Every hunt poses a risk of injury to sharks, so they need to make every meal count. That's why they go for animals with a lot of high-calorie fat and blubber—they get more energy for less effort. Humans are usually too lean and bony to be worth the risk.

Sharks are loners. That depends on the shark. Some species, such as the great white, are rarely seen in the company of other sharks. However, many other species aren't so antisocial. Blacktip reef sharks hunt in packs, working together to drive fish out of coral beds so every shark in the group gets a meal. Near Cocos Island off Costa Rica, hammerheads have been filmed cruising around in schools that consist of hundreds of sharks.

You have a greater chance of being killed by a falling coconut than by a shark. True! Falling coconuts kill close to 150 people every year. In comparison, sharks kill only five people per year on average. The International Shark Attack File estimates that the odds of a person being killed by a shark are approximately 1 in 264 million.

Sharks have poor vision, and most attacks are cases of mistaken identity. As popular as this belief is, it's wrong. Scientists have observed that sharks' behavior when they are hunting differs significantly from what most people report when a bite occurs. Sharks are extremely curious creatures and, since they don't have hands, they frequently explore their environment with the only things they have available—their mouths. Unfortunately for humans, a curious shark can do a lot of damage with a "test" nibble, especially if it's a big shark.

Most shark attacks are not fatal. True! There are approximately 60 shark attacks around the world each year, and, on average, just 1 percent of those are fatal. What we usually call "attacks" are really only bites. Scientists report that an inquisitive shark that bites a surfboard (or an unlucky swimmer) shows far less agression than when it is on the hunt and attacks fiercely and repeatedly.

Shark cartilage is an effective treatment for cancer. False! Anyone toting the benefits of shark cartilage as a nutritional supplement to cure cancer is selling snake oil. Multiple studies by Johns Hopkins University and other institutions have shown that shark cartilage has no benefit. This myth got started with the popular but incorrect notion that sharks don't get cancer.

Most shark attacks occur in water less than six feet deep. True! And the reason is obvious—that's where the majority of people are. It makes sense that most of the interactions between humans and sharks happen where the concentration of people is greatest.

Sharks have to swim constantly or they drown. There are a few species that need to keep moving, but most sharks can still get oxygen when they're "motionless." They just open their mouths to draw water in and over their gills.

Most sharks present no threat to humans. True! There are more than 400 species of sharks, and approximately 80 percent of them are completely harmless to people. In fact, only four species are responsible for nearly 85 percent of unprovoked attacks: bull sharks, great white sharks, tiger sharks, and great hammerhead sharks.

INDEX

❋ ❋

A

Abbott, William (Bud), 301
Aborigines, 138–39
Academy Awards, 26, 137
Accidents, aviation, 18
Acne, 381
Adjules, 232
Agriculture and civilization, 210
Ahura Mazda, 35
Airplanes. *See* Aviation.
Akhenaten (Egyptian pharaoh), 36
Alamo, Battle of, 283
Alaska, 369–70
Alcohol
  drunk driving, 284
  evaporation, 126
  mixing types of, 126–27
  Prohibition and, 95
  Puritans and, 31
  Rolling Rock beer, 13
  sake, 86
  ulcers and, 398
  wines, 125
Ali, Muhammad, 70
Allen, Ethan, 322
Allen, Euphemia, 44
Allende, Carlos, 272–73
All Quiet on the Western Front, 182
Althing (Parliament of Iceland), 437

American Revolution
  Arnold, Benedict, and, 361
  Boston and, 93–94, 325
  Hale, Nathan, and, 280
  Revere, Paul, and, 168–69
American West
  advice to go to, 109
  gunfights, 278
  law enforcement, 320
  in movies, 239, 278
  outlaws, 239, 359
Amityville Horror, The, 181
Anasazi, 145–46
Andean wolves, 232
Animals, 80–81, 435
  bulls, 393
  legendary, 231–33
  lions and tigers, 80
  moon and, 412
  Nazis and, 364–65
  primates, 337
  statues, 85
  See also specific types.
Anne of Cleves (queen of England), 348
Anson, Jay, 181
Antarctica, 22
Antelope, gilled, 232
Antony, Mark, 285
Apes, 337
Apollo moon missions, 311

Magazines, 368
Magi, 35, 423
Mallon, Mary, 128
Malta, prehistoric temples, 96
Mandarin Chinese, 397
Manhattan Project, 372
Manson, Charles, 200
Manson, Marilyn, 160
Marey, Etienne-Jules, 23
Marie Antoinette (queen of
    France), 382
Marriage
    of Lucrezia Borgia, 74–75
    of movie stars, 58
    of priests, 71–72
    at sea, 436
Marx, Karl, 227, 384
Mary, Queen of Scots, 242
Mayflower, 302–3
Mayonnaise, 103
Mazuku, 271
McCain, John, 366
McClintock Effect, 407
McDonald's restaurants, 248–49
Memorial Day, 206
Mending Wall, 416
Menstrual synchrony, 407
Merchant of Venice, The, 241
Mermaids, 197
Mice, 84
Mickey Mouse, 84
Middle Ages, 265–66
Milk, 249, 251
Mindanao, Philippines, 99–100

Minnesota Vikings, 77
Misquotes
    about misleading appearances,
        241
    advice, 109
    American Revolution, 220,
        280, 322
    baseball, 15
    freedom of speech, 377
    Golden Rule, 334
    government, 165, 186
    hard work, 401
    movies, 155, 342, 355
    patriotism, 148, 361
    plays, 203
    space travel, 332
    television programs, 121–22
    women, 307
Mokele-mbembe, 233
Moment magnitude scale, 329
Mona Lisa, 201–2
Monkees (band), 200
Monkeys, 337
Monotheism, 35–36
Monroe, Marilyn, 274–75
Monsters, 123–24, 196–97
Montagu, John, Fourth Earl of
    Sandwich, 228–29
Montreal Canadiens, 293
Moon
    distance to Earth, 42
    full, 412
    human behavior and, 349
    men on, 310–11

Presidents (American)
Atchison as, 37
baseball and, 110
Constitutional requirements, 366
Inaugural Address, 421
Presidents' Day, 243
Prince, The, 305–6
Proctor & Gamble, 286–87
Prohibition, 95
Provence II, 379–80
Proverbs, 129–30
Puebloans, 145–46
"Puff, the Magic Dragon," 160
Puffins, 80
Punxsutawney Phil, 324
Puritans, 31, 303
Pyramids of Egypt, 96, 136

Q
Quicksand, 429

R
Rabbits, 405
Rack (torture), 266
Rackham, "Calico" Jack, 308–9
Radiation, 312, 403–4
Rats, 117–18, 295
Read, Mary (Mark), 308–9
Reagan, Ronald, 63
Recycling, 248
Redwood trees, 174–75
"Religion is the opiate...," 384
Remarque, Erich, 182

Revere, Paul, 168–69
Richards, Keith, 161
Richter scale, 329
Rivers, 157
RMS *Titanic,* 379–80
Robinson Crusoe, 162
Rockne, Knute, 342
Rocs, 232
Role-playing games (RPGs), 433–34
Rolling Rock beer, 13
Rome, ancient
burned, 367
emperors, 408
gladiators, 427
sacked, 237
soldiers, 282
Roosevelt, Franklin Delano, 95, 189–90, 421
Roosevelt, Theodore, 59, 401
Ross, Elizabeth (Betsy), 207
Roswell, New Mexico, 326
Royal houses, 257–58
Rukh, 232
Rum, 31
Russian Academy of Sciences, 61
Ruth, George Herman "Babe," 38, 166, 224, 422

S
Sacajawea, 106–7
Sake (alcohol), 86
Salem, Massachusetts, 134
Salem witch trials, 134

CONTRIBUTING WRITERS

Jeff Bahr is an author and motorcycle journalist who generally focuses on the world of the strange and unusual. With *Myths & Misconceptions*, he has found that there are others out there nearly as misunderstood as he.

Tom DeMichael, a frequent contributor to Publications International, Ltd., projects, has authored several books on American history and holds a degree in the subject. He also has published books and magazine articles in subjects as diverse as American film, American firefighting, and collectible toys.

Katherine Don is a freelance writer who hails from a Chicago suburb and currently lives in Wrigleyville. When not typing away on her trusty Macbook, she volunteers for nonprofit organizations that deal with health-care and penal-system reform, does research for her book-in-progress, and in general hones her skills for world domination—or, at the very least, graduate school.

James Duplacey is an author and sports historian currently residing in the flatlands of Alberta, Canada, in the home of the Calgary Stampede. He is an avid fan of baseball, film, and all things jazz and has written more than 60 books on sports, culture, and entertainment.

Emily Dwass lives in Los Angeles, where she has written for TV and newspapers. When not at her computer, she can be found in the kitchen, baking something chocolate.

J. K. Kelley has a B.A. in history from the University of Washington in Seattle. Thus far he has contributed to seven *Armchair Reader*™ books. He resides in the desiccated sagebrush of eastern Washington with his wife Deb, his parrot Alex, Fabius the Labrador Retriever, and Leonidas the miniature Schnauzer.

Bill Martin is a freelance writer who is finally putting his B.A. in history and political science from the University of Toronto to good use. His diverse portfolio of commercial, media, and creative writing includes two previous *Armchair Reader*™ volumes: *World War Two* and *The Amazing Book of History*.

Susan McGowan is a poet who, despite her best efforts, has found employment as a college instructor, game developer, media consultant, freelance writer, and functionality expert. She lives in Columbus, Ohio, with her husband, impish daughter, and three orange cats.

Bill Sasser is a freelance writer and journalist based in New Orleans. He writes for Salon.com and *The Christian Science Monitor,* among other publications.

Ken Sheldon is a humorist, author, and singer/songwriter. He has appeared on television, radio, and at the homes of most of his friends, usually around dinnertime. In addition to articles, plays, stories, and songs, he has written hundreds of checks, most of which passed the bank with no trouble whatsoever. He has also written several books, which are currently sitting on the desks of editors from coast to coast.

Lawrence Robinson is a Los Angeles–based novelist and screenwriter. Although he admits to being technologically challenged, it's a myth that he has never figured out how to update his Web site, britwriter.com.

Ilene Springer has written for *Cosmopolitan, Ladies' Home Journal, The Boston Globe,* and many other national publications. She currently lives in Malta (just below Sicily). Visit her blog: An-American-in-Malta.com.

Donald Vaughan is a veteran freelance writer based in Raleigh, North Carolina. His work has appeared in an eclectic array of publications, including *Military Officer* magazine, *Cat Fancy, Mad* magazine, *Nursing Spectrum,* and the *Weekly World News.* He tries not to believe everything he reads.

Jennifer Plattner Wilkinson is a part-time poet and former expatriate who finds grappling with misconceptions to be a way of life.

More great titles from West Side Publishing

Yesterday & Today™ is a collection of gift-oriented hardcover books featuring stunning photography that captures the essence and chronicles the history of cherished sports teams, beloved cities, and beyond.

YESTERDAY & TODAY™

**Cleveland Indians • Detroit Tigers
Chicago Cubs • St. Louis Cardinals
New York Yankees • Boston Red Sox**

Coming Attractions

BASEBALL
New York Mets

FOOTBALL
University of Arkansas Razorbacks • University of Florida Gators • University of Georgia Bulldogs • University of Texas Longhorns • USC Trojans • NFL: Chicago Bears • Green Bay Packers • New England Patriots • New York Giants

CITIES
Charleston • Nashville • New York City • Portland

www.armchairreader.com

Hope you enjoyed this Armchair Reader™

You'll find the rest of the crop quite exciting.
Please look for these titles wherever books are sold.

ARMCHAIR
• READER™ •

The Gigantic Reader • The Last Survivors • The Origins of Everything • The Book of Myths & Misconceptions • Weird, Scary & Unusual • The Colossal Reader • The Book of Incredible Information • The Amazing Book of History • The Extraordinary Book of Lists • Civil War • World War II • Grand Slam Baseball

Coming Attractions

Armchair Reader™ Goes Hollywood
Armchair Reader™ *USA Today* The Best Places to Go

Visit us at *www.armchairreader.com*
to learn all about our other great books from
West Side Publishing, or just to let us know
what your thoughts are about our books.
We love to hear from all our readers.

WEST
SIDE
PUBLISHING

www.armchairreader.com